— *The* BIG BOOK *of* —

GLUTEN-
FREE
RECIPES

The BIG BOOK *of*
GLUTEN-FREE RECIPES

**More Than 500 Easy Gluten-Free Recipes
for Healthy and Flavorful Meals**

Kimberly A. Tessmer, RD, LD

Aadamsmedia
Avon, Massachusetts

Published by Adams Media, a division of F+W Media, Inc.
57 Littlefield Street, Avon, MA 02322. U.S.A.
www.adamsmedia.com

ISBN 10: 1-4405-6239-3
ISBN 13: 978-1-4405-6239-6
eISBN 10: 1-4405-6240-7
eISBN 13: 978-1-4405-6240-2

Printed in the United States of America.

10 9 8 7 6 5 4 3 2

Contains material adapted and abridged from *The Everything® Gluten-Free Cookbook*, by Rick Marx and Nancy T. Maar, copyright © 2005 by F+W Media, Inc., ISBN 10: 1-59337-394-5, ISBN 13: 978-1-59337-394-8; *The Everything® Gluten-Free Slow Cooker Cookbook*, by Carrie S. Forbes, copyright © 2012 by F+W Media, Inc., ISBN 10: 1-4405-3366-0, ISBN 13: 978-1-4405-3366-2; and *The Everything® Wheat-Free Diet Cookbook*, by Lauren Kelly, CN, copyright © 2013 by F+W Media, Inc., ISBN 10: 1-4405-5680-6; ISBN 13: 978-1-4405-5680-7.

Always follow safety and commonsense cooking protocol while using kitchen utensils, operating ovens and stoves, and handling uncooked food. If children are assisting in the preparation of any recipe, they should always be supervised by an adult.

Many of the designations used by manufacturers and sellers to distinguish their products are claimed as trademarks. Where those designations appear in this book and F+W Media was aware of a trademark claim, the designations have been printed with initial capital letters.

This book is available at quantity discounts for bulk purchases.
For information, please call 1-800-289-0963.

DEDICATION

I dedicate this great collection of gluten-free recipes to all the people who dutifully follow their gluten-free diet. My hope is that all of these yummy recipes will help them to realize that a life without gluten doesn't have to mean a life without delicious foods!

ACKNOWLEDGMENTS

Thanks to the team at Adams Media, especially Ross Weisman for all his help with this project.

CONTENTS

3   Quick Breads and Spreads

4 Snacks...89

5 Appetizers 115

8 Beef and Veal 231

11 Vegetarian Mains.. 323

12   Pasta and Rice 355

13   Beans and Lentils 389

14 Side Dishes 419

INTRODUCTION

Gluten-free living has become a way of life for millions of people whether it is due to a gluten intolerance, a condition known as celiac disease, or personal preference. Whatever the case, cooking a variety of healthy and great-tasting gluten-free meals that the whole family will love on a daily basis can become quite a challenge. And don't forget creating menus for holidays and parties or just simple everyday snacks. We know that variety is key in any type of eating style to better nutritional intake, palatability, and just overall pleasure in eating. This book helps solve that problem and provides you with a large and diverse collection of wonderful gluten-free recipes right at your fingertips. You will find a huge variety of recipes you need both for everyday use and for those special occasions.

There is much to learn when it comes to leading a gluten-free life. Your first goal should be to learn all you can from a specialized health care professional. Second, you should take what you learn and turn it into healthy and satisfying meals. I hope this book will help make your gluten-free lifestyle a little less daunting and assist you in creating good health and delicious family meals.

CHAPTER 1

THE GLUTEN-FREE WAY OF LIFE

A gluten-free way of life has become more popular than ever before. There are presently just over 2 million people who have a condition called celiac disease and must medically adhere to a strict gluten-free diet for life. Add to that people who suffer from food allergies, gluten intolerances, and those who use this type of diet as a nonmedical way to manage autism spectrum disorders. In addition some people choose a gluten-free diet to improve their health and increase their energy. That makes for a lot of people who either need or choose to follow a gluten-free way of life.

What Is Gluten?

The word *gluten* has been popping up a lot more lately, including at our local grocery chains, restaurants, and in the news. So what exactly is this mysterious ingredient? *Gluten* is a general term used for a group of proteins, or *prolamins*, that are found in certain grains—specifically wheat, rye, barley, and any of their derivatives. Gluten is the part of flour that gives dough its structure and leavening abilities. It can be found in a wide variety of foods including baked goods (such as breads, cookies, and cakes), pasta, cereals, sauces, soups, seasonings, candy, and even some medications, just to name a few.

Oats were once included on the list of prohibited foods for a gluten-free diet. The concern in the past was not so much oats themselves, but instead, cross-contamination with grains that contained gluten. In light of recent research, however, most people with celiac disease can safely eat pure, uncontaminated oats in moderation. However there are those who show sensitivity to oats whether they are pure or not. Because it remains questionable whether oats are safe for all people with celiac disease you should work with your health care provider before adding oats to your daily diet to assure that the addition of oats is not causing any damage.

People who cannot medically tolerate gluten are instructed to always read food labels no matter what the food product and no matter how many times they have bought it. Manufacturers tend to change their products frequently, including ingredients and/or how food products are manufactured. What was once gluten-free can change at a moment's notice.

What Is Celiac Disease?

As mentioned earlier, many people choose to avoid gluten because of lifestyle preferences, but there are many more who must avoid gluten for medical reasons. The most prevalent reason for those people is celiac disease. Celiac disease is an autoimmune inflammatory disorder of the small intestine and is much more common than once thought. In fact, one out of every 133 people in the United States has celiac disease. This translates to just over 2 million people. This disease can affect both adults and children. Researchers believe several genes work together to cause celiac disease rather than a single missing or altered gene. Since our immune system is partly controlled by heredity, it goes without saying that celiac disease has a strong chance of running in the family.

For people with celiac disease, consuming any amount of gluten sets off an autoimmune response that causes the destruction of the villi within the lining of the small intestine as well as the destruction of digestive enzymes. The body of such a person produces antibodies that attack the small intestine, causing damage, debilitating symptoms, and illness. As a result of the destruction of the villi, the body can no longer absorb nutrients that are needed for good health, such as carbohydrates, protein, fat, and essential vitamins and minerals. In turn these nutritional deficiencies can deprive the brain, nervous system, bones, liver, heart, and other organs of the nourishment they need and cause many types of health issues and illnesses.

Symptoms of celiac disease can vary greatly among individuals and can include symptoms such as:

- Abdominal bloating and pain
- Nausea
- Vomiting
- Diarrhea
- Weight loss
- Iron-deficiency anemia
- Nutritional deficiencies
- Edema
- Excessive gas
- Chronic fatigue
- Weakness
- Depression
- Bone or joint pain
- Muscle cramps
- Constipation
- Balance problems
- Migraine headaches
- Seizures
- Memory issues
- Dental defects
- Infertility
- Failure to thrive in children

Celiac disease is sometimes misdiagnosed as its symptoms very closely mirror other health issues, such as irritable bowel disease, Crohn's disease, and diverticulitis. The first step in diagnosis is a blood antibody test. If these tests come back positive, the next step is an endoscopy, in which a biopsy of the small intestine is taken to check for actual damage to the villi. **Never follow a gluten-free diet before you have had blood tests and/or a biopsy done because this can interfere with test results and therefore a correct diagnosis.**

If, after proper testing, you are diagnosed with celiac disease, you will be educated and placed on a 100-percent gluten-free diet for life. Currently, this is the only form of treatment available for people who suffer from the disease. You must strictly adhere to the diet and must be completely gluten-free to allow for the small intestine to heal and for no further damage to occur. Most people find improvement in symptoms within days of following a gluten-free diet, but it usually takes a good three to six months or more for the small intestine to heal properly. It is vital for people with celiac disease to work closely with their health care provider and a registered dietitian who specializes in this area.

Who Else Needs to Follow a Gluten-Free Diet?

Gluten-free diets are also used to treat a condition called dermatitis herpetiformis (DH). DH is a chronic and severe disease of the skin that causes itchy skin blisters on the elbows, knees, buttocks, scalp, and/or back. DH is also a genetic autoimmune disease and can be linked to celiac disease, though both are separate conditions. However, research shows that about 5 percent of people with celiac disease will develop DH, either before being diagnosed or within the first year on the diet. Although the majority of people with DH do not have obvious gastrointestinal symptoms, such as with celiac disease, almost all have some type of damage to the small intestine. Therefore they also have the potential for all of the nutritional deficiency problems of a person with celiac disease. Both celiac disease and DH are permanent, and if you have either of these conditions and consume gluten, damage will occur.

In addition to celiac disease and DH some people suffer from a less aggressive form of gluten intolerance. General gluten intolerance is even harder to diagnose than celiac disease because there are no established diagnostic criteria. People who may have a general intolerance to gluten do not display severe symptoms such as those with celiac disease, but a gluten-free diet can substantially improve their health and quality of life.

How Do I Start a Gluten-Free Diet?

Getting started on a gluten-free diet can seem like a daunting task. There are some foods where the presence of gluten is obvious, but the challenge is learning how to spot its hidden sources. To get started, collect all the information you can about gluten-free diets. Talk to your health care provider, search reputable sites on the Internet, read books and pamphlets written by reputable sources, purchase specialized gluten-free cookbooks such as this one, and become familiar with gluten-free associations and support groups. Knowledge is power, so the more you know, the more control you have and the easier your gluten-free lifestyle will become. Educate your spouse and family members so that they too understand the basics and can help to support you. Seek out others who follow a gluten-free diet and can help support you through the tough times. There are plenty of local support groups as well as forums and message boards on the Internet that can help provide the support you will need. Most importantly, seek the guidance of a professional. Starting a gluten-free diet can be a very overwhelming task. A registered dietitian who specializes in this area can help you sort through the foods you are allowed and not allowed and provide you with valuable information. Such a professional can help you take it step by step and help to make you feel more at ease with the process. You can contact the Academy of Nutrition and Dietetics (formerly the American Dietetic Association) at *www.eatright.org* to find a dietitian in your area, or ask your health care provider to refer you to one.

Is a Gluten-Free Diet Healthier?

Following a gluten-free diet can be a healthy option depending on the choices you make. Your main focus, as with any healthy diet, should be to eat a variety of foods daily from all of the food groups. The key is to choose foods from each group that don't contain gluten. Therefore, you need to build your healthy eating plan using alternative grains that are free of gluten and to learn about all the hidden sources of gluten.

Since wheat is a large contributor of dietary fiber in the average diet, and because many gluten-free grain foods are low in fiber, it is important to ensure that you consume the recommended amount of fiber daily. Aim to consume daily a variety of high-fiber, naturally gluten-free foods, such as fresh fruits, fresh vegetables, legumes, nuts, seeds, and brown rice. Higher-fiber gluten-free flours and grains include amaranth, cornmeal, flax seed, chickpea (garbanzo) flour, garfava flour, millet seeds, rice bran, and soy flour (defatted).

A gluten-free diet can be a healthy diet for those who need to follow one. However, don't believe the hype that a gluten-free diet is automatically healthier than a diet including gluten. Making the right choices in either type of diet can lead to a healthy way of life, but choosing incorrectly can also make either type of diet an unhealthy choice.

Tips for Following a Gluten-Free Diet

Adjusting to anything new takes time. Don't expect to learn all you need to know about gluten-free eating overnight. It is very normal to feel overwhelmed and upset about foods you can no longer eat. Instead of concentrating on what you can't have, think about all the foods you *can* still eat and all of the new foods you will discover. There are tons of gluten-free foods available at your local supermarkets with new ones reaching the market all the time. With new labeling laws it is becoming easier and easier to find foods at the store that are naturally gluten-free.

Label reading is an important first step. You must make it a habit to read all labels before eating a food. While you are beginning to learn about all the foods you can or cannot eat, stick with foods that are naturally gluten-free such as plain poultry, fish, meats, legumes, nuts, seeds, fresh potatoes, rice, fresh fruits, and fresh vegetables. All these foods are healthy and delicious and pose no worries! The key is being careful to prepare these foods without other gluten-containing products. Most dairy products can also be consumed as long as you are not lactose intolerant.

Use some of these other helpful tips to make starting a gluten-free diet easier:

- As you learn which foods you can and cannot eat, keep a list of "safe" foods to serve as a quick reference.
- If you are unsure whether you can eat a food, take the safe path and don't eat it until you can do some more research on it.
- Don't gauge if you can consume a food or not by whether it produces symptoms of gluten intolerance. Many people don't experience symptoms when consuming small amounts of gluten but they are still damaging their small intestine. If a food contains gluten *do not* eat it!
- Get in the habit of always reading food labels and questioning any ingredient of which you are not 100-percent sure.
- Watch for cross-contamination between utensils, toasters, counters, food storage bins, jars, and any other place people may leave crumbs. Just a small amount of crumbs from a knife or toaster with gluten-containing products are enough to contaminate your gluten-free foods and cause damage to your body.

- Be aware that just because a food is "wheat-free" does *not* mean it is "gluten-free."
- When eating in a restaurant don't be afraid to ask questions about how the food is prepared. If necessary, ask to have your foods specially prepared for you. Many restaurants now offer gluten-free entrees so it may be a good idea to seek out these places in your area.
- Look for gluten-free cookbooks to help you get started. They can be a lifeline to a more normal way of eating for the whole family.
- Last, hang in there. It will get easier and become second nature in no time. If you put the time into it, it will pay off in the long run!

Note: When using the recipes in this book, even if an ingredient does not state "gluten-free," always double check food labels to ensure you are using a gluten-free product. Some foods in the book that state "gluten-free" do so because not all brands are gluten-free, so read labels closely.

Helpful Resources

Celiac.com: *www.celiac.com*

The University of Maryland Center for Celiac Research: *www.celiaccenter.org*

The North American Society for Pediatric Gastroenterology, Hepatology and Nutrition (NASPGHAN): *www.naspghan.org*

Mayo Clinic: *www.mayoclinic.com*

U.S. Department of Health and Human Services, National Institutes of Health: *www.nih.gov*

Gluten Free Drugs: *www.glutenfreedrugs.com*

Celiacs, Inc.: *www.e-celiacs.org*

FinerHealth & Nutrition: *www.finerhealth.com*

Glutenfreeda.com, Inc.: *www.glutenfreeda.com*

R.O.C.K. Raising Our Celiac Kids: *www.celiackids.com*

GFCF (Gluten Free Casein Free) Diet Support Group: *www.gfcfdiet.com*

Gluten Free Checklist: *www.glutenfreechecklist.com*

Academy of Nutrition and Dietetics (formerly the American Dietetic Association): *www.eatright.org*

So Simple Gluten Free: *www.gfreelife.com*

Celiac Disease Foundation: *www.celiac.org*

National Digestive Diseases Information Clearinghouse (NDDIC): *www.digestive.niddk.nih.gov/ddiseases/pubs/celiac*

CHAPTER 2

BREAKFAST AND BRUNCH

CRUSTLESS VEGETABLE QUICHE CUPS

This protein-packed breakfast can be made with whatever vegetables you have on hand. It's also the perfect way to sneak in your daily dose of vegetables.

Serves 12

INGREDIENTS:

1 tablespoon canola oil

½ cup finely chopped onion

1 cup fresh organic spinach

1 cup fresh grape or cherry tomatoes, halved

2 cups fresh mushrooms, diced

2 large whole eggs, beaten

6 egg whites, beaten

1 cup Cheddar cheese

¼ teaspoon thyme

½ teaspoon sweet basil

¼ teaspoon oregano

¼ teaspoon salt

⅛ teaspoon pepper

1. Preheat the oven to 350°F. Lightly spray a 12-cup muffin tin with nonstick cooking spray or line with cupcake liners.

2. Heat oil in a large skillet over medium-high heat. Add the onions and cook, stirring occasionally, until onions are soft, about 2–3 minutes. Stir in spinach, tomatoes, and mushrooms, and continue cooking until veggies have wilted, about 3–4 minutes.

3. In a large bowl, combine the eggs, egg whites, cheese, thyme, basil, oregano, salt, and pepper. Add spinach mixture and stir to blend. Pour into prepared muffin tins.

4. Bake in preheated oven until eggs have set, about 30 minutes. Let cool for 10 minutes before serving.

Powerful Protein

Studies show that people who consume a breakfast that contains protein tend to eat less throughout the day. One quiche cup has over 6 grams of protein!

VEGETABLE-EGG SCRAMBLE WITH FONTINA CHEESE

This light dish will be a favorite way to meet your daily requirements of vegetables. If you don't have broccoli or tomatoes, use whatever vegetables you have in the house.

Serves 1

INGREDIENTS:

1 tablespoon grapeseed oil

1 clove garlic, chopped

1 cup chopped broccoli

½ cup sliced grape tomatoes

1 large whole egg

2 egg whites

2 tablespoons fresh basil

½ teaspoon sea salt

1 teaspoon oregano

1 tablespoon shredded fontina cheese

1. Heat the oil in a medium skillet over medium-high heat. Sauté the garlic for 1 minute, then add the broccoli and tomatoes. Cook for 2–3 minutes until broccoli is tender, but still crunchy.

2. Whisk egg and egg whites in a bowl until frothy.

3. Pour egg and egg whites into skillet and continue to mix thoroughly while eggs cook. Add basil, salt, oregano, and cheese and cook for 3–4 minutes until eggs have light brown edges. Remove from heat and serve immediately.

Don't Pass on the Yolks, Folks

Are you using only egg whites? The yolks have a bad reputation, but they really are quite healthy. Yes, yolks do contain cholesterol and fat, but moderate consumption of yolks will not put you at higher risk for heart diseases as was once thought. Egg yolks also contain large amounts of protein, calcium, and zinc so don't be afraid to have some whole eggs once in a while too!

RICOTTA TORTE WITH SERRANO HAM AND PARMESAN

If you can't find serrano ham, substitute prosciutto. Do not, however, use low-fat ricotta—it just doesn't taste the same.

Serves 6

INGREDIENTS:

2 shallots, peeled and minced

2 tablespoons butter

3 large eggs

1 pound gluten-free ricotta cheese

½ cup freshly grated Parmesan cheese

¼ cup finely chopped gluten-free serrano ham or prosciutto

4 tablespoons butter, melted

1 teaspoon dried oregano

1 teaspoon dried basil

⅛ teaspoon nutmeg

½ teaspoon salt

½ teaspoon pepper

1. In a skillet over medium heat, sauté the shallots in the butter for 2–3 minutes. Place shallots in a pie pan prepared with nonstick spray. Preheat the oven to 325°F.

2. In a large bowl add the eggs and the rest of the ingredients, and beat constantly until well mixed and frothy. Pour into prepared pie pan and bake for 35 minutes, or until set and golden. Cut into wedges and serve.

SHIRRED EGGS AND ASPARAGUS ÀU GRATIN

This is a very easy brunch or supper dish. Fresh asparagus is definitely better in this recipe. The trick is arranging the asparagus evenly in the pan.

Serves 4

INGREDIENTS:

1 pound fresh asparagus, ends trimmed, or 2 (10-ounce) packages frozen

8 large eggs

1 cup crumbled Roquefort cheese

½ teaspoon salt

½ teaspoon pepper

1. Preheat oven to 350°F.

2. Blanch the asparagus in boiling water for 5 minutes. Remove immediately from boiling water, place in ice water, and drain.

3. Prepare a gratin pan or dish with nonstick spray and arrange the asparagus in the bottom in a single layer. Break the eggs over the top. Sprinkle with Roquefort, salt, and pepper, and bake until eggs are done and cheese is hot and runny (about 12 minutes). Serve hot.

BANANA PANCAKES

For a lighter pancake, separate the eggs and beat the whites stiffly. The bananas can be either sliced onto the cakes or mashed and incorporated into the batter.

Makes 16 pancakes

INGREDIENTS:

½ cup milk

2 large eggs

1½ tablespoons butter, melted

1 tablespoon gluten-free baking powder

1 banana

1 cup rice flour (or substitute corn, chickpea, or tapioca flour)

Extra butter for frying pancakes

1. In the bowl of a food processor, process all of the liquid ingredients together. Slowly add the baking powder, banana, and flour and process until smooth.

2. Heat a griddle pan or large frying pan over medium heat. Drop a teaspoon of butter on it and when the butter sizzles, pour batter into pan until about 2 inches in diameter.

3. When bubbles come to the top, turn the pancakes and continue to fry until golden brown. Place on a plate in a warm oven to keep the pancakes warm while you make the others.

Flour Substitutions

Try substituting rice or potato flour in some recipes, and chickpea flour also makes an excellent savory pancake. You have so many gluten-free options—it's fun to exercise them.

EGG-AND-CHEESE-STUFFED TOMATOES

These are simple but look sophisticated. Their presentation is pretty and is perfect for a brunch with friends and family.

Serves 4

INGREDIENTS:

8 medium tomatoes

2 cloves garlic, minced or put through a garlic press

4 tablespoons butter

1 teaspoon salt

1 teaspoon black pepper

1 teaspoon dried oregano

1 teaspoon cumin powder

8 large eggs

½ cup grated Monterey jack or Cheddar cheese

8 teaspoons gluten-free corn bread crumbs

1. Cut the tops off the tomatoes, core, and using a melon baller, scoop out seeds and pulp. Place the tomatoes on a baking sheet covered with parchment paper or sprayed with nonstick spray.

2. Preheat the oven to 350°F.

3. In a skillet over medium heat, sauté the garlic in the butter for 2 minutes.

4. In a small bowl, mix together the salt, black pepper, oregano, and cumin. Spread ½ of the mixture on the insides of the tomatoes, saving the rest for topping.

5. Spoon the butter and garlic mixture into the tomatoes. Sprinkle with ½ of the *remaining* spice mixture.

6. Break an egg into each tomato. Sprinkle with the rest of the spice mixture.

7. Loosely spoon the cheese over the eggs, then sprinkle 1 teaspoon corn bread crumbs over each tomato.

8. Bake for 20 minutes. The tomatoes should still be firm, the eggs soft, the cheese melted, and the bread crumbs browned.

Priceless Heirlooms

There are good tomatoes in the supermarket and good tomatoes in cans, but the best tomatoes are homegrown. Recently there has been a trend toward growing ancient varieties of tomato. These heirlooms, as they are called, have more flavor—sweetness paired with acid—than ordinary tomatoes do. You can buy the seeds and grow them yourself, and some farmers' markets have them too.

APPLE-CINNAMON CREPES

The aroma of these delicious crepes will be sure to please children and adults alike. And yes, they taste as delightful as they smell. For a special treat, top them with Cool Whip or gluten-free ice cream.

Serves 6

INGREDIENTS:

2 large tart apples, such as Granny Smith, peeled, cored, and chopped

1 tablespoon butter

1 teaspoon cinnamon

¼ teaspoon ground cloves

2 tablespoons brown sugar, or to taste

4 ounces cream cheese, at room temperature

12 Chestnut Flour Crepes (see recipe in this chapter), made with sugar

1. Preheat oven to 350°F.

2. In a large skillet over medium heat, sauté the apples in butter for 20 minutes. Stir in cinnamon, cloves, and brown sugar.

3. Blend the cream cheese into the hot mixture.

4. Lay out crepes and place a spoonful of filling on each. Roll them and place in a baking dish prepared with nonstick spray.

5. Bake in oven until hot, about 8–10 minutes. Serve warm.

CHESTNUT FLOUR CREPES

Chestnut flour is sweet and nutty, making the most delicious crepes you can imagine. Stuff them with fruit and Cool Whip or with savory fillings.

Makes 12 crepes

INGREDIENTS:

2 large eggs

1 cup milk

½ teaspoon salt

½ cup chestnut flour

½ cup rice flour

2 teaspoons sugar (optional)

2 tablespoons butter, melted (plus more for pan)

1. In a food processor, add the eggs, milk, and salt, and process until blended.

2. With the motor on low, slowly add the flours, stopping occasionally to scrape down the sides of the container.

3. Add the sugar if you are making sweet crepes with sweet filling; omit if you are going to fill them with savory delights.

4. Heat 1 tablespoon butter in a nonstick sauté pan over medium heat. Pour in batter by the half-cupful into the hot pan. Tilt the pan to spread the batter thinly.

5. Fry the crepes, turning, until browned, about 3–4 minutes on both sides; place on wax paper and sprinkle with a bit of rice flour to prevent them from sticking.

6. When the crepes are done, you can fill them right away or store them in the refrigerator or freezer for later use.

Using Nonstick Sauté Pans

Nonstick pans take all the grief out of making crepes. However, even if your pan is quite new, it's important to use a bit of butter for insurance and extra flavor. Keep the pan well buttered and you have an almost foolproof method for making perfect crepes.

BLUEBERRY OR STRAWBERRY PANCAKES

These are a healthy and delicious way to get a serving of fruit in at breakfast or brunch. You will get some caramelization from the sugar and fruit—it's delicious. Top with more berries and Cool Whip.

Makes 12 pancakes

INGREDIENTS:

½ pint blueberries or strawberries

1 teaspoon sugar

1 teaspoon grated orange zest

1½ tablespoons butter

1 batch Banana Pancakes batter (see recipe in this chapter)

1. In a bowl, mix the fruit, sugar, and orange zest. Mash with a potato masher or fork.

2. Heat a griddle over medium heat. Add butter. Pour half-cupfuls of pancake batter on the hot griddle and spoon some berries on top.

3. When bubbles rise to the top of the cakes, flip them over and brown on the other side.

Freezing Fruit in Its Prime

There's nothing like blueberry pie in January, and you don't have to use sugary canned blueberry pie filling. When fresh blueberries are available, just rinse a quart and dry on paper towels. Place the berries on a cookie sheet in the freezer for a half hour and then put them in a plastic bag for future use.

EGG AND AVOCADO BREAKFAST BURRITO

Breakfast burritos are easy enough to make even on your busiest mornings.

Serves 4

INGREDIENTS:

3 large whole eggs

3 egg whites

¼ cup shredded Cheddar cheese

⅓ cup milk

1 tablespoon grapeseed oil

¼ yellow onion, finely chopped

½ green pepper, diced

2 avocados, peeled, pitted, and mashed

¼ teaspoon salt

½ teaspoon pepper

4 gluten-free corn or rice flour tortillas, warmed

⅔ cup crumbled goat cheese

¼ cup gluten-free salsa

1. In a medium bowl, beat together the eggs, egg whites, cheese, and milk until frothy.

2. Heat the oil in a medium skillet over medium-high heat. Sauté the onion and green pepper until onion is translucent, about 2–3 minutes.

3. Pour the egg mixture into skillet and cook, stirring, until eggs are scrambled.

4. Season the mashed avocados with salt and pepper.

5. Place tortillas one at a time in a separate skillet and cook until warm, about 2–3 minutes.

6. Spread equal amounts of avocado on one side of tortillas and layer with equal amounts of goat cheese and scrambled eggs. Roll up into burritos and serve immediately with salsa on the side.

EGG AND TURKEY SAUSAGE CASSEROLE

This healthy and simple dish is perfect to make the night before, for brunch or breakfast. Feel free to experiment with different types of vegetables and cheeses too.

Serves 6

INGREDIENTS:

1 tablespoon extra-virgin olive oil

1 (16-ounce) package gluten-free lean turkey breakfast sausage

2 cups baby spinach, rinsed and dried

¼ cup shredded Cheddar cheese

6 large whole eggs

6 egg whites

½ cup skim milk

1. Spray a 9" × 13" casserole dish with cooking spray to prevent sticking. Preheat the oven to 350°F.

2. In a large skillet, heat oil over medium-high heat. Cook breakfast sausage for about 5–7 minutes, or until no longer pink inside. Place on a plate covered with paper towels to drain. Let cool, then cut into 1" slices.

3. Place the spinach on the bottom of casserole dish. Top with sausage slices and sprinkle shredded cheese on top.

4. In a large bowl, whisk eggs and egg whites with milk. Continue to beat until frothy.

5. Pour egg and milk mixture over spinach and sausage slices and bake for 35 minutes, until completely set.

EASY BREAKFAST QUINOA

Move over oatmeal, breakfast just got a little healthier! Quinoa has more high-quality protein and fiber than oatmeal and other hot breakfast options and is gluten-free. In addition, it is high in iron, magnesium, phosphorus, potassium, and zinc.

Serves 2

INGREDIENTS:

½ cup uncooked quinoa

1 cup milk of choice (fat-free suggested)

1 tablespoon chopped walnuts

1 teaspoon cinnamon

1 tablespoon almond butter

¼ cup fresh blueberries

1. Place the quinoa in a fine mesh strainer. Rinse and drain quinoa. Combine quinoa and milk in a medium saucepan. Bring to a boil. Cover and reduce heat to a gentle simmer. Cook 10–15 minutes until the milk is absorbed and the quinoa is tender.

2. Add walnuts, cinnamon, and almond butter. Mix thoroughly. Let cool. Add fresh blueberries on top.

Variations

This recipe has so many options. You can use different kinds of milks, nuts, fruits, or nut butters to get creative. To save time on busy mornings, keep cooked quinoa in the refrigerator. Simply reheat quinoa with desired toppings and enjoy.

CHESTNUT CREPES WITH PROSCIUTTO AND PEACH SAUCE

If you can't find mascarpone cheese, use cream cheese. You can make the crepes and sauce and fill the crepes in advance. Just heat everything up at the last moment.

Serves 4

INGREDIENTS:

2 tablespoons cornstarch

¼ cup cold water

2 peaches, blanched, peeled, and sliced

Juice of ½ lemon

1 teaspoon hot red pepper sauce, or to taste

½ cup sugar

Plenty of freshly ground black pepper

8 small Chestnut Flour Crepes (see recipe in this chapter)

8 teaspoons mascarpone or cream cheese

8 paper-thin slices of gluten-free prosciutto

1. Mix the cornstarch in cold water until very smooth. Place in a saucepan with the peaches, lemon juice, hot sauce, and sugar. You may need to add some more water if the peaches are not very juicy. Bring to a boil, stirring constantly, until very thick and syrupy. Taste for seasonings and add black pepper to taste.

2. Preheat oven to 300°F.

3. Lay the crepes on a baking sheet and spread with the cheese. Place a slice of ham over each and roll. Use nonstick spray on a pie pan or baking dish.

4. Arrange the rolls, seam-side down, in the pan and bake for 10–15 minutes or until the crepe rolls are hot. Serve with the peach syrup.

Blanching

When you blanch a peach, a tomato, or a nectarine, you plunge it into boiling water for a minute. You don't cook it, you just loosen the skin. If you are blanching a great many pieces, have a colander next to your pot of boiling water and a pot of ice water in the sink. Use a slotted spoon to remove the fruit from the boiling water, put it into the colander, and then plunge it into the ice water. After it is cool enough to handle, slip off the skin and cut it up.

MUSHROOM, HAM, AND CHEESE CREPES

This filling is excellent for brunch, lunch, or a light supper. You can vary the herbs.

Makes 12 crepes

INGREDIENTS:

2 cups mushrooms, brushed clean and chopped

2 tablespoons olive oil

6 sage leaves, shredded

Salt and pepper, to taste

½ cup gluten-free ricotta cheese

1 large egg, lightly beaten

12 Chestnut Flour Crepes (see recipe in this chapter)

1 batch Basic Cream Sauce (see recipe in this chapter)

½ cup freshly grated Parmesan cheese

1. Sauté the mushrooms in oil until softened. Add the sage leaves, salt, and pepper. In a bowl, mix the mushroom mixture with the ricotta cheese and egg.

2. Preheat oven to 350°F.

3. Lay out the crepes. Put a tablespoon of filling on one side of each. Roll and put in a baking dish. Cover with Basic Cream Sauce and sprinkle with Parmesan cheese.

4. Bake for 20 minutes, and serve hot.

BASIC CREAM SAUCE

This cream sauce is the basis for a lot of cooking. You can use milk instead of cream, but don't substitute margarine for butter.

Makes 2 cups

INGREDIENTS:

3 tablespoons unsalted butter

3 tablespoons corn flour

2 cups milk or cream, warmed

Salt and pepper, to taste

⅛ teaspoon nutmeg, 1 teaspoon gluten-free Dijon mustard, or 1 tablespoon snipped fresh chives (optional)

1. Melt the butter and stir in the flour. Sauté, stirring for 4–5 minutes over medium-low heat. Add the warm milk or cream, whisking constantly until thickened to desired consistency.

2. Just before serving, add salt and pepper. Optional ingredients can be added at this time.

Beyond the Basics

Once you learn to make a basic cream sauce, you can add gluten-free mustard, sautéed mushrooms, oysters, shrimp, herbs, and all kinds of luscious things. You can pour the sauce over fish or shellfish, poultry, or vegetables.

CORN CREPES WITH EGGS, CHEESE, AND SALSA

These Mexican-style crepes make a fantastic brunch!

Makes 12 crepes

INGREDIENTS:

1 batch Corn Crepes (see recipe in this chapter)

12 thin slices jack or pepper jack cheese

12 large eggs, poached or fried sunny-side up

12 teaspoons gluten-free salsa

12 teaspoons Parmesan cheese, freshly grated

1. Place the crepes on cookie sheets prepared with nonstick spray. Put a slice of cheese on each crepe. Place one egg on each piece of cheese. Spoon a bit of salsa on top of each egg.

2. Preheat the broiler to 400°F. Sprinkle the crepes with Parmesan cheese and broil for about 5 minutes, until cheese is hot and starting to melt.

3. You can put the jack cheese on top of the eggs if you wish, and serve the salsa on the side.

CORN CREPES

You can make these crepes in advance and store them in the refrigerator or freezer.

Makes 12 crepes

INGREDIENTS:

2 large eggs

1 cup milk or buttermilk

1 teaspoon salt

1 cup corn flour

2 teaspoons sugar (optional)

2 tablespoons butter, melted

1 tablespoon vegetable oil, plus more if needed

1. Place the eggs, milk, and salt in your food processor and process until smooth.

2. With the motor on low, slowly add the flour, and spoon in the sugar (if you are making sweet crepes). Scrape down the sides of the container often. Add the melted butter.

3. Heat oil in a nonstick pan over medium heat. Pour in 1 cup batter. Tilt the pan to spread the batter evenly. Cook for 3–4 minutes, turning once. Repeat with remaining batter.

4. Place crepes on sheets of wax paper that have been dusted with extra corn flour.

5. To store, place in a plastic bag in refrigerator or freezer. You can stuff these with gluten-free salsa, jack cheese, and gluten-free sour cream, or you can stuff them with mashed fruit such as blueberries.

Storing Crepes

To store crepes, simply put a bit of corn flour on sheets of wax paper and stack the crepes individually. Then put the whole thing in a plastic bag and store in the refrigerator for up to 3 days.

CORN CREPES WITH SALMON AND CREAM CHEESE

Love the taste of smoked salmon and cream cheese? These crepes will hit the spot. You can substitute unsweetened, gluten-free whipped cream for the cream cheese.

Serves 4

INGREDIENTS:

12 Corn Crepes (see recipe in this chapter)

4 ounces cream cheese, room temperature

4 ounces sliced smoked salmon

½ sweet onion, sliced thin

Gluten-free condiments, such as gluten-free horseradish, chopped chives, gluten-free mustard

1. Toast the crepes on a baking sheet under the broiler at 350°F for about 5 minutes. Spread with cream cheese.

2. Place the sliced salmon over the cheese and let people help themselves to onion slices and condiments.

Corn Is a Crucial Food

Cornmeal is an ancient grain, first raised in South and Central America. It made its way north, with seeds passed by native tribes. By the time the Pilgrims got to Plymouth, corn was a staple in North America. It's hardy, sustaining, and a "hot" food, warming the body. Without corn, or maize, supplied by sympathetic Indians, settlers in this country would not have survived.

CORN CREPES WITH RICOTTA AND HERB FILLING

Try a variety of herbs in the filling, such as fresh basil, sage, oregano, or chopped rosemary.

Makes 12 crepes

INGREDIENTS:

1½ cups gluten-free ricotta cheese

2 large eggs

¼ cup fresh, finely grated Parmesan cheese

Salt and freshly ground black pepper, to taste

¼ cup basil leaves (or your favorite herbs), finely chopped

1 batch Corn Crepes (see recipe in this chapter)

1 batch Basic Cream Sauce (see recipe in this chapter)

1 cup shredded white American cheese

1. In food processor, whirl the ricotta cheese, eggs, Parmesan cheese, salt and pepper, and basil.

2. Preheat oven to 325°F. Lay crepes out and prepare a large baking dish with nonstick spray. Place a tablespoon of filling on the end of each crepe and roll, arranging them in baking dish.

3. Pour sauce over crepes. Sprinkle with white American cheese. Bake for 25 minutes. Serve hot.

The Ties That Bind

Gluten is the glue that holds breads, cakes, and pie crusts together. When you substitute gluten-free flours for gluten-containing flours, you must use eggs or other stabilizers such as guar gum or xanthan gum to hold things together.

BASIC PANCAKES

For a lighter pancake, separate the eggs and beat the whites stiffly. These pancakes are great with mashed fresh peaches, strawberries, and/or blueberries.

Makes 16 pancakes

INGREDIENTS:

½ cup milk

2 large eggs

1½ tablespoons butter, melted

1 tablespoon gluten-free baking powder

1 cup rice flour (or substitute corn, chickpea, or tapioca flour)

Extra butter for frying pancakes

1. In the bowl of a food processor, whirl all of the liquid ingredients. Slowly add the baking powder and flour.

2. Heat griddle pan or large frying pan to medium. Drop a teaspoon of butter on it and when the butter sizzles, pour batter into pan until about 2 inches in diameter.

3. When bubbles come to the top, turn the pancakes and continue to fry until golden brown. Place on a plate in a warm oven to keep warm while you make the others.

LUSCIOUS RICOTTA GRIDDLECAKES

Preparing the batter in your blender makes it velvety smooth. You can serve with fruit, or dress with a berry coulis. The ricotta adds protein.

Makes 12 griddlecakes

INGREDIENTS:

1 cup gluten-free ricotta cheese

2 whole large eggs plus 1 egg yolk

⅓ cup plus 1 tablespoon rice or tapioca flour

1 teaspoon vanilla

1 teaspoon gluten-free baking soda

½ teaspoon salt

⅛ teaspoon nutmeg

⅛ teaspoon cinnamon

2 tablespoons unsalted butter, melted

Extra butter for sautéing the cakes

1. Whirl the ingredients in your blender, adding them in the order given, finishing with the melted butter.

2. Set your griddle over medium heat and melt a liberal amount of butter on it. When the butter foams, start pouring batter, by ¼ cupfuls, on the griddle.

3. After 4 minutes, turn and cook the other side. Stack on a platter in a low (200°F) oven to keep warm until ready to serve. Serve with fruit, syrup, or a fruit coulis.

ITALIAN RICOTTA/CHESTNUT FRITTERS

This is a traditional Italian recipe. These fritters are a wonderful side dish at brunch with bacon or ham. They're easier to make than home fries.

Serves 4

INGREDIENTS:

2 large eggs

½ cup sugar

1 teaspoon vanilla extract

1 teaspoon gluten-free baking soda

1 cup gluten-free ricotta cheese

½ cup chestnut flour

½ cup rice flour

Vegetable oil for frying

Powdered sugar to dust fritters

1. In a large bowl, beat the eggs and sugar until thick. Slowly add the rest of the ingredients except the vegetable oil and the powdered sugar. Cover the bowl and let stand for 1 hour.

2. Heat 2 inches of oil over medium-high heat to 375°F. Drop the fritters by tablespoonfuls into the oil. Do not overfill the pot. Fry for about 2 minutes, turning as they brown.

3. Drain on brown paper or paper towels and dust with powdered sugar.

Vanilla

You can use vanilla beans to make flavored sugar: Simply slit open a bean and place it in a jar with 2 cups sugar, seal, and let sit for a week. Whatever you do, don't use imitation vanilla extract.

BANANA NUT PANCAKES

The bananas can be either sliced onto the cakes or mashed and incorporated into the batter.

Serves 4

INGREDIENTS:

1 banana

Extra butter for frying cakes

1 batch Basic Pancakes batter (see recipe in this chapter)

1 cup coarsely chopped walnuts

1 cup heavy cream, whipped with 1 tablespoon sugar

1. Whirl the banana in a food processor until smooth.

2. Heat pan or griddle over medium heat. Add butter and pour the batter, a half cup at a time. Sprinkle nuts on top of each cake.

3. Turn when the pancakes begin to bubble on top. Place on a warm platter. Serve with freshly whipped cream.

Bananas: One of the Perfect Foods

Bananas have almost everything needed for survival, plus a healthy dose of potassium. Colicky babies thrive on goat's milk blended with bananas. Even during droughts and famines, banana trees continue to flourish. Their larger form, the plantain, is wonderful fried or baked, and is eaten as a complete starch.

SOUTHERN FRIED GREEN OR YELLOW TOMATOES

Use tomatoes that are very firm. They usually aren't very large, so count on two per person. Serve with thick slices of gluten-free country ham or Irish bacon.

Serves 4

INGREDIENTS:

1 cup corn flour

1 teaspoon salt

Coarsely ground black pepper, to taste

1 cup gluten-free cornmeal

2 whole large eggs, whisked in a large flat soup bowl

8 green or yellow tomatoes, cores removed, cut in ⅓" slices

Oil for frying

1. Spread the flour mixed with salt and pepper on one sheet of wax paper and the cornmeal on another. Place the whisked eggs in a bowl between the two.

2. Dip the tomato slices first in the flour, then in the egg, and coat them with cornmeal.

3. Heat ½ inch of oil in a frying pan to 350°F. Slide the tomato slices in and fry for 4 minutes or until well browned. Turn and finish frying.

4. Drain on paper towels. Serve as a side dish with eggs and bacon. As an extra fillip, you can add a dollop of gluten-free sour cream to each tomato slice.

SHIRRED EGGS WITH CRUMBLED CHEDDAR TOPPING

These are just plain cute and so appealing. For an extra touch, you can place a thin slice of tomato in the bottom of each ramekin.

Serves 6

INGREDIENTS:

12 extra-large eggs

Salt and pepper, to taste

4 tablespoons butter

¾ cup grated Cheddar cheese

1. Preheat the oven to 350°F. Prepare 12 small 4-ounce ramekins or 6 larger 6-ounce ramekins with nonstick spray. Place the ramekins on a cookie sheet. Break 1 egg into each of 12 or 2 eggs into each of 6 larger ramekins.

2. Sprinkle the eggs with salt and pepper and dot with butter.

3. Sprinkle with Cheddar cheese and bake for 8–12 minutes. Serve immediately.

An Elegant Touch

If you are having a crowd of people to brunch, place ramekins on a cookie sheet and bake for 10 minutes. Then, serve with a big bowl of fruit on the side. You can use glass custard cups, but individual ramekins made of white porcelain are more elegant.

HAM AND ASPARAGUS ROLLS WITH CHEESE

This is excellent for a cool morning. It's tasty enough to get things going, and hearty enough to stay with you for a morning of skiing or sledding outdoors.

Serves 6

INGREDIENTS:

1 10-ounce package frozen asparagus

½ pound gluten-free smoked ham, sliced thin

½ pound white American cheese, sliced thin

1 recipe Creamy Cheddar Sauce with Ham and Sherry (see recipe in this chapter)

1. Preheat oven to 350°F. Drop frozen asparagus in boiling water for 1 minute, remove from water, and dry on paper towels. Lay out the slices of ham. Place a slice of cheese and then an asparagus spear on each ham slice. Roll up and secure with toothpicks if necessary.

2. Place the rolls in a glass baking pan treated with nonstick spray. Pour cheese sauce over the top.

3. Bake for 25 minutes or until lightly browned on top and heated through. Serve hot.

CREAMY CHEDDAR SAUCE WITH HAM AND SHERRY

This is excellent over vegetables, spaghetti squash, or rice.

Makes 2½ cups

INGREDIENTS:

3 tablespoons unsalted butter

3 tablespoons corn flour

2 cups milk or cream, warmed

⅔ cup grated sharp Cheddar cheese

¼ cup minced gluten-free smoked ham

2 teaspoons sherry

Salt and pepper, to taste

1. In a medium saucepan, melt the butter and stir in the flour. Sauté, stirring for 4–5 minutes over medium-low heat. Add the warm milk or cream, whisking constantly until thickened to desired consistency.

2. Remove from the heat and stir in the cheese, ham, sherry, salt, and pepper. Serve.

Sherry as a Flavoring

There are two kinds of sherry used in cooking, dry and sweet. Sweet sherry is often called cream sherry, as in Harveys Bristol Cream. High-quality sherry is made in Spain by British companies who export it all over the world. The Chinese love it in sauces and soups, and it does add a wonderful flavor. It's also good in shrimp bisque, lobster Newburg, and other seafood dishes.

GLUTEN-FREE BREAKFAST GRANOLA

Finding gluten-free granola can be a challenge in most grocery stores, but it's super easy to make your own in the slow cooker. Make sure to stir the ingredients about every 30 minutes to prevent uneven cooking or over-browning.

Serves 10

INGREDIENTS:

2½ cups gluten-free rolled oats

¼ cup ground flaxseeds

½ cup unsweetened shredded coconut

½ cup pumpkin seeds

½ cup walnuts, chopped

½ cup sliced almonds

1 cup gluten-free dried cranberries

¾ cup brown sugar

⅓ cup coconut oil

¼ cup honey

½ teaspoon salt

1 teaspoon ground cinnamon

1. Mix all ingredients together and place in a greased 4-quart slow cooker.

2. Cover slow cooker and vent with a wooden spoon handle or a chopstick. Cook on high for 4 hours, or on low for 8 hours, stirring every hour or so.

3. When granola is toasty and done, pour it onto a cookie sheet that has been lined with parchment paper. Spread the granola out evenly over the entire sheet of parchment paper. Allow granola to cool and dry for several hours.

4. Once cooled, break granola up and place in an airtight container or a tightly sealed glass jar and store in pantry for up to 1 month. For longer storage keep granola in freezer for up to 6 months.

Change It Up

Don't like pumpkin seeds, walnuts, or dried cranberries? Use the seeds, nuts, and gluten-free dried fruit that you prefer in your own granola. Use raisins, sunflower seeds, cocoa nibs, or even dried bananas. The different variations are endless. You can even add chocolate chips if you'd like, but only after the granola has been cooked and cooled!

BLUEBERRY FRENCH TOAST CASSEROLE

Store-bought gluten-free bread is too expensive to waste if it becomes stale. This recipe shows you how to make a frugal but delicious breakfast or dessert using leftover or stale gluten-free bread.

Serves 6

INGREDIENTS:

7 cups gluten-free bread, cubed

1⅓ cups almond milk

5 large eggs, whisked

1 tablespoon vanilla

1 tablespoon 100% pure maple syrup

½ teaspoon salt

2 tablespoons butter (melted) or coconut oil

2 teaspoons cinnamon

3 tablespoons sugar

1½ cups blueberries, fresh or frozen

1. In a large bowl mix together the cubed gluten-free bread, almond milk, whisked eggs, vanilla, maple syrup, and salt.

2. Pour mixture into a greased 4-quart slow cooker.

3. Drizzle melted butter or coconut oil over the casserole. Sprinkle cinnamon and sugar evenly over the bread. Top with blueberries.

4. Cover slow cooker and vent with a wooden spoon handle or chopstick. Cook on high for 2½–3 hours or on low for 5–6 hours.

5. Remove lid and allow liquids to evaporate the last 20 minutes of cooking. Serve warm.

HAM AND CHEESE SLOW COOKER OMELET

Eggs are one of the most affordable proteins available and they are naturally gluten-free. If you make a large family-sized omelet like this on Sunday evening, you'll have ready-made breakfasts for the rest of the week.

Serves 5

INGREDIENTS:

10 large eggs

½ teaspoon gluten-free ground mustard

½ teaspoon salt

½ teaspoon paprika

½ teaspoon ground pepper

½ teaspoon dill weed

1½ cups gluten-free ham, diced

1½ cups shredded Cheddar cheese

½ cup chopped green onions (scallions)

1. Whisk eggs in a large bowl. Add in ground mustard, salt, paprika, ground pepper, and dill weed. Stir in diced ham.

2. Pour egg mixture into a greased 2½-quart slow cooker.

3. Sprinkle cheese and scallions over the top of the egg mixture.

4. Cover and cook on high for 1½–2 hours or on low for 2½–3 hours.

How to Store Fresh Green Onions

Green onions have small white bulbs and long green stalks. Both parts of the onion can be eaten. They are also referred to as spring onions or scallions. Either way, they will often go bad if left in the fridge. To preserve them, buy two or three bunches, slice them all up and place them in the freezer in a zip-top bag.

EASTERN NORTH CAROLINA CHEESY GRITS CASSEROLE

Cheesy grits is a favorite dish to bring to church potlucks and luncheons. This recipe combines eggs, bacon, and cheesy grits all in one pot.

Serves 8

INGREDIENTS:

1½ cups gluten-free Bob's Red Mill regular yellow grits (also known as "polenta style"; not quick-cooking)

4¼ cups water

1 teaspoon salt

½ teaspoon ground pepper

4 tablespoons butter, divided

6 large eggs

1 pound gluten-free bacon, cooked and crumbled

1 cup Cheddar cheese, shredded

1. Pour grits, water, salt, pepper, and 2 tablespoons of butter into a greased 4-quart slow cooker.

2. Cover and cook on high for 3 hours or on low for 6 hours.

3. Thirty minutes before serving, whisk eggs together and cook them in a saucepan over medium heat in the remaining 2 tablespoons of butter for 4–5 minutes until eggs are cooked through. Fold scrambled eggs into the cooked grits in the slow cooker. Add crumbled bacon and cheese.

4. Cook on high an additional 30 minutes to melt cheese and heat bacon through.

BREAKFAST SPANISH TORTILLA

Traditionally served as tapas (an appetizer) in Spanish restaurants and bars, this version of the Spanish tortilla removes a lot of the fat and makes a healthy breakfast casserole. Conventionally it does not contain cheese, but feel free to sprinkle some on top in the last 30 minutes of cooking.

Serves 6

INGREDIENTS:

2 small onions, finely diced

3 tablespoons olive oil

10 large eggs

1 teaspoon salt

1 teaspoon ground pepper

3 large baking potatoes, peeled and thinly sliced

1. In a skillet over medium heat, slowly cook onions in olive oil until lightly brown and caramelized, about 5–6 minutes.

2. In a large bowl whisk together the eggs, salt, and pepper.

3. Layer half of the potatoes and fried onions in a greased 4-quart slow cooker. Pour half the eggs over the layers. Repeat layers ending with the last of the whisked eggs.

4. Cover and cook on low for 6–7 hours or on high for 3½–4 hours.

Spanish Tapas

It's common practice in Spain to visit a bar or restaurant and order several types of tapas, which are usually appetizer-type foods that can be served hot or cold.

BREAKFAST BURRITO FILLING

Serve in a large gluten-free brown rice tortilla or corn tortilla with your favorite breakfast burrito toppings, such as diced avocados, gluten-free sour cream, or salsa.

Serves 4

INGREDIENTS:

1¼ pounds lean boneless pork, cubed

12 ounces diced tomatoes with green chilies (or plain diced tomatoes if you prefer a less spicy filling)

1 small onion, diced

1 jalapeño, seeded and diced

½ teaspoon ground chipotle

¼ teaspoon gluten-free cayenne pepper

2 cloves garlic, peeled and minced

Place all ingredients into a greased 2½-quart slow cooker. Stir together. Cover and cook on low for 8 hours. Stir before serving.

CRUSTLESS QUICHE LORRAINE

Ham is often already salty, so take that into consideration when deciding how much salt to add to the egg mixture. The gluten-free bread "crust" in this recipe is optional; the quiche is just as delicious without it.

Serves 4

INGREDIENTS:

4 slices gluten-free bread, toasted

4 teaspoons butter

2 cups Swiss cheese, grated

½ pound cooked gluten-free ham, cut into cubes

6 large eggs

1 tablespoon gluten-free mayonnaise

½ teaspoon gluten-free Dijon mustard

1 cup heavy cream

½ teaspoon salt

½ teaspoon freshly ground black pepper

Dash of gluten-free cayenne pepper

1. Grease a 4-quart slow cooker with nonstick spray. If desired, remove the crusts from the gluten-free toast. Butter each slice with 1 teaspoon of butter, tear the toast into pieces, and arrange the toast pieces butter-side down in the slow cooker.

2. Spread half of the cheese over the toast pieces, and then spread the ham over the cheese, and top the ham layer with the remaining cheese.

3. In a bowl, beat the eggs together with the mayonnaise, mustard, cream, salt, black pepper, and cayenne pepper. Pour the egg mixture into the slow cooker.

4. Cover and cook on high for 1½–2 hours or on low for 3–4 hours, until the eggs are set.

EGGS FLORENTINE

Freshly ground black pepper goes well in this dish. You can use up to a teaspoon in the recipe. If you prefer to go lighter on the seasoning to accommodate individual tastes, be sure to have a pepper grinder at the table for those who want to add more.

Serves 4

INGREDIENTS:

9 ounces (2 cups) Cheddar cheese, grated, divided

1 (10-ounce) package frozen spinach, thawed

1 (8-ounce) can sliced mushrooms, drained

1 small onion, peeled and diced

6 large eggs

1 cup heavy cream

½ teaspoon gluten-free Italian seasoning

½ teaspoon garlic powder

½ teaspoon freshly ground black pepper

1. Grease a 4-quart slow cooker with nonstick spray. Spread 1 cup of the grated cheese over the bottom of the slow cooker.

2. Drain the spinach and squeeze out any excess moisture; add in a layer on top of the cheese. Next add the drained mushrooms in a layer and then top them with the onion.

3. In a small bowl beat together the eggs, cream, Italian seasoning, garlic powder, and pepper. Pour over the layers in the slow cooker. Top with the remaining cup of cheese.

4. Cover and cook on high for 2 hours or until eggs are set.

Make It Dairy-Free

To make egg casseroles dairy-free, replace the cream with full-fat coconut milk. For the Cheddar cheese, there are many dairy-free alternatives available now; one in particular, called Daiya, is sold in shreds and melts beautifully in dishes like this.

SAUSAGE AND CHEESE CASSEROLE

A big bowl of freshly prepared fruit salad would be the perfect accompaniment to this savory casserole.

Serves 8

INGREDIENTS:

1 tablespoon extra-virgin olive oil or vegetable oil

1 large onion, peeled and diced

1 green pepper, seeded and diced

1 pound ground sausage

4 cups frozen gluten-free hash brown potatoes, thawed and drained of all liquid

8 large eggs

¼ cup water

½ teaspoon salt

½ teaspoon freshly ground pepper

½ pound Cheddar cheese, grated

1. Preheat a deep 3½-quart nonstick sauté pan over medium-high heat and add the oil. Once the oil is heated, add the onion and pepper and sauté until the onion is transparent, about 5 minutes.

2. Add the sausage, browning (and crumbling) and cook for 5 minutes. Remove any excess fat, if necessary, by carefully dabbing the pan with a paper towel.

3. Stir the hash browns into the sausage mixture, and then transfer the mixture to a 4-quart slow cooker treated with nonstick spray.

4. In a medium bowl, whisk together the eggs, water, salt, and pepper. Pour over the sausage–hash brown mixture in the slow cooker. Cover and cook on low for 4 hours.

5. Turn the cooker to warm. About 45 minutes before you'll be serving the casserole, sprinkle the cheese over the cooked mixture in the slow cooker. After 30 minutes, uncover the casserole and let stand for 15 minutes before serving.

Feeding a Crowd

You can stretch this recipe to even more servings by increasing the amount of chopped peppers you sauté with the onion. In fact, a mixture of red, green, and yellow peppers makes for a delicious combo.

BREAKFAST QUINOA WITH FRUIT

Take a break from oatmeal and try this fruity quinoa instead!

Serves 4

INGREDIENTS:

1 cup quinoa

2 cups water

½ cup gluten-free dried mixed berries

1 pear, thinly sliced and peeled if desired

½ cup dark brown sugar

½ teaspoon ground ginger

¼ teaspoon cinnamon

⅛ teaspoon cloves

⅛ teaspoon nutmeg

Place all ingredients into a 4-quart slow cooker. Stir. Cook for 2½ hours on high or around 4 hours on low or until the quinoa has absorbed most of the liquid and is light and fluffy.

What Is Quinoa?

Pronounced "keen-wah," this crop is grown as a grain, although it's actually a seed. It's become very popular in recent years, being touted as a health food. The grain itself has actually been used for thousands of years in South America. It's a perfect addition to the gluten-free diet because of its high nutritional content.

CHEESY HASH BROWN CASSEROLE

This is a perfect slow cooker recipe that is easy to put together the night before. Place it in the fridge and it can be slow cooked for a little over 2 hours on high in the morning.

Serves 4

INGREDIENTS:

1 package shredded hash browns, squeezed dry of all water

2 large eggs

2 cups shredded Cheddar cheese, divided

1 cup gluten-free mayonnaise

¼ cup chopped onion

½ cup melted butter or margarine, divided

1½ cups gluten-free Rice Chex cereal, crushed

1. Grease a 2½- or 4-quart slow cooker.

2. In a large bowl, mix together the drained hash browns, eggs, 1½ cups cheese, mayonnaise, chopped onions, and ¼ cup melted butter. Pour into greased slow cooker.

3. In small bowl stir together crushed Rice Chex, remaining melted butter, and remaining cheese. Spread topping evenly over hash browns. Cover slow cooker and vent the lid with a chopstick or the handle of a wooden spoon.

4. Cook on high for 2½ hours or on low for 4 hours, until casserole is cooked through and is firm and cheese has melted on the top.

SPICED CIDER

The aroma of this warming cider will fill your whole house!

Serves 20

INGREDIENTS:

2 cinnamon sticks

1" chunk fresh ginger, peeled

1 tablespoon whole cloves

1 gallon apple cider

1 tablespoon dark brown sugar

½ teaspoon ground nutmeg

1. Place the cinnamon sticks, ginger, and cloves into a cheesecloth packet. Place the packet, the cider, brown sugar, and nutmeg into a 6-quart slow cooker. Stir until the sugar dissolves.

2. Cook on high for 2–3 hours or until very hot. Reduce to low to keep hot until serving. Remove packet after cooking if desired.

How to Make a Cheesecloth Packet

Place the items to be enclosed in the packet on a length of cheesecloth. Cut out a square about three times larger than the area the items take up. Pull all ends toward the middle and tie closed with kitchen twine.

HOT CRANBERRY-PINEAPPLE PUNCH

If you prefer, you can omit the brown sugar and water and sweeten the punch with 2 cups of apple juice instead.

Serves 20

INGREDIENTS:

8 cups cranberry juice

8 cups unsweetened pineapple juice

2 cups brown sugar, packed

2 cups water

2 (3") cinnamon sticks

2 teaspoons whole cloves

1. Add the cranberry juice, pineapple juice, brown sugar, and water to a 6-quart slow cooker.

2. Break the cinnamon sticks into smaller pieces and add them along with the whole cloves to a muslin spice bag or wrap them in cheesecloth tied shut with cotton string or kitchen twine. Add to the slow cooker. Cover and cook on low for 1 hour.

3. Uncover and stir until the brown sugar is dissolved into the juice. Cover and cook for another 7–8 hours.

4. Uncover the cooker and lift out the spice bag or cheesecloth. Holding it over the slow cooker, squeeze it to extract the seasoned juice. To serve, ladle into heatproof mugs.

Chilled Cranberry-Pineapple Punch

After slow cooking, allow the punch to cool to room temperature and then chill until needed. Add 3–4 cups lemon-lime soda or Mountain Dew. Serve in punch cups or in tall glasses over ice, garnished with a maraschino cherry.

CHAPTER 3

QUICK BREADS AND SPREADS

WINTER CRANBERRY ORANGE CORN BREAD

This is wonderful with turkey and can also be chopped and used as stuffing.

Serves 8–10

INGREDIENTS:

1 cup gluten-free cornmeal (yellow or white)

1 cup corn or rice flour

¼ cup light brown sugar

3 teaspoons gluten-free baking powder or baking soda

1 teaspoon salt

1 cup milk

2 large eggs, beaten

3 tablespoons unsalted butter, melted

½ cup gluten-free dried cranberries

Zest of 1 orange

½ cup chopped walnuts (optional)

1. Preheat the oven to 400°F. Spray an 8" square baking pan with nonstick spray.

2. In a large bowl, mix all of the dry ingredients together. Slowly stir in the rest of the ingredients.

3. Turn into the pan and bake for 20–25 minutes. Cool for a few minutes before cutting into squares and serving.

INDIAN CORN CAKES

This is delightful as a side dish or as an easy snack.

Makes about 12 cakes

INGREDIENTS:

7 cups water

1 tablespoon salt, or to taste

2 cups gluten-free cornmeal

½ teaspoon freshly ground black pepper, or to taste

1 teaspoon molasses

4 tablespoons butter or lard

1. Bring the water to a boil and add salt. Stir in the cornmeal and cook for about 20 minutes, stirring occasionally. Add the pepper and molasses.

2. Prepare an 11" × 13" glass lasagna pan with nonstick spray. Spread the corn mixture in the pan and cover. Refrigerate for 1–2 hours, or until very stiff.

3. Heat butter or lard in a large frying pan. Cut the corn cakes into twelve squares and fry until golden on both sides, about 3–4 minutes per side.

Corn Lore

Native Americans saved early settlers in this country with their stores of corn. Native Americans taught the colonists how to grow, dry, and mill corn into meal. Interestingly, corn, as a crop, started in ancient Mexico and Central America. The valuable crop went all the way to Canada, indicating tribal movement and sharing.

MAPLE CORN CAKES

This is a wonderful quick meal for the kids. Serve with gluten-free bacon, sausages, or ham and eggs, if you are really hungry.

Makes 12 medium-sized pancakes

INGREDIENTS:

2 cups rice flour

5 teaspoons gluten-free baking powder

1 teaspoon salt

2 tablespoons 100% pure maple syrup

2 cups milk

2 large eggs

1 tablespoon butter, melted

1½ cups corn kernels (fresh or frozen)

Butter or oil for the griddle

1. Mix the dry ingredients together in a bowl.

2. Slowly add the syrup, milk, eggs, and butter, whisking to keep it light. Fold in the corn.

3. Heat the skillet or griddle to medium. Drop the batter on the buttered griddle using a ladle. Fry until little bubbles form on the tops of the cakes. Turn and fry on the reverse side until golden brown. Serve with maple syrup, or fresh berries and gluten-free whipped cream.

APPLE BROWN BETTY WITH CORN BREAD

Now you know what to do with old, stale bread. You can make it into a delicious, homey, baked pudding.

Serves 4

INGREDIENTS:

4 large tart apples, peeled, cored, and sliced

Juice of ½ lemon

2 cups corn bread cubes

2 large eggs, lightly beaten

1½ cups milk

1 teaspoon vanilla extract

¼ teaspoon ground nutmeg

¼ teaspoon ginger

1 teaspoon ground cinnamon

⅛ teaspoon ground cloves

½ teaspoon salt

½ cup dark brown sugar, or to taste

½ cup butter

1. Preheat the oven to 350°F. Liberally butter a 2-quart casserole dish or treat it with nonstick spray.

2. Put the apples in the casserole and sprinkle with lemon juice. Add the bread cubes. Mix well.

3. In a medium bowl, beat together the eggs, milk, vanilla, spices, salt, and sugar. Mix with the apples and bread cubes. Dot with butter.

4. Bake for 45 minutes, or until brown on top and very moist inside. Serve warm with gluten-free whipped cream or gluten-free ice cream.

Why Not Use Canned Whipped Cream?

Whipped cream that comes in aerosol spray cans is much sweeter than the cream you would whip yourself. Also, there is more air than cream, so you are paying a premium for the spray convenience. When you do your own cream whipping, you will get a lot more flavor, no additives, and a healthier end product. And you will be sure it is gluten-free as well!

CRUNCHY CORN BREAD SQUARES

These can also be cut into rectangles and used as bases for dips and spreads.

Makes 15–20 squares

INGREDIENTS:

1 cup gluten-free cornmeal

1 cup corn flour

2 teaspoons baking soda

1 teaspoon cream of tartar

1 teaspoon salt, or to taste

4 tablespoons white or brown sugar

1 cup gluten-free sour cream

¼ cup buttermilk

2 large eggs, beaten

1. Prepare a 9" × 13" baking pan with nonstick spray and preheat oven to 425°F. Mix all of the dry ingredients together in a bowl. Stir in sour cream, buttermilk, and eggs. (You can add various herbs and spices to change the flavors, such as oregano and garlic powder for an Italian flavor or chili and cumin for a Mexican taste.)

2. Pour into the prepared baking pan and bake for 20 minutes or until lightly browned.

Snacking

Always a part of American eating habits, snacks should be a healthful addition to the diet. Overly sweet snacks such as cakes and candies are not all that helpful, as they produce a sugar high followed by more hunger. Healthy foods such as fruits, vegetables, gluten-free whole grains, and dairy products are satisfying and help to keep away hunger.

FRIED POLENTA SQUARES WITH SALSA

Make the polenta a day in advance, then refrigerate it until just before you eat it.

Makes 12–24 squares

INGREDIENTS:

6½ cups water

2 tablespoons salt

2 cups yellow gluten-free cornmeal

2–4 ounces unsalted butter

2 tablespoons dried herbs or 1 tablespoon each fresh: basil, rosemary, and parsley

½ cup freshly grated Parmesan cheese

Freshly ground black pepper, to taste

2 tablespoons unsalted butter and 2–4 tablespoons vegetable oil, for frying

1 (8-ounce) jar of your favorite gluten-free salsa or homemade Guacamole (see recipe in Chapter 4) for dipping

1. Bring the water to a boil.

2. Add salt, and using your hand, drop the cornmeal into the boiling water, letting it slip slowly between your fingers to make a very slim stream. You should be able to see each grain. Do not dump the cornmeal into the water or you will get a mass of glue.

3. Stir constantly while adding the cornmeal. Reduce heat to a simmer and keep stirring for about 20 minutes as it thickens.

4. Stir in the butter, herbs, Parmesan cheese, and pepper. Spread in a 9" × 13" glass pan prepared with nonstick spray.

5. Chill for 3 hours or overnight. Cut into squares and fry until golden brown over medium heat in a combination of butter and oil. If you are having an outdoor party, you can grill the squares over low flame for a smoky flavor. Serve with gluten-free salsa or Guacamole.

GLUTEN-FREE MILLET BREAD

Some people who are sensitive to gluten are also sensitive to other grains such as corn. This bread is free of gluten, corn, dairy/casein, soy, and rice and is a perfect alternative for those with multiple food sensitivities.

Serves 12

INGREDIENTS:

⅓ cup sorghum flour

⅓ cup arrowroot starch

1 cup millet flour

1 teaspoon xanthan gum

1 teaspoon gluten-free baking soda

¼ teaspoon salt

3 tablespoons sugar

3 tablespoons oil

2 large eggs

1 cup almond milk

1 tablespoon lemon juice or apple cider vinegar

1. In a large bowl whisk together sorghum flour, arrowroot starch, and millet flour. Add xanthan gum, baking soda, salt, and sugar. Mix together thoroughly.

2. In a smaller bowl mix together the oil, eggs, almond milk, and lemon juice or apple cider vinegar.

3. Mix wet ingredients into dry ingredients with a fork, until you have a thick batter.

4. Grease 3 emptied and cleaned (15-ounce) aluminum cans and place ⅓ of the bread batter into each can. The cans will be about half full.

5. Place the cans in a 4-quart slow cooker. Pour ½ cup of water around the cans.

6. Cover the slow cooker and vent the lid with a chopstick. Cook on high for 3–3½ hours or on low for 6–7 hours. Bread should rise, double in size, and become golden brown on top when done.

7. Remove cans of bread carefully from slow cooker and allow the bread to cool before removing from cans. Slice each loaf into 4 round pieces of bread. Serve warm.

Use Recycled Cans for Slow Cooker Baking

When using recycled aluminum cans for baking, make sure to carefully cut away sharp edges with wire cutters so that you do not chance cutting your fingers when filling or emptying the cans. Clean cans carefully between each use with a baby bottle cleaner.

GLUTEN-FREE CORN BREAD

When you're following a gluten-free diet, one of the hardest foods to replace can be bread. This easy recipe for gluten-free corn bread is baked right in your slow cooker. Perfect as a side for weeknight meals or to use in stuffing for the holidays!

Serves 12

INGREDIENTS:

⅓ cup brown rice flour

⅔ cup arrowroot starch

⅔ cup gluten-free cornmeal

1 teaspoon xanthan gum

2 teaspoons gluten-free baking powder

½ teaspoon salt

3 tablespoons sugar

¼ cup oil

2 large eggs

1 cup milk or dairy-free substitute

1. In a large bowl whisk together brown rice flour, arrowroot starch, and cornmeal. Add xanthan gum, baking powder, salt, and sugar. Mix together thoroughly.

2. In a smaller bowl mix together the oil, eggs, and milk.

3. Mix wet ingredients into dry ingredients with a fork, until you have a thick batter.

4. Grease 3 emptied and cleaned (15-ounce) aluminum cans and place ⅓ of the corn bread batter into each can. The cans will be about half full.

5. Place the cans in a 4-quart slow cooker. Pour ½ cup of water around the cans.

6. Cover the slow cooker and vent the lid with a chopstick. Cook on high for 3–3½ hours or on low for 6–7 hours. Bread should rise, double in size, and become golden brown on top when done.

7. Remove cans of bread carefully from slow cooker and allow bread to cool before removing from cans. Slice each loaf into 4 round pieces of bread. Serve warm.

Gluten-Free Cornmeal

Many companies that process cornmeal also make mixes that include wheat flour. It's important to find a company that makes cornmeal that has been tested to have less than 20 ppm (parts per million) of gluten. This recipe was tested using Bob's Red Mill brand gluten-free cornmeal.

PULL-APART CINNAMON RAISIN BISCUITS

Who ever thought you could make gluten-free biscuits in the slow cooker? Well you can, and they turn out light and soft with a perfect crumb! To prevent the biscuits on the edge from browning too quickly you can line the slow cooker with parchment paper.

Serves 9

INGREDIENTS:

1 cup brown rice flour

1 cup arrowroot starch

1 tablespoon gluten-free baking powder

1 teaspoon xanthan gum

½ teaspoon salt

⅓ cup sugar

½ teaspoon ground cinnamon

⅓ cup vegetable shortening

2 large eggs

¾ cup whole milk

½ cup raisins

1. In a large bowl whisk together the brown rice flour, arrowroot starch, baking powder, xanthan gum, salt, sugar, and cinnamon.

2. Cut in the vegetable shortening using a fork and knife, until it resembles small peas within the gluten-free flour mixture.

3. In a small bowl whisk together eggs and milk. Pour into the flour mixture and mix with a fork to combine, until the dough is like a very thick, sticky cake batter. Fold in the raisins.

4. Grease a 4-quart slow cooker and/or line with parchment paper.

5. Drop biscuit dough in balls, about the size of a golf ball, into the bottom of the greased slow cooker. The biscuits will touch each other and may fit quite snugly.

6. Cover slow cooker and vent lid with the handle of a wooden spoon or a chopstick. Cook biscuits on high for about 2–2½ hours or on low for around 4–4½ hours. Biscuits around the edge of the slow cooker will be browner than those in the center. The biscuits should have doubled in size during cooking. The biscuits are done when a toothpick inserted in the center of the middle biscuit comes out clean.

7. Turn the slow cooker off and remove the insert to a heat-safe surface such as the stovetop or on top of potholders. Allow the biscuits to cool for several minutes before removing from slow cooker insert. They will "pull apart" individually.

Quick Vanilla Glaze

Impress your family by making a quick powdered sugar glaze for these lightly sweetened biscuits/buns. Mix together 1 cup of powdered sugar with 1½ tablespoons of water or milk and ½ teaspoon of vanilla extract. Drizzle artistically over warm buns and serve immediately.

PEAR CLAFOUTI

Clafouti is a soft, pancake-like breakfast with cinnamon and pears. If you choose to use a larger slow cooker than the specified 2½-quart, you will need to reduce the cooking time. When the sides are golden brown and a toothpick stuck in the middle comes out clean, the clafouti is done.

Serves 4

INGREDIENTS:

2 pears, stem and seeds removed, cut into chunks, and peeled if preferred

½ cup brown rice flour

½ cup arrowroot starch

2 teaspoons gluten-free baking powder

½ teaspoon xanthan gum

¼ teaspoon salt

⅓ cup sugar

1 teaspoon ground cinnamon

2 tablespoons vegetable shortening, melted

2 large eggs

¾ cup whole milk

1 tablespoon vanilla extract

1. Place cut-up pears into a greased 2½-quart slow cooker.

2. In a large bowl whisk together the brown rice flour, arrowroot starch, baking powder, xanthan gum, salt, sugar, and cinnamon.

3. Make a well in the center of the dry ingredients and add melted shortening, eggs, milk, and vanilla. Stir to combine wet with dry ingredients.

4. Pour batter over pears. Cover slow cooker and vent lid with a chopstick or the handle of a wooden spoon.

5. Cook on high for 2½–3 hours or on low for 5–6 hours. Serve warm or cold, drizzled with maple syrup.

Gluten-Free Baking Shortcut

Don't want to mix up all these ingredients? You can replace the brown rice flour, arrowroot starch, baking powder, and xanthan gum with 1 cup of Bob's Red Mill Gluten-Free Pancake Mix, or your favorite gluten-free pancake mix.

GLUTEN-FREE SLOW COOKER YEAST BREAD

Did you know you can make gluten-free sandwich bread right in your slow cooker? If using the loaf pan for this bread, make sure to use the size recommended in the recipe. Otherwise, your bread can rise too high and then fall while baking.

Serves 12

INGREDIENTS:

⅓ cup arrowroot starch

⅓ cup blanched almond flour

3 tablespoons millet flour

1½ cups brown rice flour

1 teaspoon salt

1 tablespoon xanthan gum

2 teaspoons bread machine yeast (try: Saf, Red Star, or Fleischmann's)

3 tablespoons sugar

1 large egg, plus 2 egg whites, room temperature

1⅓ cups whole milk, heated to 110°F

3 tablespoons olive oil

1. In a large bowl whisk together arrowroot starch, blanched almond flour, millet flour, brown rice flour, salt, xanthan gum, yeast, and sugar.

2. In a smaller bowl whisk together the egg, egg whites, milk, and oil.

3. Pour wet ingredients into whisked dry ingredients. Stir with a wooden spoon or a fork for several minutes until dough resembles a thick cake batter. First it will look like biscuit dough, but after a few minutes it will appear thick and sticky.

4. Line an 8½" × 4½" metal or glass loaf pan with parchment paper or spray with nonstick cooking spray. Pour bread dough into the pan. Using a spatula that's been dipped in water or coated with oil or nonstick cooking spray, spread the dough evenly in the pan. Continue to use the spatula to smooth out the top of the bread dough. Place the loaf pan in a 6-quart or larger oval slow cooker.

5. Cover the slow cooker and vent the lid with a chopstick or the handle of a wooden spoon. Cook on high for 3½–4 hours. The bread will rise and bake at the same time. The bread should be about double in size, and the sides should be a light golden brown; the bread will not "brown" as much as it would in the oven.

6. Remove the bread from the pan and cool on a wire rack. Slice and keep in an airtight plastic bag on the counter for 2 days. Freeze any remaining bread.

Free-Form Oval Bread

If you don't have a large 6-quart slow cooker, simply line a 2½- or 4-quart slow cooker with parchment paper. Spray it with nonstick cooking spray. Coat your hands or a large spoon with cooking spray or olive oil and shape the dough into an oval loaf. Place loaf in the middle of the parchment paper and bake as directed below. You will need to keep a close eye on the loaf as it can burn around the edges since it's closer to the heating element.

SLOW COOKER GLUTEN-FREE YEAST ROLLS

This recipe proves how versatile gluten-free yeast dough can be, even in the slow cooker! You will need 2 (4-quart) slow cookers or 1 (6-quart) slow cooker for this recipe.

Serves 12

INGREDIENTS:

1 batch Gluten-Free Slow Cooker Yeast Bread dough (see recipe in this chapter)

3 tablespoons olive oil or melted butter

½ teaspoon garlic powder

½ teaspoon toasted sesame seeds

½ teaspoon gluten-free Italian seasoning

1. Using an ice cream scoop, scoop dough into 12 balls and place each ball in a greased cupcake liner. Place the cupcake liners on the bottom of one large or two smaller slow cookers.

2. Brush rolls with oil or melted butter and sprinkle garlic powder, sesame seeds, and/or Italian seasoning over the tops.

3. Cover and vent the lid with a chopstick or the handle of a wooden spoon. Cook on high for 1½–2½ hours until dough has almost doubled in size and the rolls are cooked through. You will need to watch the rolls at the end of the cooking period as they can get overdone on the edges since they are so close to the cooking element.

Drop Rolls

Instead of using cupcake liners you can simply line the slow cooker with parchment paper. Spray the parchment paper with nonstick cooking spray and drop the scoops of dough onto the parchment paper. Bake as directed.

BUTTERMILK GLUTEN-FREE DROP BISCUITS

Buttermilk adds a tangy flavor to these fluffy gluten-free biscuits.

Serves 10–12

INGREDIENTS:

2 cups brown rice flour

¼ cup sorghum flour

½ cup arrowroot starch

¼ cup potato starch or cornstarch

2 tablespoons sugar

4 teaspoons gluten-free baking powder

1 teaspoon salt

1 teaspoon gluten-free baking soda

1 teaspoon xanthan gum

½ cup chilled butter

1¼ cups buttermilk

1 large egg

1. In a large bowl whisk together all dry ingredients. Cut butter into the dry ingredients with two knives or with a pastry cutter until it resembles small peas throughout the dry ingredients.

2. In a smaller bowl mix together buttermilk and egg. Pour buttermilk mixture into the dry ingredients and mix with a fork. Biscuit dough will be slightly stiff when thoroughly mixed.

3. Line a 6-quart slow cooker with parchment paper and spray it with nonstick cooking spray.

4. Using an ice cream scoop, scoop out 10–12 drop biscuits and place them on the parchment paper on the bottom of the slow cooker.

5. Cover and vent the lid of the slow cooker with a chopstick or the end of a wooden spoon. Cook on high for 2–2½ hours until the biscuits have risen by about half and are cooked through.

Dairy-Free "Buttermilk"

For a dairy-free buttermilk alternative mix 2 tablespoons of lemon juice or apple cider vinegar with 1¼ cups almond milk or coconut milk.

BRAZILIAN CHEESE BREAD

This cheesy, naturally gluten-free bread is made from tapioca starch, a flour often used in Brazilian cooking and baking.

Serves 10–12

INGREDIENTS:

1 teaspoon salt

2 cups tapioca starch

2 teaspoons garlic powder

⅔ cup freshly grated Parmesan cheese

½ cup olive oil

⅔ cup 2% milk

2 large eggs, beaten

1. In a large bowl whisk together salt, tapioca starch, garlic powder, and Parmesan cheese.

2. Make a well in the center of the ingredients and add olive oil, milk, and eggs. Mix together until you have a sticky dough.

3. Line a 6-quart slow cooker with parchment paper and spray it with nonstick cooking spray.

4. Using a greased ice cream scoop, scoop out 10–12 balls of dough and place them on the parchment paper on the bottom of the slow cooker.

5. Cover and vent the lid of the slow cooker with a chopstick or the end of a wooden spoon. Cook on high for 2–2½ hours until the rolls have risen by about half and are cooked through.

NO GRAIN BREAD

This bread is perfect for sandwiches, toast, or even grilled cheese. The flaxseed adds antioxidants and fiber, making this bread nutritious and delicious.

Serves 12

INGREDIENTS:

2½ cups golden flaxseed meal

½ cup almond meal

1 tablespoon gluten-free baking powder

¼ teaspoon gluten-free baking soda

1 teaspoon salt

1½ tablespoons sugar

1 teaspoon cinnamon

3 large eggs, beaten

½ cup water

3 tablespoons extra-virgin olive oil

1. Preheat oven to 350°F. Place parchment paper in a 9" × 5" × 3") loaf pan.

2. In a large bowl, mix flaxseed meal, almond meal, baking powder, baking soda, salt, sugar, and cinnamon.

3. Add eggs, water, and oil to dry ingredients and combine well. Let batter set for 2–3 minutes to thicken up, then pour into the prepared pan.

4. Bake for about 20 minutes, until the top is brown, and the loaf springs back when you touch the top.

5. Cool and cut into slices. Store leftovers in the refrigerator to preserve freshness for up to 5 days.

THE BEST GRAIN-FREE BANANA BREAD EVER

Even those who don't need to be on a gluten-free diet will adore this banana bread. It tastes just as good with or without the walnuts.

Serves 10

INGREDIENTS:

¼ cup butter, softened

⅔ cup turbinado sugar

2 large eggs

3 tablespoons plain nonfat gluten-free Greek yogurt

2 tablespoons water

1 teaspoon vanilla extract

2 tablespoons ground flaxseed

2 cups brown rice flour or rice flour

1 teaspoon gluten-free baking powder

½ teaspoon gluten-free baking soda

½ teaspoon salt

½ teaspoon cinnamon

1 cup mashed ripe banana (approximately 3 large bananas)

⅓ cup finely chopped walnuts (optional)

1. Preheat the oven to 350°F.

2. In a large bowl, beat the butter and sugar until creamy. Beat in the eggs, one at a time.

3. Stir in yogurt, water, and vanilla extract and mix well.

4. In a separate bowl combine the flaxseed, rice flour, baking powder, baking soda, salt, and cinnamon. Add this mixture to the butter mixture.

5. Stir in the bananas and mix well.

6. Spoon the mixture into two or three greased mini loaf pans (5½" × 3") or one large loaf pan (5" × 10").

7. Bake 50–55 minutes, or until a wooden pick inserted into the center of the bread comes out clean.

8. Cool in the pans for 2 minutes, then turn out and cool completely.

Brown Rice Flour

Brown rice flour has more fiber and B vitamins than regular rice flour. It also offers a nutty, slightly sweet taste as opposed to regular rice flour so it may be a better alternative than cookies and baked goods.

DARK CHOCOLATE–COCONUT SCONES

These gluten-free scones are perfect with a cup of coffee or tea. You can use carob chips to make them dairy-free as well.

Serves 8

INGREDIENTS:

1½ cups gluten-free, all-purpose flour

¼ cup coconut flour

½ teaspoon xanthan gum

¼ cup turbinado sugar

2 teaspoons gluten-free baking powder

⅛ teaspoon salt

¾ cup finely shredded coconut, unsweetened

½ cup coconut oil

2 large eggs

⅓ cup coconut milk

1 teaspoon vanilla extract

¼ cup dark chocolate chunks or chips

Coconut or additional turbinado sugar for sprinkling (optional)

1. Preheat the oven to 400°F. Line a baking sheet with parchment paper or use a silicone mat.

2. In a large bowl, mix together the flours, xanthan gum, sugar, baking powder, salt, and coconut. Work in the coconut oil until the mixture is crumbly.

3. In a separate bowl, whisk together the eggs, milk, and vanilla extract until frothy. Add to the dry ingredients, stirring until well blended. The dough will be sticky. Fold in the chocolate chunks.

4. Drop the dough onto the parchment paper or silicone mat and form into a circle in the center of baking sheet. Cut circle into 8 triangles.

5. Sprinkle the scones with coconut or turbinado sugar if desired. Bake for 15–20 minutes, or until golden brown. Remove from the oven and let cool for 5 minutes before serving.

CHOCOLATE CHIP–ZUCCHINI BREAD

You will never know that there are vegetables in this yummy bread or that it's gluten-free. It's a perfect way to sneak vegetables into picky children!

Serves 8

INGREDIENTS:

2 large eggs

½ cup turbinado sugar

½ cup grapeseed oil

½ cup unsweetened applesauce

1 tablespoon vanilla extract

1 cup brown rice flour

½ cup almond flour

½ cup cornstarch

1 teaspoon xanthan gum

½ teaspoon gluten-free baking soda

¼ teaspoon gluten-free baking powder

½ teaspoon salt

1 tablespoon cinnamon

¼ teaspoon ground cloves

¼ teaspoon nutmeg

1½ cups fresh zucchini, shredded

½ cup chocolate chips

1. Preheat oven to 350°F. Grease a 9" × 5" loaf pan with cooking spray.

2. In a large mixing bowl, beat together the eggs, sugar, oil, and applesauce. Add the vanilla extract and mix well.

3. In a separate bowl, combine the flours, cornstarch, xanthan gum, baking soda, baking powder, salt, cinnamon, cloves, and nutmeg.

4. Add the dry ingredients to wet ingredients and mix well.

5. Add zucchini and chocolate chips and stir to combine.

6. Pour into the greased loaf pan and bake for 60–70 minutes. Place a toothpick in center of bread and if it comes out clean, it's done.

DOUBLE CHOCOLATE-QUINOA MUFFINS

Quinoa adds a wonderful texture and a good amount of protein to these delicious chocolate muffins.

Makes 12 muffins

INGREDIENTS:

1¾ cups pure, gluten-free buckwheat flour

¼ cup unsweetened cocoa powder

½ cup fine sugar

1½ teaspoons gluten-free baking powder

1 teaspoon sea salt

1 teaspoon cinnamon

¼ cup grapeseed oil

1 large egg

1 cup reduced fat buttermilk

1¼ teaspoons vanilla

2 cups cooked quinoa, cooled

⅓ cup semisweet chocolate chips

¼ cup chopped almonds or whatever nuts you like

1. Preheat the oven to 350°F. Line muffin tins with cupcake liners or spray with baking spray.

2. Combine all the dry (the first 6) ingredients in a bowl and mix with a wire whisk.

3. In a separate, larger bowl, combine the wet ingredients (including the chocolate chips and nuts) and mix thoroughly.

4. Carefully fold in the dry ingredients and mix just until they are combined.

5. Fill muffin tins ¾ full with batter. Bake for 25 minutes, or until the insertion of a toothpick in the center comes out clean. Let cool slightly before removing from the pan.

Boost the Antioxidant Power

Why not add some ground flaxseed to increase your fiber and antioxidants? Simply add 2 tablespoons ground flaxseeds to the second step and add omega-3 fatty acids, antioxidants, fiber, and protein.

PUMPKIN SPICE MUFFINS

You will love these muffins, as they will leave you satisfied, and you will never miss gluten, wheat, or dairy.

Makes 18–24 muffins, depending on their size

INGREDIENTS:

1 (15-ounce) can of puréed pumpkin

2 large eggs

¼ cup canola oil

1 teaspoon gluten-free baking powder

½ cup turbinado sugar

½ cup 100% pure maple syrup

¼ teaspoon salt

1 tablespoon pumpkin pie spice

1 teaspoon ground cinnamon

½ teaspoon ground cloves

⅛ teaspoon ground ginger

1¼ cups flaxseed, ground

1 cup all-purpose, gluten-free flour

1. Preheat the oven to 375°F. Spray muffin tins with baking spray or line with cupcake liners.

2. In a large bowl, mix all the ingredients together except for the ground flaxseed and the flour until thoroughly combined.

3. Add the ground flaxseed and flour slowly and mix to combine.

4. Bake for 35–40 minutes, until toothpick comes out clean when inserted in the middle of muffin.

SPICY CORN BREAD, STUFFED WITH CHILIES AND CHEESE

This is perfect with soup, fried chicken, stews, and chowders. You can easily adjust the spices according to your taste.

Serves 6–8

INGREDIENTS:

1 cup gluten-free cornmeal (yellow or white)

1 cup corn or rice flour

¼ cup light brown sugar

3 teaspoons gluten-free baking powder or baking soda

1 teaspoon salt

¼ teaspoon cumin

1 teaspoon dried red pepper flakes, or to taste

½ cup buttermilk

½ cup gluten-free sour cream

2 large eggs, beaten

2 tablespoons unsalted butter, melted

½ cup chipotle chilies, chopped

½ cup grated pepper jack or Cheddar cheese

1. Preheat oven to 400°F. In a large bowl, mix together the cornmeal, flour, sugar, baking powder or baking soda, salt, cumin, and red pepper flakes.

2. Mix in the buttermilk, sour cream, eggs, and melted butter.

3. Prepare an 8" square baking pan with nonstick spray. Place half of the batter in the pan. Sprinkle with peppers and cheese. Cover with the rest of the batter. Bake for 20–25 minutes.

The Word on Chipotle

Chipotle chilies are jalapeño chili peppers that have been smoked and preserved in brine or vinegar. They are useful in cooking and baking, adding a smoky zing to recipes.

AMISH APPLE BUTTER

Traditionally flavored with warm spices and sweetened with honey, this condiment is called "butter" due to its thick consistency and soft texture. Since apple butter needs a long, unhurried cooking period to caramelize the fruit and deepen the flavors, the slow cooker is the most suitable modern cooking appliance to make it.

Yields 8 cups

INGREDIENTS:

10 cups (about 5 pounds) Gala apples, peeled, cored, and quartered

1 cup honey

3 tablespoons lemon juice or apple cider vinegar

1½ teaspoons ground cinnamon

½ teaspoon ground cloves

½ teaspoon allspice

1. Place apples in a greased 4-quart slow cooker.

2. Pour honey and lemon juice over apples and add cinnamon, cloves, and allspice. Stir to coat apples.

3. Cover and cook on low for 14–16 hours (yes, 14–16 *hours*), until the apple butter is a deep, dark brown and is richly flavored.

4. Ladle into pint jars and store in the refrigerator for up to 6 weeks. You can also process and can the apple butter if you prefer.

Old-Fashioned Apple Butter Making

Apple butter used to be made in large copper pots while simmering over a hot fire all day long. It was often done by a church group, or by a large family who could share the responsibility of stirring the pot throughout the long day to prevent it from burning. Once finished, the apple butter would be canned and sold to raise money for a good cause or shared among all who helped make it.

APPLE AND PEAR SPREAD

Make the most of in-season apples and pears in this easy alternative to apple or pear butter.

Yields 1 quart

INGREDIENTS:

4 Winesap apples, cored, sliced, and peeled

4 Bartlett pears, cored, sliced, and peeled

1 cup water or pear cider

¼ cup brown sugar

¼ cup sugar

¼ teaspoon ginger

¼ teaspoon cinnamon

¼ teaspoon nutmeg

¼ teaspoon allspice

1. Place all ingredients into a 4-quart slow cooker. Cook on low for 10–12 hours.

2. Uncover and cook on low for an additional 1–2 hours or until thick and most of the liquid has evaporated.

3. Allow to cool completely then pour into the food processor and purée. Pour into clean glass jars. Refrigerate up to 6 weeks.

Do-It-Yourself Brown Sugar

Brown sugar is simply white sugar that has been mixed with molasses. Make brown sugar by combining 1 cup granulated sugar with ¼ cup molasses. Store in an airtight container.

BLACKBERRY JAM

This easy low-sugar jam does not need to be canned; it will keep up to a month in the refrigerator.

Yields about 1 quart

INGREDIENTS:

3 cups fresh blackberries

1¾ ounces low-sugar/no-sugar pectin

½ cup sugar

¾ cup water

1. Place all ingredients in a 2-quart slow cooker. Stir.

2. Cook on high, uncovered, for 5 hours. Using a fork or potato masher, smash the berries a bit until they are the texture you prefer. Pour jam into an airtight container.

3. Refrigerate overnight before using.

PEACH MARMALADE

You can spread this on gluten-free toast or biscuits. It can also be used to turn an ordinary gluten-free cracker (Glutino is a wonderful brand) into a delicious snack or appetizer.

Yields about 8 cups

INGREDIENTS:

2 pounds peaches, peeled, pitted, and chopped

½ cup (about 6 ounces) gluten-free dried apricots, chopped

1 (20-ounce) can pineapple tidbits in unsweetened juice, undrained

2 medium oranges

1 small lemon

2½ cups granulated cane sugar

2 (3") sticks cinnamon

1. Add peaches to a food processor or blender along with the apricots and pineapple (with juice).

2. Remove the zest from the oranges and lemon. Add to the food processor or blender. Cut the oranges and the lemon into quarters and remove any seeds, then add to the food processor or blender. Pulse until entire fruit mixture is pulverized. Pour into a greased 4–6-quart slow cooker.

3. Add the sugar to the slow cooker and stir to combine with the fruit mixture. Add the cinnamon sticks. Cover and, stirring occasionally, cook on low for 4 hours or until the mixture reaches the consistency of applesauce. When finished cooking remove cinnamon sticks.

4. Unless you process and seal the marmalade into sterilized jars, store in covered glass jars in the refrigerator for up to 3–4 weeks. The marmalade can also be frozen for up to 6 months.

Innovative Peach Marmalade Uses

By keeping this marmalade the consistency of applesauce you have the added versatility of using it as a condiment to top cooked chicken breasts, easily mixing it together with barbecue or chili sauce to create a sweet and savory dipping sauce, or using it to replace applesauce in many different recipes.

CHAPTER 4

SNACKS

AVOCADO–WHITE BEAN HUMMUS

Simple yet impressive, this snack or appetizer will wow your family and guests. It also makes a delicious and healthy alternative to mayonnaise on your favorite sandwich.

Serves 10

INGREDIENTS:

1 (15-ounce) can cannellini beans, drained and rinsed

1 ripe avocado, peeled, pitted, and diced

1 large garlic glove, coarsely chopped

¼ cup water, plus more as needed

Juice of 1 lemon

2 tablespoons extra-virgin olive oil

1 teaspoon kosher salt

2 tablespoons coarsely chopped fresh cilantro

Freshly ground black pepper

1. Place the cannellini beans, avocado, garlic, water, lemon juice, olive oil, salt, chopped cilantro, and pepper in a food processor fitted with a blade attachment or a high-speed blender.

2. Process until smooth, scraping down the sides of the bowl as needed. If the dip is too thick, pulse in more water, a tablespoon at a time, until the desired consistency is reached. Serve with Baked Corn Tortilla Chips (see recipe in this chapter).

BAKED CORN TORTILLA CHIPS

Who says tortilla chips have to be laden with fat and calories to taste good? These tasty chips are perfect with all kinds of gluten-free dips and salsas.

Serves 6

INGREDIENTS:

24 gluten-free corn tortillas

1 teaspoon kosher salt

1. Preheat the oven to 350°F.

2. Cut tortillas into large triangular slices. Lay slices out in a single layer on a baking sheet and sprinkle with salt.

3. Bake 8–12 minutes, or until chips start to lightly brown. Repeat with remaining tortilla slices. Let cool for 10 minutes before eating.

Read the Label!

Some corn tortillas are made with wheat gluten! Thoroughly reading the labels will help keep you informed, because sometimes they don't advertise that they contain wheat.

GOLDEN PARMESAN CRISPS

It's important to use a block of fresh Parmesan cheese for this recipe. The bottled stuff won't work as well because it's too fine and too dry. Use the coarse grating blade of a food processor or box grater.

Makes 12 crisps

INGREDIENTS:

2 tablespoons unsalted butter (more if necessary)

12 heaping tablespoons coarsely grated fresh Parmesan cheese

1 teaspoon thyme

Freshly ground black or gluten-free cayenne pepper, to taste

1. Heat the butter in a large fry pan over medium heat until it bubbles.

2. Spoon the cheese by tablespoonfuls onto the butter, pressing down lightly with the back of the spoon to spread, making 12 tablespoon-sized crisps.

3. After about 2 minutes, turn and cook until both sides are lightly golden brown. Add more butter if necessary.

4. Sprinkle with thyme and black pepper or cayenne, or both. Serve at once.

RASPBERRY YOGURT SMOOTHIE

Smoothies are a wonderful, healthy, and filling alternative to standard snack or even breakfast options. They are so versatile and can be used with so many different ingredients.

Serves 2

INGREDIENTS:

1 cup plain nonfat gluten-free Greek yogurt

½ cup frozen raspberries

½ cup fat-free milk (almond, soy, or milk of your choice)

½ banana

2 tablespoons ground flaxseed

Place all of the ingredients in blender for 1–2 minutes until thoroughly blended. Serve immediately.

The Benefits of Flax

Flax is a seed that is packed with more antioxidants, fiber, and omega-3 fatty acids than just about anything its size. These omega-3 fatty acids are the ones that fight inflammation in the body and help prevent diseases and chronic illnesses. Ground flaxseed can be found in most supermarkets and health food stores.

CHOCOLATE PEANUT BUTTER SMOOTHIE

This smoothie is so delicious you won't even believe that it is healthy!

Serves 2

INGREDIENTS:

2 tablespoons unsweetened cocoa powder

2 tablespoons natural creamy gluten-free peanut butter

½ banana, frozen

½ cup almond milk (or milk of your choice)

½ cup plain gluten-free Greek low-fat yogurt

½ teaspoon vanilla extract

4–5 ice cubes

Combine all ingredients in a blender and blend until thick and creamy. Serve immediately.

Looking to Add More Protein to Your Smoothie?

Protein powder is an easy way to increase your protein, especially in smoothies. There are many varieties of protein powders. Read your labels carefully to make sure the protein powders have no ingredients containing gluten.

BLUEBERRY-OATMEAL SMOOTHIE

Gluten-free rolled oats add a wonderful texture to your average smoothie.

Serves 2

INGREDIENTS:

½ cup gluten-free rolled oats

1 cup soy milk

1 banana, frozen

¾ cup fresh or frozen organic blueberries

1 teaspoon honey (optional)

4–5 ice cubes (if using fresh blueberries)

Place the oats in a blender and blend for 1–2 minutes until they are ground into a fine powder. Add the rest of the ingredients, blend, and enjoy!

Freeze-Ahead Fruit

Frozen fruit is perfect for smoothies and you can always keep it in your freezer. Feel free to mix it up and use whatever fruit you have on hand.

SNEAKY KIWI-PINEAPPLE SMOOTHIE

This smoothie is a terrific way to "sneak" vegetables into your kids' smoothie! If they are suspicious of the bright green color, tell them that it's the kiwi that turned the smoothie green.

Makes 2 smoothies

INGREDIENTS:

1 cup pineapple chunks, fresh or frozen

2 kiwis, peeled and chopped

½ banana

6 ounces plain gluten-free Greek yogurt

½ cup pineapple juice

Ice (you can use less if you use frozen pineapple)

2 tablespoons chia seed or flaxseed (optional)

1 cup spinach or kale (optional)

Place all the ingredients in a blender. Blend until smooth. Serve immediately.

MIXED BERRY SMOOTHIE

This smoothie is ideal for breakfast or as a snack. You can substitute different frozen fruits if you do not have frozen berries on hand.

Serves 2–3

INGREDIENTS:

2 cups unflavored almond milk, or milk of your choice

1 tablespoon 100% pure maple syrup

1 teaspoon vanilla extract

½ cup frozen raspberries

½ cup frozen strawberries

1 tablespoon coconut oil

½ teaspoon cinnamon

½ cup blueberries, frozen

1. Place all ingredients into a blender container in the order listed.

2. Blend until smooth, about 1 minute. Pour into glasses and serve.

POPCORN WITH PARMESAN TOPPING

There is no need to add butter to this popcorn. Parmesan cheese adds a delightful flavor to your typical, ordinary popcorn.

Serves 8

INGREDIENTS:

1 tablespoon grapeseed oil

1 cup popcorn kernels

½ teaspoon sea salt

½ cup Parmesan cheese, freshly grated

1. Place grapeseed oil in bottom of a large pot.

2. Place popcorn kernels on top of the oil in the pan. Do *not* turn stove on yet. Stir kernels to make sure they are evenly coated with the oil.

3. Place heat on medium and, with the pot uncovered, shake the kernels around in the pot until the first kernel pops. Quickly place the lid on top and wait until all the kernels pop.

4. Once done, remove from heat and add salt and Parmesan cheese. Stir to mix thoroughly. You can store popcorn in an airtight container for up to 6 months.

HOMEMADE SWEET POTATO CHIPS

Sweet potatoes are loaded with vitamin A and are very delicious when fried and salted. (You can substitute plantains for a taste of the islands.)

Makes about 3 dozen chips

INGREDIENTS:

2 large sweet potatoes, peeled

3 cups canola oil

Salt and pepper, to taste

1 teaspoon cinnamon (optional)

1. Slice the potatoes thinly with a mandoline.

2. Heat the oil in a deep-fat fryer to 375°F.

3. Fry potato slices for about 3–4 minutes, depending on the thickness of the chips. When the chips are very crisp, remove from the oil and drain.

4. Add salt, pepper, and cinnamon if desired. Serve with a gluten-free dip or eat plain.

Veggie-Chips!

These "chips" can be prepared with a variety of different vegetables. You can make eggplant, zucchini, or even parsnip chips. The kids won't even suspect they are healthy!

APPLE AND PEAR NACHOS

Children will not only love eating these, but they will have so much fun preparing them too.

Serves 4

INGREDIENTS:

1 sliced apple, cored

1 sliced pear, seeds and stem removed

2 tablespoons raw almond butter, slightly heated

2 ounces pecans, walnuts, almonds, or nuts of choice

Chocolate chips, to taste

Golden raisins, to taste

Shredded coconut

1. Arrange apple and pear slices on a plate.

2. Pour the melted nut butter over the top. Then add nuts, chocolate chips, raisins, coconut, or any other of your favorite toppings, and serve immediately.

PARMESAN-KALE CHIPS

Low calorie and nutritious, these make the perfect snack for the little ones. Just like potato chips, you can eat the whole bowl in one sitting.

Serves 6

INGREDIENTS:

1 bunch kale (the curly kind is less bitter)

1 tablespoon extra-virgin olive oil in Misto sprayer

1 teaspoon salt

1 tablespoon finely, freshly grated Parmesan cheese

1. Preheat oven to 350°F. Line a non-insulated cookie sheet with parchment paper.

2. With a knife or kitchen shears, carefully remove the kale leaves from the thick stems and tear into bite-sized pieces. Wash and thoroughly dry kale with a salad spinner.

3. Spray the kale with olive oil from Misto sprayer and sprinkle with salt and Parmesan.

4. Bake until the edges brown, but are not burned, 10–15 minutes.

BANANA-NUTTER SANDWICH

Move over PB & J, there's a new sandwich in town. This one is gluten-free and uses bananas instead of jelly.

Serves 6

INGREDIENTS:

1 loaf No Grain Bread (see recipe in Chapter 3)

½ cup natural gluten-free peanut butter

3–4 large bananas, sliced

1. Slice loaf of bread into 12 slices.

2. Spread peanut butter on 6 slices, then add sliced bananas. Place remaining bread slices on top to make a sandwich.

Wrap It Up!

These sandwiches are just as delicious when you use gluten-free wraps. Simply spread peanut butter on wrap, top with banana slices, and wrap it up! Feel free to substitute other nut butters as well.

SWEET CHERRY-QUINOA GRANOLA BARS

Your kids will be asking for these granola bars over and over again. Feel free to use whatever dried fruits you have on hand as a substitute for cherries.

Makes 18 bars

INGREDIENTS:

1½ cups gluten-free puffed rice cereal

1 cup pure rolled oats (make sure they are gluten-free)

1 cup cooked quinoa

½ cup gluten-free dried cherries, unsweetened

⅓ cup sunflower seeds

⅓ cup sliced walnuts

¼ cup pumpkin seeds

2 tablespoons flax, ground

2 tablespoons chia seed, ground

1 teaspoon ground cinnamon

½ teaspoon sea salt

⅓ cup sunflower seed butter

6 tablespoons 100% pure maple syrup

1. Preheat the oven to 325°F. Line a baking sheet with parchment paper and set aside.

2. In a large mixing bowl, combine all ingredients, *except* the sunflower seed butter and maple syrup.

3. In a small saucepan, heat the sunflower seed butter and syrup over medium low heat until it becomes liquefied and smooth.

4. Pour the liquid ingredients over the dry ingredients and mix together until fully combined and everything is coated evenly.

5. Spread the granola out on the parchment-lined baking sheet, into a thin ¼" layer.

6. Bake in the center of a warmed oven for 25 minutes, until the granola is browned and slightly crispy. (Don't cook any longer; it may not look burned but it will be.)

7. Let the granola cool for about 10 minutes on the baking sheet.

8. Transfer to a flat surface and cut into bars and finish cooling on a wire rack. Enjoy either in bar form or crumble as granola pieces. Store in an airtight container, for up to 5 days.

PEPPERONI PIZZA QUESADILLAS

What happens when pizza meets a gluten-free tortilla? You get Pizza Quesadillas that your whole family will love.

Serves 4

INGREDIENTS:

8 gluten-free corn or brown rice flour tortillas

2 cups Easy Pizza Sauce (see recipe in this chapter), plus extra for dipping

8 ounces shredded mozzarella cheese

⅓ pound gluten-free pepperoni

Sliced mushrooms, peppers, onions (optional)

1. Brush each tortilla with a thin layer of pizza sauce (so thin that if you turned it over, none would drip).

2. Sprinkle cheese on top of the sauce on the bottom tortilla. Top with pepperoni and other toppings, if desired. Sprinkle with another layer of cheese and place the other tortilla on top (sauce side in).

3. Lay out tortilla and place it on a griddle or in a pan sprayed with cooking spray and cook for 3–5 minutes on each side, until cheese is melted and tortillas are crispy.

4. Slice into quarters and serve with a little bowl of pizza dipping sauce.

EASY PIZZA SAUCE

This delicious sauce will enhance the flavor of any type of pizza you make. This also makes a wonderful dipping sauce for quesadillas, chicken tenders, or even French fries.

Makes 2¾ cups

INGREDIENTS:

1 teaspoon extra-virgin olive oil

1–2 cloves garlic, finely chopped

½ medium onion, finely chopped

1 (15-ounce) can tomato sauce

1 (6-ounce) can tomato paste

1 tablespoon ground oregano

1 teaspoon ground basil

½ teaspoon turbinado sugar

½ teaspoon salt

1. In a skillet over medium heat, place the oil, garlic, and onions. Simmer until they soften, about 2–3 minutes.

2. In a medium bowl, mix together tomato sauce and tomato paste until smooth. Stir in oregano, basil, sugar, and salt. Add the cooked garlic and onions. Makes sauce for about 4 (10") pizzas.

FRUIT KEBABS WITH YOGURT DIPPING SAUCE

This is a really fun way to get the little ones to eat fruit. Be sure to cut the ends off the skewers for safety.

Makes 4–6 kebabs

INGREDIENTS:

1 (16-ounce) container strawberries, sliced

1 kiwi, sliced

¼ cantaloupe, scooped out with melon baller

1 apple, cut into squares

¼ honeydew, scooped out with melon baler

Juice of ½ a lemon

Yogurt Dipping Sauce (see recipe in this chapter)

1. Place sliced fruit in any order on skewers with ends cut off.

2. Sprinkle with fresh lemon juice to ensure the fruit stays fresh.

3. Serve with yogurt dipping sauce, or even melted chocolate or nut butter.

It's a Marshmallow World

Why not add some mini marshmallows to these fun kebabs? Marshmallows turn this delicious snack into a wonderful dessert.

YOGURT DIPPING SAUCE

The thickness of Greek yogurt and the sweetness of the honey make this a perfect dip for any fruit out there.

Makes 2 cups

INGREDIENTS:

2 cups vanilla gluten-free Greek yogurt

½ cup honey

¼ teaspoon lemon juice

½ teaspoon cinnamon

Mix all the ingredients in a small bowl. Serve immediately or store, covered, in the refrigerator.

Why Greek Yogurt?

Greek yogurt adds significantly more protein than regular yogurt. The thick texture of Greek yogurt is perfect for any type of dipping sauce.

ALMOND DELIGHT YOGURT DIP

This dip is a favorite of kids and grownups alike. This dip goes wonderfully with sliced apples, bananas, carrots, or celery.

Serves 4

INGREDIENTS:

4 tablespoons almond butter

16 ounces vanilla gluten-free Greek yogurt

½ teaspoon cinnamon

1 tablespoon honey

½ teaspoon vanilla extract

¼ cup chocolate chips (optional)

1. Place all ingredients (except chocolate chips if you are adding them) in a medium-sized bowl and stir until well combined.

2. Serve with sliced fruits and vegetables immediately. Top with chocolate chips if desired.

Dippers

This dip is super easy and can be used with a wide variety of foods besides fruits and vegetables. You can also dip gluten-free sliced pancakes, waffles, graham crackers, or even pretzels for a sweet/salty snack. Feel free to also substitute peanut, cashew, or sunflower seed butter for the almond butter. This is a great snack for kids' lunchboxes as well.

CORN DOG MUFFINS

The whole family will love these. These make a delicious kid-friendly meal or a simple appetizer.

Makes 24 muffins or 48 mini muffins

INGREDIENTS:

1 (16-ounce) package of gluten-free hot dogs (beef, turkey, chicken, or veggie)

1 cup all-purpose gluten-free flour

1 cup yellow gluten-free cornmeal

¼ cup turbinado sugar

2 teaspoons gluten-free baking powder

½ teaspoon salt

1 cup milk or buttermilk

2 large eggs

¼ teaspoon vanilla extract

¼ cup butter, softened

¼ cup unsweetened applesauce

1. Preheat the oven to 425°F. Spray muffin tins with nonstick cooking spray or line with muffin liners.

2. Cut hot dogs into ¼" pieces.

3. In a medium-sized bowl, mix together flour, cornmeal, sugar, baking powder, and salt.

4. Stir in milk, eggs, vanilla extract, butter, and applesauce, and mix until smooth.

5. Pour chopped hot dogs into corn bread batter. Stir well. Fill ¾ of each muffin tin with corn bread/hotdog batter.

6. Bake until muffins become light brown and center is thoroughly cooked, about 12–15 minutes. Cool for a few minutes before serving.

QUINOA GRANOLA WITH DRIED CRANBERRIES

This granola is the perfect breakfast, snack, or dessert.

Serves 8

INGREDIENTS:

1 cup gluten-free pure whole rolled oats

1 cup gluten-free buckwheat groats

⅓ cup uncooked quinoa, rinsed and drained

2 tablespoon ground chia seeds

¾ cup raw chopped pecans

¼ cup raw chopped walnuts

¼ cup raw pumpkin seeds

¼ cup raw sunflower seeds

½ cup shredded coconut, unsweetened

2 teaspoons cinnamon

1 teaspoon ground ginger

1 teaspoon allspice

½ cup 100% pure maple syrup

1 tablespoon vanilla extract

¼ cup organic coconut oil, melted

⅓ cup chopped dates

⅓ cup gluten-free dried cranberries, unsweetened

1. Preheat the oven to 225°F.

2. In a large bowl, combine the dry ingredients (first 4 ingredients). Add the nuts, seeds, and coconut. Mix well.

3. Stir to combine thoroughly while adding in the cinnamon, ginger, and allspice.

4. Mix in maple syrup, vanilla, melted coconut oil, dates, and cranberries. Make sure everything is evenly distributed and coated well.

5. Spoon and press mixture onto baking sheet lined with wax paper or parchment paper. Bake for 60 minutes.

6. Let cool after removing from oven then pull corners of wax paper together to crumble granola. Store in airtight container when cooled for up to 3 days.

COCONUT-ALMOND ICE CREAM

Even those who are not on a gluten-free or dairy-free diet will love this ice cream! You can also add dairy-free carob chips (instead of chocolate chips) to this ice cream.

Serves 6

INGREDIENTS:

4 cups coconut milk (full fat)

½ cup honey

1 tablespoon vanilla extract

½ cup toasted almonds, slivered

1. Combine all the ingredients in a large mixing bowl. You might have to whisk to get the milk and honey to combine.

2. Prepare following your ice cream maker instructions. Store in the freezer for up to 2 weeks.

No Ice Cream Maker?

What happens if you don't have an ice cream maker? Don't fret. You can easily make this without one. Add all the ingredients except almonds in a blender or food processor and blend for 2–3 minutes, until thoroughly mixed. Make sure you stop to scrape the sides of the blender too. Take mixture out of the blender and pour into an airtight freezer safe container. Toss in almonds and stir to combine. Freeze for 6–8 hours, until it hardens.

NO BAKE PEANUT BUTTER–FLAX BITES

These simple bars are an easy afterschool snack for children or for a quick treat. These are so much healthier than other treats with a long list of ingredients.

Makes 20 bites

INGREDIENTS:

1 cup dry old-fashioned gluten-free pure oats

½ cup dark chocolate chips

½ cup gluten-free natural peanut butter

½ cup ground flaxseed

⅓ cup honey

1 teaspoon vanilla extract

1. Stir all ingredients together in a medium-sized bowl until thoroughly mixed. Spread mixture in a 9" × 9" pan and place in the refrigerator to cool.

2. Cut the bites into small squares. Store in an airtight container and keep refrigerated for up to 1 week.

Alternatives

This recipe is so versatile that the possibilities are endless. You can use sunflower seed butter, cashew butter, or almond butter in place of the peanut butter. You can substitute chopped dried cranberries, raisins, cherries, or nuts for the chocolate chips. You can also roll them into little balls instead of cutting them into squares. This is a fun activity kids will enjoy helping with.

BLUEBERRY FROZEN YOGURT

This wonderful, light dessert can be made with any berries you have on hand. You can also use frozen berries and defrost them before you mix with the yogurt.

Serves 14

INGREDIENTS:

¾ cup milk

¼ cup turbinado sugar

4 cups vanilla gluten-free Greek yogurt

2 cups strawberries, puréed

1. In a medium bowl, mix the milk and sugar until the sugar is dissolved, about 1–2 minutes on low speed.

2. Stir in the yogurt and strawberry purée.

3. In an ice cream maker, freeze according to manufacturer's instructions. You can spoon the frozen yogurt into a tall, upright plastic container to place in the freezer for up to a week.

Simply Homemade

Store-bought frozen yogurt and ice creams may have over twenty ingredients in them! This recipe is a perfect example of how easy it is to make your own frozen yogurt at home with only four ingredients.

POPCORN WITH SPICY BUTTER

This is an excellent change from regular buttered popcorn. You can add more heat to it if you like, as well as seasoned salt.

Serves 2

INGREDIENTS:

½ stick (¼ cup) butter or margarine

1 teaspoon Tabasco sauce

½ teaspoon freshly ground black pepper

1 teaspoon salt

1 package microwave popcorn or 4 cups popped corn, unflavored and unbuttered

Melt the butter and add seasonings. Pour over hot popcorn, mixing vigorously.

Get Creative with Your Popcorn!

There are so many different seasonings you can add to popcorn that won't add calories, fat, or artificial additives. Chili powder, curry, garlic powder, lemon pepper, or even sugar and cinnamon, are among the many options you have. This is a perfect opportunity for children to experiment with new flavors too.

SAVORY CHICKEN SPREAD

You can use leftover roast chicken or turkey for an excellent substitution. This works nicely as a canapé, a stuffing for celery, or a spread for tea sandwiches.

Makes 3 cups

INGREDIENTS:

2 cups cooked white or dark chicken

1 stalk celery, coarsely chopped

1–2 scallions, white parts peeled

2 shallots, peeled

⅔ cup gluten-free mayonnaise (not low-fat)

1 teaspoon madras curry powder

1 teaspoon gluten-free Dijon mustard

1 teaspoon dried thyme leaves

½ teaspoon celery salt

Salt and freshly ground black pepper, to taste

½ cup fresh parsley, rinsed and chopped

Place all ingredients in a food processor and whirl until coarsely blended. Scrape into an attractive bowl and chill until ready to serve. Good with toasted gluten-free baguette slices, chips, or on lettuce as a first course. Possible garnishes include chopped chives, capers, sliced green or black olives, or baby gherkin pickles.

Capers

These tiny berries are pickled in brine or packed in salt. The islands of the Mediterranean are lush with the bushes that produce them and they are used in profusion in many fish, meat, and salad dishes. The French love them, as do the Italians, Greeks, Sardinians, and Maltese. Try some in a butter sauce over a piece of fresh striped bass and you'll understand their popularity.

CHILI BEAN DIP WITH DIPPING VEGETABLES

This is the perfect afterschool snack for hungry children. Feel free to eliminate the jalapeño if it's too spicy for the little ones.

Makes 1 quart

INGREDIENTS:

½ pound ground beef

1 medium onion, chopped

2 jalapeño peppers, or to taste, cored, seeded, and chopped

2 cloves garlic, chopped

1 tablespoon extra-virgin olive oil

¼ teaspoon ground pepper

4 teaspoons gluten-free chili powder, or to taste

1 (13-ounce) can crushed tomatoes with juice

1 (13-ounce) can red kidney beans, drained and rinsed

½ cup flat gluten-free beer

Cheddar cheese, shredded for topping (optional)

Assortment of carrots, celery pieces, radishes, broccoli, spears of zucchini, etc.

1. Sauté the beef with the onion, peppers, and garlic in the oil in a large skillet, breaking up any clumps with a spoon.

2. When the vegetables are soft, add the rest of the ingredients (except the cheese and vegetables for dipping). Cover and simmer for 1 hour.

3. Serve warm. Top with shredded cheese if desired. Or cool, and turn this into a dip by pulsing it in the food processor. Do not make it smooth. Serve alongside veggies.

Chili and Beans

There are endless variations of the chili-and-bean combination. Some people use turkey, others add dark chocolate and cinnamon and vary the amounts of beans and tomatoes. Some forms of chili don't have any beans. Different regions use various amounts of spice, heat, and ingredients.

STUFFED CELERY WITH GORGONZOLA AND GREEN PEPPERCORNS

Celery is a great replacement for, not to mention healthier than, crackers when you are on a gluten-free diet.

Makes 1½ cups

INGREDIENTS:

1 bunch celery, washed and cut into 2" lengths

¾ cup gluten-free sour cream

½ cup crumbled Gorgonzola cheese

1 tablespoon lemon juice

1 tablespoon chopped onion

1 teaspoon celery salt

1 teaspoon Tabasco or other hot pepper sauce

2 tablespoons green peppercorns, in brine

1. Arrange the celery on a platter, cover, and refrigerate.

2. Mix the rest of the ingredients together. Stuff the celery and serve. You can put this together two or three hours in advance.

3. Garnish with small shrimp, pieces of roasted red pepper, halved black olives, and/or herbs such as parsley, chives, or oregano.

GUACAMOLE

There are many recipes for guacamole. This a delicious recipe where the flavors unite wonderfully. Serve with Baked Corn Tortilla Chips (see recipe in this chapter).

Makes 1–1½ cups

INGREDIENTS:

3 medium Hass or 2 large, smooth-skinned avocados, peeled and seeded

Juice of 2 limes

½ cup finely minced sweet onion

½ cup grape or cherry tomatoes, halved

½ teaspoon Tabasco sauce, or to taste

½ teaspoon salt, or to taste

2 tablespoons finely chopped fresh cilantro

⅛ teaspoon gluten-free cayenne pepper (optional)

1. In a large bowl, using a fork, mash the avocados.

2. Mix in the rest of the ingredients until well blended.

Choosing Avocados

Most store-bought avocados are as hard as stones. That's fine; if you buy ripe ones, they generally have many blemishes. Just buy them a few days before you plan to serve them. Place them on a sunny windowsill or in a brown paper bag, or wrap them in a newspaper. The paper seems to hasten ripening. The avocado should not have oily black spots in it when you cut it open but should be a uniform green. One or two black spots can be cut out, but don't use an avocado that is full of black spots or gray-brown areas.

ALMOND AND DRIED CHERRY GRANOLA

This variation of breakfast/snack granola focuses more on gluten-free whole grains and has less sugar in the overall recipe than most granolas.

Serves 24

INGREDIENTS:

5 cups old-fashioned gluten-free pure rolled oats

1 cup slivered almonds

¼ cup mild honey

¼ cup canola oil

1 teaspoon vanilla

½ cup gluten-free dried tart cherries, raisins, or dried cranberries

¼ cup unsweetened flaked coconut

½ cup sunflower seeds

1. Place the oats and almonds into a 4-quart slow cooker. Drizzle with honey, oil, and vanilla. Stir the mixture to distribute the syrup evenly. Cook on high, uncovered, for 1½ hours, stirring every 30 minutes.

2. Add the cherries, coconut, and sunflower seeds. Reduce heat to low. Cook for 4 hours, uncovered, stirring every 30 minutes.

3. Allow the granola to cool fully, and then store it in an airtight container for up to 1 month in the pantry.

HOT CINNAMON CHILI PEANUTS

These seasoned peanuts are a surprising hit with chili powder and cinnamon and just a hint of sweetness from the honey and brown sugar.

Yields 1½ cups

INGREDIENTS:

1½ cups peanuts

¼ cup brown sugar

2 teaspoons cinnamon

1½ teaspoons gluten-free chili powder

¼ teaspoon salt

2 teaspoons honey

2 teaspoons oil

1. Combine all ingredients and place in a greased 2½-quart slow cooker.

2. Cover slow cooker and vent lid with a chopstick or the handle of a wooden spoon. Cook on high for 2 hours or on low for 4 hours. If using a larger slow cooker, you will probably need to reduce the cooking time to only 1 hour on high or 2 hours on low.

3. Pour peanut mixture out onto a baking sheet lined with parchment paper. Allow to cool and dry and then transfer to a container with an airtight lid. Store in the pantry for up to 2 weeks.

BALSAMIC ALMONDS

These sweet and sour almonds are a great addition to a cheese platter or appetizer plate.

Serves 15

INGREDIENTS:

2 cups whole almonds

½ cup dark brown sugar

½ cup balsamic vinegar

½ teaspoon kosher salt

1. Place all ingredients into a 4-quart slow cooker. Cook uncovered on high for 4 hours, stirring every 15 minutes or until all the liquid has evaporated. The almonds will have a syrupy coating.

2. Line 2 cookie sheets with parchment paper. Pour the almonds in a single layer on the baking sheets to cool completely. Store in an airtight container in the pantry for up to 2 weeks.

Healthy Almonds

Botanically speaking, almonds are a seed, not a nut. They are an excellent source of vitamin E and have high levels of monounsaturated fat, one of the two "good" fats responsible for lowering LDL cholesterol.

LOW-CARB SNACK MIX

For this recipe, use raw almonds, cashews, pecans, shelled pumpkin seeds, shelled sunflower seeds, walnuts, and raw or dry roasted peanuts. The amounts you use of each kind of nut is up to you, although because of their size, ideally the recipe shouldn't have more than 1 cup of sunflower seeds.

Serves 24

INGREDIENTS:

4 tablespoons butter, melted

3 tablespoons gluten-free Worcestershire sauce

1½ teaspoons garlic powder

2 teaspoons onion powder

½ teaspoon sea salt

8 cups raw nuts

1. Add all ingredients to 4-quart slow cooker. Stir to coat the nuts evenly. Cover and cook on low for 6 hours, stirring occasionally.

2. Uncover and continue to cook on low for another hour to dry the nuts and seeds, stirring occasionally, and then evenly spread them on a baking sheet lined with aluminum foil or parchment paper until completely cooled. Store in an airtight container in the pantry for up to 2 weeks.

Toasted Pumpkin Seeds

Pumpkin seeds make a healthy and crispy topping for salads, casseroles, and stir-fries. Simply add ½ cup of pepitas to a hot, heavy-bottomed skillet. Drizzle with 2 tablespoons olive oil and ⅛ teaspoon salt, and stir for about 5 minutes until lightly toasted.

CINNAMON AND SUGAR PECANS

Not only a tasty snack, these chopped sweet pecans are also delicious sprinkled over French toast.

Serves 12

INGREDIENTS:

3 cups pecan halves

3 tablespoons butter, melted

2 teaspoons vanilla extract

½ cup sugar

1 teaspoon cinnamon

½ teaspoon salt

1. Add all ingredients to a 4-quart slow cooker. Stir to coat the nuts evenly. Cover and cook on low for 4–5 hours or on high for 2 hours, stirring occasionally.

2. Uncover and continue to cook on low for another hour, stirring occasionally, to dry the nuts. Next, evenly spread the nuts on a baking sheet lined with parchment paper or aluminum foil until completely cooled. Store in an airtight container in the pantry for up to 2 weeks.

ROASTED PINK PEPPER NUTS

These will keep for up to one week in a tight plastic or tin container. You can also substitute black or white pepper with only slightly different results.

Makes 2½ cups

INGREDIENTS:

½ stick (¼ cup) unsalted butter

¾ cup golden brown sugar (not "Brownulated")

4 teaspoons water

½ teaspoon ground cloves

⅛ teaspoon ground nutmeg

¼ teaspoon cinnamon

2 teaspoons salt

1 tablespoon freshly ground pink peppercorns

2½ cups blanched almonds

1. Preheat the oven to 350°F. Line a cookie sheet with aluminum foil and treat with nonstick spray.

2. In a saucepan over medium heat, melt the butter, add sugar and water, and mix well.

3. Add the spices, salt, and peppercorns. When well blended, add the almonds and stir to coat.

4. Transfer the nuts to the cookie sheet. Bake for about 10 minutes, until well browned. Cool and store in airtight container.

COCONUT MILK YOGURT

If you're intolerant to dairy proteins like casein or dairy sugar (lactose), this coconut milk yogurt is a perfect alternative—and you can make it right in your slow cooker! Serve the yogurt plain or with any flavor jam or fresh fruit.

Serves 8

INGREDIENTS:

6 cups full-fat coconut milk

6 capsules of allergen-free probiotics or yogurt starter

3 tablespoons plain gelatin

½ cup sugar, optional

½ cup blackberry jam, optional

1. Pour the coconut milk into a 4-quart slow cooker. Turn the slow cooker on low and let it cook for 3 hours.

2. Turn the slow cooker off and let it sit for 3 hours. (Cooking the mixture first will help to kill off any bad bacteria that may be in the coconut milk.) Once the coconut milk has cooled after 3 hours, remove 1 cup of the warm coconut milk and mix it in a glass bowl with the contents of the probiotics capsules and the gelatin.

3. Return the probiotic/coconut milk mixture back to the slow cooker. Whisk thoroughly to distribute the probiotics and gelatin throughout the mixture. Place the lid back on the slow cooker.

4. Leave the slow cooker turned *off*, but wrap the slow cooker in several layers of bath towels to give the probiotics a warm environment to grow in. Leave the towel-wrapped slow cooker alone for 8–10 hours.

5. After 8 hours, stir in the sugar, if desired, and place the covered slow cooker insert into the fridge. Allow the yogurt to chill for 6–8 hours. This will allow the gelatin to thicken the yogurt, so it has the proper texture. Serve cold topped with blackberry jam.

Using Probiotics to Make Yogurt

You will need to purchase a yogurt starter or probiotics that contain "live active cultures" for them to work properly to create this yogurt. Alternately, if you have a grocery store nearby that sells yogurt made from coconut milk, you can simply purchase a small container of plain coconut milk yogurt and use that as your starter instead of using probiotic capsules.

MAPLE PUMPKIN SPICE LATTES

This warm latte is reminiscent of a drink you would pay big bucks for at a local coffee chain. By making your own, you're not only saving money, but you'll have enough for a whole week's worth of breakfasts or after-dinner coffees. Try it with a whipped cream topping.

Serves 8

INGREDIENTS:

2 cups very strong coffee or espresso

4 cups whole milk

¾ cup plain pumpkin purée

⅓ cup 100% pure maple syrup

1 tablespoon vanilla extract

2 teaspoons pumpkin pie spice

In a 4-quart slow cooker whisk together all ingredients. Cover and cook on high for 1½ hours or on low for 3 hours. When serving, turn slow cooker to the warm setting for up to 2 hours. Serve warm.

Make Your Own Pumpkin Pie Spice

If you don't have pumpkin pie spice, mix together 3 tablespoons ground cinnamon, 2 tablespoons ground ginger, 2 teaspoons ground nutmeg, 1½ teaspoons ground allspice, and 1½ teaspoons ground cloves. Store in an airtight container.

SALTED CARAMEL MOCHA LATTES

The slight hint of salt in this warm, creamy drink balances out the sweetness of the caramel. When serving this sweet drink, offer whipped cream, additional caramel sauce, chocolate syrup, or sea salt for toppings.

Serves 6

INGREDIENTS:

3 cups whole milk

3 cups strongly brewed coffee

2 tablespoons unsweetened cocoa powder

⅓ cup sugar

¼ teaspoon salt

1 teaspoon vanilla extract

⅓ cup caramel sauce (gluten-free)

1. Place all ingredients in a 4-quart slow cooker. Use a whisk to combine ingredients thoroughly.

2. Cover slow cooker and cook on high for 1–2 hours or on low for 2–3 hours, until mixture is hot and simmering.

Strongly Brewed Coffee

To get a very strong coffee flavor in this drink use about 3–4 tablespoons of ground coffee per cup of water. The coffee will be diluted when combined with the milk in this recipe and will be creamy and delicious.

PEPPERMINT MOCHA LATTES

A refreshing coffee drink made right in your slow cooker. You could also make a chilled peppermint mocha latte by refrigerating the leftovers and serving the drink over ice the next day!

Serves 6

INGREDIENTS:

3 cups whole milk

3 cups strongly brewed coffee

¼ cup unsweetened cocoa powder

⅓ cup sugar

½ teaspoon peppermint extract

⅛ teaspoon salt

2 cups whipped heavy cream

1. Add milk, coffee, cocoa, sugar, peppermint extract, and salt to a 4-quart slow cooker. Use a whisk to combine ingredients thoroughly.

2. Cover slow cooker and cook on high for 1–2 hours or on low for 2–3 hours, until mixture is hot and simmering.

3. Serve in large mugs or coffee cups with whipped cream.

How Much Peppermint?

Peppermint extract is made from the essential oils of the peppermint plant. It is a *very* strongly flavored extract and a little goes a long way. Start with using ½ teaspoon in this batch of peppermint lattes and if you prefer more add ⅛ teaspoon at a time until it's as minty as you like! For more peppermint flavor, crush 2 candy canes or a few peppermint hard candies to sprinkle on top.

VANILLA BEAN WHITE HOT CHOCOLATE

Children love this creamy, rich, warm vanilla-y drink made with white chocolate baking pieces.

Serves 8

INGREDIENTS:

8 cups whole milk

1 (12-ounce) package white chocolate chips

2 tablespoons vanilla extract

⅛ teaspoon salt

1 vanilla bean

2 cups whipped heavy cream

1. Add milk, white chocolate chips, vanilla, and salt to a 4-quart slow cooker. Use a whisk to combine ingredients thoroughly.

2. Using a sharp knife, cut the vanilla bean in half and scrape out the tiny seeds and add them to the milk mixture.

3. Cover slow cooker and cook on high for 1–2 hours or on low for 2–3 hours, until mixture is hot and simmering.

4. Serve in large mugs or coffee cups with whipped cream on top.

CHAPTER 5

APPETIZERS

TINY CHICKPEA CREPES

The chickpea (garbanzo bean) flour gives a slightly nutty flavor that goes well with many dips and fillings.

Serves 12

INGREDIENTS:

2 cups chickpea flour

2 cloves garlic, crushed

1 teaspoon Tabasco sauce or other red hot sauce

1 teaspoon salt

1½ cups water

¼ cup olive oil, for frying

1. Mix flour, garlic, hot sauce, salt, and water in a blender, pulsing and scraping the mixture down the sides.

2. Heat the oil in a nonstick pan over medium-high heat. Add 1 tablespoon of the batter for 1½" crepes.

3. Cook until very crisp on the bottom, about 3–4 minutes; do not turn. Remove from pan and place on paper towels or a platter. Now you can add fillings of your choice, such as cheese or vegetables, and close, or fold each crepe in half.

Rich in Soluble Fiber

Nutritionists say chickpeas (also called garbanzo beans) are rich in soluble fiber, which is the best type of fiber, actually helping to eliminate cholesterol from the body. Chickpeas are a good source of folate, vitamin E, potassium, iron, manganese, copper, zinc, and calcium. As a high-potassium, low-sodium food, they can help to reduce blood pressure.

SICILIAN EGGPLANT ROLLS

These make the perfect appetizer or entrée that will definitely impress your guests.

Serves 6

INGREDIENTS:

1 medium eggplant (about 1 pound), peeled

Salt

½ cup extra-virgin olive oil

½ cup rice flour

1 cup gluten-free ricotta cheese

¼ cup Sicilian olives, pitted and chopped

1–2 cloves garlic, chopped

¼ cup Parmesan cheese, freshly grated or be sure gluten-free

1. Cut the eggplant in very thin (⅛") slices with a mandoline or a vegetable peeler. Salt the slices and stack them on a plate; let sit under a weight for 30 minutes to let the brown juices out.

2. Pat the eggplant slices dry with paper towels.

3. Heat the oil in a large skillet or fry pan to 300°F. Dip the eggplant slices in rice flour and fry until almost crisp, about 2 minutes per side.

4. Drain the slices and then place a spoonful of the ricotta cheese and some chopped olives and garlic on the end of each slice. Roll and secure with a toothpick. Place in a greased baking pan.

5. Heat oven to 300°F. Sprinkle the rolls with Parmesan cheese and bake for 8 minutes. Serve warm.

Drain the Bitterness

Eggplant can be sliced thin lengthwise or crosswise and then fried, broiled, or baked. Salting and stacking eggplant slices under a weight will drain off the bitterness that some seem to harbor. Be sure to use a plate with steep sides or a soup bowl under the eggplant—it will release a lot of juice when salted.

LIGHT GORGONZOLA AND RICOTTA TORTE APPETIZER

This appetizer is light and delicious. You will find that this works best in a springform pan. Serve warm or at room temperature.

Serves 6

INGREDIENTS:

16 ounces fresh whole-milk gluten-free ricotta cheese

4 ounces Gorgonzola cheese, crumbled

1 teaspoon fresh oregano, or ¼ teaspoon dried

1 teaspoon fresh lemon juice

1 teaspoon freshly grated lemon zest

1 teaspoon salt

½ teaspoon pepper

3 egg whites, beaten stiff

½ cup walnuts, chopped and toasted

1. Preheat the oven to 350°F.

2. Place the cheeses, oregano, lemon juice, zest, salt, and pepper in a food processor and process until very smooth.

3. Place the mixture in a bowl and fold in the beaten egg whites.

4. Spray the inside of a 10" springform pan with nonstick cooking spray. Add the cheese mixture, and bake for about 30 minutes or until slightly golden.

5. Sprinkle with the walnuts. Cool slightly and serve in wedges.

DEVILISH EGG-STUFFED CELERY

This is a different take on deviled eggs—you devil the whole egg. Try garnishing these eggs with either 3 teaspoons salmon caviar, 3 teaspoons capers, 3 teaspoons green peppercorns, chopped fresh parsley, or hot or sweet Hungarian paprika.

Serves 12

INGREDIENTS:

6 large eggs, hard-boiled, cooled in water, cracked, and peeled

2 tablespoons gluten-free mayonnaise

6 drops Tabasco sauce

½ teaspoon freshly ground white pepper

1 teaspoon celery salt

1 tablespoon gluten-free Dijon mustard

2 tablespoons chopped onion

1 clove garlic, chopped

1 teaspoon salt

2 tablespoons half-and-half

4 stalks celery, washed and cut into thirds

1. Place all the ingredients except the celery in a food processor and blend until smooth.

2. Spread the resulting mixture into the celery and cover with foil or plastic wrap and chill for 1 hour.

3. Add garnishes of your choice just before serving.

An International Flavor

Chili sauce and mayonnaise will add a Russian flavor to the eggs. Salmon caviar as a garnish will add a Scandinavian touch. Change the amount of heat and the herbs and you will have a different taste sensation. Experiment to find the flavor combinations you like best.

PIQUANT ARTICHOKE AND SPINACH DIP

This is the perfect dip for parties and entertaining. Serve with corn or rice crackers or sliced vegetables.

Yields 2 cups

INGREDIENTS:

1 (10-ounce) package frozen chopped spinach, thawed

2 tablespoons extra-virgin olive oil

1 (12-ounce) jar artichoke hearts, drained and chopped

4 ounces cream cheese

8 ounces gluten-free sour cream

2 cloves garlic, finely chopped

½ bunch scallions, chopped

2 tablespoons fresh lemon juice

¼ teaspoon freshly grated nutmeg

1 tablespoon shredded or grated fresh Parmesan cheese

1. Drain the thawed spinach, squeezing it with paper towels, until the extra liquid is gone.

2. Heat the olive oil in a large skillet over medium heat and add the spinach; cook until just soft, about 5 minutes.

3. Remove pan from heat and add the rest of the ingredients, stirring to mix. Serve warm or cold.

The Artichoke Quandary

Some people absolutely adore artichokes that come in cans or jars; others prefer fresh or frozen. Cooking artichokes requires a bit more work, but even a busy person can cook ahead. After cooking baby artichokes, you can use them in a number of ways, after simply removing the outside leaves.

HEALTHY SHRIMP SCAMPI APPETIZER

Shrimp scampi can be healthy and delicious. It's perfect on its own for an appetizer, or you can serve it over gluten-free noodles and steamed spinach for a complete entrée!

Serves 6

INGREDIENTS:

3 tablespoons extra-virgin olive oil

1 pound cleaned, large shrimp, deveined and patted dry

4 cloves garlic, minced

1 cup reduced sodium gluten-free chicken broth

¾ teaspoon salt

¾ teaspoon pepper

1 tablespoon unsalted butter

½ cup chopped parsley

½ teaspoon grated lemon zest

Juice of ½ lemon (optional)

1. Heat oil in a 12" heavy skillet over medium-high heat until it simmers, then add the shrimp and sauté them, turning once, until just cooked through, about 2 minutes each side. Transfer shrimp with a slotted spoon to a large bowl.

2. Add the garlic, chicken broth, salt, and pepper to the skillet and bring to a boil. Continue boiling until the liquid is reduced to ½ cup, about 5–7 minutes.

3. Add the butter and stir until melted, then remove skillet from heat and stir in shrimp.

4. Add the mixture to a large bowl and toss with parsley and lemon zest. Squeeze lemon juice on top if desired.

TZATZIKI DIP

This Greek cucumber-yogurt dip is light and delightful with sliced vegetables. This is a delicious, simple dip for children.

Serves 12

INGREDIENTS:

8 ounces plain Greek low-fat gluten-free yogurt

2 tablespoons extra-virgin olive oil

1 tablespoon lemon juice

½ teaspoon salt

½ teaspoon ground black pepper

1 tablespoon fresh dill, chopped

2 cloves garlic, minced

2 tablespoons peeled, seeded, and minced English cucumber

1 tablespoon chopped fresh mint

In a medium bowl, mix all the ingredients together until thoroughly combined. Refrigerate for at least 1 hour to let the flavors settle in. Serve cold with sliced raw vegetables.

Tzatziki

Tzatziki—pronounced "tsah-ZEE-kee"—is a Mediterranean sauce made with yogurt and cucumbers. It is traditionally served as a meze (an appetizer). It can also be used as a spread on gyros (Greek sandwiches) or souvlaki (Greek fast food consisting of meat and vegetables).

DEVILED EGGS

This protein-packed recipe is a perfect afternoon snack for children and adults alike or as a yummy appetizer.

Makes 10 deviled eggs

INGREDIENTS:

5 large hard-boiled eggs

½ cup low-fat gluten-free mayonnaise

1 teaspoon gluten-free Dijon mustard

1 teaspoon Tabasco sauce or other hot red pepper sauce

½ bunch of chives, snipped finely

2 teaspoons capers, the smallest available

Paprika, for garnish (optional)

1. Peel eggs, cut them in half, and remove the yolks to your food processor. Arrange the whites on a platter.

2. Add the mayonnaise, mustard, Tabasco or pepper sauce, chives, and capers to the food processor and process until blended.

3. Stuff the egg whites with the yolk mixture, and sprinkle with paprika, as desired.

Olive Oil in Spray Bottles

This is a very easy and economical way to use olive oil. Just buy a bottle used for spraying plants with water and fill it with olive oil instead. Use it for spraying your food, salads, and so on. Or you can get olive oil–flavored nonstick spray at the supermarket. The nonstick spray, however, is not suitable for salads.

GRILLED CHICKEN WINGS

Traditional Buffalo wings are generally fried. This recipe, done with a rub and some olive oil, is a lot less fattening. Double the recipe and refrigerate half for delicious cold snacks.

Serves 4–8

INGREDIENTS:

4 pounds chicken wings, split at the joint, tips removed

1 tablespoon onion powder

1 tablespoon garlic powder

¼ teaspoon cinnamon

2 teaspoons dark brown sugar

½ teaspoon paprika

½ teaspoon ground black pepper

¼ cup freshly squeezed lime juice

¼ cup extra-virgin olive oil

1 teaspoon salt

Ground black pepper, to taste

1. Rinse the wings, and set them on paper towels to dry.

2. In a large bowl, mix the rest of the ingredients together. Coat the chicken with the spice mixture, cover, and refrigerate for 1 hour.

3. Grill over medium-hot coals or broil at 350°F for 20 minutes, turning every few minutes, or until well browned.

QUINOA MEATBALLS WITH CREAMY PESTO DIPPING SAUCE

These meatballs make the perfect appetizer or main dish. Serve with zucchini noodles or gluten-free pasta.

Serves 6

INGREDIENTS:

¼ cup uncooked quinoa, rinsed and drained

½ cup gluten-free chicken broth

1 teaspoon extra-virgin olive oil

1 small onion, chopped

2–3 cloves garlic, chopped

1 (20-ounce) package lean ground chicken (or lean turkey or ground beef)

1 tablespoon tomato paste

2 teaspoons gluten-free Worcestershire sauce

1 large egg, and 1 egg white

1 teaspoon ground rosemary

1 teaspoon ground basil

¾ teaspoon red pepper flakes

2 tablespoons fresh Parmesan cheese, grated

½ teaspoon salt

1 teaspoon ground black pepper

Creamy Pesto Dipping Sauce (see recipe in this chapter)

1. Preheat the oven to 350°F.

2. Bring the quinoa and broth to a boil in a saucepan over high heat. Reduce heat to medium-low, cover, and simmer until the quinoa is tender and the broth has been absorbed, about 15–20 minutes. Set aside to cool.

3. Heat the olive oil in a skillet over medium heat. Stir in the onion; cook and stir until the onion has softened and turned translucent, about 5 minutes. Add the garlic and cook for another minute; remove from heat to cool.

4. In a large bowl, combine the chicken, cooked quinoa, onions, garlic, tomato paste, Worcestershire sauce, egg and egg white, seasonings, Parmesan cheese, salt, and pepper. Mix until well combined. The mixture will be very moist.

5. Roll into 1½" balls. Place on a baking sheet lined with parchment paper.

6. Bake until no longer pink in the center, 20–25 minutes. Serve with pesto dipping sauce.

CREAMY PESTO DIPPING SAUCE

This sauce is perfect for dipping chicken or other meat in, or to use on top of gluten-free pasta.

Serves 10–12

INGREDIENTS:

4 ounces extra-virgin olive oil

3 cloves garlic

1½ ounces pine nuts

2 ounces Parmesan cheese, fresh or gluten-free

2 ounces fresh basil leaves, torn

4 ounces half-and-half

1. Add all the ingredients to food processor or high-powered blender in the order listed.

2. Blend for 2–3 minutes, until smooth. Serve immediately, or store in the refrigerator until ready to serve.

STUFFED ARTICHOKES WITH LEMON AND OLIVES

Artichokes have a way of making everything around them taste delicious. They can be eaten with just a little lemon juice.

Serves 4 as an entrée, or 8 as an appetizer

INGREDIENTS:

4 large artichokes, trimmed and split lengthwise

4 quarts water

½ lemon

1 cup cooked rice

10 green olives, chopped

10 kalamata olives, chopped

2 tablespoons minced parsley

3 tablespoons grapeseed oil

1 teaspoon garlic salt

Pepper, to taste

1 large egg (optional)

1. Boil the artichokes in 4 quarts of water with squeezed lemon, and including rind, for 20 minutes. Drain and lay on a baking sheet, cut-side up.

2. Preheat the oven to 350°F.

3. Mix the rest of the ingredients (including the egg, if using) together in a large bowl.

4. Spoon the filling over the artichokes, pressing between the leaves. Bake for 15 minutes, until hot.

SPICY GORGONZOLA DIP WITH RED PEPPER "SPOONS"

This is very flavorful—the more fresh herbs, the better. Try using fresh chives, basil, and oregano.

Yields 2 cups

INGREDIENTS:

6 ounces Gorgonzola cheese, at room temperature

4 ounces gluten-free mayonnaise

4 ounces cream cheese, at room temperature

2 ounces roasted red peppers (jarred is fine)

2 teaspoons freshly chopped herbs (such as oregano, basil, and chives)

Salt, black pepper, and Tabasco sauce, to taste

4 sweet red bell peppers

1. Put all but the raw red peppers into the food processor and blend until smooth. Scrape into a serving bowl.

2. Wash, core, and seed the red bell peppers, and then cut into chunks (these will be your "spoons"). Place the red pepper spoons around the dip.

Exciting and Distinctive—and Healthy—Party Fare

Many of the party appetizers in this chapter are less fattening than plain old cheese and crackers. They are definitely not ho-hum, and many are full of healthful vitamins, minerals, and phytochemicals. Bright red and yellow peppers are an excellent source of vitamin C.

HEARTY MUSHROOMS STUFFED WITH SPICY BEEF

This recipe is wonderful on a chilly night. You can even increase the portions and serve the mushrooms for lunch with a bowl of soup on the side.

Serves 4

INGREDIENTS:

6 ounces lean ground beef

1 large egg

2 tablespoons gluten-free chili sauce

1 teaspoon minced fresh garlic

½ cup chopped red onion

1" fresh gingerroot, peeled and minced

⅛ teaspoon ground cinnamon

½ teaspoon dried red pepper flakes, or to taste

½ teaspoon freshly ground black pepper

Salt, to taste

8 very large fresh mushrooms

Water or white wine (enough to cover bottom of pan)

8 teaspoons freshly grated Parmesan cheese for topping

¼ cup pine nuts, for topping

1. To make the filling, place the beef, egg, chili sauce, garlic, onion, spices, and salt in the food processor and mix thoroughly.

2. Carefully remove the stems from the mushrooms and pack them with the filling.

3. Preheat the oven to 325°F. Place the mushrooms in a baking pan and add enough water or white wine to cover the bottom of the pan.

4. Sprinkle with cheese and pine nuts. Bake for 35 minutes.

The Versatile Mushroom

Today, you can get really excellent commercially grown exotic mushrooms. Mushrooms can be called wild only if gathered in the wild. Try baby bellas, which are small portobello mushrooms. Shiitake are very fine in flavor, and oyster mushrooms are delicious. If you have no budgetary constraints, buy morels or chanterelles.

MINI QUICHES

A wonderful cocktail party snack. You can vary the ingredients, using Cheddar cheese instead of Jarlsberg and chopped cooked bacon instead of ham.

Makes 12

INGREDIENTS:

1 package gluten-free pie crust mix (made by the Gluten Free Pantry)

2 large eggs

½ cup grated Jarlsberg cheese

¼ cup minced gluten-free prosciutto or smoked ham

⅔ cup cream

⅛ teaspoon grated nutmeg

2 tablespoons minced fresh chives

Freshly ground black pepper, to taste

1. Preheat the oven to 325°F. Spray a mini-muffin pan with nonstick spray and prepare the pie crust mix according to box directions. Roll out thinly. With the rice-floured rim of a juice glass or a 2" biscuit cutter, cut dough into 12 rounds and line the muffin cups with dough.

2. Mix the rest of the ingredients in a food processor.

3. Fill the cups three-quarters full with the cheese mixture.

4. Bake for about 10 minutes, or until the quiches are set. Let rest for 5 minutes. Carefully lift the Mini Quiches from the cups. Serve warm.

Mincing Chives

Of course, you can use a knife to mince chives; however, a pair of sharp kitchen scissors works faster and better than a knife. The scissors work well with any number of other ingredients too, such as scallions, bacon, etc. As with any cutting tool, the sharper, the better—and safer. Dull tools are dangerous—they can slip off a tomato, for example—and inefficient.

STIR-FRIED SHRIMP AND VEGETABLES IN RICE CREPE WRAPS

These are wonderful as an appetizer or as an entrée. Feel free to dip them in teriyaki sauce (but read the label to make sure it is gluten-free).

Serves 4

INGREDIENTS:

1 tablespoon sesame seed oil

¼ cup peanut oil

4 scallions, sliced

4 cloves garlic, minced

1 zucchini squash, finely chopped

1 medium onion, finely chopped

⅔ pound raw shrimp, shelled and deveined

½ cup almonds, chopped

1 tablespoon fish sauce (gluten-free)

¼ cup dry sherry

1 teaspoon wasabi powder mixed with 2 teaspoons water to make a paste

1 batch Rice Flour Crepes (see recipe in this chapter)

1 large egg, beaten

1. Heat the sesame and peanut oils in a wok or frying pan and add the vegetables and shrimp. Stir and cook until the shrimp turn pink, about 2–3 minutes.

2. Add the rest of the ingredients except for the crepes and the egg. Mix well. Place the shrimp and vegetables in a bowl and cool.

3. Put a spoonful of filling on half of a crepe. Paint the rim of the circle with the beaten egg. Fold over and press to seal.

4. Broil on high heat or steam the filled crepes for 10 minutes, or until they are steaming hot. Serve hot.

RICE FLOUR CREPES

Use 1½ cups of rice milk instead of water if you want a richer crepe.

Serves 4

INGREDIENTS:

2 large eggs

1½ cups water or rice milk

½ teaspoon salt

¼ teaspoon freshly ground white pepper

1 cup rice flour

Peanut or canola oil

1. Place the eggs, water or rice milk, and salt in a blender and process them together. Add pepper and flour, stopping once to scrape the sides of the container.

2. Oil a nonstick pan, set heat to medium, and slowly pour or ladle small amounts (about ¼ cup) of the batter into the pan, lifting and tipping to spread the batter.

3. When the edges start to get brown, after about 3 minutes, flip the crepe. Cook for only 1 minute on the reverse side or it will become crisp and not pliable.

4. Cool and stack between sheets of wax paper.

Crepes, Pancakes, and Tortillas—Ripe for the Stuffing

While gluten-free flours can be a disaster under certain circumstances, they are a great success when it comes to crepes, pancakes, and corn tortillas, which are made like crepes. You can stuff them like wontons, make tubes and fill them, or fold them and dip them into a spicy sauce. Experiment.

MANGO SALSA

This is quick and easy. Try it with cold chicken, seafood, or grilled fish.

Makes about 1 cup

INGREDIENTS:

2 ripe mangoes, peeled, seeded, and chopped

1 jalapeño chili, or to taste, minced

Juice of 1 lime

1 teaspoon lime zest

2 tablespoons minced red onion

1 teaspoon sugar

Salt, to taste

¼ cup chopped fresh mint or parsley

Mix all ingredients together and let stand for 2 hours or in the fridge overnight. Serve at room temperature or cold.

SPICY TOMATO SALSA

Salsa made with fresh tomatoes and herbs is such a treat. Of course, you can vary it tremendously. Have fun with it, adding extras from your garden.

Makes about 1½ cups

INGREDIENTS:

10 large, fresh plum (Roma) tomatoes, blanched in boiling water, skinned

¼ cup lemon juice

3 cloves garlic, minced

2 ears cooked corn, kernels cut from the cob

1 teaspoon cumin

2 medium onions, peeled, cut into quarters

Salt and hot pepper sauce, to taste

½ cup chopped fresh cilantro or parsley, to taste

Mix all ingredients in a food processor, pulsing until coarsely chopped. Refrigerate until ready to serve.

HOT AND SWEET PEPPERS WITH JACK CHEESE STUFFING

This is an easy snack or cocktail nibble.

Serves 4

INGREDIENTS:

4 sweet red bell peppers, cut in quarters, cored, and seeded

4 teaspoons olive oil, or spray bottle of olive oil

4 ounces Monterey jack or pepper jack cheese, shredded

½ cup Crunchy Corn Bread Squares (see recipe in Chapter 3), crumbled in the blender or food processor

Freshly ground black pepper and cayenne pepper, to taste

4 teaspoons Parmesan cheese for topping (fresh or gluten-free)

Shredded lettuce and gluten-free sour cream, for garnish

1. Preheat oven to 350°F.

2. Prepare a baking dish with nonstick spray. Lay the peppers in the dish. Spray or drizzle them with olive oil. Divide the jack cheese between the peppers.

3. Mix the crumbs, pepper, cayenne pepper, and Parmesan cheese together and spoon over the jack cheese in the peppers. Bake until the cheese melts, about 10 minutes. Serve garnished with shredded lettuce and a dollop of gluten-free sour cream.

PEPPERS WITH JALAPEÑO JELLY AND CREAM CHEESE STUFFING

This can also be served on gluten-free crackers or Crunchy Corn Bread Squares (see recipe in Chapter 3). The combination of sweet, hot, and creamy is irresistible.

Makes 32 pieces

INGREDIENTS:

4 large, ripe red bell peppers, cored, seeded, cut into quarters, and then halved

1 (8-ounce) package cream cheese

1 (8-ounce) jar jalapeño jelly

Arrange the cut pepper "spoons" on a platter. Place a dab of cream cheese on each, add a dab of the hot/sweet jalapeño jelly, and serve.

DEVILED EGGS WITH CAVIAR OR SHRIMP

There is nothing more delightful than a deviled egg with a dab of caviar on top and a dab of gluten-free sour cream on top of that.

Make 10 deviled eggs

INGREDIENTS:

5 hard-boiled eggs

½ cup whole or low-fat gluten-free mayonnaise

1 teaspoon gluten-free Dijon mustard

1 teaspoon Tabasco sauce or other hot red pepper sauce

½ bunch of chives, snipped finely

2 teaspoons capers, the smallest available

2 ounces red salmon caviar or 10 small cooked shrimp

Gluten-free sour cream if you are using caviar

1. Peel eggs, cut them in half, and remove the yolks to your food processor. Arrange the whites on a platter.

2. Add the mayonnaise, mustard, Tabasco or pepper sauce, chives, and capers to the food processor and whirl until blended.

3. Stuff the egg whites with the yolk mixture and place ¼ teaspoon caviar on top of each, or a small shrimp. Serve with sour cream on the side to go with the caviar.

CHEESE FONDUE WITH DIPPING VEGETABLES

This is an "interactive" party appetizer, or you can serve it as a main course.

Serves 12–14

INGREDIENTS:

1 clove garlic

1 cup dry white wine

1 pound imported Swiss cheese, such as Jarlsberg, coarsely grated

¼ teaspoon ground nutmeg

Freshly ground pepper, to taste

3 tablespoons kirsch (liqueur)

Salt, to taste

2 egg yolks, beaten

2 tablespoons gluten-free flour, such as potato flour

½ cup cream

2 tablespoons butter

1 loaf gluten-free French-style bread, cubed and toasted

1 broccoli crown, blanched in boiling water for 2 minutes, cooled and cut in pieces

2 sweet red peppers, cored, seeded, and cut into chunks

½ pound sugar snap peas, rinsed

2 zucchini and/or 12 very thin asparagus tips, cut up

1. Mash the garlic, and in a large earthenware pot or chafing dish over a burner, heat the garlic in the wine.

2. Stir in the cheese, nutmeg, pepper, kirsch, and salt. Mix slowly over low flame.

3. In a separate bowl, whisk together the egg yolks, flour, and cream. Stir into the cheese mixture.

4. Serve with buttered bread cubes and vegetables, keeping the heat low under the chafing dish water basin. Or use a really heavy flameproof earthenware casserole, keeping a low flame under it.

5. When the cheese mixture has melted, enjoy by spearing veggies or bread on a long-handled fork and dipping into the cheese mixture. If the cheese gets too thick, add a bit more warm white wine.

Fondue Facts

Ever wonder where fondue first came from? It was first created in Switzerland, where it was used as a way of using up hardened cheese. Traditionally a peasant dish, fondue became popular in America in the 1950s, as a result of chef Konrad Egli's Chalet Swiss restaurant fondue method of cooking meat cubes in hot oil. Later on came chocolate fondue.

PARMESAN ARTICHOKE DIP

For a more savory dip, reduce the amount of mayonnaise to 2 cups and stir in 2 cups of room-temperature sour cream immediately before serving. For fewer servings, cut the recipe in half and reduce the cooking time.

Serves 24

INGREDIENTS:

2 (13½-ounce) jars marinated artichoke hearts

4 cups gluten-free mayonnaise

2 (8-ounce) packages of cream cheese, cubed

12 ounces (3 cups) freshly grated Parmesan cheese

4 cloves garlic, peeled and minced

1 teaspoon dried dill

½ teaspoon freshly ground black pepper

1. Drain and chop the artichoke hearts. Add to a 2½-quart slow cooker along with the mayonnaise, cream cheese, Parmesan cheese, garlic, dill, and pepper. Stir to combine. Cover and cook on low for 1 hour; uncover and stir well.

2. Re-cover and cook on low for an additional 1–1½ hours or until the cheese is melted completely and the dip is heated through. To serve, reduce the heat setting of the slow cooker to warm. Serve with gluten-free tortillas, rice crackers, or gluten-free toast points.

Instead of . . .

Instead of using artichokes, you can use fresh or frozen spinach (drained of all liquids). For a more hearty dip, add 1 pound fresh lump crabmeat and ½ teaspoon Old Bay Seasoning.

TEX-MEX TACO DIP

This is a super-easy gluten-free taco dip made with everyday pantry ingredients.

Serves 6

INGREDIENTS:

1 (8-ounce) package cream cheese

1 (14½-ounce) can diced tomatoes, drained, reserving 4 tablespoons juice

½ cup refried beans

1 package gluten-free taco seasoning

¼ cup black olives, sliced

1. Grease a 1½-quart slow cooker with nonstick cooking spray.

2. Add cream cheese, drained diced tomatoes, reserved tomato juice, refried beans, and taco seasoning. Mix together, cover, and cook on low for 4–5 hours or on high for 2–2½ hours.

3. Right before serving, sprinkle sliced black olives on top of dip. Serve with gluten-free corn chips, rice chips, or gluten-free toast points.

Make Your Own Taco Seasoning

You can create your own taco seasoning to keep on hand by mixing together: 1 tablespoon chili powder, ¼ teaspoon garlic powder, ¼ teaspoon onion powder, ¼ teaspoon dried oregano, ½ teaspoon paprika, 1½ teaspoons cumin, 1 tablespoon sugar, ½ teaspoon salt, and ½ teaspoon ground pepper. Store in an airtight container.

SPICY CHEDDAR HAMBURGER DIP

A hearty dip with ground beef and garlic, this dish could also be served over cooked rice for a Mexican-inspired gluten-free meal.

Serves 6

INGREDIENTS:

1 pound lean ground beef

½ cup finely chopped onion

4 cloves garlic, peeled and crushed

½ jalapeño pepper, seeded and minced

¼ teaspoon salt

1 (15-ounce) can tomato sauce

½ teaspoon oregano

1 (8-ounce) package cream cheese

1 cup Cheddar cheese, shredded

1 teaspoon gluten-free chili powder

1. Brown ground beef in a skillet with the onion, garlic, and jalapeño. Pour browned ground beef mixture into a greased 2½-quart slow cooker.

2. Add salt, tomato sauce, oregano, cream cheese, Cheddar cheese, and chili powder.

3. Cover and cook on high for 2–3 hours or on low for 5–6 hours.

4. Serve with gluten-free corn tacos, gluten-free corn tortilla chips, or rice chips.

Handling Hot Peppers

Make sure to wear gloves when deseeding and mincing hot peppers such as jalapeños. Those with sensitive skin can actually get a chemical burn from touching the seeds and/or the membrane surrounding the seeds.

SWEDISH MEATBALLS WITH GRAVY

No one will ever guess these uniquely spiced meatballs simmering in a savory gravy are gluten-free. To easily make them dairy-free, use almond milk in place of the whole milk and coconut oil in place of the butter.

Serves 4

INGREDIENTS:

1 slice gluten-free bread

4 tablespoons whole milk, divided

¼ cup finely diced onion

2 tablespoons butter, divided

1 pound lean ground beef

1 large egg

¼ teaspoon ground pepper

¼ teaspoon ground allspice

¼ teaspoon ground nutmeg

2 tablespoons brown rice flour

1 cup gluten-free beef broth

1. In a small bowl crumble up the bread and add 2 tablespoons milk to soften it. Set aside. In a small skillet soften the onions in 1 tablespoon of butter for about 3–5 minutes until softened and translucent.

2. In a large bowl mix together the softened bread, onions cooked in butter, ground beef, egg, pepper, allspice, and nutmeg. Mix together thoroughly and roll tablespoons of the meat mixture into small meatballs.

3. Brown meatballs (in small batches) in a nonstick skillet and then transfer them to a greased 4-quart slow cooker.

4. In the same skillet you browned the meatballs in, whisk together the remaining tablespoon of butter and the brown rice flour. Whisk for 1–2 minutes to toast the flour. Slowly pour in the beef broth, whisking constantly. Cook for 3–5 additional minutes until you have a thickened gravy. Whisk in remaining 2 tablespoons of milk.

5. Pour gravy over the meatballs in the slow cooker. Cover and cook on high for 3–4 hours or on low for 6–8 hours.

SWEET AND SOUR MINI HOT DOG SNACKERS

Sometimes it can be difficult to make sure certain brands of sandwich meats and hot dogs are gluten-free. To make it easier, instead of searching high and low for mini gluten-free hot dogs, simply use a brand of regular gluten-free hot dogs you trust and cut them into bite-sized pieces.

Serves 4

INGREDIENTS:

1 package gluten-free hot dogs, cut into bite-sized pieces

½ cup grape jelly

½ cup gluten-free barbecue sauce

2 tablespoons orange juice

½ teaspoon ground white pepper

1 tablespoon gluten-free Worcestershire sauce

½ teaspoon gluten-free ground mustard

1. Place cut-up hot dogs into a greased 2½-quart slow cooker.

2. In a bowl, mix together the jelly, barbecue sauce, orange juice, pepper, Worcestershire sauce, and mustard. Pour over the hot dogs in the slow cooker.

3. Cover and cook on high for 3–4 hours or on low for 6–8 hours.

HOT CHICKEN BUFFALO BITES

Love buffalo wings? Then you will love these chicken bites even more; they are made with juicy chicken breasts so you won't have to worry about bones. They are super easy and much less messy!

Serves 6

INGREDIENTS:

3 large chicken breasts, cut into 2" strips

2 tablespoons brown rice flour

¼ cup melted butter

3 cloves garlic, peeled and minced

⅓ cup Frank's RedHot sauce

¼ cup gluten-free ranch dressing

1. Place chicken pieces into a greased 2½-quart slow cooker.

2. In a saucepan whisk together the brown rice flour and melted butter for 2–3 minutes to toast the flour.

3. Slowly whisk in the garlic and Frank's RedHot sauce. Pour sauce over chicken in the slow cooker.

4. Cover and cook on high for 3 hours or on low for 6 hours. Serve with ranch dressing for dipping. If using a larger slow cooker, make sure to reduce cooking time by about half.

Fresh Garlic Versus Garlic Powder

In a pinch, use 1½ teaspoons garlic powder in this recipe. The garlic flavor won't be quite as pungent and rich as it is when you use fresh garlic, but it will still be easy and enjoyable.

MANGO PORK MORSELS

In this recipe, the mango provides natural sweetness and a tropical flair. Plate and pierce each morsel with a toothpick.

Serves 10

INGREDIENTS:

1½ pounds lean pork loin, cubed

2 mangoes, cubed (see sidebar)

3 cloves garlic, minced

1 jalapeño, seeded and minced

1 tablespoon gluten-free salsa

¼ teaspoon salt

¼ teaspoon freshly ground black pepper

2 teaspoons ground chipotle

1 teaspoon New Mexican gluten-free chili powder

½ teaspoon oregano

2 tablespoons orange juice

2 tablespoons lime juice

1. Quickly brown the pork in a nonstick skillet. Add the browned pork and cubed mango to a 4-quart slow cooker.

2. In a small bowl, whisk together the garlic, jalapeño, salsa, salt, pepper, chipotle, chili powder, oregano, and the orange and lime juices. Pour over the mango and pork. Stir.

3. Cook on low for 6 hours; remove the cover and cook on high for 30 minutes. Stir before serving.

How to Cut Up a Mango

Slice the mango vertically on either side of the large flat pit. Then, using the tip of a knife, cut vertical lines into the flesh without piercing the skin. Make horizontal lines in the flesh to form cubes. Use a spoon to scoop out the cubes. Repeat for the other side.

GLUTEN-FREE "SHAKE IT AND BAKE IT" DRUMSTICKS

Remember that wonderful chicken seasoning from your childhood? You can now make it gluten-free for crispy chicken drumsticks right in your slow cooker!

Serves 6

INGREDIENTS:

1 cup gluten-free corn tortilla chips, finely crushed

1½ tablespoons olive oil

½ teaspoon salt

½ teaspoon paprika

¼ teaspoon celery seeds

¼ teaspoon ground black pepper

¼ teaspoon garlic powder

½ teaspoon dried onion flakes

¼ teaspoon dried basil

¼ teaspoon dried parsley

¼ teaspoon dried oregano

6 chicken drumsticks

1. In a heavy-duty gallon-sized zip-top bag, mix together the seasoning ingredients: crushed tortilla chips, olive oil, salt, paprika, celery seeds, pepper, garlic powder, onion flakes, basil, parsley, and oregano.

2. To prepare the slow cooker either wrap 4–5 small potatoes in foil and place them in the bottom of a greased 4-quart slow cooker, or make 4–5 foil balls about the size of a small potato and place them in the bottom of the slow cooker. (This will help the chicken to get a little bit crispy in the slow cooker instead of cooking in its juices.)

3. Place 2 drumsticks in the bag with the seasoning mix, seal it tightly, and shake the bag to coat the chicken. Place coated chicken drumsticks on top of the foil balls. Repeat with remaining drumsticks, 2 at a time.

4. Cover slow cooker and vent the lid with a chopstick to help release extra moisture. Cook on high for 4 hours or on low for 8 hours.

Make It and Shake It for Later

Double or triple the batch of the seasoned coating ingredients so in the future you can prepare this delicious gluten-free appetizer or light meal in a snap.

PINEAPPLE TERIYAKI DRUMSTICKS

Serve this crowd-pleasing favorite as a hearty appetizer. Pair leftovers with steamed rice for a great lunch.

Serves 12

INGREDIENTS:

12 chicken drumsticks

1 (8-ounce can) pineapple slices, in juice

¼ cup gluten-free teriyaki sauce or gluten-free soy sauce

1 teaspoon ground ginger

¼ cup gluten-free hoisin sauce

1. Arrange the drumsticks in a single layer on a broiling pan. Broil for 10 minutes on high, flipping the drumsticks once halfway through the cooking time.

2. Drain the juice from the pineapple into a 4–6-quart slow cooker. Add the teriyaki sauce, ginger, and hoisin sauce. Stir to combine.

3. Cut the pineapple rings in half. Add them to the slow cooker.

4. Add the drumsticks to the slow cooker and stir to combine. Cover and cook on low for 4–6 hours or on high for 2–3 hours.

GRILLED PORTOBELLO MUSHROOMS WITH BALSAMIC GLAZE

This vegan salad is so filling and hearty any time of the year. If you haven't tried to grill portobellos, now is the time!

Serves 6

INGREDIENTS:

4 cups arugula, rinsed and dried

3 large portobello mushrooms

1 cup balsamic vinegar

1 tablespoon turbinado sugar

1 teaspoon gluten-free soy sauce

1. Place the arugula on a large platter.

2. Clean mushrooms and remove stems and any debris. Grill over a hot grill for 10 minutes, turning once. Place mushroom caps on top of the arugula.

3. In a small saucepan, heat the vinegar, sugar, and soy sauce to a boil. Reduce heat to low and simmer for about 15–20 minutes, or until the mixture thickens. Remove from heat and let cool.

4. Once balsamic glaze has cooled a bit, pour evenly over portobellos and arugula. Serve immediately or at room temperature.

FRESH TOMATO AND BASIL BRUSCHETTA OVER PORTOBELLOS

Don't use canned tomatoes or dried basil for this recipe. The fresh tomato and basil really make a difference. Serve as an appetizer, as a side dish, or in a salad.

Serves 12

INGREDIENTS:

6 plum (Roma) tomatoes, seeded and chopped

2 tablespoons extra-virgin olive oil

½ red onion, chopped finely

4 cloves garlic, minced

2 tablespoons balsamic vinegar

3 tablespoons fresh basil, torn

1 tablespoon Parmesan cheese, freshly grated

½ teaspoon salt

½ teaspoon pepper

6 large portobello mushroom caps, wiped clean, stems removed

Extra-virgin olive oil in Misto sprayer

8 ounces fresh mozzarella, thinly sliced

1. Preheat the oven to 425°F.

2. In a large bowl, combine the tomatoes, olive oil, onion, garlic, vinegar, basil, and Parmesan cheese. Add salt and pepper and mix well.

3. Slice each mushroom cap in half, leaving two half circles, and place on a baking sheet sprayed with nonstick cooking spray. Lightly spray each portobello mushroom cap with Misto sprayer filled with olive oil. Bake for 5 minutes. Remove from oven.

4. Spoon bruschetta mixture on each mushroom half. Top with mozzarella and bake for 2–3 minutes more, until cheese is melted. Serve warm.

GRAVLAX (SALMON CURED IN SUGAR AND SALT)

This is a year-round Swedish specialty—good on any buffet at any special occasion. The salmon will "cook" or "cure" in the salt and sugar.

Serves 12–15

INGREDIENTS:

1 (3-pound) salmon fillet, skin removed

⅔ cup salt

½ cup granulated sugar

20 white peppercorns, crushed

6 thick slices fresh gingerroot, peeled

5 large fronds fresh dill weed

Sprigs of watercress and hard-boiled egg slices, for garnish

1 batch Cucumber Sauce for Gravlax (see recipe in this chapter)

1 batch Mustard Sauce for Gravlax, Ham, or Roast Beef (see recipe in this chapter)

1. Rinse the salmon and dry on paper towels.

2. In a large glass baking pan, mix together the salt, sugar, and peppercorns. Place the salmon in the pan and turn it to cover with the mixture.

3. Arrange the gingerroot over and under the fish. Place fronds of dill over and under the fish. Cover tightly and refrigerate for 16–24 hours.

4. Scrape off the salt and sugar, wiping the fish with paper towels. Slice thinly, on the diagonal, and serve with sprigs of watercress, hard-boiled egg slices, and the dressings.

CUCUMBER SAUCE FOR GRAVLAX

This is such a great side with Gravlax. It's also good with cold roast beef, roasted filet mignon, or gluten-free ham.

Makes 3 cups

INGREDIENTS:

1 long English cucumber (also known as Burpee's Burpless), peeled

1 red onion, chopped finely

1½ cups gluten-free sour cream

½ cup minced fresh dill

Juice and minced zest of 1 lemon

1 teaspoon champagne vinegar or other white wine vinegar (no malt vinegars)

1 teaspoon salt

Black or white pepper, freshly ground, to taste

Chopped chives and parsley, for garnish

1. Slice the cucumber in half lengthwise and scoop out the seeds and discard. Chop the cucumber finely.

2. Add the rest of the ingredients, except the chives and parsley, and store in the refrigerator for at least 2 hours to "marry," which will bring out the flavors.

3. Serve in a chilled bowl alongside the gravlax. Garnish with chives and parsley.

MUSTARD SAUCE FOR GRAVLAX, HAM, OR ROAST BEEF

This is so simple and good you won't ever go wrong by making it. You can also serve it with salads.

Makes 1 cup

INGREDIENTS:

⅔ cup olive oil

⅓ cup white wine vinegar

1 tablespoon gluten-free Dijon-style mustard

1 teaspoon sugar

Salt and pepper, to taste

Fresh herbs such as dill, oregano, parsley, or basil

Place all ingredients in a blender and whirl until emulsified. Serve in a glass bowl or sauceboat. Store in a glass jar, covered, in the refrigerator. Will keep for a week, depending on the freshness of the herbs. It will keep longer with dry herbs.

CHAPTER 6

SALADS, SOUPS, AND CHILI

APPLE, WALNUT, CRANBERRY, AND SPINACH SALAD

The wonderful combination of fruit and nuts makes this salad perfect any time of year. The dressing can be used for any salad or as a marinade for chicken or vegetables.

Serves 4

INGREDIENTS:

Dressing:

½ cup extra-virgin olive oil

½ cup balsamic vinegar

1 clove garlic, crushed

1 teaspoon ground mustard

1 teaspoon honey

1 teaspoon salt

½ teaspoon pepper

Salad:

1 (6-ounce) bag organic baby spinach

2 tablespoons chopped walnuts

2 tablespoons gluten-free dried, unsweetened cranberries

1 Fuji apple, cored and chopped

½ medium orange bell pepper, seeded and chopped

2 plum (Roma) tomatoes, chopped

½ cup kidney beans, thoroughly rinsed and drained

1 tablespoon chia seeds

1. Wisk all the dressing ingredients together in a small bowl. You can also pour into a small, airtight container and shake vigorously.

2. In a large bowl, mix the salad ingredients. Add the dressing and toss before serving.

LEMONY GARLIC KALE-LENTIL SALAD

This light salad tastes wonderful the first day—and even better as leftovers. The lemon and kale create a delightful combination.

Serves 6

INGREDIENTS:

1 tablespoon extra-virgin olive oil

3 cloves garlic, chopped

¼ cup chopped onion

2 cups kale, stems removed

½ cup sliced tomatoes

1–2 tablespoons fresh basil

½ teaspoon kosher salt

8 ounces lentils, soaked and cooked

2 tablespoons fresh lemon juice

2 tablespoons shaved Asiago cheese, or any other hard cheese

1. Heat oil in a large skillet over medium-high heat. Add the garlic and onion and sauté for 2 minutes.

2. Add the kale and tomatoes and sauté for 2–3 minutes more, until kale is softened but still crisp. Add basil and salt, and stir until blended.

3. In a large bowl, combine the kale mixture with the cooked lentils. Stir well.

4. Stir in lemon juice and cheese. Serve hot or cold.

A Valuable Source of Protein and Fiber

Lentils are an inexpensive way to get protein and fiber in your diet. They are also packed with crucial vitamins and minerals such as folate, vitamin B6, and magnesium, which are important for maintaining proper functioning of your body. Make sure you thoroughly rinse lentils before you cook them to ensure you have removed all dirt and debris.

GRILLED PEAR-KALE SALAD WITH FETA CHEESE

These grilled pears are wonderful along with the crisp texture of kale. Kale has become popular for its health benefits and delicious taste.

Serves 6

INGREDIENTS:

Juice of 1 small lemon

5 tablespoons grapeseed oil, divided

½ teaspoon coarse salt

½ teaspoon ground black pepper

4 pears, halved and cored, Bartlett or Bosc work the best here

4 cups finely chopped curly kale leaves

¼ red onion, finely chopped

1 tablespoon gluten-free dried cranberries, unsweetened

¼ cup walnuts

¼ cup feta cheese

1. For the dressing, whisk together the lemon juice, 4 tablespoons oil, salt, and pepper in a small bowl. Set aside.

2. Prepare a grill to medium-high heat (you should be able to hold your hand an inch over the cooking grate for 2–3 seconds). Make sure the cooking grate is well oiled.

3. Brush cut sides of pears with remaining grapeseed oil. Put pears, cut-side down, on the grill. Cover and cook until pear halves are grill-marked and heated through, about 10 minutes. Let them cool and slice into strips.

4. In a large bowl, add the kale, onion, cranberries, and walnuts. Stir to combine. Top with pears, feta cheese, and dressing.

Super Kale

Did you know that one serving of kale has 200 percent of your vitamin C daily requirement? Kale has even more vitamin C per serving than an orange! Kale is packed with fiber, vitamins, minerals, and antioxidants.

AVOCADO EGG SALAD

You will not miss the mayonnaise that traditional egg salads have when you taste the creaminess of the avocado in this recipe. Serve it on a bed of lettuce or wrapped up in a gluten-free tortilla.

Serves 6

INGREDIENTS:

7 hard-boiled eggs, peeled and cooled

1 avocado, peeled, pitted, and cut into 1" pieces

2 tablespoons plain gluten-free Greek low-fat yogurt

2 tablespoons lemon juice

1 green onion, finely chopped

1 celery stalk, finely chopped

1 teaspoon paprika

½ teaspoon salt

½ teaspoon pepper

1. Separate the whites and the yolks of the eggs. Set aside 3 yolks for another use.

2. Dice the egg whites.

3. In a large bowl, combine the avocado, 4 egg yolks, and yogurt. Mash until the mixture is creamy and smooth.

4. Mix in the lemon juice, onion, celery, paprika, salt, and pepper.

5. Gently add the chopped egg whites and combine. Refrigerate or serve immediately.

GRILLED CORN SALAD

When you grill corn, it becomes juicy, sweet, and crispy. This salad is so simple and flavorful, you will want to make it again and again.

Serves 8

INGREDIENTS:

4 ears un-shucked corn

2 avocados, peeled, pitted, and cut into 1" squares

½ cup grape or cherry tomatoes, halved

1 green pepper, diced

6 cups arugula, divided

Cilantro-Lime Vinaigrette (see recipe in this chapter)

2 tablespoons fresh cilantro leaves, torn

1. Pull back the husks of the corn and remove the silk. Pull husks back over corn. Lightly brush grates on grill with olive oil and heat grill to medium.

2. Place corn on the grill and cook for 15–20 minutes, turning occasionally. Remove from the grill and let corn cool.

3. When corn has cooled, shuck corn completely. With a sharp knife, cut down sides of each corn cob to remove kernels, and place grilled corn kernels in a large bowl.

4. Add the avocados, tomatoes, pepper, and 3 cups of arugula to the bowl. Mix well.

5. Add Cilantro-Lime Vinaigrette and stir thoroughly to combine. Refrigerate at least 1 hour to let the flavors soak in.

6. When ready to serve, place remaining 3 cups of arugula on a large platter and top with corn salad. Garnish with cilantro.

QUINOA-AVOCADO SALAD

This dish makes a hearty meal in itself or can be made as a side dish for chicken or fish. It tastes best when it is prepared the night before. Just make sure to save a little extra dressing to toss right before serving.

Serves 8

INGREDIENTS:

1½ cups uncooked quinoa, rinsed and drained

3 cups water

2 (15-ounce) cans black beans, rinsed and drained

1 (14-ounce) box of frozen corn, defrosted

2 avocados, peeled and cut into ½" pieces

2 pints grape tomatoes, halved

Cilantro-Lime Vinaigrette (see recipe in this chapter)

1. Cook the quinoa with the water according to package directions. Let cool to room temperature.

2. In a medium bowl, combine the beans, corn, avocados, and tomatoes. Toss with cooled quinoa.

3. Pour Cilantro-Lime Vinaigrette over the salad. Refrigerate for several hours or overnight.

CILANTRO-LIME VINAIGRETTE

This dressing is so wonderful you will want to make more of it and keep it in your refrigerator. It's perfect for all kinds of salads or even as a marinade.

Makes 8–10 servings

INGREDIENTS:

1 clove garlic, minced

¼ cup grapeseed oil

¾ teaspoon minced fresh gingerroot

¼ cup fresh lime juice

Zest of 1 lime

2 teaspoons balsamic vinegar

¼ cup fresh-packed cilantro leaves

Salt, to taste

Mix all ingredients together in a small bowl. Refrigerate until ready to serve. Store in an airtight container in the refrigerator for several days.

Cilantro, Love It or Hate It?

If you are among those who do not like cilantro, you are not alone. Feel free to substitute Italian parsley, mint, basil, or any other herb for cilantro in a recipe.

GREEK QUINOA SALAD

This is a wonderful re-creation of a classic Greek salad.

Serves 4–6

INGREDIENTS:

2 cups low-sodium gluten-free chicken broth

1 cup uncooked quinoa, rinsed and drained

½ cup grape or cherry tomatoes, halved

½ cup chopped red or yellow sweet bell pepper

¼ cup chopped cucumber

2 teaspoons chopped, pitted kalamata olives

1 tablespoon extra-virgin olive oil

½ teaspoon lemon zest

1 teaspoon fresh juice of lemon

1 teaspoon red vinegar (no malted)

½ teaspoon basil, ground

½ teaspoon oregano

1 tablespoon garlic, minced

¼ cup feta cheese

1. Heat the broth in a medium saucepan until it comes to a boil. Add quinoa and cover. Cook for 15–20 minutes, until all broth is absorbed. Remove from heat. Fluff with a fork.

2. Place the tomatoes, pepper, cucumber, and olives in large bowl. Set aside.

3. In a small bowl, combine the olive oil, lemon zest, lemon juice, vinegar, basil, oregano, and garlic. Mix thoroughly.

4. Add the quinoa to the vegetables and cover with the dressing. Top with feta cheese, stir to combine.

CLASSIC CAESAR SALAD WITH GLUTEN-FREE CROUTONS

Caesar salad has become unbelievably popular—it is served with fried calamari, grilled chicken, shrimp, fish, and vegetables.

Serves 4

INGREDIENTS:

1 head romaine lettuce, washed, dried, and chopped into bite-sized pieces

1 whole large egg and 1 egg yolk, beaten

Freshly squeezed juice of ½ lemon

2 cloves garlic, minced

1 teaspoon gluten-free English mustard

1" anchovy paste or 2 canned anchovies, packed in oil, mashed

¾ cup extra-virgin olive oil

Salt and freshly ground black pepper, to taste

6 tablespoons freshly grated Parmesan cheese

24 Fresh Gluten-Free Croutons (see recipe in this chapter)

1. Wash and spin-dry the lettuce; then chop, wrap in a towel, and place in the refrigerator to crisp.

2. Whisk together the egg, egg yolk, lemon juice, garlic, mustard, anchovy paste, and olive oil until very smooth. Add salt and pepper to taste. Add the greens and toss.

3. Sprinkle with Parmesan cheese and croutons, and serve.

Not *That* Caesar

According to the JNA Institute of Culinary Arts in Philadelphia, Caesar salad was originally created in 1924 by Caesar Cardini, an Italian restaurateur in Tijuana, Mexico. The salad is named after its creator—a chef—not Julius Caesar of the Roman Empire.

FRESH GLUTEN-FREE CROUTONS

These can be made in advance and stored in the refrigerator, then crisped up at the last moment. Double the recipe for extras.

Makes 24 croutons

INGREDIENTS:

½ cup olive oil

2 cloves garlic, minced or put through a garlic press

4 slices gluten-free bread, thickly cut, crusts removed

Salt and pepper, to taste

1. Preheat the broiler to 350°F.

2. Mix the oil and garlic. Brush both sides of the bread with the garlic oil. Sprinkle with salt and pepper to taste.

3. Cut each slice of bread into 6 cubes, to make 24 cubes. Spray a cookie sheet with nonstick spray. Place the cubes on the sheet and broil until well browned on both sides.

4. Put the cookie sheet on the bottom rack of the oven. Turn off the oven and leave the croutons to dry for 20 minutes.

5. Store in an airtight container until ready to use.

For the Love of Garlic

Garlic will give you various degrees of potency depending on how you cut it. Finely minced garlic, or that which has been put through a press, will be the strongest. When garlic is sliced, it is less strong, and when you leave the cloves whole, they are even milder.

THICK AND RICH CREAM OF BROCCOLI SOUP

This hearty soup is perfect on a cold winter day. Feel free to add diced chicken or turkey to make it more of a meal.

Serves 4–6

INGREDIENTS:

1 pound broccoli

1 tablespoon extra-virgin olive oil or butter

1 large sweet onion, chopped

2 cloves garlic, chopped

1 stalk celery, chopped

2 tablespoons cornstarch dissolved in ⅓ cup cold water

3 cups low-salt gluten-free chicken broth

½ cup dry white wine

¼ teaspoon freshly grated nutmeg

Juice and rind of 1 lemon

Salt and freshly ground pepper, to taste

1 cup heavy cream

¾ cup minced prosciutto or other gluten-free smoked ham

1. Rinse, trim, and coarsely chop the broccoli; set aside in a colander to drain.

2. In a large soup pot, heat the oil or butter, and add onion, garlic, and celery. Sauté until softened, about 3–4 minutes.

3. Stir in the cornstarch/water mixture and other liquid ingredients.

4. Mix in the broccoli, nutmeg, juice and rind of lemon, salt, and pepper.

5. Simmer the soup, covered, until the broccoli is tender, about 15 minutes.

6. Remove the lemon rind. In blender, purée in batches, or use immersion blender directly in soup pot. Stir in the cream and ham. Reheat but do not boil. Serve hot.

Adding Depth of Flavor to Soup

Adding gluten-free sausage, ham, or bacon to a soup enriches the flavor of soup. The salt and smoke in the curing process of pork plus the herbs and spices used in sausage also add to the flavor of a soup or stew. Smoked ham hocks are a classical tasty touch in Southern cooking. They are inexpensive and meaty, but the skin and bones must be removed before the soup is served. Just make sure your addition is gluten-free!

ITALIAN SAUSAGE, BEAN, AND VEGETABLE SOUP

There's nothing like a bowl of good soup, especially when you are in a hurry. This hearty soup can be made quickly and will not disappoint.

Serves 4–6

INGREDIENTS:

1 pound gluten-free Italian sausage, either sweet or hot, cut into 1" pieces

1 large red onion, chopped

4 cloves garlic, minced

¼ cup extra-virgin olive oil

1 (28-ounce) can crushed tomatoes with their juice

1 bunch of escarole, washed, base stems removed, chopped

2 (13-ounce) cans gluten-free beef broth

2 (13-ounce) cans white beans, drained and rinsed

1 tablespoon fresh rosemary, crumbled

1 tablespoon dried oregano

⅓ cup grated Parmesan cheese, freshly grated or gluten-free

1. In a large skillet, sauté the sausage, onion, and garlic in the olive oil for 5–6 minutes.

2. When the onion and garlic are soft, add the rest of the ingredients, except the Parmesan cheese. Cover and simmer over very low heat for 30 minutes.

3. Garnish with Parmesan cheese and serve.

TASTY TACO SOUP

This wonderful soup can be made into a chili if you reduce the amount of broth.

Serves 8

INGREDIENTS:

2 tablespoons extra-virgin olive oil

1½ pounds lean ground beef (you can also use lean ground turkey or chicken)

1 tablespoon extra-virgin olive oil

1 medium onion, chopped

3 cloves garlic, minced

1 red or yellow bell pepper, chopped

1 cup diced tomatoes

1½ cups frozen corn

1 tablespoon gluten-free chili powder

¼ teaspoon red pepper flakes

¼ teaspoon oregano, dried

½ teaspoon paprika

1 tablespoon cumin

2–3 tablespoons fresh cilantro, chopped

Salt and pepper, to taste

1 (15-ounce) can red kidney beans, thoroughly rinsed and drained

1 can green chili peppers

3 cups gluten-free chicken broth

1½–2 cups water (depending on how much liquid you want)

Juice of ½ lime

Cheddar cheese, gluten-free sour cream, extra cilantro, for garnish

1. In a large stockpot or Dutch oven, heat 2 tablespoons oil and add the ground meat. Cook for 5–8 minutes, until completely browned and no longer pink. Remove from heat and place meat into a bowl.

2. In the same pot, heat 1 tablespoon oil, onion, and garlic for 3–4 minutes, until they soften.

3. Add the bell pepper, tomatoes, corn, spices, and cilantro. Season with salt and pepper and mix well.

4. Add the kidney beans and chili peppers and mix again.

5. Add the meat back to the pot along with chicken broth, water, and lime juice. Mix well and bring to a boil.

6. Cover and reduce heat to low. Season with additional salt and pepper, if desired. Simmer for 30 minutes. Garnish with cheese, sour cream, and extra cilantro, if desired.

Do You Love Sour Cream?

If you are looking for a healthier alternative, why not substitute plain Greek yogurt for sour cream? Greek yogurt is thick and creamy but has much less fat and fewer calories. Greek yogurt is also much higher in protein.

CREAMY HAM AND POTATO SOUP

This is comfort food at its finest and is filling enough for an entrée. This is a great way to use leftover ham too. Go ahead and add whatever vegetables you'd like—cauliflower, asparagus, and corn would be delicious in this soup.

Serves 8

INGREDIENTS:

3½ pounds Yukon Gold potatoes, peeled and diced

2 medium onions, chopped

2 medium carrots, sliced

2 celery stalks, diced

1 cup gluten-free smoked ham, diced

⅛ teaspoon gluten-free cayenne pepper, ground

½ teaspoon sage, dried

1 teaspoon parsley, dried

2 cloves garlic, minced

3 cups gluten-free chicken broth

2 cups water

Salt and pepper, to taste

4 tablespoons butter

5 tablespoons gluten-free, all-purpose flour

1½ cups milk

¼ cup shredded Cheddar cheese, for garnish (optional)

Chopped fresh chives, for garnish

1. In a large stockpot, place the potatoes, onions, carrots, celery, ham, cayenne pepper, sage, parsley, garlic, broth, and water over high heat. Bring to a boil, then lower heat to medium, and cook for 15 minutes, until potatoes soften. Add salt and pepper to taste.

2. To make a roux, melt butter over medium-low heat in a medium saucepan. Slowly add flour, stirring continuously until thick, about 1 minute. Gradually add milk while continuing to stir. Continue stirring until thick and no lumps remain, about 4 minutes.

3. Stir the milk mixture into stockpot and mix well. Cook until thoroughly combined. Add shredded cheese, if desired, and garnish with chopped chives. Serve immediately.

What Is a Roux?

A roux is very simple to make and is crucial for thickening soups and sauces. A roux is prepared by using equal parts fat and flour and mixing them together until they are completely smooth.

LENTIL AND SAUSAGE SOUP WITH QUINOA AND KALE

This soup is hearty enough for a complete meal. It is packed with protein and can be easily frozen in an airtight container.

Serves 6–8

INGREDIENTS:

1 tablespoon grapeseed oil

3 cloves garlic, minced

1 pound gluten-free turkey sausage, casings removed (can also use pork or chicken sausage)

½ cup diced carrots

½ cup diced celery

½ cup diced onion

1 tablespoon dried basil

1 tablespoon dried oregano

1 teaspoon dried rosemary

½ teaspoon dried thyme

8 cups low sodium gluten-free chicken broth

16 ounces dried lentils, rinsed

1½ cups cooked quinoa

5 cups kale, rinsed and stems removed

4 tablespoons freshly grated Parmesan cheese or gluten-free (optional)

1. Place oil and garlic in large stockpot or Dutch oven. Cook for 1–2 minutes, until garlic softens.

2. Add sausage and cook over medium-low heat until browned and no longer pink inside, about 5–8 minutes. Break the sausages up into bite-sized pieces.

3. Add diced vegetables and seasonings. Stir well and slowly add the broth, lentils, and quinoa. Turn heat to high and bring to a boil. Cover soup and reduce heat to low. Simmer for 45–60 minutes, until lentils become soft.

4. Add kale in the last 5–10 minutes. Serve immediately. Top with Parmesan cheese if desired.

Are You Familiar with Kale?

Kale is a powerhouse of nutrition as well as being a member of the cabbage family. Kale is packed with fiber, calcium, vitamin B6, vitamin A, vitamin K, and vitamin C. Kale can be eaten raw or cooked and can replace your other leafy greens in all varieties of recipes.

SUMMER CUCUMBER SOUP

This is very refreshing on a hot day. This soup is so simple to prepare, you can make an elegant and healthy summer soup in no time.

Serves 4

INGREDIENTS:

2 English cucumbers, peeled and chopped

2 cups reduced fat buttermilk

1 cup gluten-free Greek yogurt

2 teaspoons salt

Juice of 1 lemon

Rind of ½ lemon

⅔ tablespoon snipped fresh dill weed

½ cup snipped fresh chives (snipped to ¼" pieces)

Freshly ground pepper, to taste

Mix all ingredients in a non-reactive ceramic or porcelain bowl. Chill overnight. Serve in chilled bowls.

FRESH TUSCAN TOMATO AND BASIL SOUP

This taste is so fresh and delightful you will want to serve it year round.

Serves 4

INGREDIENTS:

4 tablespoons butter

¼ cup cornstarch

2 cups cherry or grape tomatoes

2 cups fresh basil leaves, stems removed

2 tablespoons fresh oregano leaves

1½ cups milk

1 cup cream

Salt and pepper, to taste

1. Make a roux with the butter and cornstarch; cook over medium heat for 5 minutes. Whirl the tomatoes, basil, and oregano in the blender until smooth. Stir the tomatoes into the hot butter mixture.

2. Bring to a boil and add the milk and cream. Heat over low flame and sprinkle with salt and pepper to taste.

Do Not Boil

When a recipe calls for cream, it's important to heat it without boiling. If you boil it, you may get curdled soup. If it does get away from you, add a few tablespoons of boiling water and blend until the curds come back together.

YELLOW SQUASH AND APPLE SOUP

A refreshing summer soup with loads of flavor. Make a lot and serve it the next day to beat the heat.

Serves 4

INGREDIENTS:

2 shallots, minced

1 Granny Smith apple, peeled, cored, and chopped

2 medium yellow squash, washed and chopped

4 tablespoons butter

3 cups fresh orange juice

1 cup apple juice

Juice of 1 fresh lime

¼ teaspoon ground cumin

⅛ teaspoon ground nutmeg

Salt and freshly ground white pepper, to taste

4 tablespoons gluten-free sour cream, for garnish

In a large pot, sauté the shallots, apple, and squash in the butter. Then add the rest of the ingredients except the sour cream. Purée the soup, bring to a boil, and serve hot or cold. Garnish with sour cream.

TUSCAN POTATO, KALE, AND SAUSAGE SOUP

An easy and delicious gluten-free version of a popular soup at a well-known Italian restaurant chain, this soup is so good you won't miss the breadsticks!

Serves 6

INGREDIENTS:

1 tablespoon olive oil

3 slices gluten-free bacon, diced

1 pound gluten-free Italian sausage, cut into bite-sized pieces

1 medium onion, chopped

2 cloves garlic, minced

3 tablespoons white wine

2 large russet potatoes, peeled and diced

4 cups gluten-free chicken broth

¼ teaspoon red pepper flakes

½ teaspoon salt

½ teaspoon ground black pepper

2 cups fresh kale, chopped

1 cup heavy cream

1. In a large skillet, heat olive oil and cook bacon and sausage until crisp, and fat has been rendered, about 5 minutes. Remove bacon and sausage and add to a greased 4-quart slow cooker.

2. Sauté onion and garlic in the bacon fat until softened, 3–5 minutes.

3. Deglaze the pan with wine. Scrape the pan to remove all bits of vegetables and meat. Add all of the pan contents to the slow cooker.

4. Add potatoes, chicken broth, pepper flakes, salt, and ground pepper. Cover and cook on high for 4 hours or on low for 8 hours, until potatoes are very tender.

5. An hour before serving, stir in the kale and the cream. Continue to cook for 45–60 minutes, until kale has softened and cream is warmed through. Be careful not to overcook at this point as the cream can curdle and separate if heated for too long.

Instead of Kale . . .

If you aren't fond of kale, try adding 2 cups fresh baby spinach to the soup in the last hour of cooking.

SIMPLE GROUND TURKEY AND VEGETABLE SOUP

This soup is easy to throw together with pantry ingredients.

Serves 6

INGREDIENTS:

1 tablespoon olive oil

1 pound lean ground turkey

1 medium onion, diced

2 cloves garlic, minced

1 (16-ounce) package frozen mixed vegetables

4 cups gluten-free chicken broth

½ teaspoon pepper

½ teaspoon salt

1. In a large skillet over medium heat, add olive oil and heat until sizzling. Cook ground turkey until browned, about 5–6 minutes, stirring to break up the meat. Add meat to a greased 4-quart slow cooker. Sauté onion and garlic until softened, about 3–5 minutes. Add to the slow cooker.

2. Add remaining ingredients. Cover and cook on high for 4 hours or on low for 8 hours. Serve with gluten-free crackers.

Pick Your Favorite

There are tons of different types of frozen vegetable mixes on the market today. One that works well with this soup is a mix of potatoes, carrots, celery, corn, and garden peas. However, if you don't like those vegetables, try a stir-fry mix or a southwestern vegetables mix instead! Alternatively, you can use two cans of mixed vegetables such as Veg-All.

CREAMY POTATO SOUP

This is a simple, comforting potato soup. For a unique flavor, stir in a few teaspoons of McCormick's Greek Seasoning about an hour before serving.

Serves 6

INGREDIENTS:

6 medium russet potatoes, peeled and diced

2 medium onions, diced

2 carrots, peeled and finely diced

2 celery stalks, washed and finely diced

6 cups gluten-free chicken broth

1 teaspoon dried basil

½ teaspoon salt

½ teaspoon ground white pepper

¼ cup brown rice flour

1½ cups half-and-half

1. Add potatoes, onions, carrots, celery, broth, basil, salt, and pepper to a greased 4–6-quart slow cooker. Cover and cook on high for 4 hours or on low for 8 hours.

2. One hour prior to serving, mix the brown rice flour and the half-and-half in a medium bowl and whisk together. Set aside.

3. Using a potato masher, roughly mash potatoes in the slow cooker until they give the soup a creamy texture.

4. Stir half-and-half mixture into the potato soup.

5. Cover and continue to cook for 45–60 minutes, until cream has been heated through and soup has thickened slightly.

COMFORTING CHICKEN AND RICE SOUP

To keep the chicken in this soup extra moist, remove it from the slow cooker after 2 hours on high or after 4 hours on low. Shred or cut the chicken, store it in the fridge, and then add it back to the soup an hour before serving.

Serves 8

INGREDIENTS:

1 tablespoon extra-virgin olive oil

1 medium onion, chopped

2 cloves garlic, minced

2 celery stalks, halved lengthwise, and cut into ½"-thick slices

2 medium carrots, cut diagonally into ½"-thick slices

4 fresh thyme sprigs

1 bay leaf

2 quarts (8 cups) gluten-free chicken broth

1 cup water

1 cup long-grain white rice, uncooked

4 large boneless, skinless chicken breasts

1 teaspoon salt

1 teaspoon ground pepper

1. In a large skillet heat olive oil. Add the onion, garlic, and celery. Cook and stir for about 6 minutes, until the vegetables are softened but not browned.

2. Add softened vegetables to a greased 6-quart slow cooker. Add remaining ingredients to the slow cooker.

3. Cover and cook on high for 4–6 hours or on low for 8–10 hours.

4. One hour prior to serving, use 2 forks to shred cooked chicken in the slow cooker and stir throughout the soup.

GREEK LEMON CHICKEN SOUP

Lemon juice and egg yolks make this soup a lovely yellow color. It's a unique soup that's perfect for a spring luncheon.

Serves 4

INGREDIENTS:

4 cups gluten-free chicken broth

¼ cup fresh lemon juice

¼ cup shredded carrots

¼ cup chopped onion

¼ cup chopped celery

⅛ teaspoon ground white pepper

2 tablespoons butter

2 tablespoons brown rice flour

4 egg yolks

½ cup cooked white rice

½ cup diced, cooked boneless chicken breast

8 slices lemon

1. In a greased 4-quart slow cooker combine the chicken broth, lemon juice, carrots, onion, celery, and pepper. Cover and cook on high for 3–4 hours or on low for 6–8 hours.

2. One hour before serving, blend the butter and the flour together in a medium bowl with a fork. Remove 1 cup of hot broth from the slow cooker and whisk with the butter and flour. Add mixture back to the slow cooker.

3. In a small bowl, beat the egg yolks until light in color. Gradually add some of the hot soup to the egg yolks, stirring constantly. Return the egg mixture to the slow cooker.

4. Add the rice and cooked chicken. Cook on low for an additional hour. Ladle hot soup into bowls and garnish with lemon slices.

ITALIAN WEDDING SOUP

This is a delicious, light soup with spinach and meatballs. When making the meatballs, use a light touch or they will become tough during cooking.

Serves 8

INGREDIENTS:

1 slice gluten-free bread, crumbled

¾ cup 1% milk

½ pound lean ground beef

1 cup gluten-free grated Parmesan cheese, divided

1 large egg

½ small onion, finely minced

⅓ cup chopped fresh parsley

2 tablespoons chopped fresh basil

1 teaspoon dried oregano

1 teaspoon garlic powder

1 teaspoon salt

⅛ teaspoon red pepper flakes

1 cup chopped celery

1 cup chopped onion

8 cups gluten-free chicken broth

1 (10-ounce) package frozen spinach, defrosted and drained

3 cups cooked small gluten-free pasta

1. Place bread in a medium bowl and pour milk over it. Let sit 10 minutes then gently squeeze out excess liquid. Put bread in a large bowl; discard milk.

2. Add the ground beef, ½ cup Parmesan cheese, egg, minced onion, parsley, basil, oregano, garlic powder, salt, and red pepper flakes to bowl with bread. Gently toss to combine. Roll the meat mixture in your hands to create tiny meatballs, ½" to 1", depending on the number you want to make.

3. Add celery, onion, chicken broth, meatballs, and spinach to a greased 6-quart slow cooker and cook on high for 4 hours or on low for 8 hours.

4. Add ½ cup cooked pasta to each bowl of hot soup and garnish with 1 tablespoon Parmesan cheese.

Gluten-Free Pasta

When choosing gluten-free pasta for the soup, look for small shapes such as ditalini or anellini. You can find these specialty pasta shapes from a gluten-free company called Le Veneziane and can order them through Amazon.com. Check your local grocery store as many now carry a variety of gluten-free items.

CLASSIC MINESTRONE

A traditional vegetarian Italian soup, minestrone can withstand long cooking periods and tastes even better on the second day.

Serves 12

INGREDIENTS:

3 tablespoons olive oil

1 cup minced white onion

3 stalks celery, chopped

4 cloves garlic, minced

1 small zucchini, chopped

4 cups gluten-free vegetable broth

2 (14-ounce) cans diced tomatoes, drained

2 (15-ounce) cans red kidney beans, drained

2 (15-ounce) cans cannellini (white) beans, drained

1 (28-ounce) can Italian-style green beans

½ cup julienne carrots

1 cup red wine (Chianti or Cabernet Sauvignon)

2 (6-ounce) cans tomato paste

2 tablespoons minced fresh parsley

1½ teaspoons dried oregano

2 teaspoons salt

½ teaspoon ground black pepper

1 teaspoon garlic powder

½ teaspoon gluten-free Italian seasoning

4 cups fresh baby spinach

1 cup cooked small gluten-free pasta

1. In a large skillet heat the olive oil over medium heat. Sauté onion, celery, garlic, and zucchini in the oil for 3–5 minutes, until the onions are translucent.

2. Add sautéed vegetables and vegetable broth to a 6-quart slow cooker, along with tomatoes, red and white beans, green beans, carrots, wine, tomato paste, parsley, oregano, salt, pepper, garlic powder, and Italian seasoning.

3. Cover and cook on high for 8 hours.

4. One hour prior to serving, stir in spinach. Add 1 tablespoon of cooked gluten-free pasta to each cup of soup.

TORTILLA SOUP

This soup tastes even better the next day. Have it for dinner one day and lunch the next.

Serves 8

INGREDIENTS:

1 teaspoon cumin

1 teaspoon gluten-free chili powder

1 teaspoon smoked paprika

⅛ teaspoon salt

25 ounces canned crushed tomatoes

14 ounces canned fire-roasted diced tomatoes

3 cups gluten-free chicken broth

2 cloves garlic, minced

1 medium onion, diced

4 ounces canned diced green chilies, drained

2 habanero peppers, seeded and diced

1 cup fresh corn kernels

2 cups cubed cooked boneless chicken breast

1. Place cumin, chili powder, paprika, salt, tomatoes, broth, garlic, onion, chilies, and peppers in a 4-quart slow cooker. Cover and cook on low for 6 hours.

2. Add the corn and cooked chicken. Cover and cook for an additional 45–60 minutes.

Put the Tortilla in Tortilla Soup

Slice 4 gluten-free corn tortillas in half, then into ¼" strips. Heat ½ teaspoon canola oil in a shallow skillet. Add the tortilla strips and cook, turning once, until they are crisp and golden. Drain on paper towel–lined plates. Blot dry. Divide evenly among the bowls of soup before serving.

SPLIT PEA SOUP

A comforting recipe for a creamy split pea, vegetable, and ham soup, this recipe can also be made vegetarian by using vegetable broth and leaving out the ham.

Serves 6

INGREDIENTS:

1 pound dried split green peas

1 large carrot, diced

1 large parsnip, diced

1 stalk celery, diced

1 medium onion, diced

2 shallots, minced

1½ cups gluten-free cooked ham, diced into 1" cubes

½ teaspoon dried sage

¼ teaspoon celery seed

¼ teaspoon gluten-free ground cayenne pepper

6 cups gluten-free chicken broth

3 tablespoons fresh lemon juice

1. Place all ingredients into a 4-quart slow cooker. Stir. Cook on low for 8–10 hours.

2. If the soup is thinner than desired, uncover and cook on high for 30 minutes before serving.

Using Split Peas

Carefully pick over split peas to remove any stones or stems that might be present. Rinse them off and they are ready to use. Split peas are one of the few legumes that do not need to be presoaked or cooked before slow cooking.

TURKEY AND WILD RICE SOUP

This is the perfect soup for leftover turkey after the holidays. Wild rice gives this soup an earthy, nutty flavor. A nice addition would be to garnish each serving with sautéed baby bella mushrooms.

Serves 6

INGREDIENTS:

6 cups gluten-free chicken broth

1 cup water

½ cup finely chopped green onions

½ cup uncooked wild rice

⅓ cup butter

¼ cup brown rice flour

½ teaspoon salt

¼ teaspoon gluten-free poultry seasoning

⅛ teaspoon ground black pepper

2 cups half-and-half

8 slices gluten-free bacon, cooked and crumbled

1½ cups diced gluten-free cooked turkey breast

2 tablespoons dry sherry

1. In a greased 4–6-quart slow cooker combine chicken broth, water, green onions, and wild rice. Cover and cook on high for 4 hours or on low for 8 hours.

2. One hour prior to serving, melt the butter in a medium saucepan over medium-low heat. Whisk in flour, salt, poultry seasoning, and pepper all at once. Cook, stirring, until smooth and bubbly.

3. Stir the half-and-half into the saucepan and cook until thickened, about 2 minutes.

4. Add thickened cream to soup. Then stir in the bacon, turkey, and sherry. Cook on low for an additional hour and serve.

Storing Cooked Bacon

You can buy precooked and crumbled bacon next to the salad dressings in the grocery store or you can make your own. Cooked and crumbled bacon will keep for several months in the freezer in a sealed zip-top bag.

GUMBO

Serve this Cajun classic over white or brown rice.

Serves 8

INGREDIENTS:

2 tablespoons butter

2 tablespoons brown rice flour

1 large green pepper, diced

4 cloves garlic, diced

1 medium onion, diced

2 carrots, diced

2 stalks celery, diced

1 quart gluten-free chicken broth

2 tablespoons gluten-free Cajun seasoning

4 chicken andouille sausages (gluten-free), sliced

1½ cups diced fresh tomatoes

2 cups diced okra

1. In a nonstick skillet, melt the butter. Add the flour and stir until the flour is golden brown. Add the pepper, garlic, onion, carrots, and celery. Sauté for 3–5 minutes.

2. Add the mixture to a 4-quart slow cooker. Add the broth, seasoning, sausage, and tomatoes. Cook on low for 8–10 hours.

3. Add the okra for the last hour of cooking. Stir prior to serving.

SOUTHWESTERN CHEESE SOUP

Serve this soup with a tossed salad and gluten-free corn chips. Use hot or mild green chilies (or leave them out altogether), according to your personal preference.

Serves 8

INGREDIENTS:

2 pounds lean ground beef

1 package gluten-free taco seasoning mix

1 (15-ounce) can whole kernel corn, undrained

1 (15-ounce) can kidney beans, undrained

1 (15-ounce) can diced tomatoes, undrained

2 (15-ounce) cans stewed tomatoes, undrained

1 (7-ounce) can green chilies, minced and drained

2 pounds Velveeta cheese, cut into cubes

1. Fry the ground beef in a large nonstick skillet over medium-high heat, for approximately 5–6 minutes, breaking it apart as you do so. Drain and discard any fat rendered from the beef.

2. Transfer the ground beef to a greased 4-quart slow cooker and stir in the taco seasoning mix.

3. Add the corn, beans, tomatoes, and chilies to the slow cooker. Stir to combine. Cover and cook on low for 4 hours.

4. Stir the cheese into the soup. Cover, stirring occasionally; continue to cook on low until the cheese is melted and blended into the soup.

TUXEDO SOUP

This soup, which gets its name from the bowtie pasta, is one that kids will love. If you cannot find gluten-free bowtie pasta, simply use your favorite shape of gluten-free pasta. Serve this thick and hearty soup with a tossed salad and gluten-free garlic bread.

Serves 8

INGREDIENTS:

1 pound lean ground beef

1 medium onion, diced

1 small green pepper, seeded and diced

1 stalk celery, diced

1 medium carrot, diced

4 cloves garlic, peeled and minced

2 (15-ounce) cans diced tomatoes, undrained

1 cup water

1 (26-ounce) jar gluten-free spaghetti sauce

1 tablespoon sugar

½ teaspoon gluten-free Italian seasoning

2 cups cooked gluten-free bowtie pasta

1 teaspoon salt

½ teaspoon freshly ground black pepper

½ cup grated Parmesan cheese (fresh or gluten-free)

¼ cup minced fresh flat-leaf parsley

1. Add the ground beef, onion, green pepper, celery, and carrot to a nonstick skillet and sauté over medium heat for about 8 minutes, or until the vegetables are tender and the meat is no longer pink.

2. Stir in the garlic and sauté for an additional 30 seconds. Drain and discard any excess fat. Transfer to a greased 4–6-quart slow cooker.

3. Stir in the undrained tomatoes, water, spaghetti sauce, sugar, and Italian seasoning. Cover and cook on low for 6–8 hours.

4. Stir pasta into the soup. Thin the soup with additional hot water if needed. Add salt and pepper. Ladle into soup bowls. Sprinkle cheese and flat-leaf parsley over each serving.

Extra Vegetables

Thanks to the spaghetti sauce, you can hide more vegetables in Tuxedo Soup and the kids won't even notice. For example, dice a few more carrots and stir them in with the other ingredients in Step 1.

HATTERAS CLAM CHOWDER

This cozy, creamy chowder is thickened only by potatoes. Serve it with a fresh green salad and homemade gluten-free bread.

Serves 4

INGREDIENTS:

4 slices gluten-free bacon, diced

1 small onion, diced

2 medium russet potatoes, peeled and diced

1 (8-ounce) bottle clam broth, gluten-free

2–3 cups water

½ teaspoon salt

½ teaspoon freshly ground pepper

2 (6½-ounce) cans minced clams (do not drain)

1. In a 2-quart or larger saucepan, sauté bacon until crispy and browned. Add onion and sauté until translucent, about 3–5 minutes. Add cooked onions and bacon to a greased 2½-quart slow cooker.

2. Add potatoes, clam broth, and enough water to cover (2–3 cups). Add salt and pepper.

3. Cover and cook on high for 3 hours, until potatoes are very tender.

4. One hour prior to serving, add in the clams, along with broth from the cans, and cook until heated through.

BACON CORN CHOWDER

This corn and potato chowder is given extra flavor with crunchy crumbled bacon.

Serves 4

INGREDIENTS:

4 slices gluten-free bacon, diced

1 medium red onion, chopped

½ jalapeño chili, seeded and finely chopped

1 clove garlic, minced

2 tablespoons brown rice flour

½ teaspoon salt

¼ teaspoon pepper

2 (15-ounce) cans sweet corn kernels, drained, or 4 cups frozen sweet corn

3 red potatoes (about 1 pound), peeled and diced

4 cups gluten-free chicken broth

2 cups half-and-half

1 cup chopped cherry tomatoes

3 tablespoons sliced fresh basil leaves

1. In a large pan, sauté bacon until crispy and browned. Remove bacon and set aside. Cook onion in bacon grease and sauté until translucent, about 3–5 minutes.

2. Whisk in jalapeño, garlic, flour, salt, and pepper and cook for 1 minute more until flour is toasted.

3. Grease a 4- or 6-quart slow cooker with nonstick cooking spray. Add onion mixture to the slow cooker. Add corn, potatoes, and chicken broth. Stir ingredients together.

4. Cover and cook on high for 4 hours or on low for 8 hours.

5. One hour before serving, stir in half-and-half. Add additional salt and pepper if desired. Serve chowder by ladling into large bowls and garnishing with bacon, chopped tomatoes, and fresh basil.

WHITE CHICKEN CHILI

This is the perfect comfort food any time of the year. Gluten-free corn bread would go perfectly with this dish.

Serves 6

INGREDIENTS:

1 tablespoon grapeseed oil

1 medium onion, chopped

4 cloves garlic, chopped

1 cup mushrooms, chopped

1½ cups frozen corn

½ cup chopped green bell pepper

1 (4-ounce) can chopped green chili peppers

1½ teaspoons ground cumin

¼ teaspoon gluten-free ground cayenne pepper

½ teaspoon gluten-free chili powder

1 teaspoon oregano

3 (15-ounce) cans navy white beans, rinsed and drained

2 (14½-ounce) cans gluten-free chicken broth

1½ pounds cooked skinless, boneless chicken breast, chopped

1 tablespoon cilantro, chopped

Chopped scallions or chopped cilantro, for garnish

1. Heat oil in a large pot or Dutch oven over medium-low heat, and add onion and garlic. Cook for 3–4 minutes, until onions become translucent.

2. Add mushrooms, corn, and bell pepper, and cook until they soften a bit, about 2–3 minutes.

3. Add chili peppers, cumin, cayenne pepper, chili powder, and oregano. Stir to combine.

4. Take 1 can of white beans and place in a blender or food processor until completely blended. You might need to add a bit of water if it becomes too thick.

5. Pour blended bean mixture into pot along with chicken broth, remaining 2 cans of beans, cooked chicken, and 1 tablespoon chopped cilantro, and stir. Reduce heat to low and continue to simmer about 10–15 minutes, stirring occasionally.

6. Top with chopped scallions or chopped cilantro.

Spice It Up

Do you like your chili a little spicier? Just add a fresh jalapeño (seeded and diced), or increase the cayenne pepper and chili powder. This dish can be made to suit your taste.

HEARTY BEEF CHILI

The key to this hearty chili is keeping the ground beef in larger chunks (instead of breaking it up into very small pieces) when you are browning it for the slow cooker. If you prefer a spicier version, add an additional tablespoon of chili powder, 1 teaspoon cumin, and ½ teaspoon cayenne pepper.

Serves 6

INGREDIENTS:

1 pound lean ground beef

1 cup chopped onion

¾ cup chopped green pepper

1 clove garlic, minced

1 (16-ounce) can diced tomatoes

1 (16-ounce) can pinto beans, drained and rinsed

1 (8-ounce) can tomato sauce

2 teaspoons gluten-free chili powder

½ teaspoon crushed basil

1. Brown ground beef and onion in a large skillet, approximately 5–6 minutes. Leave the ground beef in larger chunks when cooking, instead of breaking it down into very small pieces. Add cooked beef and onion to a greased 4-quart slow cooker.

2. Add remaining ingredients. Cover and cook on high for 4 hours or on low for 8 hours.

Where's the Beef?

Some people prefer to use all beef in their chili. For a full beef, bean-free chili, use 2 pounds of lean ground beef and leave out the pinto beans. Quartered button mushrooms can also add a meaty texture to this chili.

BLACK BEAN AND BUTTERNUT SQUASH CHILI

This is a spicy and filling vegetarian chili. Feel free to use spinach for the greens in this recipe instead of kale.

Serves 8

INGREDIENTS:

2 tablespoons olive oil

1 medium sweet onion, chopped

3 cloves garlic, minced

3 tablespoons gluten-free chili powder

2 teaspoons cumin

2½ cups butternut squash, peeled, cooked, and cubed

2 (15-ounce) cans black beans, rinsed and drained

4 cups gluten-free vegetable broth

1 (14-ounce) can diced tomatoes in juice

2–3 cups fresh kale, washed, patted dry, chopped

1 teaspoon salt

½ teaspoon freshly ground pepper

1. In a skillet, heat olive oil. Sauté onion and garlic until soft, about 3–5 minutes. Add chili powder and cumin and cook for 1–2 minutes to release the aroma of the spices. Add onion mixture to a greased 4-quart slow cooker.

2. Add squash, beans, broth, and tomatoes to the slow cooker. Cover and cook on high for 4 hours or on low for 8 hours.

3. An hour prior to serving, stir in the chopped kale, salt, and pepper.

Instead of Butternut . . .

Any type of cubed winter squash (other than spaghetti squash), or even peeled and cubed sweet potatoes would work perfectly in this vegetarian stew.

SPICY VEGETARIAN CHILI

Have a chili party and offer diners their choice of a hearty beef chili and this zesty and flavorful vegetarian chili.

Serves 8

INGREDIENTS:

2 tablespoons olive oil

1½ cups chopped yellow onion

1 cup chopped red bell pepper

2 tablespoons minced garlic

2 serrano peppers, seeded and minced

1 medium zucchini, diced

2 cups frozen corn

1½ pounds portobello mushrooms (about 5 large), stemmed, cleaned, and cubed

2 tablespoons gluten-free chili powder

1 tablespoon ground cumin

1¼ teaspoons salt

¼ teaspoon gluten-free cayenne pepper

2 (15-ounce) cans diced tomatoes

2 (15-ounce) cans black beans, drained and rinsed

1 (15-ounce) can tomato sauce

2 cups gluten-free vegetable broth, or water

¼ cup chopped fresh cilantro leaves

1. In a large, heavy pot, heat the oil over medium-high heat. Add the onions, bell peppers, garlic, and serrano peppers, and cook, stirring, until soft, about 3 minutes.

2. Add softened vegetables to a greased 4–6-quart slow cooker. Add remaining ingredients, except for cilantro.

3. Cover and cook on high for 4–6 hours or on low for 8–10 hours. Stir in cilantro before serving.

Pick Your Own Garnishes

A fun way to serve this chili is to prepare and chill bowls of chopped avocados, gluten-free sour cream, shredded cheese, crushed gluten-free tortilla chips, and gluten-free salsa. Allow diners to garnish their own bowls of chili when it's time to eat.

EASY TURKEY AND RICE CHILI

This easy chili can be quickly put together in the slow cooker for a last-minute dinner since it's hot and ready in 2–3 hours.

Serves 4

INGREDIENTS:

1 pound lean ground turkey

¼ cup chopped onion

1 (14-ounce) can diced tomatoes

2–3 teaspoons gluten-free chili powder

1 teaspoon cumin

1 teaspoon garlic

1 (27-ounce) can kidney beans, undrained

1½ cups water

1 cup cooked white rice

1. Brown ground turkey in a large skillet, for about 5–6 minutes until cooked through. Add onion and cook for 2–3 minutes until softened.

2. Place browned ground turkey and onions in a greased 4-quart slow cooker. Add tomatoes, chili powder, cumin, garlic, kidney beans, and water. Stir to combine. Cover and cook on high for 2–3 hours or on low for 5–6 hours.

3. An hour before serving, stir in cooked rice.

CHAPTER 7

POULTRY

CREAMY CHICKEN STEW

This rich and creamy chicken stew is an excellent dish to serve with Buttermilk Gluten-Free Drop Biscuits (see recipe in Chapter 3).

Serves 8

INGREDIENTS:

2 tablespoons olive oil

3 pounds boneless skinless chicken breasts, cut into 1" cubes

1 teaspoon salt

1 teaspoon pepper

1 teaspoon paprika

2 cups white potatoes, peeled and cubed

3 large carrots, peeled and diced

2 cups frozen whole kernel corn

1 cup chopped green pepper

1 cup chopped sweet red pepper

1 cup diced celery

1 medium onion, diced

2 teaspoons dried basil

1 bay leaf

¼ teaspoon celery salt

7 cups gluten-free chicken broth

½ cup butter

⅓ cup brown rice flour

1. In a large skillet, heat olive oil over medium heat. Sauté chicken pieces in small batches until they are browned, about 1–2 minutes per side. Add browned chicken to a greased 6-quart slow cooker.

2. Add salt, pepper, paprika, potatoes, carrots, corn, green and red peppers, celery, onion, basil, bay leaf, celery salt, and chicken broth to the slow cooker. Cover and cook on high for 4 hours or on low for 8 hours. One hour before serving, remove bay leaf.

3. In a large saucepan, melt butter; whisk in flour until smooth. Cook and stir for 2 minutes. Gradually whisk in 2 cups of hot broth from the slow cooker. Bring to a boil; cook and stir for 2 minutes or until thickened. Whisk thickened sauce into stew in the slow cooker. Cook an additional hour.

BISCUIT-TOPPED CHICKEN PIE

Pure comfort food! This creamy chicken and vegetable pie is topped with homemade Buttermilk Gluten-Free Drop Biscuits. To make the pie extra rich, drizzle a few tablespoons of melted butter over the biscuit topping right before cooking.

Serves 6

INGREDIENTS:

4 tablespoons brown rice flour

4 tablespoons butter

1 cup whole milk

1 cup gluten-free chicken broth

1 teaspoon salt

½ teaspoon ground black pepper

2 cups cooked chicken breast, cut or torn into bite-sized pieces

1 (12-ounce) can mixed vegetables, drained

1 prepared batch of dough for Buttermilk Gluten-Free Drop Biscuits (see recipe in Chapter 3)

1. In a small saucepan over medium heat, whisk together flour and butter. When butter has melted, slowly stir in milk, chicken broth, salt, and pepper. Cook on medium heat for 5–10 minutes, whisking constantly until mixture is thick, with a gravy consistency.

2. Add chicken and vegetables to a greased 4-quart slow cooker. Pour cream soup mixture into the slow cooker and mix with chicken and vegetables.

3. Using an ice cream scoop, drop biscuit dough over chicken, vegetables, and sauce.

4. Cover slow cooker and vent lid with a chopstick. Cook on high for 3–4 hours or on low for 6–8 hours until chicken sauce is bubbling up around the biscuits, and the biscuits are cooked through.

Gluten-Free Baking Mixes

Instead of homemade biscuits, you can also use your favorite gluten-free biscuit baking mix. It must be an all-purpose mix that includes xanthan gum and a leavening ingredient such as gluten-free baking powder or baking soda. Use a recipe on the package that will make 8–10 gluten-free biscuits as a topping for chicken pie.

CHICKEN ALFREDO PASTA

Quartered artichokes add a tangy flavor to this easy pasta casserole.

Serves 4

INGREDIENTS:

1 pound boneless, skinless chicken thighs, cut into ¾" pieces

1 (14-ounce) can quartered artichokes, drained

1 (16-ounce) jar gluten-free Alfredo pasta sauce

1 cup water

½ cup sun-dried tomatoes, drained and chopped

8 ounces gluten-free pasta, uncooked

2 tablespoons shredded Parmesan cheese, gluten-free

1. In a greased 4-quart slow cooker, mix chicken, artichokes, Alfredo sauce, and water. Cover and cook on high for 3 hours or on low for 6 hours.

2. About 45 minutes before serving, stir tomatoes and uncooked pasta into chicken mixture.

3. Cover lid and continue to cook until pasta is al dente. Sprinkle Parmesan cheese over individual servings.

Make Your Own Alfredo Sauce

Most Alfredo sauces are naturally gluten-free: they're usually made with butter, cheese, cream, and spices. To make your own, whisk together over medium heat: ½ cup butter, 8 ounces light cream cheese, 1 cup whole milk or half-and-half, ⅓ cup gluten-free Parmesan cheese, and 1 tablespoon garlic powder. Allow the mixture to cool. It will thicken as it cools.

SPANISH CHICKEN AND RICE

Have Spanish extra-virgin olive oil at the table for those who wish to drizzle a little over the rice. For more heat, sprinkle some additional dried red pepper flakes on top.

Serves 4

INGREDIENTS:

1 tablespoon olive or vegetable oil

4 bone-in chicken thighs

4 bone-in split chicken breasts

2 tablespoons lemon juice

4 ounces gluten-free smoked ham, cubed

1 medium onion, peeled and diced

1 red bell pepper, seeded and diced

4 cloves garlic, peeled and minced

2½ cups water

1¾ cups gluten-free chicken broth

1 teaspoon oregano

½ teaspoon salt

¼ teaspoon saffron threads, crushed

⅛ teaspoon dried red pepper flakes, crushed

2 cups converted long-grain rice, uncooked

1. Bring the oil to temperature in a large nonstick skillet over medium-high heat. Put the chicken pieces in the skillet skin-side down and fry for 5 minutes or until the skin is browned. Transfer the chicken to a plate and sprinkle the lemon juice over the chicken.

2. Pour off and discard all but 2 tablespoons of the fat in the skillet. Reduce the heat under the skillet to medium. Add the ham, onion, and bell pepper; sauté for 5 minutes or until the onion is transparent. Stir in the garlic and sauté for 30 seconds.

3. Grease a 6-quart slow cooker with nonstick spray. Pour the cooked ham and vegetables into the slow cooker. Add the water, broth, oregano, salt, saffron, red pepper flakes, and rice. Stir to combine.

4. Place the chicken thighs, skin-side up, in the slow cooker and add the breast pieces on top of the thighs. Cover and cook on low for 6 hours or until the rice is tender and the chicken is cooked through. Place a split chicken breast and thigh on each serving plate. Stir and fluff the rice mixture and spoon it onto the plates.

Adding a Vegetable to Spanish Chicken and Rice

After you've removed the chicken from the slow cooker in Step 4, stir in 1 cup (or more) of thawed baby peas. Stir into the mixture remaining in the cooker when you fluff the rice. The heat from the rice should be sufficient to warm the peas so you can serve immediately.

MEDITERRANEAN CHICKEN CASSEROLE

Raisins may seem like an odd ingredient to add to a main dish, but they provide a slightly sweet flavor that beautifully complements the tomatoes and spices.

Serves 4

INGREDIENTS:

1 medium butternut squash, peeled and cut into 2" cubes

1 medium bell pepper, seeded and diced

1 (14½-ounce) can diced tomatoes, undrained

4 boneless, skinless chicken breast halves, cut into bite-sized pieces

½ cup mild gluten-free salsa

¼ cup raisins, gluten-free

¼ teaspoon ground cinnamon

¼ teaspoon ground cumin

2 cups cooked rice, for serving

¼ cup chopped fresh parsley

1. Add squash and bell pepper to the bottom of a greased 4-quart slow cooker. Mix tomatoes, chicken, salsa, raisins, cinnamon, and cumin together and pour on top of squash and peppers.

2. Cover and cook on low for 6 hours, or on high for 3 hours, until squash is fork tender.

3. Remove chicken and vegetables from slow cooker with slotted spoon. Serve over cooked rice. Ladle remaining sauce from slow cooker over the vegetables. Garnish with parsley.

CREAMY CHICKEN IN MUSHROOM AND WHITE WINE SAUCE

Many traditional slow cooker recipes call for using canned cream soups, which often contain wheat flour as an ingredient. For a gluten-free version, this recipe shows you how to make a simple homemade cream soup using cornstarch and milk.

Serves 4

INGREDIENTS:

4 boneless chicken breasts, cut into chunks

3 tablespoons cornstarch

1 cup 2% milk

½ cup white wine

½ teaspoon salt

½ teaspoon ground pepper

1½ teaspoons gluten-free poultry seasoning

½ teaspoon garlic powder

½ teaspoon salt-free, gluten-free, all-purpose seasoning

2 (4-ounce) cans sliced mushrooms, drained and rinsed

1½ cups frozen peas

2 cups cooked gluten-free pasta

1. Grease a 4-quart slow cooker with nonstick cooking spray. Place chicken into the slow cooker.

2. In a saucepan whisk together the cornstarch, milk, and white wine. Whisk in salt, pepper, poultry seasoning, garlic powder, and salt-free seasoning. Cook over medium heat whisking constantly until sauce thickens. Pour sauce over chicken.

3. Add mushrooms on top of the chicken. Cook on low for 6 hours or on high for 3 hours.

4. One hour before serving, stir in the frozen peas.

5. Serve over pasta.

ORANGE CHICKEN

You can use light or dark brown sugar, depending on your preference. (Dark brown sugar will impart more molasses flavor to the dish.) Serve this dish over cooked rice or stir-fry vegetables, or with both.

Serves 8

INGREDIENTS:

3 pounds boneless, skinless chicken breasts

1 small onion, peeled and diced

½ cup orange juice

3 tablespoons orange marmalade

1 tablespoon brown sugar

1 tablespoon apple cider vinegar

1 tablespoon gluten-free Worcestershire sauce

1 teaspoon gluten-free Dijon mustard

1 tablespoon cornstarch mixed with 2 tablespoons cold water

2 tablespoons grated orange zest

1. Grease the slow cooker with nonstick cooking spray. Cut the chicken breasts into bite-sized pieces. Add the chicken and the onion to the slow cooker.

2. In a small bowl, mix together the orange juice, marmalade, brown sugar, vinegar, Worcestershire sauce, and mustard. Pour over the chicken in the slow cooker.

3. Cover and cook on low for 5–6 hours, or until chicken is cooked through. About 10 minutes before serving, whisk in the cornstarch slurry. Uncover the slow cooker, turn the temperature to high, and continue to cook for 10 minutes to thicken the sauce. Serve with orange zest sprinkled on top.

CHICKEN AND GLUTEN-FREE DUMPLINGS

Fluffy gluten-free dumplings float on top of a savory chicken stew. You can make the biscuit topping from scratch or use your favorite all-purpose gluten-free baking mix.

Serves 4

INGREDIENTS:

4 chicken breasts, cut into chunks

4 cups gluten-free chicken broth

¾ teaspoon salt, divided

1 teaspoon ground pepper

2 celery stalks, thinly sliced

2 carrots, thinly sliced

½ medium onion, finely chopped

1 cup brown rice flour

1 cup arrowroot starch

1 teaspoon xanthan gum

1 tablespoon sugar

3 teaspoons gluten-free baking powder

⅓ cup vegetable shortening

2 large eggs, lightly beaten

1 cup 2% milk

1. Place the chicken in a greased 4–6-quart slow cooker. Add chicken broth, ½ teaspoon salt, pepper, celery, carrots, and onion. Cook on high for 3–4 hours or on low for 6–8 hours.

2. In a mixing bowl whisk together the flour, arrowroot starch, xanthan gum, sugar, baking powder, and remaining ¼ teaspoon salt.

3. Cut the shortening into the dry ingredients with two knives or a pastry cutter until the mixture resembles small peas. Make a well in the center of the dry ingredients and add the eggs and milk. Gently mix the wet ingredients into the dry ingredients until you have a fluffy dough.

4. Thirty minutes before serving, drop the dough in golf ball–sized spoonfuls into the hot chicken broth. Place the lid on the slow cooker and do not open it for 30 minutes so the dumplings will rise and cook through.

5. Serve dumplings with broth and chicken in large bowls.

Using a Gluten-Free All-Purpose Mix

If you prefer to use your favorite all-purpose gluten-free baking mix for the topping, simply follow the directions on the package for a batch that makes 6–8 biscuits. Then follow the directions, adding the uncooked dumplings to the slow cooker 30 minutes before you are ready to serve.

ROAST CHICKEN WITH LEMON AND ARTICHOKES

This is an elegant twist on a simple roast chicken. Marinated artichoke hearts add a hint of zest while fresh lemons give the dish a bright flavor reminiscent of summer.

Serves 4

INGREDIENTS:

1 small onion, quartered

1 large carrot, sliced

1 large lemon

3 cloves garlic

1 (4-pound) whole chicken

½ teaspoon salt

½ teaspoon freshly ground pepper

2 tablespoons olive oil

1 (6-ounce) jar marinated artichoke hearts

1. Grease a large 6-quart slow cooker with nonstick cooking spray.

2. Place the onion and carrot in the slow cooker. Cut the lemon in half. Place half of the lemon, along with the garlic cloves, into the cavity of the chicken.

3. Cut the remainder of the lemon into 4–5 large slices.

4. Place the chicken on top of the onions and carrots. Place lemon slices on top of the chicken. Sprinkle salt and pepper over the chicken. Drizzle olive oil over chicken. Cook on low for 6–8 hours or on high for 3–4 hours.

5. An hour before serving, place artichokes (discarding the oil) over the top of the chicken.

Make a Quick Lemon Sauce

Make a sauce using the liquids from the cooked chicken by straining them into a saucepan. Whisk in 2 tablespoons of brown rice flour or garbanzo bean flour and cook on low heat until thickened. The resulting sauce will have a fragrant aroma of lemon, artichokes, and garlic. Serve over rice or gluten-free pasta with green beans or a salad.

HAWAIIAN CHICKEN

Pineapple and green peppers give this chicken dish a distinctive and fruity flavor.

Serves 4

INGREDIENTS:

4 boneless, skinless chicken breasts

1 (15-ounce) can sliced pineapple, drained (reserve juice)

½ green pepper, sliced

½ red pepper, sliced

¼ teaspoon cinnamon

½ teaspoon gluten-free Chinese five-spice powder

½ teaspoon crushed red pepper

1. Place chicken breasts in a greased 4-quart slow cooker.

2. Add 2 slices of pineapple on top of each piece of chicken. If there are leftover pieces, simply set them alongside the chicken.

3. Place green and red pepper slices evenly over all the pieces of chicken. Sprinkle the cinnamon, Chinese five-spice powder, and crushed pepper evenly over the chicken.

4. Finally, pour ½ cup of the reserved pineapple juice over the chicken.

5. Cook on high for 2½–3 hours or on low for 5–6 hours.

Using Pineapple Juice

When buying canned fruit, try to buy varieties that are canned in "natural juices" or "its own juices" instead of corn syrup. The leftover juice can be saved in the refrigerator to use later as juice to drink, or even as a natural sweetener for a glass of iced tea or a bowl of warm oatmeal.

HONEY GLAZED CHICKEN DRUMSTICKS

It can be a challenge to eat at Chinese restaurants when you are avoiding gluten. But this Asian-inspired chicken is a great substitute for take out! Serve with white rice, a salad, and egg drop soup.

Serves 4

INGREDIENTS:

2 pounds chicken drumsticks

1 tablespoon melted butter

¼ cup lemon juice

¾ cup honey

1 teaspoon sesame oil

3 cloves garlic, crushed

½ teaspoon ground ginger

½ teaspoon salt

1. Place chicken drumsticks in a greased 4-quart slow cooker.

2. In a glass measuring cup whisk together the melted butter, lemon juice, honey, sesame oil, garlic, ginger, and salt.

3. Pour the honey sauce over the drumsticks. Cook on high for 3–4 hours or on low for 6–8 hours.

Sesame Oil

Sesame oil is a highly flavored oil made from pressing either toasted or plain sesame seeds. It provides a uniquely nutty and earthy flavor to savory dishes. A little goes a long way and it's not very expensive. It can be found at most grocery stores in the Asian foods aisle.

EASY ITALIAN CHICKEN

To add vibrant color to this one-pot meal, use a red or orange pepper instead of green.

Serves 4

INGREDIENTS:

4 boneless, skinless chicken breasts

1 cup gluten-free Italian salad dressing

½ teaspoon salt

1 cup diced green peppers

1 cup diced onions

4 medium potatoes, peeled and quartered

1 (14½-ounce) can green beans, drained and rinsed

1. Place chicken in a greased 4-quart slow cooker. Add Italian dressing, salt, green peppers, onions, and potatoes.

2. Cook on high for 3 hours or on low for 6 hours.

3. Add green beans during the last hour of cooking.

CHICKEN PAPRIKASH

If you prefer not to cook with wine, replace it with an equal amount of gluten-free chicken broth. You can also substitute an equal amount of drained plain yogurt or full-fat coconut milk for the sour cream.

Serves 8

INGREDIENTS:

1 tablespoon butter

1 tablespoon extra-virgin olive oil

1 large yellow onion, peeled and diced

2 cloves garlic, peeled and minced

3 pounds boneless, skinless chicken thighs

½ teaspoon salt

¼ teaspoon freshly ground pepper

2 tablespoons Hungarian paprika

½ cup gluten-free chicken broth

¼ cup dry white wine

1 (16-ounce) container gluten-free sour cream

4 cups cooked gluten-free pasta

1. Add the butter, oil, and onion to a microwave-safe bowl; cover and microwave on high for 1 minute. Stir, re-cover, and microwave on high for another minute or until the onions are transparent. Stir in the garlic; cover and microwave on high for 30 seconds. Add to a greased 4–6-quart slow cooker.

2. Cut the chicken thighs into bite-sized pieces. Add the chicken to the slow cooker. Stir in the salt, pepper, paprika, broth, and wine. Cover and cook on low for 6 hours or on high for 3 hours.

3. Stir in the sour cream; cover and continue to cook long enough to bring the sour cream sauce to temperature, about 30 minutes. Serve over pasta. Sprinkle each serving with additional paprika if desired. Serve immediately.

Thickening or Thinning

If the resulting sauce for the chicken paprikash is too thin, add more gluten-free sour cream. If it's too thick, slowly whisk in some milk.

TARRAGON CHICKEN

This rich French dish can stand on its own when served with just a tossed salad and some crusty gluten-free bread.

Serves 4

INGREDIENTS:

½ cup plus 2 tablespoons brown rice flour or garbanzo bean flour

½ teaspoon salt

8 bone-in chicken thighs, skin removed

2 tablespoons butter

2 tablespoons olive oil

1 medium yellow onion, peeled and diced

1 cup dry white wine

1 cup gluten-free chicken broth

½–1 teaspoon dried tarragon

1 cup heavy cream

1. Add ½ cup flour, salt, and the chicken thighs to a gallon-sized plastic bag; close and shake to coat the chicken.

2. Add the butter and oil to a large sauté pan and bring it to temperature over medium-high heat. Add the chicken thighs and brown them by cooking for about 5 minutes on each side. Drain the chicken on paper towels and then place in a 4–6-quart slow cooker. Cover the slow cooker. Set temperature to low.

3. Add the onion to the sauté pan; sauté until the onion is transparent, about 3–5 minutes. Stir in 2 tablespoons of brown rice flour, cooking until the onion just begins to brown. Slowly pour the wine into the pan, stirring to scrape the browned bits off of the bottom of the pan and into the sauce. Add the broth. Cook and stir for 15 minutes or until the sauce is thickened enough to coat the back of a spoon. Stir the tarragon into the sauce, and then pour the sauce over the chicken in the slow cooker. Cover and cook for 3 hours on high or 6 hours on low.

4. Pour the cream into the slow cooker; cover and cook for an additional 15 minutes or until the cream is heated through. Test for seasoning and add additional salt and tarragon if needed. Serve immediately.

Tarragon Chicken Cooking Times

After 3 hours on high, the chicken will be cooked through and ready to eat. Yet, if you prefer to leave the chicken cooking for a longer period, after 7–8 hours on low, the meat will be tender enough to fall away from the bone. You can then remove the bones before you stir in the cream.

MOROCCAN CHICKEN

This dish was inspired by traditional North African tagines and adapted for the slow cooker. Serve over cooked rice or mashed sweet potatoes

Serves 6

INGREDIENTS:

½ teaspoon coriander

½ teaspoon cinnamon

¼ teaspoon salt

1 teaspoon cumin

3 pounds (about 8) boneless, skinless chicken thighs, diced

1 medium onion, thinly sliced

4 cloves garlic, minced

2 tablespoons fresh ginger, minced or ½ teaspoon dried ginger

½ cup water

4 ounces gluten-free dried apricots, halved

15 ounces canned chickpeas, drained and rinsed

1. In a large bowl, combine the coriander, cinnamon, salt, and cumin. Toss chicken in the spice mixture.

2. Place onion, garlic, ginger, and water into a 4-quart slow cooker. Place chicken on top of vegetables. Place dried apricots and chickpeas on top of chicken.

3. Cover and cook on low for 5–6 hours.

Fresh Ginger or Ground?

Fresh ginger has a strong, pungent flavor, which is hard to replicate with dried ginger. Yet, if you need to substitute simply use about ¼ teaspoon dried ginger for 1 tablespoon of freshly minced ginger. Tightly wrapped fresh ginger will keep in your refrigerator for approximately 3 weeks and will stay fresh in the freezer for up to 6 months.

CHICKEN PICCATA

Serve over mashed potatoes or gluten-free egg noodles.

Serves 4

INGREDIENTS:

2 large boneless, skinless chicken breasts, cut into very thin slices

1 cup brown rice flour

1 tablespoon olive oil

¼ cup lemon juice

3 tablespoons nonpareil capers

¾ cup gluten-free chicken broth

¼ teaspoon freshly ground black pepper

1. Dredge both sides of the sliced chicken breasts in the flour. Discard leftover flour.

2. Heat olive oil in a nonstick pan. Quickly sear the chicken on both sides to brown, approximately 1 minute per side.

3. Place the chicken, lemon juice, capers, broth, and pepper into a greased 4-quart slow cooker.

4. Cook on high for 2–3 hours or on low for 4–6 hours, until the chicken is cooked through and the sauce has thickened.

Dredge Details

Dredging is a process in which food is dragged through dry ingredients like cornstarch or gluten-free bread crumbs to coat it. Dredging can be a one-step process, but if a thicker crust or coating is desired, the food is dredged in flour once, dipped in egg or milk, then dredged through gluten-free flour, gluten-free cornmeal, or gluten-free bread crumbs again. In slow cooking, dredging often has a dual purpose of coating the meat and thickening the sauce.

BUTTER CHICKEN

This dish is also called Chicken Makhani. The common name, "Butter Chicken," is a bit of a misnomer as the dish traditionally only includes about a tablespoon of butter.

Serves 4

INGREDIENTS:

2 shallots, minced

2 cloves garlic, minced

½ knob of fresh ginger, peeled and minced

2 tablespoons lemon juice

2 teaspoons garam masala (gluten-free)

2 teaspoons ground cumin

½ teaspoon gluten-free cayenne

½ teaspoon fenugreek

¼ teaspoon salt

½ teaspoon freshly ground black pepper

1 tablespoon butter

1 tablespoon tomato paste

1 pound boneless, skinless chicken breasts

¾ cup plain low-fat gluten-free Greek yogurt

1. Mix together shallots, garlic, ginger, lemon juice, garam masala, cumin, cayenne, fenugreek, salt, pepper, butter, and tomato paste in a 4-quart slow cooker. Stir to combine and add chicken breasts. Cook on low for 5 hours or on high for 2½ hours.

2. About 10 minutes before serving, stir in the yogurt.

Do-It-Yourself Greek Yogurt

Greek yogurt is super thick and creamy, but is also low in fat. It is available in many grocery stores but can be tricky to find in some areas. A reasonable facsimile can be made by lining a colander with cheesecloth and straining low-fat plain yogurt overnight. Be sure to start with twice as much yogurt as the final product should be because the yogurt will reduce by half.

CHICKEN CACCIATORE

If you prefer, you can remove the skin from a 3-pound chicken and cut it into 8 serving pieces and substitute that for the chicken thighs. Serve the chicken and sauce over cooked rice or gluten-free pasta.

Serves 4

INGREDIENTS:

¾ cup brown rice flour, divided

½ teaspoon salt

8 bone-in chicken thighs, skin removed (if using boneless reduce cooking time by 1 hour)

3 tablespoons olive oil

1 medium yellow onion, diced

4 cloves garlic, minced

3 tablespoons coarsely chopped oil-packed sun-dried tomatoes

1 cup dry white wine

⅛ teaspoon dried sage

¼ teaspoon dried rosemary

Pinch dried red pepper flakes

½ teaspoon freshly ground black pepper

1. Add ½ cup of the flour, salt, and the chicken thighs to a gallon-sized plastic bag; close and shake to coat the chicken.

2. Add the oil to a large sauté pan and bring it to medium-high heat. Add the chicken thighs and brown them by cooking for about 5 minutes on each side. Drain the chicken on paper towels and then place in a 4–6-quart slow cooker. Cover the slow cooker and set the temperature to low.

3. Add the onion to the sauté pan and cook until the onions begin to soften, about 3–5 minutes. Stir in the garlic and sauté for 30 seconds. Add the sun-dried tomatoes. Slowly pour the wine into the pan to deglaze (stirring to scrape the browned bits off the bottom of the pan). Stir in the sage, rosemary, pepper flakes, and black pepper, and then pour the sauce over the chicken in the slow cooker.

4. Cover and cook on high for 3–4 hours or on low for 6–7 hours.

CHICKEN IN PLUM SAUCE

For this rich, sweet entrée, you can use commercial gluten-free plum sauce or make your own Plum Sauce (see recipe in this chapter). Top each serving with toasted sesame oil and gluten-free soy sauce if desired.

Serves 4

INGREDIENTS:

1¾ cups gluten-free plum sauce

2 tablespoons butter, melted

2 tablespoons orange juice concentrate, thawed

1 teaspoon gluten-free Chinese five-spice powder

8 bone-in chicken thighs, skin removed

1. Grease a 4-quart slow cooker with nonstick cooking spray. Add the plum sauce, butter, juice concentrate, and five-spice powder to the slow cooker; stir to combine.

2. Add the chicken thighs. Cover and cook on low for 6 hours or on high for 3 hours.

PLUM SAUCE

Plum sauce is usually served with egg rolls, which are generally not gluten-free. But this delicious sauce is also wonderful brushed on chicken or pork ribs; doing so near the end of the grilling time will add a succulent glaze to the grilled meat.

Yields 4 cups

INGREDIENTS:

8 cups (about 3 pounds) plums, pitted and cut in half

1 small sweet onion, finely diced

1 cup water

1 teaspoon fresh ginger, peeled and minced

1 clove garlic, peeled and minced

¾ cup sugar

½ cup rice vinegar or cider vinegar

1 teaspoon ground coriander

½ teaspoon salt

½ teaspoon cinnamon

¼ teaspoon gluten-free cayenne pepper

¼ teaspoon ground cloves

1. Add plums, onion, water, ginger, and garlic to a 4-quart slow cooker. Cover and, stirring occasionally, cook on low for 4 hours or until plums and onions are tender.

2. Use an immersion blender to pulverize the contents of the slow cooker before straining it or pressing the cooked plum mixture through a sieve.

3. Return the liquefied and strained plum mixture to the slow cooker and stir in sugar, vinegar, coriander, salt, cinnamon, cayenne pepper, and cloves. Cover and, stirring occasionally, cook on low for 2 hours or until the sauce reaches the consistency of applesauce.

TUSCAN CHICKEN AND SAUSAGE STEW

You don't need a lot of ingredients to create a stew full of hearty and warm Tuscan flavors.

Serves 4

INGREDIENTS:

1 pound boneless, skinless chicken thighs

8 ounces gluten-free turkey sausage, cut into ½" slices

1 (26-ounce) jar gluten-free pasta sauce

1 (14.5-ounce) can green beans, drained

1 teaspoon dried oregano

1. Cut chicken thighs into bite-sized pieces. Place chicken into a greased 4-quart slow cooker.

2. Add remaining ingredients. Stir to combine and cook on high for 4 hours or on low for 8 hours.

Change It Up

Don't like green beans or don't have them available in your pantry? Use navy beans, cannellini beans, or even black beans.

SALSA CHICKEN

This chicken is easy, versatile, and always delicious. Serve it any way you would like: in gluten-free corn taco shells, over a salad, over cooked rice, or in a casserole.

Serves 4

INGREDIENTS:

4 boneless, skinless chicken breasts

1 (12-ounce) jar mild gluten-free salsa

Add chicken and salsa to a greased 2½- or 4-quart slow cooker. Cook on high for 3–4 hours or on low for 6–8 hours.

No Salsa?

Use gluten-free spaghetti sauce, taco sauce, pizza sauce, or jarred pesto in place of the salsa. Use whatever sauce you like to create a super-easy chicken dish with flavors you love, but be sure to first check that it is gluten-free.

QUINOA MEAT LOAF

You won't miss the bread crumbs in this recipe. Quinoa adds protein and texture to your typical meat loaf.

Serves 6

INGREDIENTS:

¼ cup uncooked quinoa, rinsed and drained

½ cup gluten-free chicken broth

1 teaspoon extra-virgin olive oil

1 small onion, chopped

2–3 cloves garlic, chopped

1 (20-ounce) package lean ground chicken (or lean ground turkey or lean ground beef)

1 tablespoon tomato paste

2 teaspoons gluten-free Worcestershire sauce

1 large egg, and 1 egg white

½ teaspoon salt

1 teaspoon ground black pepper

1 teaspoon ground rosemary

1 teaspoon ground basil

¾ teaspoon red pepper flakes

2 tablespoons Parmesan cheese, grated, fresh or gluten-free

1. Bring the quinoa and broth to a boil in a saucepan over high heat. Reduce heat to medium-low, cover, and simmer until the quinoa is tender and the water has been absorbed, about 15–20 minutes. Set aside to cool.

2. Preheat the oven to 350°F.

3. Heat the olive oil in a skillet over medium heat. Add in the onion; cook and stir until the onion has softened and turned translucent, about 5 minutes. Add the garlic and cook for another minute; remove from heat to cool.

4. In a large bowl add the chicken, cooked quinoa, onions, garlic, tomato paste, Worcestershire sauce, egg and egg white, salt, pepper, seasonings, and Parmesan cheese. Mix until well combined. The mixture will be very moist. Shape into a loaf on a foil-lined baking sheet.

5. Bake until no longer pink in the center, 50–60 minutes. An instant-read thermometer inserted into the center should read at least 160°F. Let the meat loaf cool for 10 minutes before slicing and serving.

CHICKEN DIVAN

Chicken lovers will be asking for second helpings after trying this mouthwatering dish.

Serves 6

INGREDIENTS:

3 pounds chicken breasts, boneless and skinless, cut into 1" strips

1 cup corn flour

1 tablespoon sea or kosher salt

Ground black pepper, to taste

½ cup extra-virgin olive oil, or more as needed

1 pound broccoli florets, cut into bite-sized pieces, cooked, and drained

1½ cups Incredible Hollandaise Sauce (see recipe in this chapter)

2 tablespoons Parmesan cheese, fresh or gluten-free

Sprinkle of paprika (optional)

1. Preheat oven to 350°F.

2. Roll the chicken in the flour, sprinkle with salt and pepper.

3. Heat the olive oil in a sauté pan over medium heat. Sauté the chicken for 5 minutes on each side until golden brown, adding more oil if the pan gets dry.

4. Butter a 2-quart casserole or prepare it with nonstick spray. Place the broccoli in the bottom and spoon some Hollandaise over the top. Arrange the chicken over the broccoli and pour on the rest of the sauce. Sprinkle with Parmesan cheese and paprika. Bake for 30 minutes.

INCREDIBLE HOLLANDAISE SAUCE

This sauce is so adaptable and can be used on fish, lobster, or hot vegetables, especially asparagus, artichokes, and broccoli.

Makes 1¼ cups

INGREDIENTS:

2 sticks (1 cup) unsalted butter

1 large whole egg, plus 1 or 2 egg yolks, depending on the richness desired

1 tablespoon freshly squeezed lemon juice

⅛ teaspoon gluten-free cayenne pepper

Salt, to taste

1. Melt the butter in a small, heavy saucepan over very low heat.

2. Place the eggs, egg yolks, lemon juice, and cayenne in a blender or food processor. Blend well.

3. With the motor running on low, add the hot butter, a little at a time, to the egg mixture.

4. Return the mixture to the pan you used to melt the butter. Whisking, thicken the sauce over low heat, adding salt to your taste, about 5–7 minutes. As soon as it's thick, pour the sauce into a bowl, a sauce boat, or over the food. (Reheating the sauce to thicken it is the delicate part. You must not let it get too hot or it will scramble the eggs, or even curdle them. If either disaster happens, add a tablespoon of boiling water and whisk vigorously.)

Hollandaise Sauce

The name implies that this sauce was created in Holland, a land of high butter use. However, it is one of the five master sauces in French cuisine. It is believed to have been created by French chefs to mimic a Dutch sauce. But in any area where there is plentiful butter, hollandaise sauce, with its rich, smooth texture, will reign. And although people tend to think of it in terms of eggs Benedict, it's good on most green vegetables.

CRISPY POTATO-CRUSTED CHICKEN

When you use this crust on your baked chicken, you'll find it's really crispy and crunchy. Don't add salt as potato chips are already salty.

Serves 4

INGREDIENTS:

12 ounces potato chips, gluten-free

4 boneless, skinless chicken breasts

⅔ cup gluten-free sour cream

1 teaspoon freshly ground black pepper

2 tablespoons snipped fresh chives

1 teaspoon dried thyme

1. In a food processor, chop up potato chips until you have 1 cup of crumbs.

2. Rinse the chicken, dry on paper towels, and lay it in a baking dish prepared with nonstick spray.

3. Preheat the oven to 350°F. Spread the chicken with sour cream; sprinkle with the potato-chip crumbs mixed with the pepper, chives, and thyme; and bake for 25 minutes or until brown and crispy.

Alternatives to Bread Crumbs

Try using your food processor to make crumbs of goodies such as corn bread, potato chips, or popcorn. Check various rice cereals, such as puffed rice and rice crisps, to make sure they are gluten-free, then put them in your food processor to make crumbs. Store the crumbs in resealable plastic bags in the refrigerator.

CLASSIC SOUTHERN FRIED CHICKEN

Fried chicken is perfectly delicious for entertaining or for a quiet meal at home with the family.

Serves 4

INGREDIENTS:

1 (6-pound) chicken, cut into 8 pieces (drumsticks, thighs, breasts, and wings)

1 cup buttermilk

1½ cups corn flour

1 clove garlic, chopped

1 teaspoon salt

1 teaspoon black pepper

1 teaspoon gluten-free baking powder

1 large egg, beaten

½ cup gluten-free, buckwheat beer

1½ cups gluten-free cornmeal

½ cup vegetable oil

1. Rinse the chicken pieces and dry on paper towels, then place in a resealable plastic bag with the buttermilk and marinate for 2–3 hours.

2. In a large paper bag, mix together the corn flour, garlic, salt, pepper, and baking powder. Add the chicken pieces to the corn flour mixture one at a time, then close the bag and shake until the chicken is well coated.

3. In a medium bowl, whisk the egg and beer together. Spread the cornmeal on a large piece of wax paper. Dip the chicken in the beaten egg/beer mixture. Then roll in the cornmeal, pressing it down into the mixture.

4. Bring 1" of oil to 365°F in a fryer, or ½" of oil in a frying pan. Fry the chicken for 20–25 minutes, turning every 4–5 minutes. Watch the chicken carefully to make sure that it doesn't burn. Drain on paper towels.

Frying with Corn Flour

When you use corn flour or cornmeal for frying, you can mix it with either rice flour or potato flour for good results. For a light, tempura-like crust, try cornstarch mixed with water and egg as a coating. Gluten-free cooking does require a whole new chemistry.

OLD-FASHIONED CHICKEN CACCIATORE WITH SPAGHETTI SQUASH

You can vary this dish by adding fresh mint, red vermouth rather than red wine, capers, and lemon zest.

Serves 4–6

INGREDIENTS:

1 (3½-pound) chicken, cut into 8 pieces

1 cup potato or corn flour

Salt and pepper, to taste

1 teaspoon oregano, crumbled

¼ cup olive oil

1 teaspoon butter

1 medium onion, peeled and diced

2–3 cloves garlic, peeled and minced

2 tablespoons fresh rosemary

2 cups mushrooms, brushed off and chopped

1 (16-ounce) jar gluten-free marinara sauce or 16 ounces canned tomatoes

4 ounces dry red table wine or to taste

½ cup Parmesan cheese, freshly grated or gluten-free

1 bunch fresh parsley, chopped, for garnish

1. Dredge the chicken in the combined flour, salt, pepper, and oregano. Heat the oil and butter together until butter melts. Sauté chicken in the oil-and-butter mixture. Add the onion, garlic, rosemary, and mushrooms. Sauté for 5 minutes.

2. Add the tomato sauce or tomatoes and the red wine. Cover and simmer over very low heat for 1 hour. Remove cover, place chicken on a platter, and continue to simmer sauce until reduced by half.

3. Spoon sauce over the chicken and sprinkle with cheese and fresh parsley.

SPICY OLIVE CHICKEN

The key to this flavorful dish is simmering while covered for a while. Don't forget to pour the extra sauce on top of the chicken and over your side dish as well.

Serves 4

INGREDIENTS:

1 (3-pound) chicken, cut into 8 pieces

½ teaspoon salt, divided

½ teaspoon pepper, divided

4 tablespoons unsalted butter

2 cloves garlic, chopped

⅔ cup chopped sweet onion

½ cup gluten-free chicken broth

½ cup dry white wine

24 green olives, pitted

1 teaspoon prepared gluten-free Dijon mustard

¼ teaspoon hot sauce

Fresh parsley, chopped

1 tablespoon capers

1. Sprinkle the chicken pieces with ¼ teaspoon salt and ¼ teaspoon pepper. Heat butter in a skillet over medium-high heat. Brown chicken pieces for about 5 minutes per side. Remove from pan and set aside.

2. In the same pan, sauté the garlic and onion for 5–10 minutes, until onions are soft. Add the broth, wine, and olives. Using a fork, whisk in the mustard.

3. Return chicken to the pan. Cover and simmer until the chicken is done, about 45 minutes. Add hot sauce and remaining salt and pepper to taste.

4. Pour sauce and olives over mashed potatoes, rice, or rice noodles. Garnish with chopped parsley and capers.

Capers

Capers are flavorful berries. Picked green, they can be packed in salt or brine. Try to find the smallest—they seem to have more flavor than the big ones do. Capers are great on their own or incorporated into sauces. They are also good in salads and as a garnish on many dishes that would otherwise be dull.

SESAME CRUSTED CHICKEN BREASTS

Serve this with rice and lots of vegetables. Leftovers can be chopped, mixed with a spicy sauce, and used to fill Rice Flour Crepes (see recipe in Chapter 5) as a delicious snack.

Serves 4

INGREDIENTS:

¼ cup pineapple juice

¼ cup orange juice

1 tablespoon lime juice

½ cup gluten-free soy sauce

1 inch gingerroot, peeled and minced

2 cloves garlic, or to taste, minced

1 teaspoon chili oil, or to taste

2 large boneless, skinless chicken breasts, halved

1 large egg, beaten

½ cup sesame seeds

1. In a non-reactive bowl or glass pan large enough to hold the chicken, whisk together the juices, soy sauce, gingerroot, garlic, and chili oil. Rinse the chicken breasts and pat dry with paper towels. Add the chicken to the sauce and turn to coat. Cover and refrigerate for 4 hours.

2. Drain the chicken; dip in beaten egg and then in sesame seeds. Grill or sauté in oil for 6 minutes per side, depending on thickness of meat. Serve hot.

Chili and Other Hot Sauces

Cooks in China, India, and other countries in Asia, Southeast Asia, and Asia Minor make their own versions of chili for cooking. Chili oil is extremely hot. Chili paste comes in green and red and is popular in Thailand. The Chinese make a chili-and-garlic paste that is called Sichuan chili. Tabasco sauce, fresh chopped chilies (red and/or green), gluten-free cayenne pepper, and red pepper flakes can be substituted.

GINGER, SOY, AND KALE CHICKEN

This recipe has a wonderful combination of ginger and soy. Marinate it the night before to let the chicken thoroughly absorb the flavors.

Serves 2

INGREDIENTS:

4 tablespoons low-sodium gluten-free soy sauce

1 tablespoon toasted sesame oil

1 tablespoon honey

½ teaspoon fresh grated gingerroot

2 cloves garlic, crushed

2 boneless, skinless organic chicken breasts, cut into 1" cubes

1 tablespoon extra-virgin olive oil

2 cups kale

1. In a small bowl, whisk together the soy sauce, sesame oil, honey, gingerroot, and garlic.

2. Place chicken in a zip-top plastic bag and pour half of the soy mixture into bag. Make sure the bag is closed and shake it up so all the chicken is covered. Let marinate for at least a half hour or overnight.

3. Remove chicken from the marinade. Heat olive oil in a skillet over medium-high heat. Sauté the chicken for 5–8 minutes, until fully cooked and no longer pink.

4. Add the kale and cook until it is still bright green but only a little soft, about 2 minutes. Add remaining soy mixture and mix well.

Fresh Gingerroot

You can use fresh gingerroot in all kinds of dishes, from dinners to desserts. Dried ground ginger, ginger snaps, and candied ginger are often used in cooking. Unpeeled fresh ginger freezes beautifully and can be added to sauces, salad dressings, and desserts such as puddings. When you want to use it, cut off an inch or two and peel it, then grate it, mince it, or chop it finely.

BALSAMIC CHICKEN WITH SUN-DRIED TOMATOES AND ROASTED RED PEPPERS

This tangy chicken dish can be served over rice or quinoa for a perfect, balanced meal.

Serves 6

INGREDIENTS:

3 boneless, skinless chicken breasts, rinsed and sliced in half

½ teaspoon salt

½ teaspoon pepper

1 tablespoon vegetable oil

1 small onion, chopped

2 cloves garlic, chopped

¼ cup balsamic vinegar

½ teaspoon brown sugar

¼ cup low-sodium gluten-free chicken broth

1 teaspoon dried rosemary

1 teaspoon dried basil

1 teaspoon dried oregano

1 (6-ounce) bag sun-dried tomatoes, sliced in quarters

1 (12-ounce) jar roasted red peppers, drained and sliced

1. Season the chicken breasts with salt and pepper.

2. Heat the oil in a skillet over medium heat. Add the onion and garlic and sauté for 2–3 minutes, until tender. Add chicken and brown about 5 minutes per side.

3. In a small bowl, combine the balsamic vinegar, brown sugar, chicken broth, rosemary, basil, and oregano.

4. Add the tomatoes and red pepper to the chicken. Pour the balsamic mixture over the chicken and vegetables. Turn heat to high and let the liquid come to a boil. Reduce heat to medium-low and simmer for about 15 minutes, or until the chicken is no longer pink inside.

What Kind of Balsamic Vinegar Do You Use?

All balsamic vinegars are *not* the same. Just like fine wine, balsamic vinegar tastes better when aged. The longer it ages, the thicker and sweeter it becomes. Although the aged balsamic vinegars may be more expensive, you have to remember that a little goes a long way.

PARMESAN-FLAX-CRUSTED CHICKEN TENDERS

These tenders are so tasty, the whole family will love them. Kids love to dip, so experiment with different dipping sauces too.

Serves 4

INGREDIENTS:

2 egg whites and 1 whole large egg, beaten

1 cup ground flaxseed

1 teaspoon dried basil

1 teaspoon dried oregano

1½ teaspoons red pepper flakes

2 cloves garlic, minced

½ teaspoon salt

½ teaspoon ground black pepper

⅓ cup Parmesan cheese, freshly grated

1 (16-ounce) package organic chicken tenderloins

1. Preheat the oven to 350°F. Spray 9" × 13" casserole dish with cooking spray.

2. Place egg whites and egg in a large bowl.

3. In a separate large bowl, place ground flaxseed, basil, oregano, red pepper flakes, garlic, salt, pepper, and cheese. Stir until mixed.

4. Start by placing each chicken tender in egg mixture, then coat with flax mixture, and make sure it is thoroughly coated on both sides. Place in prepared casserole dish.

5. Place casserole dish in the oven and cook for 35 minutes, making sure to turn tenders over halfway through cooking time. Serve with your favorite dipping sauce!

Homemade Is Better

Chicken tenders you find in the grocery store can have a lot of preservatives and ingredients in them that you may not expect. This recipe is a perfect example of how easy they are to make at home.

CHICKEN PESTO POLENTA

This recipe uses precooked polenta that is cut and layered in a casserole lasagna-style. Most prepared polenta comes in tube form and is naturally gluten-free. Make sure to read the ingredients and call the manufacturer if you have any questions.

Serves 6

INGREDIENTS:

4 boneless, skinless chicken breasts, cut into bite-sized pieces

1 cup prepared pesto, divided

1 medium onion, finely diced

4 cloves garlic, minced

1½ teaspoons gluten-free dried Italian seasoning

1 (16-ounce) tube prepared polenta, cut into ½" slices

2 cups chopped fresh spinach

1 (14½-ounce) can diced tomatoes

1 (8-ounce) bag shredded low-fat Italian cheese blend

1. In large bowl, combine chicken pieces with ½ cup pesto, onion, garlic, and Italian seasoning.

2. In a greased 4-quart slow cooker, layer half of chicken mixture, half the polenta, half the spinach, and half the tomatoes. Continue to layer, ending with tomatoes. Cover and cook on low for 4–6 hours or on high for 2–3 hours.

3. An hour before serving, drizzle remaining pesto over casserole and top with shredded cheese. Cover and continue to cook for 45–60 minutes, until cheese has melted.

Make Your Own Pesto

Instead of using prepared pesto, you can easily make your own: In a high-powered blender or food processor add 2 cups fresh basil leaves, ½ cup extra-virgin olive oil, ½ cup gluten-free Parmesan cheese, ½ cup pine nuts, 3 garlic cloves, and salt and pepper to taste. Blend on high for a few minutes until mixture is creamy. You can use blanched almond flour in place of the Parmesan cheese, if you are intolerant to dairy.

CHICKEN IN LEMON SAUCE

This recipe is for a one-pot meal. By completing a simple step at the end of the cooking time, you have meat, potatoes, vegetables, and sauce all ready to serve and eat.

Serves 4

INGREDIENTS:

1 (16-ounce) bag frozen cut green beans, thawed

1 small onion, peeled and cut into thin wedges

4 boneless, skinless chicken breast halves

4 medium potatoes, peeled and cut in quarters

2 cloves garlic, peeled and minced

¼ teaspoon freshly ground black pepper

1 cup gluten-free chicken broth

4 ounces cream cheese, cut into cubes

1 teaspoon freshly grated lemon peel

1. Place green beans and onion in the slow cooker. Arrange the chicken and potatoes over the vegetables. Sprinkle with the garlic and pepper. Pour broth over all. Cover and cook on low for 5 or more hours or until chicken is cooked through and moist.

2. Evenly divide the chicken, potatoes, and vegetables between 4 serving plates or onto a serving platter; cover to keep warm.

3. To make the sauce, add the cream cheese cubes and grated lemon peel to the broth in the slow cooker. Stir until cheese melts into the sauce. Pour the sauce over the chicken, potatoes, and vegetables.

Gluten-Free Chicken Broth

Reading food labels will become second nature when you are following a gluten-free diet. Remember to check the label on your canned chicken broth. Some brands add wheat starch or wheat flour as a thickener. Two readily available gluten-free brands are Swanson and Kitchen Basics.

SMOKED TURKEY SAUSAGE AND VEGETABLE CASSEROLE

Prepared Italian dressing adds great flavor to the vegetables in this simple casserole. For a complete meal serve this with Gluten-Free Millet Bread (see recipe in Chapter 3).

Serves 4

INGREDIENTS:

5 tablespoons gluten-free bottled zesty Italian salad dressing

2 tablespoons gluten-free Dijon mustard

2 medium potatoes, cut into ½" slices

2 medium onions, sliced

2 medium carrots, cut into ½" slices

2 cups green cabbage, chopped

1 ring (1 pound) fully cooked gluten-free smoked turkey sausage, cut into 1" slices

1 (14½-ounce) can petite-diced tomatoes with Italian seasonings

1. In small bowl whisk together dressing and mustard.

2. In a 4-quart slow cooker, arrange potato slices on the bottom. Drizzle with one-third of the dressing mixture. Lay onion slices evenly over potatoes and drizzle with one-third of the dressing mixture. Top with carrots and cabbage; drizzle with remaining dressing.

3. Arrange sausage slices on top of vegetables. Pour diced tomatoes over the casserole.

4. Cover and cook on low for 8 hours or on high for 4 hours.

Make Your Own Seasoned Tomatoes

Sometimes it can be hard to find canned petite-diced tomatoes with seasoning added to them. Instead, you can use a can of plain petite-diced tomatoes and add 1 teaspoon Italian seasoning, ½ teaspoon garlic powder, and ½ teaspoon crushed basil.

ITALIAN TURKEY SAUSAGE WITH PEPPERS AND ONIONS

The colorful variety of peppers in this recipe makes a beautiful dinner presentation. Feel free to substitute chicken sausage for the turkey sausage if it is more readily available in your area. Also, this recipe has no added salt since processed sausage contains a lot of sodium.

Serves 4

INGREDIENTS:

1 large red pepper, sliced, with seeds removed

1 large yellow pepper, sliced, with seeds removed

1 sweet onion, sliced

2 tablespoons olive oil

2 teaspoons garlic powder

2 teaspoons oregano

20 ounces gluten-free lean Italian turkey sausage

1. Mix peppers and onion in a large glass or microwave-safe bowl. Drizzle with olive oil, garlic powder, and oregano.

2. Microwave on high for 2–3 minutes, until vegetables are slightly softened and have become fragrant. Pour half of the onion/pepper mixture into the bottom of a greased 4-quart slow cooker.

3. Place the sausages side by side on top of the vegetables. Pour the remaining onion and pepper mixture on top of the sausages.

4. Cook on low for 6 hours or on high for 3 hours.

Sautéing Vegetables in the Microwave

One easy way to enhance the flavor of aromatic vegetables such as garlic, peppers, celery, and onions is to cook them in the microwave for just a few minutes before adding them to the slow cooker. This method softens the vegetables, releases their aroma, and begins the cooking process.

GROUND TURKEY JOES

This easy sweet-and-sour sandwich filling comes together quickly and is ready when you are. If you prefer, you can also use ground chicken or ground beef as a substitute for ground turkey.

Serves 4

INGREDIENTS:

2 teaspoons olive oil

1 pound lean ground turkey

½ cup onion, finely chopped

½ cup green pepper, finely chopped

1 teaspoon garlic powder

1 tablespoon prepared gluten-free yellow mustard

¾ cup gluten-free ketchup

3 tablespoons brown sugar

1 tablespoon gluten-free Worcestershire sauce

¼ teaspoon salt

½ teaspoon ground pepper

4 gluten-free hamburger rolls

1. In a large skillet brown ground turkey, onion, and green pepper in olive oil for approximately 5–6 minutes. Drain off any grease.

2. Add turkey mixture to a greased 2½-quart or 4-quart slow cooker. Add garlic powder, mustard, ketchup, brown sugar, Worcestershire sauce, salt, and pepper.

3. Mix ingredients together and cook on low for 4 hours or on high for 2 hours.

4. Serve on gluten-free hamburger rolls.

Multiple Meals

Instead of using this recipe as a sandwich filling, you could also serve it over cooked rice, a baked potato, or gluten-free spaghetti noodles for a fun twist. For a Mexican-style variation, leave out the brown sugar and Worcestershire sauce and replace the ketchup with 1 cup tomato sauce along with 1 packet gluten-free taco seasoning.

TURKEY MEATBALLS WITH TANGY APRICOT SAUCE

These easy turkey meatballs are browned on the stovetop and then cooked in a mouthwatering sweet and sour sauce. For a simple variation try orange marmalade instead of apricot jam.

Serves 4

INGREDIENTS:

1 pound lean ground turkey

¾ cup almond flour

1 large egg

¼ cup finely diced onions

¼ cup finely diced celery

½ teaspoon ground pepper

½ teaspoon salt

1 tablespoon olive oil

1 cup apricot preserves

¼ cup gluten-free Dijon mustard

1. In a large bowl mix together the ground turkey, almond flour, egg, onions, celery, ground pepper, and salt. Roll into small meatballs. The meatball mixture will be slightly wet. Heat olive oil in a large skillet. Add meatballs to hot skillet and brown on all sides, about 1 minute per side.

2. Grease a 2½-quart slow cooker. Add browned meatballs to the slow cooker.

3. In a small bowl mix together the preserves and mustard. Pour the sauce over the meatballs. Cook on high for 3 hours or on low for 6 hours.

4. If using meatballs as an appetizer instead of a main course, you can turn the slow cooker to the warm setting and leave them for up to 2 hours.

Are Meatballs Gluten-Free?

Meat loaf and meatballs are usually made with wheat bread crumbs. To make meat loaf or meatballs gluten-free, simply replace the bread crumbs called for in a recipe with almond flour, crushed gluten-free tortilla chips, leftover gluten-free bread, or even potato flakes.

ASIAN-INSPIRED TURKEY BREAST

A 3-pound turkey breast or roast will yield about 8 (4-ounce) servings. If you prefer larger portions, adjust the servings or increase the size of the roast. If you do the latter, you may need to increase the cooking time to ensure the poultry reaches the correct internal temperature.

Serves 8

INGREDIENTS:

½ cup orange marmalade

1 tablespoon fresh ginger, peeled and grated

1 clove garlic, peeled and minced

½ teaspoon gluten-free Chinese five-spice powder

1 teaspoon salt

½ teaspoon freshly ground black pepper

¼ cup orange juice

1 (3-pound) turkey breast or roast

1. Add the marmalade, ginger, garlic, spice powder, salt, pepper, and orange juice to a 4–6-quart slow cooker. Stir to mix.

2. Place the turkey breast or roast into the slow cooker. Spoon some of the sauce over the meat. Cover and cook on low for 8 hours or until the internal temperature of the meat is 170°F.

TURKEY CUTLETS WITH RED ONION SAUCE

Turkey cutlets are 1" slices of uncooked turkey breast that can be purchased from many large grocery stores in the poultry section. It's a great way to prepare turkey for dinner without having to cook the whole bird.

Serves 4

INGREDIENTS:

1¼ pounds turkey cutlets

Salt and pepper, for seasoning

2 tablespoons olive oil

1 large red onion, thinly sliced

⅓ cup sweetened rice vinegar

1. Season turkey cutlets with salt and pepper and place in a greased 2½-quart slow cooker.

2. In a small bowl mix together olive oil, red onion, and sweetened rice vinegar. Pour over the turkey cutlets. Cook on high for 3–4 hours or on low for 6–8 hours until turkey is cooked through. If necessary, add salt and pepper to taste.

Make It Chicken

If your family prefers the flavor of chicken to turkey, simply use 3–4 boneless chicken breasts instead of turkey cutlets.

FAMILY STYLE TURKEY LOAF

This can be served with rice or mashed potatoes on the side. It can be adapted in many ways to suit the family's tastes, from mild to spicy.

Serves 4–6

INGREDIENTS:

1 pound lean ground turkey

1 cup ground popcorn or gluten-free corn bread crumbs

⅔ cup milk

¼ cup gluten-free chili sauce

3 large eggs

1 teaspoon thyme

½ cup chopped onion

Salt and pepper, to taste

¼ teaspoon nutmeg

2 strips gluten-free bacon

1. Preheat oven to 350°F.

2. Put all but the bacon into your food processor and whirl until well blended.

3. Pour into a 9" × 5" inch bread pan and put that pan into a much larger one (such as an 11" × 13" inch pan). Place in the oven and add boiling water to the larger pan. Cut the bacon in halves and arrange across the top of the loaf. Bake for 1 hour.

4. Serve with mashed potatoes.

TASTY TURKEY PARMESAN

Adding your favorite herbs and seasonings can modify this dish, which is a wonderful variation of the classic chicken Parmesan.

Serves 4

INGREDIENTS:

1¼ pounds boneless, skinless turkey breast

1 cup gluten-free corn bread crumbs

1 clove garlic, chopped

½ teaspoon dried oregano

½ teaspoon dried basil

1 cup gluten-free Parmesan cheese, divided

1 large egg

1 cup corn flour

1 cup extra-virgin olive oil

2 cups tomato sauce

½ pound whole-milk mozzarella, shredded or thinly sliced

1. Preheat the oven to 350°F.

2. Flatten the turkey breast with a meat pounder. Cut into 4 serving pieces.

3. In a shallow bowl, mix the corn bread crumbs, garlic, oregano, and basil with ½ cup Parmesan cheese.

4. In another shallow bowl, beat the egg.

5. Pour the corn flour onto a plate. Dip the turkey in the flour, then in the egg, and finally in the crumb mixture.

6. Heat oil in a large skillet over medium-high heat. Fry turkey in oil until golden brown, about 4–5 minutes total, flipping as needed; drain on paper towels.

7. Spray a 9" × 13" baking dish with nonstick spray. Pour a little tomato sauce into the baking dish. Add the turkey pieces. Sprinkle with remaining ½ cup Parmesan cheese. Cover with tomato sauce. Spread the mozzarella over the top.

8. Bake in oven until hot and bubbling, about 20 minutes. Serve hot.

What's in the Stuffing?

The key to buying gluten-free food is reading every label carefully. Store-bought corn bread stuffing may have wheat flour mixed in with the corn flour and cornmeal. Corn muffins, also a favorite in making home-made stuffing, can have a mixture of wheat flour and cornmeal. In the long run, the safest way to provide gluten-free stuffing is to make the corn bread yourself.

HOT AND SPICY TURKEY MEATBALLS

Meatball recipes usually include bread crumbs as a filler and sometimes for an outside coating. This recipe uses ground potato chips. The eggs will hold the meatballs together, and who doesn't love potato chips?

Makes 10–12 meatballs

INGREDIENTS:

1 pound lean ground turkey

2 large eggs

2 cloves garlic, minced

1 teaspoon dried oregano

1 teaspoon dried basil

½ teaspoon cinnamon

½ teaspoon fennel seeds

½ cup finely grated gluten-free Parmesan cheese

2 cups crushed low-salt, gluten-free potato chips, divided

½ teaspoon salt

½ teaspoon pepper

4 tablespoons canola oil

1. In a large bowl, mix the turkey, eggs, garlic, oregano, basil, cinnamon, fennel seeds, cheese, 1 cup potato chip crumbs, salt, and pepper.

2. Place a large sheet of wax paper on the counter. Sprinkle remaining cup of chip crumbs on it.

3. Form 1" meatballs from the turkey mixture. Roll meatballs in crumbs to coat.

4. Heat oil in a large skillet over medium-high heat. Fry meatballs until well browned, about 5 minutes. Drain on paper towels and then either refrigerate, freeze, or serve with the gluten-free marinara sauce of your choice.

Kick Up Those Meatballs

You can add flavor to your meatballs by grinding up some sweet or hot Italian gluten-free sausage and mixing it with the turkey. A truly great Italian sausage has aromatics like garlic and herbs, and spices such as anise seeds.

WHITE BEAN, KALE, AND TURKEY SAUSAGE STEW

Who says comfort food has to be laden with fat and calories for it to be comforting? This dish is simple enough to prepare during the week.

Serves 6

INGREDIENTS:

1 tablespoon grapeseed oil

½ cup chopped onion

1 (16-ounce) package gluten-free turkey sausage, cut into ½" slices

1 medium zucchini, quartered and cut into ½" slices

½ red bell pepper, chopped

3 cloves garlic, peeled and crushed

6 cups chopped, trimmed kale (about ½ pound)

½ cup fresh mushrooms, chopped

½ cup water

2 (16-ounce) cans cannellini beans or other white beans, rinsed and drained

3 plum (Roma) tomatoes

¼ teaspoon fennel

⅛ teaspoon dried chili flakes

½ teaspoon gluten-free Italian seasoning

¼ teaspoon rosemary

¼ teaspoon salt

¼ teaspoon freshly ground black pepper

1. Heat oil in a large Dutch oven over medium-high heat. Sauté onion and sausage 5–6 minutes or until sausage is browned.

2. Add the zucchini, pepper, and garlic, and cook for 2 minutes.

3. Add kale and remaining ingredients; bring to a boil. Cover, reduce heat, and simmer 10 minutes or until thoroughly heated. Serve immediately.

THE BEST ROASTED TURKEY

For the sweetest, juiciest bird, try to find a turkey that is between 9 and 12 pounds. Make extra gravy by adding a can of chicken broth to the basting liquid.

Serves 15

INGREDIENTS:

1 (10-pound) turkey (if the turkey has been injected with flavoring, check ingredients for any gluten-containing products)

¼ pound butter, softened

1 teaspoon dried thyme

½ cup fresh Italian flat-leaf parsley, rinsed and minced

Salt, to taste, and 1 teaspoon pepper

Giblets, including wing tips and neck

½ cup dry white wine

2 bay leaves

1 recipe Stuffing for Roasted Turkey (see recipe in this chapter)

4 strips gluten-free bacon for bottom of roasting pan

2 teaspoons cornstarch

¼ cup water

1. Rinse the turkey in cold water and pat dry. Mix the butter, herbs, salt, and pepper thoroughly. Tease it under the skin of the breast, working it into the thighs. Be careful not to tear the skin.

2. Place the giblets and wing tips in a saucepan with the wine and water to cover. Add the bay leaves. Cook for 2 hours, or while the turkey is cooking. Add extra water if the broth gets dry.

3. Stuff the turkey and skewer the legs together. Close the neck cavity with a skewer. Preheat the oven to 325°F.

4. Place the bacon on the bottom of the roasting pan and start the turkey breast-side down. After 30 minutes, turn the turkey over and arrange the bacon over the breast and legs. Roast for 3 hours, basting every 20 minutes with the giblet broth, then with the pan juices. Roast until the thickest part is 155°F on a meat thermometer. Let the turkey rest for 15 minutes before carving.

5. Make gravy by mixing 2 teaspoons cornstarch with ¼ cup water and blending with pan juices.

Roasting Turkeys

Always start the turkey breast-side down so the juices run into, rather than out of, the breast. The bacon prevents the breast from sticking to the roasting pan and adds a nice flavor to the juices. If, like most families, yours likes extra dressing (stuffing), make 3 to 4 cups extra and roast it in a casserole while you are roasting the turkey.

STUFFING FOR ROASTED TURKEY

Make your own gluten-free corn bread for stuffing a day or two before, cube, and place in the refrigerator in a plastic bag until ready to use.

Makes enough stuffing for one turkey

INGREDIENTS:

1 medium onion, finely chopped

4 stalks celery with tops, finely chopped

4 tablespoons butter

1 pound bulk breakfast sausage, gluten-free

10 cups cubed gluten-free corn bread

1 cup unsalted butter, melted with ½ cup water

2 teaspoons dried thyme

10 fresh sage leaves, minced, or 2 tablespoons dried

2 large tart apples, peeled, cored, and chopped

Salt and pepper, to taste

1. In a large frying pan, sauté the onion and celery in 4 tablespoons butter. Add the sausage and break up with a wooden spoon. Cook until sausage is done and vegetables are tender. Place in a very large bowl.

2. Add the rest of the ingredients to the bowl. With your hands inside large plastic bags, mix the ingredients well. Stuff your turkey with this mixture.

Vary Your Stuffing

You can make this stuffing really come alive with extra ingredients such as fresh oysters, shucked and chopped; gluten-free dried cranberries; and coarsely chopped pecans or walnuts.

ELEGANT DUCKLING AND FRUIT FILLED CORN CREPES

This would be a delicious dinner or lunch served over baby spinach or fresh salad greens. The sweetness of the duck works with the fruit—a marriage made in heaven.

Serves 4

INGREDIENTS:

½ cup gluten-free chicken broth

1 tablespoon cornstarch

⅔ pound boneless, skinless duck breasts

½ cup corn flour

3 tablespoons unsalted butter

Salt and 2 teaspoons freshly ground black pepper

½ cup gluten-free dried cranberries soaked in ⅔ cup apple juice or wine

¼ cup gluten-free dried cherries soaked in ½ cup orange juice

¼ cup chopped celery tops

24 pearl onions (frozen is fine)

½ cup apple brandy (such as Calvados)

1 tablespoon rosemary leaves, dried and crumbled

8 large Corn Crepes (see recipe in Chapter 2)

2 tablespoons butter, melted, or olive oil

1. Mix the chicken broth and the cornstarch and set aside.

2. Dredge the duck breasts in corn flour and sauté them in butter over medium heat. Add the salt and pepper and the chicken broth/cornstarch mixture to the pan, stirring to make a sauce.

3. Add the soaked fruit (drained), celery tops, onions, apple brandy, and rosemary. Cover and cook for 20 minutes over low heat.

4. Preheat oven to 350°F.

5. Cool and remove the duck from the pan. Cut it into small pieces and shred. Return the duck to the sauce. Divide the sauce and shredded duck mixture between the 8 crepes. Roll the crepes, place them seam-side down in a greased baking dish, and drizzle with melted butter or olive oil. Heat them in the oven for 10–15 minutes. Serve over greens or sautéed spinach.

ROASTED CORNISH GAME HENS WITH GINGER-ORANGE GLAZE

This is simple and tastes fantastic. It tastes just as delightful as leftovers the next day.

Serves 4

INGREDIENTS:

2 Cornish game hens, split open

2 tablespoons extra-virgin olive oil

½ teaspoon salt

¾ teaspoon pepper

1 tablespoon orange marmalade

2 tablespoons peanut oil

1 tablespoon gluten-free soy sauce

2 tablespoons orange juice

½ medium white onion, finely chopped

1 tablespoon minced fresh gingerroot

1. Preheat the oven to 375°F.

2. Rinse the hens, pat dry with paper towels, brush with olive oil, and sprinkle with salt and pepper.

3. In a small saucepan over low heat, stir the rest of the ingredients together to make glaze; set aside.

4. Roast the hens in a baking dish or pan, cut-side up, for 15 minutes. Turn hens and brush with glaze. Continue to roast for another 20 minutes, brushing hens with glaze every 5 minutes. Serve with roasted vegetables, rice, or mashed potatoes.

MANGO DUCK BREAST

Slow-cooked mangoes soften and create their own sauce in this easy duck dish. If you prefer, you can use 1½ cups of frozen pre-cut mango instead of fresh. Serve the duck with roasted winter vegetables and steamed asparagus.

Serves 4

INGREDIENTS:

2 boneless, skinless duck breasts

1 large mango, peeled and cubed

¼ cup gluten-free chicken broth

1 tablespoon finely grated fresh ginger

1 tablespoon minced hot pepper

1 tablespoon minced shallot

1. Place all ingredients into a 4-quart slow cooker.

2. Cook on low for 4 hours, or on high for 2 hours.

CHAPTER 8

BEEF AND VEAL

BEEF STROGANOFF

This is an elegant, historic recipe, named after the Russian general who is said to have invented it. You can serve it with potato pancakes on the side or with wild rice.

Serves 6

INGREDIENTS:

2 tablespoons extra-virgin olive oil

1 medium white onion, chopped

8 ounces tiny button mushrooms, brushed clean, stems removed

2 cloves garlic, minced

2 tablespoons tapioca flour, plus ¼ cup for coating the meat

1 teaspoon dried mustard

Salt and pepper, to taste

1½ cups gluten-free beef broth, warmed

1 cup dry red wine

1 teaspoon gluten-free Worcestershire sauce

2 pounds filet mignon, cut into bite-sized cubes

2 tablespoons unsalted butter

2 tablespoons snipped fresh dill weed

1 cup gluten-free sour cream or crème fraîche

1. In a large sauté pan, heat the oil over medium heat and add the onion, mushrooms, and garlic. Cook for 5 minutes to soften.

2. Add 2 tablespoons flour, mustard, and salt and pepper to the pan, and stir to blend.

3. Mix in the warmed beef broth, cook, and stir to thicken. Stir in the wine and Worcestershire sauce and bring to a boil. Turn off the heat.

4. On a large piece of wax paper, roll the beef in ¼ cup flour.

5. Heat the unsalted butter in a separate pan. Sear the beef in the butter over medium-high heat for 1 minute to quickly brown and seal in the juices.

6. Spoon the beef into the mushroom sauce, add the dill weed, and stir to blend. Simmer for 10–15 minutes; the beef should be medium rare.

7. Just before serving, add the sour cream. Spoon over a bed of wild rice or serve with potato pancakes on the side.

Why Should You Not Wash Mushrooms?

Mushrooms are grown in a safe and sanitary medium that has been treated with thermophilic bacteria. This process kills any germs by naturally heating the growing medium to a very high temperature. Also, washing mushrooms makes them mushy because they absorb the water. Please don't peel them, either—just brush them off with a paper towel.

CORN TORTILLA CASSEROLE

Serve this casserole along with a tossed salad. Have some additional gluten-free taco or enchilada sauce at the table along with an assortment of optional condiments, such as chopped jalapeño peppers, diced green onions, gluten-free sour cream, and guacamole.

Serves 8

INGREDIENTS:

2 tablespoons olive oil

2 pounds lean ground beef

1 small onion, peeled and diced

1 clove garlic, minced

1 envelope gluten-free taco seasoning

½ teaspoon salt

½ teaspoon freshly ground pepper

1 (15-ounce) can diced tomatoes

1 (6-ounce) can tomato paste

2 cups refried beans

9 gluten-free corn tortillas

2 cups gluten-free enchilada sauce

2 cups (8 ounces) grated Cheddar cheese

1. In a large skillet, heat olive oil. Brown ground beef for approximately 5–6 minutes and set aside in a large bowl. In the same skillet, sauté onions until softened, about 3–5 minutes. Add sautéed onions to ground beef.

2. Stir in the garlic, taco seasoning, salt, pepper, tomatoes, tomato paste, and refried beans into the ground beef and onions.

3. Grease a 4-quart slow cooker with nonstick spray. Add ⅓ of the ground beef mixture to cover the bottom of the slow cooker insert. Layer 3 tortillas on top of the ground beef mixture and cover with ⅓ of the enchilada sauce, then ⅓ of the shredded cheese. Repeat layers. Cover and cook on low for 6–8 hours. Cut into 8 wedges and serve.

STUFFED FILET MIGNON WITH RED WINE SAUCE

Stuffing a whole filet mignon with mushrooms and garlic will turn it into a luscious feast. Using chestnut flour will add a nutty and delightful flavor.

Serves 10–12

INGREDIENTS:

4 tablespoons unsalted butter

4 cups exotic mushrooms such as creminis, morels, shiitake, or oysters, brushed off, stems removed, chopped finely

6 shallots, peeled and minced

4 cloves garlic, peeled and minced

1 tablespoon gluten-free Worcestershire sauce

¼ cup chestnut flour, mixed with salt and pepper, to taste

½ cup dry red wine, divided

4 sage leaves, torn in small pieces

½ teaspoon dried rosemary

½ teaspoon dried thyme

1 (6-pound) filet mignon, fat trimmed

½ cup chestnut flour

1 tablespoon coarse salt

1 teaspoon black pepper

1 cup gluten-free beef broth

2 tablespoons extra-virgin olive oil

1. In a large skillet over medium heat, melt the butter. Add the mushrooms, shallots, and garlic, and sauté until the vegetables are soft and the mushrooms are wilted, about 3–4 minutes.

2. Add the Worcestershire sauce. Add ¼ cup flour seasoned with salt and pepper and blend. Stir in red wine and the sage, rosemary, and thyme. Reduce the mixture to about 1½ cups, about 5–7 minutes.

3. Preheat oven to 350°F.

4. Make a tunnel down the middle of the filet mignon—use a fat knitting needle or the handle of a blunt knife. Stuff the mushroom mixture into the tube. If there are extra mushrooms, save them for the sauce.

5. Coat the outside of the filet with ½ cup chestnut flour, salt, and pepper. Place the beef broth in the bottom of a roasting pan with the filet. Sprinkle with olive oil and roast in oven for 20 minutes per pound.

Drippings Make the Perfect Sauce

Use the drippings for a sauce, served on the side. If the pan juices get too reduced, add some boiling water or more gluten-free beef broth.

MARINATED SPICY BEEF AND BABY SPINACH

After you have marinated the beef, the dish takes but a few minutes to cook. Garnish with a few slices of lemon or lime.

Serves 4

INGREDIENTS:

2 cloves garlic, minced

2 tablespoons sugar

½ teaspoon salt, or to taste

1 teaspoon red pepper flakes, or to taste

2 tablespoons canola oil

1½ pounds filet mignon, trimmed and cut into ½" slices

¼ cup dry white wine

¼ cup white wine vinegar (not malt)

2 teaspoons sugar

2 tablespoons gluten-free fish sauce

2 tablespoons canola or peanut oil

4 cups fresh baby spinach, rinsed, spun dry, stems removed

1 tablespoon butter

Gluten-free soy sauce, chopped scallions, and lemon and lime slices, for garnish

1. In a large bowl or glass baking dish, mix together the garlic, 2 tablespoons sugar, salt, pepper flakes, and 2 tablespoons oil. Add the slices of filet mignon, turning to coat. Cover and refrigerate for 2 hours.

2. Mix together the wine, vinegar, 2 teaspoons sugar, and fish sauce; set aside. Heat a nonstick pan over very high heat and add 2 tablespoons oil. Quickly sauté the filets until browned on both sides, about 2 minutes per side. Arrange the meat over a bed of spinach.

3. Add the wine mixture and butter to the pan and deglaze, reducing quickly. Pour over the spinach and meat. Serve with gluten-free soy sauce and chopped scallions on the side and slices of lemon or lime.

Fish Sauce

Fish sauce, available at Asian markets, is an important ingredient in Southeast Asian, Chinese, and Indonesian cuisines. Be sure it is gluten-free before purchasing it.

GASCONY-STYLE POT ROAST

This is a traditional holiday dish, often made on Christmas Eve to serve on Christmas Day. Serve with mashed potatoes and winter vegetables.

Serves 6

INGREDIENTS:

1 (4-pound) top or bottom round beef roast

4 cloves garlic, slivered

1 teaspoon salt

1 teaspoon freshly ground black pepper

Pinch each of cinnamon and nutmeg

1 slice gluten-free bacon, cut into pieces

4 shallots, peeled and halved

2 red onions, peeled and quartered

2 ounces cognac

2 cups red wine

1 cup rich gluten-free beef broth

1 teaspoon thyme

4 whole cloves

¼ cup cornstarch mixed with ⅓ cup cold water until smooth

1. Make several cuts in the meat and put slivers of garlic in each. Rub the roast with salt, pepper, and pinches of cinnamon and nutmeg.

2. Heat the bacon on the bottom of a Dutch oven. Remove the bacon before it gets crisp, and brown the roast. Surround the roast with shallots and onions. Add the cognac, wine, beef broth, thyme, and cloves.

3. Place in a 250°F oven for 5–6 hours. When the meat is done, place the roast on a warm platter. Add the cornstarch-and-water mixture to the pan juices and bring to a boil. Slice the roast. Serve the sauce over the pot roast with the vegetables surrounding the meat.

A Hearty, Delectable Pot Roast

Crock-Pots or slow cookers are excellent for cooking a pot roast. Either a top or bottom round is great. Chuck tends to be stringy. Trim the roast well but do leave a bit of fat on it. You can also marinate a pot roast overnight in red wine and herbs. That will give you a deliciously tender piece of meat.

STUFFED, ROASTED FILET MIGNON

This can be served hot, cold, or at room temperature. The garlic and spinach stuffing is a terrific counterpoint to the meat.

Serves 10–12

INGREDIENTS:

1 pound fresh spinach, washed, cut up, blanched, and squeezed to remove extra moisture, or 2 (10-ounce) boxes frozen spinach, thawed and drained

2 tablespoons olive oil

4 cloves garlic, minced

Juice of ½ lemon

¼ teaspoon nutmeg

1 cup gluten-free soft bread crumbs mixed with seasonings such as dried oregano and salt and pepper, to taste

1 (6-pound) filet mignon, well trimmed

1 teaspoon salt and freshly ground black pepper, to taste

2 tablespoons softened butter

1 (13-ounce) can gluten-free low-salt beef broth

1. Preheat the oven to 350°F.

2. Place the spinach on paper towels to dry a bit. Heat the olive oil in a medium-sized fry pan and add the garlic; cook over medium heat to soften. Stirring, mix in the spinach, lemon juice, and nutmeg. Add the bread crumbs.

3. Using a fat knitting needle or the handle of a dull knife, make a channel through the meat. Force in the stuffing.

4. Sprinkle the meat with salt and pepper, then rub with the softened butter. Roast in oven for 60 minutes, basting every 15 minutes with the beef broth. Reserve pan juice for another use. Let the filet rest for 15 minutes before serving.

BASIC BEEF STEW

Feel free to change the seasonings in this basic but delicious beef stew. You can also add red wine in addition to the beef broth for a richer taste.

Serves 6

INGREDIENTS:

4 tablespoons vegetable oil

⅓ cup brown rice flour

1 tablespoon garlic powder

1 teaspoon salt

1 teaspoon black pepper

2 pounds beef chuck, cubed

1 medium onion, diced

6 large potatoes, peeled and diced

6 carrots, sliced

3 stalks celery, sliced

4 cups gluten-free beef broth

1. Grease a 4–6-quart slow cooker with nonstick cooking spray. In a large skillet, heat oil over medium-high heat.

2. In a zip-top plastic bag, mix together the flour, garlic powder, salt, and pepper. Add a small handful of beef and shake until well coated. Repeat until all beef is coated in the flour mixture.

3. In batches, brown beef in hot oil, about 1 minute per side. Remove the browned meat and place in the slow cooker.

4. Lower heat under skillet to medium and add onions. Cook onion until softened, about 3–5 minutes, then place on top of beef in slow cooker.

5. Add remaining ingredients to slow cooker. Cover and cook on high for 4 hours or on low for 6–8 hours.

BEEF AND SWEET POTATO STEW

This rich, deeply flavored beef stew with sweet potatoes, red wine, and cremini mushrooms is a crowd pleaser. Serve it over rice to absorb the delicious sauce.

Serves 8

INGREDIENTS:

¾ cup brown rice flour

1½ teaspoons salt, divided

1½ teaspoons ground black pepper, divided

1¼ pounds stew beef, cut into 1" chunks

¼ cup olive oil, divided

1 medium yellow onion, diced

2 cups carrots, peeled and diced

¾ pound cremini mushrooms, cleaned and cut in half

6 cloves garlic, minced

3 tablespoons tomato paste

½ cup red wine

1 pound sweet potatoes, peeled and diced

4 cups gluten-free beef broth

1 bay leaf

1½ teaspoons dried thyme

1 tablespoon gluten-free Worcestershire sauce

1 tablespoon sugar

1. In a large zip-top plastic bag, place flour, 1 teaspoon salt, and 1 teaspoon pepper. Shake gently to mix. Add beef and close the bag. Shake lightly, making sure that all of the beef is coated in flour and seasoning. Set aside.

2. In a large skillet, heat 2 tablespoons of olive oil over medium heat. Cook beef in small batches until browned on all sides, about 1 minute per side. Add beef to a greased 4–6-quart slow cooker.

3. In the same skillet, heat the remaining 2 tablespoons of olive oil. Add onion and carrots and cook until onions are translucent, about 5 minutes.

4. Add mushrooms and garlic, and cook for another 2–3 minutes.

5. Add tomato paste and heat through. Deglaze the pan with the wine, scraping the stuck-on bits from the bottom of the pan. Add cooked vegetable mixture on top of the beef in the slow cooker.

6. Add the sweet potatoes, broth, bay leaf, thyme, and Worcestershire sauce. Cover and cook on low for 8 hours or on high for 4 hours.

7. Before serving, add sugar and remaining salt and pepper.

COUNTRY HAMBURGER CASSEROLE

Using similar ingredients to "Ground Beef Foil Packets" or "Hobo Meals," this beefy vegetable casserole is simmered in a creamy sauce.

Serves 8

INGREDIENTS:

4 medium potatoes, peeled and sliced

3 carrots, peeled and sliced

1 (14½-ounce) can peas, drained

2 stalks celery, diced

2 medium onions, sliced

2 pounds lean ground beef, browned

1 (15-ounce) can evaporated milk

1 cup gluten-free chicken broth

3 tablespoons brown rice flour

½ teaspoon salt

½ teaspoon pepper

1. Place potatoes in bottom of a greased 4-quart slow cooker; top with carrots, peas, celery, and onion slices. Place ground beef on top.

2. In a medium bowl, whisk together milk, broth, flour, salt, and pepper and pour over ground beef.

3. Cover and cook on low for 6–8 hours. In the last 2 hours, vent slow cooker lid with a chopstick to allow excess water to escape.

Instead of Ground Beef . . .

Feel free to use lean ground turkey, ground pork, or ground sausage instead of ground beef. You can also make this a vegetarian casserole by using 2 cans of drained and rinsed navy beans instead of ground beef.

CABBAGE AND BEEF CASSEROLE

A lower-carbohydrate beefy casserole using cabbage and tomato sauce.

Serves 6

INGREDIENTS:

2 pounds lean ground beef

1 small onion, chopped

1 head cabbage, shredded

1 (16-ounce) can tomatoes, diced

½ teaspoon garlic salt

¼ teaspoon ground thyme

¼ teaspoon red pepper flakes

½ teaspoon oregano

1 (8-ounce) can tomato sauce

1. In a large skillet, brown the ground beef for about 5–6 minutes. Remove ground beef to a bowl and set aside. In same skillet, sauté onion until softened, about 3–5 minutes.

2. In a greased 4–6-quart slow cooker, layer cabbage, onion, tomatoes, garlic salt, thyme, pepper flakes, oregano, and beef. Repeat layers, ending with beef. Pour tomato sauce over casserole.

3. Cook on low for 8 hours or on high for 4 hours.

THE BEST MEAT LOAF

This is classic comfort food. With some mashed potatoes and gravy, your family will love it.

Serves 6–8

INGREDIENTS:

1½ pounds lean ground beef, either chuck or sirloin

½ cup gluten-free chili sauce

½ cup milk

3 large eggs

1 cup gluten-free corn bread crumbs

Salt and pepper, to taste

2 cloves garlic, minced

1 small onion, minced

1 teaspoon dried rosemary, crumbled

2 teaspoons Lea & Perrins Steak Sauce

½ teaspoon nutmeg

1. Preheat oven to 350°F.

2. In the large bowl of a food processor, whirl all ingredients together.

3. Treat a 9" × 5" inch bread pan with nonstick spray. Pour in the meat loaf mixture.

4. Place a roasting pan in the middle of the oven. Add 1 inch of water. Place the bread pan with the meat loaf in the water. Bake for 80 minutes. For an extra touch, drape 2 slices of gluten-free bacon over the top of the meat loaf.

A Hot Water Bath

Baking your meat loaf in a hot water bath enables it to stay juicy. Processing the ingredients makes a much smoother meat loaf than the coarse stuff that you have to chew for a long time. The water bath is called a bain-marie, and it keeps baked foods soft, creamy, and moist.

TAMALE PIE

A favorite of kids everywhere, this corn bread–topped ground beef and bean pie is a great weeknight dinner! To make this dish extra special, add 1 cup of shredded Cheddar cheese to the beef and bean filling.

Serves 6

INGREDIENTS:

1 pound lean ground beef

1 package gluten-free taco seasoning

½ cup warm water

1 (15-ounce) can pinto beans, drained and rinsed

1 (11-ounce) can corn, drained

1 (8-ounce) can tomato sauce

2 tablespoons melted butter

1 large egg

1 tablespoon sugar

½ cup 2% milk

¾ cup gluten-free cornmeal

1 teaspoon gluten-free baking powder

¼ teaspoon salt

1. In a large skillet, brown ground beef until cooked through, approximately 5–6 minutes. Drain excess fat and add taco seasoning and water to the skillet. Stir to combine and then pour into a greased 4-quart slow cooker.

2. Add beans, corn, and tomato sauce to the seasoned ground beef. Stir to combine.

3. In a small bowl whisk together melted butter, egg, sugar, and milk. Add cornmeal, baking powder, and salt. Using a fork, whisk thoroughly to combine batter. Pour corn bread batter over the ingredients in the slow cooker. Do not stir.

4. Cover and vent the slow cooker with a chopstick or the handle of a wooden spoon. Cook on high for 3 hours or on low for 6 hours or until corn bread is golden brown on the edges.

YANKEE POT ROAST

New England cooking is traditionally plain and straightforward. If your family prefers a heartier flavor, add a teaspoon of Mrs. Dash Garlic & Herb Seasoning Blend.

Serves 8

INGREDIENTS:

¼ pound salt pork, cut into cubes

2 stalks celery, diced

1 (4-pound) chuck or English roast

1 teaspoon salt

1 teaspoon freshly ground black pepper

2 large onions, peeled and quartered

1 (1-pound) bag of baby carrots

2 turnips, peeled and diced

8 medium potatoes, peeled

2 cups gluten-free beef broth

4 tablespoons butter

4 tablespoons brown rice flour

1. Add the salt pork and the celery to the bottom of a 6-quart slow cooker. Place the roast on top of the pork; sprinkle with salt and pepper. Add the onions, carrots, turnips, and potatoes. Pour in the beef broth. Cover and cook on low for 8 hours.

2. Use a slotted spoon to move the meat and vegetables to a serving platter; cover and keep warm.

3. In small bowl, mix the butter and flour together with ½ cup of the broth. Increase the slow cooker heat setting to high; cover and cook until the mixture begins to bubble around the edges. Whisk the flour mixture into the broth; cook, stirring constantly, for 10 minutes, or until the flour flavor is cooked out of the gravy and it's thickened enough to coat the back of a spoon. Taste the gravy for seasoning and stir in more salt and pepper if needed. Serve over or alongside the meat and vegetables.

Mocking the Maillard Reaction

Contrary to myth, searing meat before it's braised doesn't seal in the juices, but it does—through a process known as the Maillard reaction—enhance the flavor of the meat through a caramelization process. Using beef broth (or, even better, a combination of brown stock and water) mimics that flavor and lets you skip the browning step.

NEW ENGLAND BOILED DINNER

Cutting the meat into serving-sized pieces before you add it to the slow cooker will make the meat cook up more tender, but you can keep it in one piece if you prefer to carve it at the table.

Serves 8

INGREDIENTS:

1 (3-pound) boneless beef round rump roast

4 cups gluten-free beef broth

2 yellow onions, sliced

1 teaspoon gluten-free prepared horseradish

1 bay leaf

1 clove garlic, minced

6 large carrots, cut into 1" pieces

3 rutabagas, peeled and quartered

4 large potatoes, peeled and quartered

1 small head of cabbage, cut into 8 wedges

2 tablespoons butter

2 tablespoons brown rice flour

1 teaspoon salt, optional

½ teaspoon freshly ground black pepper, optional

1. Cut the beef into 8 serving-sized pieces and add it along with the broth, onions, horseradish, bay leaf, and garlic to a 6-quart slow cooker. Add the carrots, rutabagas, potatoes, and cabbage wedges. Cover and cook on low for 8 hours.

2. Remove meat and vegetables to a serving platter; cover and keep warm.

3. Increase the slow cooker setting to high; cover and cook until the pan juices begin to bubble around the edges. Mix the butter and flour in a bowl together with ½ cup of the pan juices; strain out any lumps and whisk the mixture into the simmering liquid in the slow cooker. Cook and stir for 15 minutes or until the flour flavor is cooked out and the gravy is thickened enough to coat the back of a spoon. Taste for seasoning and add salt and pepper if desired. Serve alongside or over the meat and potatoes.

Horseradish Gravy

If you prefer a more intense horseradish flavor with cooked beef, increase the amount to 1 tablespoon. Taste the pan juices before you thicken them with the butter and brown rice flour mixture, and add more horseradish at that time if you desire. Of course, you can have some horseradish or horseradish mayonnaise available as a condiment for those who want more. Ensure it is gluten-free.

ROAST BEEF FOR TWO

Couples deserve a good roast dinner just as much as larger families. So enjoy this one without having to eat leftovers for a week.

Serves 2

INGREDIENTS:

½ teaspoon freshly ground black pepper

½ teaspoon fennel seeds

½ teaspoon crushed rosemary

¼ teaspoon salt

½ teaspoon dried oregano

¾-pound bottom round roast, excess fat removed

¼ cup caramelized onions

¼ cup gluten-free beef broth

1 clove garlic, sliced

1. In a small bowl, stir the pepper, fennel seeds, rosemary, salt, and oregano. Rub it onto all sides of the meat. Refrigerate for 15 minutes.

2. Place the roast in a 2-quart slow cooker. Add the onions, broth, and garlic. Cook on low for 6 hours, or on high for 3 hours. Remove roast and slice. Serve the slices topped with the caramelized onions. Discard any cooking juices.

BARBECUE WESTERN RIBS

At the end of the 8-hour cooking time, the meat will be tender and falling off of the bones. You can stretch this recipe to 8 servings if you serve barbecue beef sandwiches instead of 4 servings of beef. Add gluten-free potato chips and coleslaw for a delicious, casual meal.

Serves 4

INGREDIENTS:

1 cup gluten-free hickory barbecue sauce

½ cup orange marmalade

½ cup water

3 pounds beef Western ribs

1. Add the barbecue sauce, marmalade, and water to greased 4–6-quart slow cooker. Stir to mix.

2. Add the ribs, ladling some of the sauce over the ribs. Cover and cook on low for 8 hours.

3. To thicken the sauce, use a slotted spoon to remove the meat and bones; cover and keep warm. Skim any fat from the sauce in the cooker; increase the heat setting to high and cook uncovered for 15 minutes or until the sauce is reduced and coats the back of a spoon.

SWISS STEAK

Minute steaks are usually tenderized pieces of round steak. You can instead buy 2½ pounds of round steak, trim it of fat, cut it into 6 portions, and pound each portion thin between 2 pieces of plastic wrap. Serve Swiss Steak over mashed potatoes.

Serves 6

INGREDIENTS:

½ cup brown rice flour or Bob's Red Mill Gluten-Free All-Purpose Flour

1 teaspoon salt

¼ teaspoon freshly ground black pepper

6 (6-ounce) beef minute steaks

2 tablespoons vegetable oil

2 teaspoons butter

½ stalk celery, finely diced

1 large yellow onion, peeled and diced

1 cup gluten-free beef broth

1 cup water

1 (1-pound) bag baby carrots

1. Add the flour, salt, pepper, and steaks to a gallon-sized plastic bag; seal and shake to coat the meat.

2. Add the oil and butter to a large skillet and bring it to temperature over medium-high heat. Add the meat and brown it for 5 minutes on each side. Transfer the meat to a 4-quart slow cooker.

3. Add the celery to the skillet and sauté while you add the onion to the plastic bag; seal and shake to coat the onion in flour. Add the flour-coated onion to the skillet and, stirring constantly, sauté for 10 minutes or until the onions are lightly browned.

4. Add the broth to the skillet and stir to scrape up any browned bits clinging to the pan. Add the water and continue to cook until the liquid is thickened enough to lightly coat the back of a spoon. Pour into the slow cooker.

5. Add the carrots. Cover and cook on low for 8 hours.

6. Transfer the meat and carrots to a serving platter. Taste the gravy for seasoning, and add more salt and pepper if desired. Serve alongside or over the meat and carrots.

Swiss Steak and Pasta

If instead of mashed potatoes, you'd prefer to serve the Swiss Steak over cooked gluten-free pasta, stir 2 tablespoons of tomato paste into the onions before you make the gravy in Step 3. Or, you can substitute 1 cup of diced tomatoes for the water.

BEEF BIRYANI

Biryani is a one-dish meal that is well spiced but not spicy. Traditionally, it is made using ghee, a type of clarified butter, but slow cooking brings out the flavor without adding fat.

Serves 6

INGREDIENTS:

1 pound top round, cut into strips

1 tablespoon minced fresh ginger

½ teaspoon ground cloves

½ teaspoon ground cardamom

½ teaspoon ground coriander

½ teaspoon freshly ground black pepper

½ teaspoon cinnamon

½ teaspoon cumin

¼ teaspoon salt

2 cloves garlic, minced

1 medium onion, minced

1 cup fat-free gluten-free Greek yogurt

1 cup frozen peas

1½ cups cooked basmati or brown rice

1. Place the beef, spices, garlic, and onion into a 4-quart slow cooker. Stir. Cook for 5–6 hours on low.

2. About 30 minutes before serving, stir in the yogurt, peas, and rice. Cook for 30 minutes. Stir before serving.

GROUND BEEF RAGOUT

Ragout *is a term that generally refers to a slow-cooked stew with a variety of vegetables that can be made with or without meat. Ground beef is used in this version for a very economical main dish. Serve over cooked rice or prepared polenta.*

Serves 4

INGREDIENTS:

1 pound lean ground beef

2 medium onions, finely chopped

1 large green pepper, diced with seeds removed

1 tablespoon olive oil

1 (14½-ounce) can Italian-style stewed tomatoes

3 medium carrots, cut into ½" slices

½ cup gluten-free beef broth

½ teaspoon salt

½ teaspoon ground pepper

1 medium zucchini, halved lengthwise and cut into ½" slices

1. Brown ground beef in a skillet, discard grease, and spoon ground beef into a greased 4-quart slow cooker.

2. In the same pan, sauté onions and green pepper in olive oil for several minutes until softened. Add onions and green pepper to slow cooker.

3. Add tomatoes, carrots, broth, salt, and pepper to the slow cooker. Stir to combine all ingredients.

4. Cook for 4 hours on high or 8 hours on low.

5. An hour prior to serving stir in zucchini and allow to cook until fork tender.

Not a Fan of Zucchini?

Instead of using zucchini, use yellow squash, precooked potatoes or sweet potatoes, parsnips, or even mushrooms. Use whatever vegetables you have on hand!

MEAT LOAF–STUFFED GREEN PEPPERS

This recipe is slightly different than traditional stuffed pepper recipes because it doesn't contain rice or potatoes to supplement the meat mixture. This is a great main dish option for those following low-carbohydrate food plans.

Serves 4

INGREDIENTS:

1 slice gluten-free bread, torn into very small pieces

¼ cup 2% milk

1 pound lean ground beef

½ teaspoon salt

½ teaspoon pepper

1½ teaspoons dried onion

1 large egg

4 green peppers

1. In a large bowl, mix together the bread and milk. Set aside for 5 minutes.

2. Add ground beef, salt, pepper, dried onion, and egg to the softened bread. Mix meat loaf ingredients together well.

3. Carefully remove the tops, seeds, and membranes of the peppers. Fill each pepper with ¼ of the meat loaf mixture.

4. Place the stuffed peppers in a greased 4-quart slow cooker. Add ⅓ cup of water around the bottom of the stuffed peppers.

5. Cook on high for 3–4 hours or on low for 6–8 hours until green peppers are softened.

Make It Grain-Free

To make this recipe completely grain-free and dairy-free (for those following a Paleo food plan or a GAPS food plan), use ¼ cup blanched almond flour in place of the gluten-free bread and use a non-dairy substitute in place of the milk.

BARBECUE MEAT LOAF

The brown sugar sprinkled on top of the meat loaf helps to caramelize the sauce.

Serves 8

INGREDIENTS:

2 pounds lean ground beef

½ pound lean ground pork

2 large eggs

1 large yellow onion, finely diced

½ teaspoon salt

¼ teaspoon freshly ground pepper

1½ cups gluten-free quick-cooking oatmeal

1 teaspoon dried parsley

1½ cups gluten-free barbecue sauce, divided

1 tablespoon brown sugar

1 teaspoon Mrs. Dash Extra Spicy Seasoning Blend

1. Add the ground beef, ground pork, eggs, onion, salt, pepper, oatmeal, parsley, and 1 cup barbecue sauce to a large bowl. Mix well with your hands. Form into a loaf that will fit into a 4–6-quart slow cooker.

2. Line the slow cooker with two pieces of heavy-duty aluminum foil long enough to reach up both sides of the slow cooker and over the edge. Grease the foil with nonstick cooking spray or olive oil.

3. Place the meat loaf on top of the foil in the slow cooker. Spread the remaining ½ cup of barbecue sauce over the top of the meat loaf. Sprinkle the brown sugar and Mrs. Dash Extra Spicy Seasoning blend over the top of the barbecue sauce. Cover and cook on low for 6–8 hours or on high for 3–4 hours, or until the center of the meat loaf registers at least 165°F.

4. Slowly lift the meat loaf out of the slow cooker and place on a large platter. Allow the meat to rest for 15–20 minutes before serving.

GROUND BEEF HASH

This dish has great potential to create a variety of meals that your family will love. You could add mushrooms, garlic, or chopped carrots, use gluten-free chili powder instead of Italian seasoning, or top each serving with shredded cheese.

Serves 6

INGREDIENTS:

2 pounds lean ground beef

2 medium onions, chopped

2 (15-ounce) cans diced tomatoes

1 large green pepper, chopped

1 cup uncooked white rice

1 tablespoon gluten-free Worcestershire sauce

2 teaspoons gluten-free Italian seasoning

½ teaspoon salt

½ teaspoon pepper

1. Brown ground beef and onions in a large skillet, for approximately 3–5 minutes. Pour into a greased 4-quart slow cooker. Add remaining ingredients and stir to combine.

2. Cook on high for 2–3 hours or on low for 4–6 hours, until rice is cooked through.

A Homemade Shortcut

Whenever you purchase your groceries, go ahead and chop up several onions, peppers, carrots, potatoes, garlic, and celery. You can freeze the diced vegetables for 3–4 months in an airtight zip-top bag or store them in the refrigerator for up to a week until you need to use them.

SLOW COOKER CHEESEBURGERS

This meal is reminiscent of sloppy joes but with a cheesy twist! Feel free to serve this cheesy ground beef not only on gluten-free buns, but over cooked rice or gluten-free pasta, or even over cooked spaghetti squash.

Serves 4

INGREDIENTS:

1 pound lean ground beef

¼ cup gluten-free ketchup

2 tablespoons gluten-free yellow mustard

1 teaspoon dried basil

2 cups mild Cheddar cheese

1. Brown ground beef in a skillet over medium heat. Pour off grease, and add cooked ground beef to a greased 2½-quart slow cooker.

2. Add ketchup, mustard, and basil to the slow cooker. Cook on high for 2–3 hours or on low for 4–5 hours.

3. Thirty minutes prior to serving add shredded Cheddar cheese to the ground beef mixture. When cheese is melted, spoon 3–4 tablespoons of cheeseburger mixture into each hamburger bun. Serve with lettuce, tomatoes, and any other hamburger toppings you desire.

REUBEN CASSEROLE

If you were a fan of the distinct tangy flavors of a Reuben sandwich before you went gluten-free, you will love this zesty, sauerkraut-filled casserole dish!

Serves 6

INGREDIENTS:

8 ounces gluten-free corned beef, cut into ½" cubes

1 Granny Smith apple, peeled, cored, and chopped

1 (14-ounce) can sauerkraut, rinsed and drained

1¼ teaspoons caraway seeds

2 cups mashed potatoes

2 cups shredded Havarti or Swiss cheese, optional

¼ cup gluten-free Thousand Island dressing, optional

1. Grease a 2½-quart or larger slow cooker. Add corned beef, apple, sauerkraut, and caraway seeds. Stir ingredients together.

2. Spoon mashed potatoes evenly over casserole ingredients. Cook on high for 3–4 hours or on low for 6–8 hours.

3. If desired, thirty minutes prior to serving, sprinkle cheese over mashed potatoes and cook until it is soft and melted. Drizzle a tablespoon of Thousand Island dressing over each serving.

BEEF BURRITO FILLING

London broil is a lean cut of meat that is perfect for the slow cooker. The longer it's cooked, the more tender and succulent it becomes. With the addition of gluten-free taco seasoning, it makes the perfect meaty filling for Mexican dishes, like burritos, enchiladas, and tacos.

Serves 6

INGREDIENTS:

1 package gluten-free taco seasoning

1 clove garlic, peeled and minced

2 pounds London broil

1 cup diced onion

2 tablespoons apple cider vinegar

1. In small bowl mix together the taco seasoning and garlic.

2. Rub London broil with the taco seasoning mixture. Place beef and onion in a greased 4-quart slow cooker. Drizzle apple cider vinegar over the meat and onions.

3. Cook on high for 4 hours or on low for 8 hours until meat can be shredded with a fork.

ENCHILADA CASSEROLE

This is definitely a crowd pleaser. You can adjust the spices according to your guests' tastes.

Serves 6

INGREDIENTS:

2 tablespoons extra-virgin olive oil

½ medium onion, chopped

1 clove garlic, minced

2 pounds lean ground beef

1 tablespoon gluten-free chili powder

1 tablespoon cumin

⅛ teaspoon gluten-free cayenne pepper, ground

1 tablespoon chopped fresh cilantro

1 (15-ounce) can black or pinto beans, thoroughly rinsed and drained

1 cup diced tomatoes or 1 (14-ounce) can diced tomatoes

½ cup green pepper, diced

1 large carrot, shredded

1 can diced green chili peppers

1 cup frozen corn

¼ teaspoon salt

8–12 gluten-free corn tortillas (amount depends on how many you want to use)

2 cups sharp Cheddar or Monterey jack cheese, shredded

2 scallions, finely chopped

1 avocado, peeled, pitted, and sliced

1 cup gluten-free sour cream

½ cup sliced black olives

1 cup gluten-free salsa

1. Preheat the oven to 425°F.

2. Heat oil in a very large, deep skillet or Dutch oven and cook onion and garlic for 3–4 minutes until they soften.

3. Add the ground beef, chili powder, cumin, cayenne pepper, and cilantro and cook for 5–8 minutes, until beef turns brown.

4. Add the beans, tomatoes, green pepper, carrot, chili peppers, and corn. Season with salt and cook additional 1–2 minutes until thoroughly combined.

5. Spray a 9" × 13" casserole dish with nonstick cooking spray. Layer the corn tortillas, then meat mixture, then cheese. Repeat again until all ingredients are used.

6. Bake for 15 minutes until the cheese is melted. Top with scallions, avocado, sour cream, olives, and salsa.

GINGER-TERIYAKI FLANK STEAK

This Asian-inspired dish pairs perfectly with steamed vegetables and rice. This marinade can be used on a variety of meats such as chicken, pork, and other cuts of beef.

Serves 4

INGREDIENTS:

½ cup water

1 tablespoon sesame oil

½ teaspoon grated gingerroot

2 cloves garlic, minced

¼ cup gluten-free soy sauce

1 tablespoon honey

1 tablespoon cornstarch

1½ pounds beef flank steak

1. In a small bowl, mix water, sesame oil, gingerroot, garlic, soy sauce, honey, and cornstarch. Stir thoroughly to ensure the cornstarch has been mixed in well.

2. Place the steak in zip-top bag and pour the marinade on top. Make sure the bag is sealed and shake until well blended. Place in refrigerator and let sit for at least 4 hours or, even better, overnight.

3. When ready to cook the steak, remove it from the bag and discard the leftover marinade.

4. Place steak on preheated grill or on a grill pan and cook on each side for about 6–8 minutes, until you have reached your desired degree of doneness. The internal temperature should read at least 145°F. Once cooked, cut steaks according to instructions.

What Does It Mean to Slice Against the Grain?

Lines in the flank steak run from right to left down the length of the steak. By cutting across these lines, the knife will cut through the fibers, which makes it easier to chew. Slicing the steak on a 45-degree angle creates an elegant presentation.

SPICY STEAK FAJITAS

Skirt steak rubbed with spicy seasoning, alongside chopped peppers, and served with warmed corn tortillas, makes for the perfect family meal.

Serves 8

INGREDIENTS:

1 tablespoon cornstarch

2 teaspoons gluten-free chili powder

1 teaspoon salt

1 teaspoon paprika

½ teaspoon red pepper flakes

1 teaspoon gluten-free Worcestershire sauce

1 teaspoon fresh lime juice

1 teaspoon turbinado sugar

¼ teaspoon cumin

4 cloves garlic, minced

3 pounds skirt steak

½ green onion, chopped

1 green bell pepper, sliced

1 red or yellow bell pepper, sliced

½ bunch fresh cilantro

Gluten-free corn tortillas

10 ounces shredded Monterey jack cheese

1. In a small bowl, mix the cornstarch, chili powder, salt, paprika, red pepper flakes, Worcestershire sauce, lime juice, sugar, and cumin.

2. Rub the steak with the garlic and the prepared seasoning mixture and then cut it into strips.

3. In a large skillet over medium heat, cook the onion, peppers, and cilantro for 3–4 minutes. Add steak strips and cook, stirring frequently, until cooked through, about 7 minutes.

4. Remove from heat and spoon the meat and vegetable mixture into corn tortillas. Top with cheese and roll them up.

HEALTHY GOULASH

This one-dish meal is filled with flavor. This is not Hungarian Goulash, which is more of a beef stew with potatoes.

Serves 8

INGREDIENTS:

2 pounds lean ground beef

2 large yellow onions, chopped

3 cloves garlic, chopped

3 cups water

2 (15-ounce) cans low-sodium tomato sauce

2 (14½-ounce) cans diced tomatoes

1 tablespoon gluten-free soy sauce

1 tablespoon gluten-free Worcestershire sauce

2 tablespoons gluten-free dried Italian herb seasoning (or 1 teaspoon each: basil, oregano, rosemary, and thyme)

3 bay leaves

½ teaspoon dry mustard

1 teaspoon paprika

¼ teaspoon salt

2 cups uncooked brown rice noodles (preferably elbows)

¼ cup shredded white sharp Cheddar cheese

1. In a large Dutch oven, cook and stir the ground beef over medium-high heat, breaking the meat up as it cooks, until the meat is no longer pink and has started to brown, about 10 minutes.

2. Skim off excess fat, and stir in the onions and garlic. Cook and stir the meat mixture until the onions are translucent, about 10 more minutes.

3. Stir in water, tomato sauce, diced tomatoes, soy sauce, Worcestershire sauce, Italian seasoning, bay leaves, dry mustard, paprika, and salt. Bring the mixture to a boil over medium heat. Reduce the heat to low, cover, and simmer 20 minutes, stirring occasionally.

4. Stir in the rice noodles, cover, and simmer, stirring occasionally, over low heat until the noodles are tender, about 25 minutes.

5. Remove from heat, discard bay leaves, and top with shredded cheese. Mix well and serve.

GARLIC-RUBBED PRIME RIB

This exquisite dish is perfect for a holiday or special occasion. Prime rib is usually served rare or medium rare.

Serves 8–10

INGREDIENTS:

10 cloves garlic, minced

2 tablespoons extra-virgin olive oil

1½ teaspoons salt

2 teaspoons ground black pepper

1 tablespoon balsamic vinegar

1 teaspoon dried thyme

1 teaspoon dried rosemary

1 (10-pound) prime rib roast

1. In a small bowl, mix together the garlic, oil, salt, pepper, balsamic vinegar, thyme, and rosemary.

2. Place the roast in a roasting pan with the fatty side up. Cut slits in the fatty layers. Rub the garlic mixture throughout the fatty side and all over the entire roast. Insert meat thermometer in the thickest part of the roast. Cover roast with aluminum foil and let sit out until it reaches room temperature.

3. Preheat oven to 450°F. Once preheated, remove foil and place the roast in the oven and bake the roast for 12 minutes.

4. Lower the temperature to 400°F and cook for 8 minutes.

5. After 8 minutes, lower the temperature to 325°F, and cook for 90 minutes or until the desired internal temperature is reached (see sidebar) when taken with a meat thermometer.

6. Remove from oven, re-cover with aluminum foil and let roast sit out for 20 minutes, or until it reaches the desired internal temperature (see sidebar). The roast will continue to cook even after it's removed from the oven.

Internal Temperatures for the Perfect Prime Rib

For a rare roast, remove from the oven at ~100°F and let it sit until it reaches ~120°F. For medium-rare prime rib, take out of the oven at ~120°F and let it sit until it reaches a final temperature of ~130°F. For a medium roast, remove from the oven at ~130°F until it reaches ~140°F.

HERB STUFFED VEAL CHOPS

This recipe calls for thick-cut chops. You can use double rib chops with a pocket for the aromatic herbs and vegetables. These can be grilled or sautéed.

Serves 4

INGREDIENTS:

½ cup minced shallots

½ medium onion, finely chopped

2 tablespoons chopped fresh rosemary

2 teaspoons dried basil, or 1 tablespoon chopped fresh basil

½ teaspoon ground coriander

2 tablespoons unsalted butter

1 teaspoon salt

Pepper, to taste

4 veal rib chops, 1½–2 inches thick, a pocket cut from the outside edge toward the bone in each

¼ cup extra-virgin olive oil

Salt and pepper for outside of chops

1. In a skillet over medium heat, sauté the shallots, onion, and herbs in butter for 2–3 minutes. Add salt and pepper. Let sit for 5 minutes.

2. Stuff the chops with herbs. Rub chops with olive oil, salt, and pepper.

3. Using an outdoor grill or broiler, sear the chops over high heat, 1–2 minutes per side.

4. Cut heat to medium and cook the chops for 4–5 minutes per side for medium chops or rare chops, depending on the thickness.

ROAST LEG OF VEAL WITH MUSTARD CRUST

You will probably have to special order the veal from your butcher—try to get one that does not exceed 7 pounds. It is the perfect dish for a special occasion.

Serves 10–12

INGREDIENTS:

½ pound unsalted butter, at room temperature

½ cup gluten-free Dijon-style mustard

1 cup rice or potato flour

1 teaspoon garlic powder

1 teaspoon dried basil

2 teaspoons dried oregano

1 (7-pound) veal leg roast, well trimmed

Salt and pepper, to taste

1 cup dry (white) vermouth

Lemon slices

Heavy cream (optional)

1. Preheat the oven to 400°F.

2. In a large bowl add the butter, mustard, flour, garlic powder, basil, and oregano. Mix together to make a paste. Rub the veal with salt and pepper. Cover the veal with the paste.

3. Place the veal in the oven in a 9" × 13" baking pan, and add the vermouth *around* (not over) the veal. Roast for 15 minutes or until the crust hardens.

4. Arrange the lemon slices on top of the veal. Baste every 15 minutes. Roast for 15 minutes per pound, until it reaches internal temperature of 145°F. Carve and serve with pan juices. (Heavy cream can be added to the pan juices to make more sauce.)

The Versatility of Veal

When you prepare veal chops, scallops, stew, or a roast, you can vary the accompanying vegetables, herbs, and spices. Veal should be very young; old veal is beef. The paler the color, the more mild and tender the meat will be. Cuts from the leg make the scallops.

SAUSAGE-FILLED VEAL ROULADES

This recipe is a snap to double for serving 8 people.

Serves 4

INGREDIENTS:

8 veal scallops, pounded very thin with a mallet

⅓ pound gluten-free sweet Italian sausage, crumbled

½ cup grated Parmesan cheese, fresh or gluten-free

1 large egg, beaten

½ teaspoon pepper

2 tablespoons unsalted butter

¼ cup gluten-free chicken broth

1 cup light cream

Parmesan cheese, parsley, or watercress, for garnish

1. Trim the pounded veal to resemble rectangles. In a bowl, mix the sausage, cheese, egg, and pepper or, if not of a fine consistency, pulse it in a food processor until it resembles coarse crumbs.

2. Spread the sausage stuffing on the veal and roll up tightly from the wide to the shorter end. Secure with kitchen string.

3. Melt the butter in a pan large enough to hold all of the roulades. Turn the veal until lightly browned. Add the broth and cover. Simmer for 30 minutes.

4. Arrange the roulades on a plate. Deglaze the pan with cream and pour it over the veal. You can add extra cheese, parsley, or watercress to garnish.

TURKISH VEAL ROULADES

Stuffing the veal with a nice tapenade (a savory paste) of olives and parsley is another excellent choice.

Serves 4

INGREDIENTS:

8 veal scallops, pounded very thin with a mallet

10 pimiento-stuffed green olives, minced

8 black olives (Spanish or Greek), pitted and minced

6 scallions, minced

½ cup minced parsley

2 tablespoons olive oil

Juice of ½ lemon

1 large egg, beaten

4 tablespoons butter

½ cup dry white wine

1. Trim the pounded veal to resemble rectangles. Lay the veal out flat. Mix the olives, scallions, parsley, olive oil, and lemon juice with the beaten egg.

2. Spread on veal scallops. Roll the veal and tie it. In a large skillet, brown veal rolls in butter. Add wine, cover, and braise over low heat for 30 minutes. Use wine in pan for sauce.

FRENCH CHEESE-FILLED VEAL ROULADES

Be creative—you can use any number of stuffings. The stuffing of Boursin cheese and oregano is very spicy, a nice counterpoint to the creamy sauce.

Serves 4

INGREDIENTS:

8 veal scallops, pounded very thin with a mallet

6 ounces pepper-flavored Boursin cheese

1 teaspoon dried oregano or 2 teaspoons fresh

1 large egg, beaten

2 tablespoons butter

½ cup dry white wine

1 cup light cream

¼ cup finely grated fresh Parmesan cheese

¼ teaspoon ground nutmeg or paprika

1. Trim the pounded veal to resemble rectangles. Combine Boursin cheese, oregano, and egg to make the stuffing. Spread on veal. Roll and tie with kitchen string.

2. In a large skillet, melt butter and lightly brown veal; add wine and cover. Cook over low to medium heat for 30 minutes.

3. Put veal on a platter and add cream, Parmesan cheese, and nutmeg or paprika to the sauce in pan; heat. Pour sauce over veal rolls and serve.

Pounding Veal

A five-pound barbell works great for pounding the meat. Whether scallops or chops, place between slices of wax paper and, working from the center to the edges, pound away! The meat will be very tender after this process.

CHAPTER 9

PORK AND LAMB

SCALLOPED POTATOES WITH LEEKS AND COUNTRY HAM

This is a great brunch or supper dish. It's filling and delicious, especially good on a cold day or nippy evening.

Serves 6

INGREDIENTS:

1½ cups grated Parmesan cheese, fresh or gluten-free

1 cup coarsely grated fontina cheese

½ cup corn flour

Salt and freshly ground black pepper, to taste

6 medium Idaho or Yukon Gold potatoes, peeled and sliced thinly

4 leeks, thinly sliced crosswise, white parts only

1 pound gluten-free deli ham, sliced and then cut crosswise into dice

3 cups fat-free milk

4 tablespoons butter (for greasing baking dish and dotting on potatoes)

1. Grease a baking dish or prepare it with nonstick spray. Preheat oven to 350°F.

2. Mix together the cheeses, corn flour, salt, and pepper.

3. Place a layer of potatoes in the baking dish, then one of leeks, and dab with bits of ham. Sprinkle with the mixture of cheeses, corn flour, and spices. Repeat until you get to the top of the baking dish. Add the milk, sprinkle with cheese mixture, and dot with butter.

4. Bake for about 90 minutes. The top should be brown and crispy, the inside soft and creamy.

Striking Yukon Gold

Yukon Gold potatoes were developed in the 1970s at the University of Guelph, Ontario, Canada. They were initially slow to capture the market but now are widely popular, particularly suited for baking, salads, and soups.

HAM, BROCCOLI, AND SHRIMP PASTA SAUCE

This is excellent over Asian rice noodles. You can substitute chicken strips for the shrimp.

Serves 4

INGREDIENTS:

1 head broccoli, stems removed, divided into small florets

2 tablespoons olive oil

1 teaspoon sesame seed oil

2 cloves garlic, thinly sliced

4 ounces gluten-free smoked ham, finely chopped

Juice of ½ lemon

½ cup dry white wine

2 tablespoons gluten-free soy sauce or gluten-free Worcestershire sauce

1 pound raw shrimp, peeled and deveined

1 teaspoon sugar

½ cup toasted pine nuts and ¼ cup chopped cilantro or parsley, for garnish

1. Bring a pot of salted water to a boil. Drop the broccoli into the boiling water and cook for 10 minutes. Drain and set aside.

2. In a large skillet over medium heat, heat the oils and add the garlic; do not brown. Stir in the ham.

3. Add the broccoli and the rest of the ingredients, except for the pine nuts and cilantro. The dish is done when the shrimp turn pink. Garnish with pine nuts and chopped cilantro or parsley and serve.

HAM, CABBAGE, AND CARROT STEW

This cabbage stew, flavored with a meaty ham bone, is a very frugal recipe and makes enough for a crowd!

Serves 8

INGREDIENTS:

1 (2–3 pound) meaty ham bone

4 large carrots, peeled and sliced into 1" circles

½ head red or green cabbage, chopped

1 medium onion, finely chopped

8 cups gluten-free chicken broth

2 teaspoons salt

2 teaspoons pepper

2 cups gluten-free cooked cubed ham

1. Add ham bone, carrots, cabbage, onion, chicken broth, salt, and pepper to a greased 4–6-quart slow cooker. Cover and cook on high for 4–6 hours or on low for 8–10 hours.

2. One hour before serving, remove the ham bone and add in the cubed ham pieces. Cook for an additional hour and serve.

HAM, SPINACH, AND RICE CASSEROLE

Use leftover ingredients to create a tasty main dish. This casserole is also ideal for a brunch or breakfast.

Serves 4

INGREDIENTS:

2 tablespoons butter

½ medium onion, chopped

2 tablespoons brown rice flour

1 cup gluten-free chicken broth

½ teaspoon salt

½ teaspoon ground pepper

¼ teaspoon dried thyme

3 large eggs, beaten

1 (10-ounce) package frozen spinach, defrosted and drained

1 cup gluten-free cooked ham, chopped

1½ cups cooked rice

½ cup crushed gluten-free Rice Chex cereal

1. In a small saucepan over medium heat, heat the butter. Whisk in onion and flour. Cook for 2–3 minutes to toast the flour.

2. Slowly whisk in the chicken broth, salt, pepper, and thyme. Cook for 3–5 minutes until sauce has thickened, and set aside.

3. In a large bowl mix together the eggs, spinach, ham, and rice. Stir in the thickened chicken broth. Pour into a greased 4-quart slow cooker. Top with crushed Rice Chex.

4. Cover and vent lid with a chopstick. Cook on high for 3 hours or on low for 6 hours, or until casserole is set.

ORANGE HONEY–GLAZED HAM

Many people are intimidated by making ham. Using the slow cooker makes it super easy and the homemade orange honey glaze is a breeze to mix up.

Serves 6

INGREDIENTS:

1 (4-pound) bone-in gluten-free ham (discard glaze or seasoning packet)

½ cup seltzer water

½ cup orange juice

¼ cup honey

1–2 tablespoons orange zest

1 teaspoon ground cloves

¼ teaspoon cinnamon

1. Place ham, seltzer water, and orange juice in a greased 4–6-quart slow cooker. Cook on low for 6–8 hours or on high for 3–4 hours.

2. In a small bowl, mix together honey, orange zest, ground cloves, and cinnamon. Spread over ham. Cook for an additional 45 minutes to an hour, venting the slow cooker lid with a chopstick or spoon handle. The ham should become golden brown and glazed. If necessary, finish off ham in 350°F oven for 15–20 minutes to get a shiny glaze.

Orange Soda or Seltzer?

You can use 1 cup of orange soda in place of the seltzer water and orange juice called for in this recipe. If you don't have orange zest you can add a splash of lime juice to the honey glaze instead.

HAM AND SWEET POTATOES

Serve this dish with a tossed salad, applesauce, a steamed vegetable, and some warm Buttermilk Gluten-Free Drop Biscuits (see recipe in Chapter 3).

Serves 6

INGREDIENTS:

1 (20-ounce) can pineapple tidbits

1 (2-pound) boneless ham steak, gluten-free

3 large sweet potatoes, peeled and diced

1 large sweet onion, peeled and diced

½ cup orange marmalade

2 cloves garlic, peeled and minced

¼ teaspoon freshly ground black pepper

½ teaspoon dried parsley

1 tablespoon brown sugar

1. Drain the pineapple, reserving 2 tablespoons of the juice.

2. Trim the ham of any fat and cut it into bite-sized pieces. Add the pineapple, 2 tablespoons pineapple juice, and ham to the slow cooker along with the sweet potatoes, onion, marmalade, garlic, black pepper, parsley, and brown sugar. Stir to combine.

3. Cover and cook on low for 6 hours.

STUFFED PORK CHOPS

Ask the butcher for thick rib chops, and to slit a pocket in each. By doing this, it will allow stuffing the pork chops to be less complicated.

Serves 4

INGREDIENTS:

1 tart apple, peeled, cored, and chopped

½ cup chopped onion

1 tablespoon dried rosemary, crumbled, or 2 tablespoons chopped fresh

¼ cup finely chopped Italian flat-leaf parsley

1 tablespoon dried basil

½ cup extra-virgin olive oil

½ cup gluten-free corn bread crumbs

Salt and pepper, to taste

4 thick-cut pork rib chops

¼ cup extra-virgin olive oil

4 cloves garlic, chopped

2 medium onions, chopped

½ cup gluten-free chicken broth

½ cup dry white wine

Zest and juice of ½ lemon

2 medium-sized ripe pears, peeled, cored, and quartered

2 teaspoons cornstarch mixed with 2 ounces cold water (to thicken the gravy)

1. Sauté the apple, onion, and herbs in ½ cup olive oil over medium heat for 5 minutes.

2. Once the apples are softened, add the corn bread crumbs, salt, and pepper. Remove from heat. When cool enough to handle, stuff into the chops and secure with toothpicks.

3. Add ¼ cup olive oil to the pan and brown the chops over medium-high heat for 4–5 minutes each side. Add the rest of the ingredients, except for the cornstarch-and-water mixture, and cover. Simmer for 40 minutes over very low heat.

4. Remove the chops and place on a warm platter. Add the cornstarch-and-water mixture to the gravy in the pan if you want it to be thicker. Add salt and pepper to taste. Serve gravy either alongside the chops or poured over the chops.

TENDERLOIN OF PORK WITH SPINACH AND WATER CHESTNUTS

For convenience, use fresh baby spinach, pre-washed and packed in a bag. This dish can be served with any variety of rice or roasted potatoes.

Serves 4

INGREDIENTS:

2 pork tenderloins, about ¾ pound each

¼ cup potato flour

1 clove garlic, minced

¼ teaspoon nutmeg

¼ teaspoon ground cloves

Salt and pepper, to taste

¼ cup extra-virgin olive oil

2 tablespoons lemon juice

1 teaspoon gluten-free Worcestershire sauce

1 (8-ounce) bag fresh baby spinach or 1 (10-ounce) box frozen chopped spinach, thawed

½ cup sliced water chestnuts

1. Trim the pork and cut into serving pieces. On a sheet of wax paper, mix together the flour, garlic, and seasonings. Dredge the pork in the mixture.

2. In a large skillet, heat olive oil over medium heat and sauté the pork for about 6 minutes per side; it should be medium.

3. Add the lemon juice, Worcestershire sauce, spinach, and water chestnuts. Stir to wilt the spinach. Sprinkle with more olive oil, if the pan is dry.

Buying Pork

You can get "heirloom" or "heritage" pork on the web. Or you can get pork tenderloin in almost any supermarket. The tenderloin is about the best and most juicy cut available.

FRUIT AND CORN-CRUSTED PORK TENDERLOIN

The colorful filling makes this a very pretty presentation. It also is very flavorful.

Serves 4–6

INGREDIENTS:

6 gluten-free dried apricots, chopped

½ cup gluten-free dried cranberries

¼ cup gluten-free white raisins (sultanas)

1 cup warm water

Juice of ½ lemon

2 pork tenderloins, about ¾ pound each

Gluten-free Worcestershire sauce

1 cup gluten-free cornmeal

1 teaspoon salt

Freshly ground black pepper, to taste

½ cup olive oil

1. Put the dried fruit in a bowl with the warm water and lemon juice. Let stand until most of the water is absorbed.

2. Preheat oven to 350°F.

3. Make a tunnel through each tenderloin using a fat knitting needle or the handle of a blunt knife. Stuff the fruit into the tunnels.

4. Sprinkle both roasts with Worcestershire. Make a paste with the cornmeal, salt, pepper, and olive oil. Spread it on the pork. Roast for 30 minutes. The crust should be golden brown and the pork pink.

Crumb and Other Crusts

Many recipes call for bread crumbs to form a crust or topping, but you don't have to pass these recipes up! You can always substitute gluten-free corn bread crumbs, potato chips, crushed popcorn, or gluten-free cereal for the bread crumbs to top almost anything. If you are using potato chips, look for a low-salt or salt-free variety so that you can adjust the saltiness to your taste. You can also make crusts with ground nuts or thinly sliced raw potatoes, which you glue to the food with a bit of beaten egg or milk.

SLOW COOKER PORK POSOLE

Posole is a spicy, Mexican stew made from pork and hominy. For a milder version, simply use plain-diced tomatoes instead of tomatoes with green chilies.

Serves 8

INGREDIENTS:

2 pounds lean cubed pork

2 cans white or yellow hominy, drained and rinsed

1 can cubed potatoes, drained and rinsed

2 (15-ounce) cans diced tomatoes with green chilies (undrained)

2 cups warm water

1 cup carrots, chopped

4 cloves garlic, minced

1 medium onion, chopped

2 teaspoons cumin

2 teaspoons gluten-free chili powder

1 teaspoon red pepper flakes

1 teaspoon dried oregano

Shredded cheese, diced avocados, sliced black olives, pico de gallo, pickled jalapeño peppers, or gluten-free sour cream, for garnish

1. Add all ingredients to a greased 4-quart slow cooker. Cook on low for 8 hours or on high for 4 hours.

2. Serve with shredded cheese, diced avocados, sliced black olives, pico de gallo, pickled jalapeño peppers, or gluten-free sour cream, if desired.

Corn by Any Other Name

Hominy is corn that has been soaked in a weak lye solution. This treatment gives the corn a creamy white texture and a distinctive taste, as it removes the germ and the bran of the grain. Hominy that has been roughly ground is known as hominy grits and is often served for breakfast.

ITALIAN PORK WITH CANNELLINI BEANS

This is an incredibly simple one-dish meal that is packed with flavor.

Serves 4

INGREDIENTS:

1½ pounds lean pork loin

28 ounces crushed tomatoes

1 head roasted garlic

1 medium onion, minced

2 tablespoons capers

2 teaspoons gluten-free Italian seasoning

15 ounces canned cannellini beans, drained and rinsed

1. Place the pork loin into a 4-quart slow cooker. Add the tomatoes, garlic, onion, Italian seasoning, and capers. Cook on low for 7–8 hours.

2. One hour before serving, add the cannellini beans and continue to cook on low for the remaining time.

How to Make Roasted Garlic

You can easily make your own roasted garlic in the oven. Simply cover a small baking sheet with aluminum foil and place 2–4 whole (unpeeled) heads of garlic on the pan. Drizzle 2 tablespoons of olive oil over the garlic and bake at 350°F for about 45 minutes. Allow to cool for 5–10 minutes and then gently squeeze garlic cloves out of the "paper" surrounding them. Alternatively, you could place the same ingredients in a 1½–2½-quart slow cooker. Cover and cook on high for 2 hours. Store roasted garlic cloves in the fridge for up to 2 weeks.

MEXICAN PORK ROAST

Serve this pork over rice with Easy "Refried" Beans (see recipe in Chapter 13) on the side, or in burritos.

Serves 4

INGREDIENTS:

1 tablespoon olive oil

1 large sweet onion, peeled and sliced

1 medium carrot, peeled and finely diced

1 jalapeño pepper, seeded and minced

1 clove garlic, peeled and minced

½ teaspoon salt

¼ teaspoon dried Mexican oregano

¼ teaspoon ground coriander

¼ teaspoon freshly ground black pepper

1 (3-pound) pork shoulder or butt roast

1 cup gluten-free chicken broth

1. Add the olive oil, onion, carrot, and jalapeño to a 4–6-quart slow cooker. Stir to coat the vegetables in the oil. Cover and cook on high for 30 minutes or until the onions are softened. Stir in the garlic.

2. In a small bowl, combine the salt, oregano, coriander, and black pepper. Rub the spice mixture onto the pork roast.

3. Add the rubbed pork roast to the slow cooker. Add the chicken broth. Cover and cook on low for 6 hours or until the pork is tender and pulls apart easily.

4. Use a slotted spoon to remove the pork and vegetables to a serving platter. Cover and let rest for 10 minutes.

5. Increase the temperature of the slow cooker to high. Cook and reduce the pan juices by half.

6. Use 2 forks to shred the pork and mix it in with the cooked onion and jalapeño. Ladle the reduced pan juices over the pork.

Mexican Pork Roast Burritos

Warm 4 large gluten-free brown rice flour tortillas (Food for Life brand tortillas can be found in the freezer section of some higher-end grocery stores). Spread refried beans on each tortilla. Divide the pork between the tortillas and top with gluten-free salsa, and, if desired, grated cheese, shredded lettuce, and gluten-free sour cream. Roll and serve.

TOMATO-BRAISED PORK

In this recipe, pork is gently cooked in tomatoes to yield incredibly tender meat.

Serves 4

INGREDIENTS:

28 ounces canned crushed tomatoes

3 tablespoons tomato paste

1 cup loosely packed fresh basil

½ teaspoon freshly ground black pepper

½ teaspoon marjoram

1¼ pounds boneless pork roast

1. Place the tomatoes, tomato paste, basil, pepper, and marjoram into a greased 4-quart slow cooker. Stir to create a uniform sauce. Add the pork.

2. Cook on low for 7–8 hours or until the pork easily falls apart when poked with a fork. Serve pork and sauce over cooked rice or polenta, with a salad on the side.

POLYNESIAN PORK CHOPS

You can substitute pork steaks for the pork chops. (Because pork steaks tend to have more marbling, there's actually less chance of pork steaks drying out when prepared this way.)

Serves 6

INGREDIENTS:

6 (6-ounce) boneless pork chops

1 green bell pepper, seeded and diced

1 large onion, diced

2 cups converted rice, uncooked

1 teaspoon sea salt

1 (20-ounce) can crushed pineapple

1 cup gluten-free honey-mustard barbecue sauce

3 cups water

½ teaspoon ground black pepper

1. Treat the slow cooker with nonstick cooking spray. Trim and discard any fat from the pork chops and then cut them into bite-sized pieces.

2. Arrange half of the pork on the bottom of the slow cooker. Top with the bell pepper, onion, and rice. Sprinkle with salt and place the remaining pork over the rice.

3. In a small bowl, combine the entire can of pineapple, barbecue sauce, water, and black pepper; stir to mix and then pour into the slow cooker. Cover and cook on low for 8 hours or until the pork is cooked through and the rice is tender.

4. Stir the mixture in the slow cooker to fluff the rice. Taste for seasoning and add additional salt, barbecue sauce, and pepper if needed.

GLAZED LEAN PORK SHOULDER

Apples and apple cider form a glaze over a long cooking time that is both flavorful and light. Use crisp, in-season apples for best results.

Serves 8

INGREDIENTS:

3 pounds bone-in pork shoulder, excess fat removed

3 apples, thinly sliced

¼ cup apple cider

1 tablespoon brown sugar

1 teaspoon allspice

½ teaspoon cinnamon

¼ teaspoon nutmeg

Place the pork shoulder into a 4-quart slow cooker. Top with the remaining ingredients. Cook on low for 8 hours. Remove the lid and cook on high for 30 minutes or until the sauce thickens.

Sautéed Fennel

Fennel is delicious as a savory, yet slightly sweet, side dish. Heat a cast-iron skillet until almost smoking and add 3 tablespoons of olive oil. When the oil is hot stir in 2 cloves of sliced garlic. Add in 2 heads of finely sliced fennel with ½ teaspoon salt and ¼ teaspoon finely ground pepper. Sauté for an additional 3–4 minutes until fennel begins to caramelize (turns golden brown). Add about a tablespoon of water and cover with a lid to allow fennel to steam for about a minute. Serve immediately.

RED WINE–BRAISED PORK TENDERLOIN ROAST

This roast is simmered in red wine and beef broth for a tender and delicious meal. Serve with Simple Garlic Mashed Potatoes (see Chapter 14) and sautéed fennel or steamed broccoli.

Serves 6

INGREDIENTS:

2 pounds boneless pork tenderloin roast

1 tablespoon dried onion flakes

¼ teaspoon freshly ground black pepper

¼ teaspoon salt

2 teaspoons garlic powder

1 cup warm water

¾ cup red wine

1 teaspoon gluten-free beef bouillon granules or 1 cube of gluten-free beef bouillon

1. Place the pork roast into a greased 4-quart slow cooker.

2. In a large bowl, whisk together the dried onion flakes, black pepper, salt, and garlic powder. Pour in the water, red wine, and bouillon and whisk everything together thoroughly.

3. Pour red wine mixture over the pork roast. Cover and cook on low for 4 hours or on high for 3 hours. Because pork tenderloin is such a lean cut you do not want to overcook this meat.

APPLES-AND-ONIONS PORK CHOPS

Try Gala apples in this sweet and savory dish; they are crisp and sweet.

Serves 4

INGREDIENTS:

4 crisp, sweet apples

2 large onions, sliced

4 thick-cut boneless pork chops (about 1 pound)

½ teaspoon gluten-free ground cayenne pepper

½ teaspoon ground cinnamon

¼ teaspoon allspice

¼ teaspoon ground fennel

1. Cut the apples into wedges. Place half of the wedges in the bottom of a greased 4-quart slow cooker along with half of the sliced onions. Top with a single layer of pork chops. Sprinkle with cayenne pepper, cinnamon, allspice, and fennel and top with the remaining apples and onions.

2. Cook on low for 8 hours.

Slow Cooking with Boneless Pork

Not only is there less waste associated with boneless pork chops or roasts, there is often less fat attached to the meat as well. Even without much fat, boneless pork is well suited to slow cooking. All of the moisture stays in the dish, ensuring tender pork.

TEX-MEX PORK

Many kids enjoy the flavors of Mexican spices as long as you don't make a dish too hot. Feel free to add more or less of the spices depending on your family's spiciness preference

Serves 6

INGREDIENTS:

1 (3-pound) boneless pork roast

1 packet gluten-free taco seasoning mix, such as McCormick's Taco Seasoning

1 teaspoon garlic powder

1 teaspoon cumin

½ teaspoon gluten-free cayenne pepper

2 tablespoons lime juice

2 tablespoons chopped green chilies with juice

¾ cup water

1. Place pork roast into a greased 4-quart slow cooker.

2. In a small bowl mix together taco seasoning, garlic powder, cumin, cayenne pepper, lime juice, chilies with juice, and water. Pour seasoning mixture over pork roast.

3. Cook on high for 4 hours or cook on low for 8 hours until pork is very tender.

Cayenne Pepper

This spicy pepper is also known as Guinea spice, cow-horn pepper, or aleva. The fruit of the plant is usually dried and ground, or the pulp is taken from the fruit, baked into a cake, and then ground and sifted to create the spice you find in your grocery store. Just be sure the brand you choose is gluten-free, such as McCormick's.

EASY APPLESAUCE PORK CHOPS

Kids and adults alike will love these tender pork chops covered in applesauce with just a hint of brown sugar. Serve with baked sweet potatoes and steamed broccoli.

Serves 4

INGREDIENTS:

4 large pork loin chops

1 cup unsweetened applesauce

¼ cup brown sugar

3 tablespoons apple cider vinegar

Salt to taste

¼ teaspoon ground pepper

1. Place pork loin chops in the bottom of a greased 4-quart slow cooker.

2. Pour applesauce over the pork chops. Sprinkle brown sugar, vinegar, salt, and pepper evenly over the applesauce.

3. Cook on high for 4–5 hours or on low for 8–9 hours, until pork is tender. If necessary, add salt to taste.

PORK ROAST WITH CRANBERRY SAUCE

This pairs wonderfully with the Wild Rice Pilaf in Chapter 12.

Serves 4

INGREDIENTS:

1 medium onion, thinly sliced

1¼ pounds pork loin

2 tablespoons sweetened gluten-free dried cranberries

1 cup gluten-free cranberry sauce

1. Place the onion slices on the bottom of a greased 4-quart slow cooker. Top with the pork and the dried cranberries, and finally the cranberry sauce to cover the whole roast.

2. Cover and cook on low for 6 hours or on high for 3 hours. Remove the pork and slice it. Discard the cooking liquids.

Cooking with Pork Loin

Pork loin is an exceptionally lean cut. If a pork does have some excess fat, it can be removed easily before cooking. Another lean cut is the tenderloin roast, which is as lean as skinless chicken breast.

GARLIC-BALSAMIC CRUSTED PORK TENDERLOIN

This is wonderful for entertaining. Mashed potatoes and roasted vegetables pair perfectly with this tenderloin.

Serves 4

INGREDIENTS:

3 cloves garlic, minced

2 tablespoons balsamic vinegar

½ teaspoon ground mustard

1 teaspoon salt

¼ teaspoon pepper

1 tablespoon extra-virgin olive oil, for marinade

1–1¼ pounds pork tenderloin

1 tablespoon extra-virgin olive oil, for sauté

2 tablespoons fresh parsley, for garnish

1. In a small bowl, mix together the garlic, balsamic vinegar, mustard, salt, pepper, and olive oil. Rub the paste all over pork. Marinate for at least 2–3 hours or overnight.

2. Preheat the oven to 400°F. Heat oil in large skillet over medium-high heat. Working in batches, if necessary, add pork and brown tenderloin all over, about 4–5 minutes. If you don't have a skillet large enough to fit the entire tenderloin, you can cut it in half and brown one piece at a time.

3. Transfer pan to preheated oven. Roast the pork, turning occasionally, until the internal temperature reaches 160°F, about 20–30 minutes.

4. Transfer the pork to a cutting board and let rest 10 minutes before slicing. Top with fresh parsley if desired.

SLOW COOKER PULLED PORK

You will love how your house smells when this is slow cooking. Feel free to use chicken if you don't eat pork.

Serves 6

INGREDIENTS:

2 medium yellow onions, chopped

5 cloves garlic, minced

1 cup gluten-free beef broth

1 tablespoon brown sugar

1 tablespoon gluten-free chili powder

2 teaspoons kosher salt

1 teaspoon cumin

½ teaspoon cinnamon

½ teaspoon dried oregano

1 (5-pound) pork shoulder, boneless or bone-in

1 cup gluten-free barbecue sauce

1 teaspoon gluten-free soy sauce

1. Place the onions, garlic, and broth in a slow cooker.

2. In a small bowl, combine the sugar, chili powder, salt, cumin, cinnamon, and oregano and mix well.

3. Pat the pork with a paper towel and rub the prepared mixture all over it. Place pork on top of broth in slow cooker.

4. In the same small bowl, mix the barbecue sauce and the soy sauce. Stir to combine. Pour on top of pork making sure the mixture is spread evenly on top. Cover and cook on low for 8 hours.

5. Remove pork from slow cooker and allow to cool slightly. If using bone-in pork, discard bone. Place pork in a 9" × 13" casserole dish.

6. Shred the pork using a fork. Add additional barbecue sauce and slow cooker mixture if you'd like. Serve warm in gluten-free buns or tortillas, with a green salad, and Raw Broccoli Slaw with Fruit, Veggies, and Walnuts (see Chapter 11) or Balsamic Roasted Vegetables (see Chapter 14).

SAUSAGE AND SHRIMP JAMBALAYA

This version of a "red" jambalaya originated in the French Quarter of New Orleans when saffron wasn't readily available. This Creole-type jambalaya contains tomatoes, whereas a rural Cajun jambalaya (also known as "brown jambalaya") does not.

Serves 8

INGREDIENTS:

2 tablespoons olive oil

1 large onion, chopped

2 medium celery stalks, chopped

1 medium green bell pepper, chopped

3 cloves garlic, minced

1 (28-ounce) can diced tomatoes, undrained

2 cups fully cooked gluten-free smoked sausage, sliced into 1" pieces

1 tablespoon parsley flakes

½ teaspoon dried thyme leaves

½ teaspoon salt

¼ teaspoon pepper

¼ teaspoon red pepper sauce

2 teaspoons gluten-free Creole seasoning

¾ pound uncooked, peeled, deveined medium-sized shrimp, thawed if frozen

4 cups hot cooked rice

¼ cup fresh parsley, chopped

1. In a large skillet, heat oil. Sauté onions, celery, and bell pepper until softened, about 3–5 minutes. Add garlic and cook 1 minute more.

2. Grease a 4-quart slow cooker and add sautéed vegetables and all remaining ingredients except shrimp, rice, and parsley.

3. Cover and cook on low for 6 hours or on high for 3 hours.

4. Add shrimp and continue to cook on low for 45 minutes to 1 hour until shrimp are bright pink. Serve jambalaya over a bed of rice and garnish with chopped fresh parsley.

Instead of Shrimp . . .

Use your favorite type of seafood instead of shrimp. Scallops, cod, or diced tilapia fillets would also work well in this dish.

ZUCCHINI AND SAUSAGE CASSEROLE

Serve this casserole on a bed of mixed greens with a fruit salad on the side.

Serves 6

INGREDIENTS:

1 pound gluten-free mild pork sausage

1¼ cups grated Parmesan cheese, fresh or gluten-free

½ teaspoon salt

½ teaspoon freshly ground pepper

2 teaspoons gluten-free Greek seasoning or 1 teaspoon dried mint, ½ teaspoon dried oregano, and ½ teaspoon basil

2 large eggs, beaten

1 cup whole milk

3 medium zucchini, sliced into ½" rounds

1 small onion, sliced

1. In a large skillet, brown ground sausage, drain the fat from the skillet, and set the sausage aside.

2. Grease a 4-quart slow cooker with nonstick spray. In a large bowl whisk together the Parmesan cheese, salt, pepper, and Greek seasoning. In another bowl whisk together the eggs and the milk.

3. Place ⅓ of the zucchini over the bottom of the slow cooker. Add ⅓ of the sliced onions over the zucchini. Add ⅓ of the cooked sausage over the onions. Add ⅓ of the milk/egg mixture over the sausage. Lastly add ⅓ of the Parmesan cheese mixture over everything. Repeat layers two more times, ending with the last of the Parmesan cheese mixture.

4. Cover, vent lid with a chopstick and cook on low for 6 hours or on high for 3 hours. Cut into squares to serve.

MOROCCAN EGGPLANT AND LAMB CASSEROLE

With this recipe, you don't have to worry about a top crust or thickening. If you like it thick, just add a bit of cornstarch or rice flour.

Serves 4

INGREDIENTS:

2 large eggplants, peeled and cut vertically into long, thin slices

Table salt

1 red onion, peeled and diced

4 cloves garlic, peeled and minced

¼ cup olive oil plus 1 tablespoon olive oil for sautéing

1¼ pounds very lean ground lamb

¼ teaspoon cinnamon

½ teaspoon ground coriander seeds

Juice of 1 lemon

½ cup golden raisins (sultanas), gluten-free

½ cup gluten-free dried apricots, chopped

1 cup crushed tomatoes, with their juice

10 fresh mint leaves, torn into small pieces

Salt and pepper, to taste

Gluten-free hot paprika or cayenne pepper, to taste

1. Stack the eggplant slices with plenty of salt between the layers. Let it rest while you prepare the filling.

2. In a large skillet sauté the onion and garlic in a tablespoon of olive oil until soft. Add the lamb when the vegetables are soft.

3. Add the rest of the ingredients and cook, stirring until well blended. The apricots will absorb much of the liquid. If still very loose, sprinkle with a teaspoon of cornstarch. Cover and simmer for 15 minutes.

4. Preheat oven to 350°F.

5. Drain any liquid from the eggplant and place one layer in a well-oiled 11" × 13" baking dish. Add some of the lamb mixture, distributing carefully. Keep making layers until you have one final layer of eggplant. Sprinkle with extra oil and bake for 45 minutes. Serve in wedges. The traditional accompaniment is rice.

Eggplants in Lavender, Purple, and White

Eggplants come in a number of sizes, shapes, and colors—they taste pretty much the same. The larger ones may have bitter seeds, thus an old method of sweetening them up is to peel and cut an eggplant paper-thin (using a mandoline, if you have one), salt the slices on each side, and stack them on a plate, under a weight. Then, a lot of brown juice comes out, and the slices are sweet.

GREEK LAMB-STUFFED EGGPLANTS

You can do most of this in advance, refrigerate, and then put it in the oven for 10 minutes. Serve on beds of lettuce or rice.

Serves 4 for lunch, 8 as appetizers

INGREDIENTS:

8 small eggplants, about 4"–5" in length

½ cup olive oil

½ cup minced onion

4 cloves garlic, minced

½ pound lean ground lamb

Salt and pepper, to taste

½ cup fresh tomato, finely chopped

3 tablespoons chopped fresh mint

¼ teaspoon ground coriander

Juice of ½ lemon

Gluten-free yogurt, extra mint leaves, and finely chopped tomato to garnish

1. Fry the whole eggplants in olive oil. When cool enough to handle, make a slit from top to bottom but do not cut through.

2. Over moderate heat, fry the onion, garlic, lamb, salt, pepper, tomato, and herbs. Moisten with lemon juice.

3. Keep stirring to blend and break up the lamb. Set aside to cool for 15 minutes. Place the eggplants on a baking sheet that has been covered with aluminum foil. Spread the eggplants open and fill with lamb stuffing.

4. Preheat oven to 400°F.

5. Bake for 10 minutes. Serve with a dollop of yogurt on each eggplant and garnish with mint and chopped tomato.

Lamb Fat

Lamb fat on a chop or roast is strong and must be trimmed away. You can always moisten lamb with gluten-free bacon, olive oil, or butter; just don't cook the fat.

THICK AND HEARTY LANCASHIRE LAMB STEW

Make a double recipe and freeze half for another busy day. Cook beans the old-fashioned way or use canned cannellini beans instead.

Serves 6

INGREDIENTS:

¼ cup olive oil

½ cup brown rice flour

1 teaspoon salt

½ teaspoon ground black pepper

2 pounds lamb stew meat

2 slices gluten-free bacon, chopped

4 cloves garlic

2 large onions, sliced or diced

2 carrots, peeled and chopped

2 bay leaves

2 cups gluten-free chicken broth

1 cup dry white wine

½ bunch parsley

2 tablespoons dried rosemary

Juice and zest of ½ lemon

2 teaspoons gluten-free Worcestershire sauce

1 (1-pound) bag great northern beans, soaked overnight and then simmered for 5 hours, or 3 (13-ounce) cans white beans, drained

1. Heat the olive oil in a large skillet.

2. In a shallow bowl, combine the flour, salt, and pepper. Dredge the lamb in the flour mixture.

3. Brown the meat in the hot oil, about 1 minute on each side. Remove from pan and drain.

4. In the same pan, cook the bacon until crisp. Place lamb and bacon in a 6-quart slow cooker. Add remaining ingredients to the slow cooker.

5. Cover and cook on high for 4 hours or on low for 8 hours.

CURRIED LAMB GRILLED ON SKEWERS

Try grilling these and serving with the your favorite dipping sauce. These were a huge crowd pleaser at my wedding reception!

Serves 4

INGREDIENTS:

½ cup peanut oil

1 teaspoon gluten-free curry powder

2 tablespoons lemon juice

4 cloves garlic, minced

½ teaspoon ground coriander

2 teaspoons hot sauce, or to taste

1 pound bite-sized lamb chunks, from the leg or shoulder

1. Soak 8–10 wooden skewers in water for at least 40 minutes.

2. Mix the peanut oil, curry, lemon juice, garlic, coriander, and hot sauce together in a bowl.

3. Add the lamb and turn to coat with the marinade. Cover and refrigerate for 2 hours.

4. String the lamb on the skewers and grill over hot coals for 4 minutes per side. Serve hot.

LAMB WITH GARLIC, LEMON, AND ROSEMARY

You can use the spice rub in this recipe as a marinade by applying it to the leg of lamb several hours (or up to one full day) before cooking. The red wine in this dish can be replaced with gluten-free chicken or beef broth.

Serves 4

INGREDIENTS:

4 cloves garlic, crushed

1 tablespoon fresh rosemary, chopped

1 tablespoon olive oil

½ teaspoon salt

1 teaspoon ground pepper

1 (3-pound) leg of lamb

1 large lemon, cut into ¼" slices

½ cup red wine

1. In a small bowl mix together garlic, rosemary, olive oil, salt, and pepper. Rub this mixture onto the leg of lamb.

2. Place a few lemon slices in the bottom of a greased 4-quart slow cooker. Place spice-rubbed lamb on top of lemon slices.

3. Add remaining lemon slices on top of lamb. Pour wine around the lamb.

4. Cook on low heat for 8–10 hours or on high for 4–6 hours.

Using Different Cuts of Affordable Meat

You could also use this spice rub on a beef rump roast, beef or lamb shanks, or any cheaper cut of meat. The flavors will infuse into the meat and make a delicious base for a stew, soup, or casserole.

HERBED LAMB CHOPS

This simple herb rub would make a fun Christmas gift to give to friends or family members who enjoy cooking! Include this recipe with a small jar of the rub.

Serves 4

INGREDIENTS:

1 medium onion, sliced

1 teaspoon dried oregano

½ teaspoon dried thyme

½ teaspoon garlic powder

¼ teaspoon salt

⅛ teaspoon ground pepper

2 pounds (about 8) lamb loin chops

1 tablespoon olive oil

1. Place onion on the bottom of a greased 4-quart slow cooker.

2. In a small bowl, mix together oregano, thyme, garlic powder, salt, and pepper. Rub herb mixture over the lamb chops.

3. Place herb-rubbed lamb chops over the sliced onions. Drizzle olive oil over the lamb chops.

4. Cook on high for 3 hours or on low for 6 hours, until tender.

BACON-WRAPPED LEG OF LAMB

Serve this holiday classic with steamed asparagus, cranberries, and mashed potatoes. Don't forget to make gravy (see sidebar) with the savory dripping from this delicious cut of meat.

Serves 4

INGREDIENTS:

1 (4-pound) bone-in leg of lamb

3 cloves garlic, slivered into small spears

½ teaspoon salt

½ teaspoon pepper

8 slices gluten-free bacon

1 tablespoon olive oil

1. Make about 24 (½"-deep) cuts evenly around the lamb. Place a garlic spear into each slit. Sprinkle salt and pepper over lamb.

2. Lay bacon evenly over and around the lamb. To keep the bacon in place, attach with toothpick halves. Drizzle lamb with olive oil.

3. Cook on high for 3–4 hours or on low for 6–8 hours, depending on how well done you prefer the lamb. Check the lamb after 2½ hours on high for a medium-rare roast. You can also use a meat thermometer. For medium rare, the internal temperature should reach 140–150°F; for well done the temperature should reach 160°F or above.

Gluten-Free Lamb Gravy

Place 1 tablespoon oil or butter in a small saucepan. Whisk in 2–3 tablespoons brown rice flour. Cook the flour for a minute, whisking constantly so it doesn't burn. Add 1–2 cups lamb drippings (and additional gluten-free chicken or beef broth if needed), and whisk over medium heat until gravy thickens. Add salt and pepper if needed. Keep gravy warm in a small 1½-quart slow cooker until dinner is served.

CHAPTER 10

SEAFOOD

SOLE FLORENTINE

Sole is an adaptable fish; mild and sweet, it goes with many different flavors. Frozen spinach works fine for this. Just make sure you completely squeeze the water out.

Serves 4

INGREDIENTS:

3 tablespoons unsalted butter

1 shallot, minced

1 clove garlic, minced

3 tablespoons cornstarch

2 (10-ounce) packages frozen chopped spinach, thawed, moisture squeezed out

⅔ cup heavy cream

¼ teaspoon nutmeg

4 sole fillets, rinsed and dried on paper towels

1 large egg, well beaten

½ cup rice or potato flour

Salt and pepper, to taste

⅔ cup extra-virgin olive oil

¼ cup Parmesan cheese, fresh or gluten-free

1. In a skillet over medium heat, melt the butter and sauté the shallot and garlic until softened, about 5 minutes. Blend in the cornstarch, cooking until smooth.

2. Add the spinach, cream, and nutmeg. Cook and stir until thickened, about 3–4 minutes. Pour into a 2-quart baking dish treated with nonstick spray and set aside.

3. Dip the pieces of sole in the beaten egg. Then, on a sheet of wax paper, mix the flour, salt, and pepper. Dredge the sole in the flour mixture.

4. In a separate skillet, heat the olive oil over medium heat. Add the sole and sauté until lightly browned, about 2–3 minutes each side.

5. Arrange the sole over the spinach in the baking dish. Sprinkle with the cheese. Run under the broiler until very brown and hot, about 3 minutes.

MARYLAND-STYLE CRAB CAKES WITH COUNTRY HAM

The addition of country ham balances the sweetness of the crabmeat and gives the whole thing a great lift.

Makes 6 crab cakes

INGREDIENTS:

½ cup gluten-free mayonnaise

2 large eggs

1 teaspoon gluten-free Dijon-style mustard

1 teaspoon gluten-free Worcestershire sauce

Salt and 1 teaspoon red pepper flakes, or to taste

1 tablespoon fresh lemon juice

1 cup gluten-free corn bread crumbs, divided

1¼ pounds lump blue crabmeat

Oil for frying

Lemon wedges, for garnish

1. In a large bowl, mix the mayonnaise, eggs, mustard, Worcestershire sauce, salt, pepper flakes, and lemon juice. Stir until well mixed.

2. Add half the corn bread crumbs and gently toss in the crabmeat. Form 8 cakes and coat each with more corn bread crumbs.

3. In a deep skillet, over medium heat, bring the oil to 300°F. Fry the cakes, turning after five minutes, until golden brown. Serve with lemon wedges.

Topping Off Crab Cakes

Some cooks add finely chopped onion to their crab cake mixture. Others use chives. You can also add finely chopped parsley. Some like their crab cakes with gluten-free tartar sauce, others with gluten-free cocktail sauce.

CRISPY BEER-BATTERED FRIED SHRIMP

You can do everything in advance but fry the shrimp. Beer batter is delicious and can be used with other seafood as well as with chicken.

Serves 4

INGREDIENTS:

½ cup corn flour

¼ teaspoon salt

1 tablespoon butter, melted

1 large whole egg

½ cup flat gluten-free beer

1¼ pounds large shrimp, peeled and deveined

¼ cup golden rum

2 tablespoons gluten-free soy sauce

1 egg white, beaten stiff

Light oil such as canola, for frying

1. Make the batter in advance by mixing together the first five ingredients. Let stand for an hour.

2. Marinate the cleaned shrimp in rum and soy sauce for 20 minutes, covered, in the refrigerator.

3. In a deep skillet or deep fryer, bring the oil for frying to 375°F. Add the final egg white to the batter. Dip the shrimp in the batter a few times to coat. Gently lower a few shrimp at a time into the oil. Fry for about 4 minutes, or until well browned. Drain on paper towels and serve.

Using Fresh Shrimp

Never use precooked shrimp for cooking. It will be rubbery and tough. Cooked shrimp is pink; raw shrimp is grayish or white. It may be a bit of trouble to peel and clean shrimp, but it's well worth it to get the succulent flavor of good fresh shrimp.

CHINESE SHRIMP BALLS

Serve with hot mustard or any other Asian sauce. For a variation, serve with tartar sauce.

Serves 8–10 as an appetizer

INGREDIENTS:

1 pound raw medium shrimp, peeled and deveined

1 large egg

1 tablespoon dry sherry

2 teaspoons gluten-free soy sauce

1 teaspoon sugar

1 tablespoon cornstarch

1 cup lean ground pork

2 scallions, chopped

3 cups oil for frying

1. Adding slowly, place the ingredients, except the cooking oil, in the food processor. Pulse, and scrape the sides often.

2. In a deep skillet or deep fryer, heat the oil to 360°F. Carefully drop balls by the teaspoonful into the oil. When golden, after about 3–4 minutes, place them on a serving platter lined with paper towels or napkins to drain. Serve and enjoy.

SEAFOOD À LA KING

You can make the sauce the day before and add the seafood at the last minute. Serve with rice or stuffed into gluten-free crepes.

Serves 4

INGREDIENTS:

½ cup shallots, minced

¼ cup unsalted butter

20 small white mushrooms, cut in half

20 pearl onions, fresh or frozen, cut in half

2 tablespoons cornstarch

2 ounces cold water

1 tablespoon tomato paste

2 tablespoons brandy

1½ cups heavy cream

Salt and pepper, to taste

½ pound medium to large shrimp, cleaned and deveined

½ pound bay scallops

2 tablespoons red salmon caviar, for garnish

1. In a large skillet, sauté the shallots in the butter over moderate heat for 5 minutes. Add the mushrooms and pearl onions. Stir, cooking for a few more minutes.

2. Mix the cornstarch with cold water and add to the pan, stirring to blend. Blend in the tomato paste and brandy. Warm the cream slightly then stir it into the sauce in the pan. (You can prepare this dish in advance up to this point. Store in the refrigerator until ready to serve.)

3. Reheat the sauce but do not boil. Add salt and pepper to taste, and then add the seafood. When the shrimp turns pink, the dish is done. Garnish with caviar and serve.

Long Live the King!

This dish was created at the Brighton Beach Hotel on Long Island, New York, by Chef George Greenwald for his boss E. Clarke King, II. It became very popular when Campbell's came out with canned cream of mushroom soup, used as a base.

SHRIMP AND LOBSTER SALAD

Try using different citrus fruits and mixing in different vegetables. Use almonds instead of peanuts. And if you like cilantro, use that instead of parsley.

Serves 4

INGREDIENTS:

1 cup gluten-free mayonnaise

1 teaspoon gluten-free Dijon mustard

Juice of ½ lime and 1 teaspoon zest

1 teaspoon gluten-free soy sauce

1 tablespoon gluten-free chili sauce

1 teaspoon minced garlic

Salt and pepper, to taste

Meat of 1 small (1½-pound) lobster, cooked

½ pound cleaned and cooked medium shrimp

¼ cup mixed, snipped fresh dill weed, and chopped fresh parsley

1 tablespoon capers

4 beds of shredded lettuce

1. Mix together the mayonnaise, mustard, lime juice and zest, soy sauce, chili sauce, minced garlic, salt, and pepper.

2. Just before serving, mix the sauce with the seafood. Garnish with snipped fresh dill weed and chopped parsley, sprinkle with capers, and serve over a bed of lettuce.

POACHED MONKFISH IN CAPER BUTTER SAUCE

Monkfish is a mild, sweet fish that is wonderful cooked in many ways. It is delicious poached, broiled, or baked.

Serves 4

INGREDIENTS:

1½ pounds monkfish, cut in 4 serving pieces

½ cup potato flour

2 tablespoons olive oil

¼ cup dry white wine

¼ cup gluten-free chicken broth

1 tablespoon butter

2 tablespoons capers

Salt and pepper, to taste

Paprika and lemon wedges, for garnish

1. Dredge the fish in flour, then in a large saute pan, sauté over medium heat in olive oil. Turn after 4 minutes.

2. Add the wine, broth, butter, and capers. Simmer (poach) for about 8 minutes, or until the fish is cooked through. Place fish on a warm plate; reduce sauce to ½ and pour over fish.

3. Sprinkle with salt, pepper, and paprika. Serve with lemon wedges.

Monkfish—Poor Man's Lobster

Oddly enough, monkfish was once considered a throwaway fish! It has a slightly hooded flange around its head, like a monk's cowl. It is delicious poached, broiled, or baked. It loves various sauces. The only thing to remember is not to overcook it. Monkfish, when poached in clam juice, water, or white wine, puffs, growing lighter and fluffier. Then all you have to do is add lemon and butter, and it's very much like lobster.

GOLDEN SAUTÉED DIVER SCALLOPS

This recipe calls for caramelizing the scallops, which is absolutely terrific! And it tastes wonderful. You'll find lots of excuses to serve these.

Serves 4

INGREDIENTS:

½ cup corn flour

2 tablespoons white sugar

1 teaspoon salt

½ teaspoon white pepper

1½ pounds large diver scallops, each about 2 inches across

2 tablespoons unsalted butter

2 tablespoons olive oil

1. On a sheet of wax paper, mix the flour, sugar, salt, and pepper. Roll the scallops in the flour mixture.

2. In a large skillet, heat the butter and oil over medium-high heat. Add the scallops and watch them. They will brown quickly. Cook for 2–3 minutes per side. Serve with any of your favorite sauces.

BAKED RISOTTO WITH SEAFOOD

This is perfect for a dinner party where you want to impress your guests but don't want to spend all day making the risotto.

Serves 6–8

INGREDIENTS:

3 tablespoons extra-virgin olive oil

1 tablespoon butter

1 small onion, minced

1 clove garlic, minced

Salt and pepper, to taste

1 tablespoon fresh rosemary, crushed, or 2 teaspoons dried, broken up

1 teaspoon saffron threads

1 cup long grain rice, uncooked

2½ cups gluten-free chicken broth

2 tablespoons Marsala or sherry wine

1 pound raw medium shrimp, peeled, deveined, and rinsed; or 1 pound bay scallops, rinsed; or 1 pound crabmeat

1. Preheat oven to 350°F.

2. In an oven-safe skillet over medium heat, heat the oil and butter. Add the onion and garlic, and sauté until softened for 2–3 minutes.

3. Add salt, pepper, rosemary, saffron, and rice, and mix to cover the rice with the oil. Add the broth, cover tightly, and place in the oven.

4. After the rice has cooked for 10 minutes, add the Marsala or sherry wine. Return to the oven and cook for another 10 minutes.

5. Add the shrimp or other seafood and continue to bake for 7 minutes more. Uncover and serve.

Instead of Mushrooms, Try . . .

You can use shrimp, scallops, crabmeat, lobster, or crayfish in place of mushrooms. The trick is to put any raw shellfish in at the end of the cooking so it will not be overdone. By the same token, you can substitute 2 cups sliced mushrooms that have been sautéed separately in butter for the seafood. Be careful of imitation seafood, such as imitation crabmeat, as it can contain gluten. Read the food labels!

OYSTER STEW À LA GRAND CENTRAL OYSTER BAR

Here's a chance to replicate the cooking at New York City's Oyster Bar, a legendary restaurant located in Grand Central Terminal.

Serves 4

INGREDIENTS:

2 tablespoons unsalted butter

2 tablespoons gluten-free Worcestershire sauce

1 cup bottled or fresh clam broth, gluten-free

2 tablespoons cornstarch mixed with 3 tablespoons cold water

⅛ teaspoon gluten-free cayenne pepper

1 quart shucked oysters, drained

2 cups fat-free milk

1 cup heavy cream

Sprinkle of celery salt and paprika

4 pats butter

Oyster crackers, gluten-free

1. Mix 2 tablespoons butter, Worcestershire, and clam broth together in a saucepan over medium heat. Whisk in the cornstarch/water mixture. Add the cayenne, oysters, milk, and heavy cream.

2. Heat carefully over a low flame until quite thick, stirring frequently for about 10 minutes. Just before serving, sprinkle with celery salt and paprika, then float a pat of butter on top of each bowl. Serve with gluten-free oyster crackers on the side.

A Secret Ingredient?

The Oyster Bar, in Grand Central Terminal in New York City, has a unique advantage in cooking soups and stews. Steam from the railroad is piped into the restaurant, with little jets heating stainless steel bowls. The steam is at exactly boiling temperature and never varies.

RHODE ISLAND CLAM CHOWDER

This recipe is very traditional. Many cooks now substitute bacon for salt pork, but it's better to make it the traditional way.

Serves 4

INGREDIENTS:

2 dozen cherrystone clams (2 inches across)

3 ounces salt pork, chopped finely

1 large onion, chopped

1 carrot, peeled and chopped

2 stalks celery with tops, chopped fine

2 large Idaho potatoes, peeled and chopped

1 tablespoon cornstarch (more if you like it really thick)

2 bay leaves

1 teaspoon dried thyme

1 teaspoon celery salt

1 tablespoon gluten-free Worcestershire sauce

3 cups gluten-free clam broth

Freshly ground black pepper, to taste

½ cup chopped fresh parsley, for garnish

1. Scrub the clams and place them in a large pot. Add 2 cups water, cover, and boil until the clams open. Remove them to a large bowl and let cool; reserve the juice. When cool, remove the clams, discard the shells, and chop the clams in a food processor.

2. In a soup pot, fry the salt pork until crisp. Drain on paper towels. Add the vegetables to the pot and sauté until soft, about 10 minutes over medium heat. Blend in the cornstarch and cook for 2 more minutes, stirring.

3. Add the reserved clam juice and the bay leaves, thyme, and celery salt to the pot. Stir in the Worcestershire sauce, clam broth, the chopped clams, and the salt pork. Cover and simmer for ½ hour. Before serving, remove bay leaf. Add black pepper to taste, garnish with chopped fresh parsley, and serve hot.

Is That Clam Alive or Dead?

Never eat a dead clam. Always run them under cold water and scrub vigorously with a brush. To test for life, tap two clams together. You should hear a sharp click, not a hollow thud. If the clam sounds hollow, tap it again, and then, if still hollow-sounding, discard it.

SHRIMP BISQUE WITH SCALLOPS

This is an elegant first course or a delicious lunch. It's very easy to make in advance, adding the cream at the last minute when heating.

Serves 4–6

INGREDIENTS:

2 minced shallots

1 clove garlic, minced

2 tablespoons butter

2 tablespoons cornstarch

1 tablespoon tomato paste

4 cups gluten-free shrimp shell broth or bottled clam broth

½ pound shrimp, cleaned and deveined

½ pound bay scallops

1 cup heavy cream

Salt and pepper, to taste

1 tablespoon dry sherry per bowl of soup

Chopped parsley, for garnish

1. In a stockpot, sauté the shallots and garlic in the butter for 2–3 minutes.

2. Blend in cornstarch and tomato paste. Add broth and bring to a boil. Then lower heat and simmer for 10 minutes.

3. Spoon in the shrimp and scallops and cook for 2–3 minutes.

4. Let cool for 5 minutes. Using blender, blend in batches until puréed. Return to the pot and add cream. Taste for salt and pepper, adding as necessary.

5. Ladle into bowls, spoon in the sherry and garnish with parsley.

SHRIMP AND COCONUT SOUP

This can be served chilled or hot. You can add 1 cup of cooked rice or quinoa to this, but it is not necessary.

Serves 4

INGREDIENTS:

2 shallots, minced

2 teaspoons peanut oil or other vegetable oil

2 tablespoons cornstarch

1½ cups gluten-free Shrimp Shell Broth (see sidebar), warmed

½ cup dry white wine

1 cup unsweetened coconut milk

1 cup cooked rice or quinoa (optional)

1 pound raw medium shrimp, shelled and deveined, chopped

1 teaspoon fresh basil, finely chopped

Salt and freshly ground white pepper, to taste

1. In a large stockpot, sauté the shallots in the oil until soft, about 10 minutes over medium heat. Stir in the cornstarch and cook until very thick.

2. Add the liquid ingredients and cook, covered, over very low heat for 30 minutes.

3. Stir in the rice or quinoa, and the shrimp; heat until the shrimp turns pink. Add basil, salt, and white pepper, to taste, and serve hot or cold.

Shrimp Shell Broth

Shrimp Shell Broth makes a flavorful addition to seafood soup. Next time you are preparing shrimp, reserve the shells. Add 1 cup water, 1 cup wine, and a bay leaf to the shells from a pound of shrimp. Bring to a boil, lower heat, and simmer, covered, for 20 minutes. Strain and use as broth in your soup.

CHINESE-STYLE CRAB IN RED CHILI SAUCE

Ever since Marco Polo brought pasta to Italy, Italians and the rest of the world have loved it. This dish could have been one that old Polo loved.

Serves 4

INGREDIENTS:

¼ cup peanut oil

4 cloves garlic, minced

1 bunch scallions, minced

2" fresh gingerroot, peeled and minced

4–6 Scotch bonnet chilies, or to taste, cored, seeded, and minced

¼ cup gluten-free dark soy sauce

2 fresh tomatoes, rinsed, cored, and chopped

1 cup canned crabmeat, gluten-free (imitation can contain gluten)

½ cup dry white wine or rice wine

1 (8-ounce) package medium-thick rice noodles

1. Heat the oil in a large frying pan or wok.

2. Add the vegetables and stir-fry for 3 minutes. Then stir in the soy sauce, tomatoes, crabmeat, and wine.

3. Boil noodles according to package directions, then add to the sauce and let the liquid soak in. Serve hot.

CURRIED SHRIMP WITH AVOCADOS

Adapting Asian flavors to American lifestyles can produce delightful dishes such as this. Quick and simply made, it's a fine lunch or light supper served with rice.

Serves 4

INGREDIENTS:

¾ cup gluten-free mayonnaise

2 teaspoons gluten-free curry powder

Juice of 1 lime

1 teaspoon hot chili oil or hot pepper sauce, such as Tabasco

½ pound raw medium shrimp, peeled and deveined

4 ripe avocados, halved, peeled, and pitted

Hungarian sweet or hot paprika, to taste

Dry roasted peanuts, for garnish

1. Preheat oven to 350°F.

2. Mix the mayonnaise with the curry, lime juice, and hot chili oil. Chop the shrimp and mix it with the mayonnaise sauce.

3. Place the avocado halves in a baking dish coated with nonstick spray. Spoon the shrimp and sauce mixture into the avocados. Sprinkle with paprika and peanuts.

4. Bake the shrimp-stuffed avocados for 20 minutes. You can vary this by adding chopped tart apple, pineapple, or red grapes.

How Hot Is Too Hot?

Any supermarket has dozens of bottles of various kinds of hot sauce, from Jamaican to Chinese to African to, of course, Asian. The degrees of heat and other flavorings such as garlic, ginger, etc., vary. However, for the flavors of the food to come through, use only as much as you find adds piquancy—don't burn your tongue or you will kill valuable taste buds. Always check labels to ensure they are gluten-free.

LOBSTER WITH SHERRY SAUCE

This adaptation is a unique way to serve lobster. Garnish with fresh lemon wedges.

Serves 4–6

INGREDIENTS:

4 chicken lobsters, 1–1¼ pounds each

1 teaspoon gluten-free Asian five-spice powder

1 clove garlic, minced

1 teaspoon parsley

¼ cup sesame seed oil

¼ cup sherry

Juice of ½ lemon

2 tablespoons minced gingerroot

1. Boil the lobsters for 20 minutes, then split them and crack the claws. Leave in shell for a beautiful presentation.

2. Preheat the broiler to 500°F.

3. In a saucepan, mix the rest of the ingredients together to make the sauce. Bring to a boil and spoon over the lobsters.

4. Broil for 3 minutes. Serve.

OLD MARYLAND CORN AND CRABMEAT PIE

You can cut the wedges as small as you like to make a wonderful appetizer, or cut the pie into fourths for a lunch or supper dish.

Serves 8 as a first course, 4–6 as a main course

INGREDIENTS:

2 tablespoons butter

1 medium onion, chopped

1 carrot, chopped

2 tablespoons cornstarch

½ teaspoon gluten-free English mustard

½ cup gluten-free chicken broth

½ cup dry white wine

1 cup heavy cream

1 teaspoon gluten-free Worcestershire sauce

1 (10-ounce) package frozen corn kernels

1 pound fresh or frozen lump crabmeat (careful to avoid imitation crabmeat that can contain gluten)

½ teaspoon dried dill or 1 teaspoon minced fresh

⅛ teaspoon freshly grated nutmeg

Salt and pepper, to taste

Gluten-free 10" pie crust or 2 cups mashed potatoes

1. Preheat oven to 350°F. In a saucepan, heat butter and add onion and carrot. Cook, stirring, until the onion and carrot are softened. Add the cornstarch and mustard. Simmer until thickened and vegetables are tender.

2. In a separate pan, warm the chicken broth and wine. Slowly add to the saucepan, stirring into the onion-and-carrot mixture. Stir until smooth and thickened.

3. Add all remaining ingredients but the crust. Stir to mix. Place in a buttered pie pan and cover with crust or mashed potatoes.

4. Place in oven and bake for about 30 minutes.

Crabmeat

There is a lot of crab and fake crabmeat around. The very best is Maryland blue crab, in lumps or flakes; it's also the most expensive, running up to $15 a pound. Fake crab, or surimi, is made from fish that has been cooked with the water and juices from crabmeat; it is cheap. Blue crabs are rounded and squat, unlike the gigantic, spider-like legs of Alaskan king crab, or the finger-like clusters of snow crab. There's nothing like a good fresh crab, whether from Alaska or Maryland. Imitation seafood can contain gluten so check the labels!

MEXICAN STYLE CORN TORTILLAS STUFFED WITH SHRIMP AND AVOCADO

This is a fine lunch or brunch dish on a hot day, and is very good with margaritas or bloody marys.

Makes 6 tortillas

INGREDIENTS:

6 gluten-free corn tortillas or 6 gluten-free crepes

24 extra-large raw shrimp, peeled and deveined

½ cup dry white wine

6 medium avocados, peeled and sliced

1 red onion, thinly sliced

Juice of 2 fresh limes

1 teaspoon freshly ground coriander seeds

1 tablespoon dried red pepper flakes

1 cup fresh or jarred gluten-free salsa

1 cup gluten-free sour cream

½ cup chopped cilantro or parsley, for garnish

1. Toast the tortillas or crepes and place on serving plates.

2. Poach the cleaned shrimp in the white wine until the shrimp is pink and curled, and drain.

3. Stack 4 shrimp on each tortilla, add the avocado and onion, and sprinkle with lime juice, coriander, and pepper flakes.

4. Spoon salsa over each tortilla, add a dollop of sour cream, and garnish with either cilantro or parsley.

The Right Flour

You can make regular corn tortillas—the only hard part is getting them to be thin and crisp as opposed to thick and hard to eat. Serious Latin cooks buy a press to stamp out their tortillas. Or you can very carefully buy "flour" tortillas, but be sure the flour is purely corn flour and gluten-free.

CORN AND LOBSTER NEWBURG

Have your fishmonger cook and remove the meat from three small (1¼ pounds each) lobsters, or buy frozen lobster meat. Serve with rice and salad.

Serves 6

INGREDIENTS:

2 tablespoons unsalted butter

2 shallots, minced

1 clove garlic, minced

4 egg yolks

2 cups heavy cream

1 cup fresh corn, cut off the cob, or frozen corn, blanched and drained

1½ pounds, or 4 cups, lobster meat (avoid imitation crabmeat that can contain gluten)

2 tablespoons dry sherry

2 tablespoons chopped parsley, for garnish

1. In a skillet over medium heat, melt the butter and sauté the shallots and garlic for 5–6 minutes, until soft.

2. In a small bowl, beat the egg yolks.

3. Put the cream into a large pan over medium heat; scald the cream but do not boil. Remove from the heat.

4. Mix 2 tablespoons of hot cream into the beaten egg yolks and whisk vigorously.

5. Pour the egg mixture into the hot cream and return to the heat. Continue to whisk until thick. Add the corn and lobster. Heat, stirring, until very hot but not boiling. Add the sherry. Serve garnished with parsley.

Extra Egg Whites or Yolks

The recipe for Lobster Newburg calls for 4 egg yolks. This gives you the opportunity to make a marvelous dessert meringue with the whites. Or if you have a recipe that calls for whites and not yolks, you can make mayonnaise or custard with the yolks. There is a use for everything but the shells.

ZUCCHINI SAUCE FOR SEAFOOD

This is excellent with grilled shrimp, scallops, or poultry.

Makes 1½ cups

INGREDIENTS:

1 cup steamed zucchini

2 cloves garlic

¼ cup gluten-free chicken broth

2 tablespoons minced shallot

2 tablespoons lime juice

¼ cup olive oil

Salt and Tabasco sauce, to taste

Put all ingredients in a blender. Purée. Serve warm or cold.

Making Interesting Sauces and Coulis

When you purée such vegetables as roasted red peppers and cooked summer squash and zucchini, you get a nice, creamy base for flavors. Add your favorite herbs and fresh lemon, lime, or orange juice. You can adjust the heat to your personal taste. You can also add cream, gluten-free sour cream, or gluten-free mayonnaise for extra smoothness.

SPICY SPINACH AND LOBSTER SAUCE

Quinoa pasta is high in protein and can be used as you would almost any pasta. Rice pasta is found in Asian markets and some supermarkets.

Serves 4

INGREDIENTS:

1 (1½-pound) lobster

2 tablespoons butter

2 tablespoons cornstarch

1 cup gluten-free hot chicken or clam broth

1 cup heavy cream

3 cups fresh baby spinach, rinsed and stems trimmed

1 tablespoon dry sherry

Pinch ground nutmeg

1 teaspoon hot red pepper flakes or gluten-free cayenne pepper

Salt and pepper, to taste

1. Plunge the lobster into plenty of boiling salted water. Cook for 15 minutes. Cool; crack the shell and remove the meat. Set the meat aside.

2. Melt the butter and add the cornstarch, stirring until smooth. Whisk in the chicken broth. Add the cream and heat.

3. Stir in the spinach and cook until wilted. Add the sherry, nutmeg, red pepper flakes, and reserved lobster. Sprinkle with salt and pepper. Serve over quinoa or rice pasta.

A Versatile Pasta

Any sauce that you would use on wheat pasta can be used on rice pasta—from a rich Alfredo sauce to a robust marinara sauce.

HERBED TILAPIA STEW

Any type of white fish fillets (such as haddock or cod) will also work in this recipe. Fish cooks very, very quickly even on the low setting in a slow cooker, so this is one recipe you will need to set a timer for.

Serves 6

INGREDIENTS:

2 pounds frozen boneless tilapia fillets

4 tablespoons butter

1 (14½-ounce) can diced tomatoes, with juice

4 cloves garlic, minced

½ cup sliced green onions

2 teaspoons gluten-free Thai fish sauce

2 tablespoons fresh thyme, chopped *or* 1 teaspoon dried thyme

1. Grease a 4-quart slow cooker with nonstick cooking spray. Place all ingredients in the slow cooker.

2. Cover and cook on high for 1½–2 hours or on low for 2½–3 hours. Watch the cooking time. If your fish fillets are very thin, you may need to reduce the cooking time.

3. When fish is cooked through, fillets will easily separate and flake with a fork. Break the fish up into the tomatoes and cooking liquids. Serve stew over cooked rice or gluten-free pasta.

SALMON WITH LEMON, CAPERS, AND ROSEMARY

Salmon is very moist and tender when cooked in the slow cooker. This is a great meal for couples or when you just need to cook something small. Serve it with steamed kale and baked potatoes.

Serves 2

INGREDIENTS:

8 ounces salmon

⅓ cup water

2 tablespoons lemon juice

3 thin slices fresh lemon

1 tablespoon nonpareil capers

½ teaspoon minced, fresh rosemary

1. Place the salmon on the bottom of a 2½-quart slow cooker. Pour water and lemon juice over the fish.

2. Arrange lemon slices in a single layer on top of the fish. Sprinkle with capers and rosemary.

3. Cook on low for 2 hours. Discard lemon slices prior to serving.

SHRIMP RISOTTO

Shrimp-flavored broth gives this risotto a flavor boost. If you don't want to take the time to make it, substitute 1 cup of additional gluten-free chicken broth and stir a pinch of crushed saffron threads directly into the slow cooker.

Serves 6

INGREDIENTS:

1 tablespoon olive oil

2 tablespoons butter, melted

2 medium white onions, peeled and diced

2 cups uncooked arborio rice

½ cup dry white wine

1 cup shrimp-infused broth (see sidebar)

5 cups gluten-free chicken broth

1½ pounds raw large shrimp, peeled and deveined

½ cup freshly grated Parmesan cheese

3 tablespoons fresh flat-leaf parsley, minced

½ teaspoon salt

1. Add the oil, butter, and onions to the slow cooker. Stir to coat the onions in the oil. Cover and cook on high for 30 minutes or until the onion is transparent.

2. Stir in the rice; continue to stir for several minutes or until the rice turns translucent. Add the wine and the shrimp-infused broth, along with the chicken broth. Stir together well. Cover and cook on high for 2½ hours or until the rice is cooked al dente.

3. Add the shrimp to the slow cooker atop the risotto. Cover and cook on high for 20 minutes or until the shrimp is pink. Stir in the cheese, parsley, and salt. Serve immediately.

Shrimp-Infused Broth

Add 1 cup gluten-free chicken broth and the shrimp shells from 1½ pounds shrimp to a saucepan. Bring to a boil over medium-high heat; reduce the heat and maintain a simmer for 15 minutes or until the shells are pink. Strain; crush a pinch of saffron threads and stir it into the broth.

COCONUT-LIME SHRIMP

This dish can be served as an appetizer or as a main dish on top of rice, quinoa, or a plate of gluten-free noodles.

Serves 4

INGREDIENTS:

1 large egg

½ cup all-purpose gluten-free flour

⅔ cup coconut milk

Juice from 2 limes

Zest from 1 lime

1½ teaspoons gluten-free baking powder

¼ cup plus 2 tablespoons coconut flour

1¼ cups finely shredded coconut

24 raw large shrimp, deveined with tails on

½ cup grapeseed oil

Fresh lime wedges, for squeezing

1. In medium bowl, combine the egg, all-purpose flour, coconut milk, lime juice, lime zest, and baking powder.

2. Place ¼ cup plus 2 tablespoons coconut flour and shredded coconut in 2 separate bowls.

3. Hold shrimp by tail, and dredge in flour, shaking off excess flour. Dip in egg/milk mixture; allow excess to drip off. Roll shrimp in coconut, and place on a baking sheet lined with wax paper. Refrigerate for 30 minutes.

4. Heat oil in grill pan or skillet.

5. Sauté the shrimp in batches: Cook, turning once, for 2–3 minutes, or until golden brown.

6. Using tongs, remove shrimp to paper towels to drain. Serve warm with fresh lime wedges.

ORANGE-GINGER SALMON

This is so simple and only has a few ingredients. This wonderful marinade can be used on various meats and fish.

Serves 6

INGREDIENTS:

¾ cup orange juice

1 tablespoon honey

1 teaspoon gluten-free soy sauce

2 teaspoons balsamic vinegar

1 teaspoon finely chopped fresh gingerroot

2 pounds salmon fillet

Salt and ground black pepper, to taste

1. Preheat the oven to 400°F.

2. Place orange juice, honey, and soy sauce in a small saucepan over medium low heat. Cook and stir 10–15 minutes, until reduced by about ½ and thickened. Remove from heat, and allow to cool.

3. Stir balsamic vinegar and gingerroot into orange juice mixture.

4. Line a baking pan with parchment paper. Place salmon filets with the skin side down. Season with salt and pepper and pour half of the orange juice mixture on top of the salmon fillets.

5. Bake salmon for about 10–15 minutes until it easily flakes with a fork.

6. Cover the cooked salmon with the remaining orange juice mixture. Serve immediately.

All Salmon Is Not the Same

There are several varieties of salmon, with wild Alaskan salmon being the healthiest. Wild Alaskan salmon has a diet that is considered safe and healthy for the environment. Atlantic farm salmon may consume antibiotics and even food coloring. Always choose "wild salmon" over "farm salmon."

COD BROILED ON A BED OF PAPER-THIN POTATOES

Cod is one of the world's most beloved and versatile fish. It can be baked, broiled, steamed, poached, salted, or cooked with milk in a stew. This dish is simple yet delicious.

Serves 4

INGREDIENTS:

2 pounds of Idaho or Yukon Gold potatoes, peeled and sliced paper-thin

¼ cup extra-virgin olive oil

2 tablespoons butter, melted

Salt and pepper, to taste

4 cod fillets or steaks, about 5 ounces each

Salt, pepper, and butter for the fish

Chopped parsley and lemon wedges, for garnish

1. Preheat the oven to 400°F.

2. In a baking pan that has been treated with nonstick spray, toss the thinly sliced potatoes with oil and melted butter, salt, and pepper.

3. Bake the potatoes for 40 minutes or until the top is brown and crisp and the inside soft.

4. When the potatoes are done, lay the fish on top, sprinkle with salt and pepper, dot with butter, and reheat the oven to broil.

5. Broil until the fish is done, 8–10 minutes, depending on the thickness of the fish. If the potatoes start to burn, move the pan to a lower shelf in the oven.

6. Sprinkle with chopped parsley and serve with lemon wedges.

PARMESAN-CRUSTED TILAPIA

These crispy tilapia fillets would be perfect served with rice and a green salad. Feel free to sprinkle extra, freshly grated Parmesan cheese on top too.

Serves 2

INGREDIENTS:

2 tablespoons extra-virgin olive oil, divided

¼ cup gluten-free bread crumbs or cornmeal

¼ cup freshly grated Parmesan cheese

1 teaspoon dried basil

½ teaspoon dried oregano

½ teaspoon onion powder

½ teaspoon red pepper flakes

½ teaspoon dried rosemary

2 cloves garlic, minced

½ teaspoon salt

¼ teaspoon ground black pepper

1 tablespoon freshly squeezed lemon juice

3–4 tilapia fillets, depending on their size, washed and dried

Extra-virgin olive oil for baking dish; can use a Misto sprayer

1. Preheat oven to 425°F.

2. Combine 1 tablespoon olive oil, bread crumbs, Parmesan cheese, seasonings, garlic, salt, and pepper in a medium-sized bowl. Stir to combine.

3. On a medium-sized plate, pour lemon juice.

4. Dip each fillet in lemon juice and then in the bread crumb mixture evenly on both sides. Place in baking dish that is well oiled. Sprinkle with remaining 1 tablespoon olive oil and additional Parmesan cheese, if you desire. Cover with aluminum foil so fish remains moist.

5. Bake for 20 minutes, or until the edges are browning. Take baking dish out of the oven and put the broiler on. Broil on medium for about 2 minutes so fillets get crispy.

CRISPY CALAMARI

This lovely dish can be served as an appetizer served with Spicy Marinara Sauce (see recipe in Chapter 12), or it can make a wonderful addition to any salad. This recipe is very simple and delicious.

Serves 10

INGREDIENTS:

1–2 cups peanut oil for frying (you may need more or less)

12 squid, cleaned and cut into small rings

¼ cup gluten-free cornmeal

¼ cornstarch

1 teaspoon sea salt

¼ teaspoon ground black pepper

2 cloves garlic, minced

½ tablespoon parsley, dried

1 teaspoon oregano

¼ cup gluten-free bread crumbs

1 lemon, sliced into wedges, for garnish

1. Preheat oil in a very large, deep-frying pan or wok. Oil must be very hot so let sit for a few minutes over medium heat.

2. While oil is heating, rinse squid with water and dry with paper towel. The calamari should be damp enough so the flour/bread crumbs will stick but not too damp or the mixture will clump.

3. In a medium-sized bowl, combine the cornmeal, cornstarch, salt, pepper, garlic, and seasonings. Dip the calamari rings into the batter, then coat with bread crumbs.

4. Deep-fry in small batches for 1–2 minutes, or until very light brown. Even if you think it may not be brown enough, stop cooking after 1–2 minutes or the calamari will be overcooked. Lay cooked calamari on paper towels to absorb any liquid. Serve with Spicy Marinara Sauce (see recipe in Chapter 12) or serve over a bed of greens in a salad.

CLASSIC CREOLE JAMBALAYA

This traditional one-dish meal is easy and scrumptious.

Serves 4

INGREDIENTS:

2 tablespoons butter

8 ounces gluten-free andouille sausage, cut into ¼" rounds

1 tablespoon paprika, ground

1 tablespoon cumin, ground

¼ teaspoon gluten-free cayenne pepper

1 teaspoon oregano, dried

2 cloves garlic, minced

1 cup diced tomatoes

1 green pepper, seeded and diced

1 celery stalk, diced

3 green onions, sliced

1 large carrot, shredded

1 bay leaf

½ teaspoon salt

1 cup brown rice, uncooked

2 cups gluten-free low-sodium chicken broth

1 pound large shrimp, peeled and deveined

Extra onion and chopped fresh parsley (optional)

1. Place the butter and sausage in a large pot or Dutch oven. Stir well and cook for 5–8 minutes, until sausage is fully cooked.

2. Stir in the paprika, cumin, cayenne pepper, oregano, and garlic. Cook for another minute until well combined.

3. Add the tomatoes, pepper, celery, onions, carrot, bay leaf, and salt.

4. Stir in the rice and broth, mix well, and bring to a boil. Cover and reduce heat to low. Let simmer about 50 minutes, until rice is fully cooked and tender.

5. Add the shrimp and let cook about 5 minutes. Remove bay leaf before serving. Garnish with extra chopped onion and fresh parsley if desired.

Jambalaya a Different Way

There are so many variations of jambalaya these days. You could add chicken, ham, or even duck. Traditional Creole Jambalaya typically uses tomatoes and chicken broth, whereas Cajun Jambalaya typically uses no tomatoes, just broth.

SOUTHERN FRIED OYSTERS

These are so crunchy on the outside and succulent on the inside, you will probably have to make an extra batch. Best when served with a squeeze of fresh lemon juice.

Serves 4

INGREDIENTS:

1 quart shucked oysters

½ cup corn flour

1 cup gluten-free cornmeal

1 teaspoon gluten-free baking powder

¼ teaspoon nutmeg

½ teaspoon dried parsley

½ teaspoon salt, or to taste

Freshly ground black pepper, to taste

2 large eggs, beaten

Oil for deep-frying

1. Place the oysters in a colander to drain.

2. In a large bowl, thoroughly mix the flour, cornmeal, baking powder, nutmeg, parsley, salt, and pepper.

3. Dip the oysters in the beaten egg and then in the flour-and-cornmeal mixture.

4. Bring the oil in a pot to 375°F and fry the oysters for about 3–4 minutes or until browned.

5. Remove with a slotted spoon. Drain on paper towels.

Seafood Loves to Be Saucy

Even the tastiest of mollusks and crustaceans love to be dipped or bathed in sauces. And there are a variety of options and substitutions. Any citrus can be substituted for just about any other—for example, limes for lemons, grapefruit for orange, and you can blend them together for intriguing outcomes using your own original flair for flavors. Throw in some ginger, gluten-free curry powder, or gluten-free mustard, and you'll add another layer of flavor.

FISH TACOS WITH TROPICAL FRUIT SALSA

These folded tacos can be stuffed with a number of different toppings. Fish tacos were derived from the Baja California region, which is actually part of Mexico.

Makes 12 tacos

INGREDIENTS:

½ teaspoon gluten-free chili powder

1 teaspoon oregano, dried

2 cloves garlic, minced

1 teaspoon cumin

1 teaspoon cilantro, minced

½ teaspoon red pepper flakes

1 pound boneless cod fillets, fresh, or frozen and thawed

Juice of one lime

Salt and pepper, to taste

12 gluten-free corn tortillas, warmed

Tropical Fruit Salsa (see Chapter 14)

Shredded lettuce, sliced avocado, gluten-free sour cream, extra cilantro, for garnish

1. Preheat oven to 375°F.

2. In a small bowl, mix chili powder, oregano, garlic, cumin, cilantro, and red pepper flakes.

3. Place cod fillets on a large sheet of aluminum foil and squeeze lime juice over top of them. With a spoon, sprinkle prepared seasonings on each side of the fillets. Season with salt and pepper. Fold the foil around the fish, and seal top to create a pouch. Place pouch on a baking tray.

4. Bake in the oven for 20 minutes or until fish easily flakes with a fork. Divide fish among the corn tortillas and top with Tropical Fruit Salsa. Serve with shredded lettuce, sliced avocado, gluten-free sour cream, and cilantro.

NEW ENGLAND CLAM CHOWDER

This delightful chowder will warm you up on the chilliest of winter days.

Serves 4–6

INGREDIENTS:

2 dozen cherrystone clams (2 inches across)

3 ounces salt pork, chopped finely

1 large onion, chopped

1 medium carrot, peeled and chopped

2 stalks celery with tops, chopped finely

2 large Idaho potatoes, peeled and chopped

1 tablespoon cornstarch (more if you like it really thick)

2 bay leaves

½ teaspoon dill weed, dried

1 teaspoon dried thyme

1 teaspoon celery salt

1 tablespoon gluten-free Worcestershire sauce

3 cups gluten-free clam broth

1 cup whole milk

1 cup heavy cream

1 tablespoon cornstarch

Freshly ground black pepper, to taste

½ cup chopped fresh parsley, for garnish

1. Scrub the clams and place them in a large pot. Add 2 cups water, cover, and boil until the clams open. Remove them to a large bowl and let cool; reserve the juice. When cool, remove the clams, discard the shells, and chop the clams in a food processor.

2. In a soup pot, fry the salt pork until crisp. Drain on paper towels, while reserving 1 tablespoon salt pork grease to cook vegetables.

3. Add the vegetables to the pot, and over medium heat, sauté until soft, about 10 minutes. Blend in the cornstarch and cook for 2 more minutes, stirring continuously.

4. Add the reserved clam juice, bay leaves, dill weed, thyme, and celery salt to the pot.

5. Stir in the Worcestershire sauce, clam broth, the chopped clams, and the salt pork. Bring to a slow boil before adding the milk, cream, and second tablespoon of cornstarch. Reduce the heat, cover, and simmer for ½ hour. After you add the milk and cream, *do not boil*. If you do, your soup is likely to curdle.

6. Taste and adjust seasonings, if necessary. Before serving, remove bay leaves. Add black pepper to taste, garnish with chopped fresh parsley, and serve hot.

MANHATTAN RED CLAM CHOWDER

With tender chunks of clam, this savory dish will satisfy the seafood lover in your family.

Serves 6

INGREDIENTS:

2 dozen cherrystone clams (2 inches across)

3 ounces salt pork, chopped finely

1 large onion, chopped

1 medium carrot, peeled and chopped

2 stalks celery with tops, chopped finely

2 large Idaho potatoes, peeled and chopped

1 tablespoon cornstarch (more if you like it really thick)

2 bay leaves

½ teaspoon dill weed, dried

1 teaspoon dried thyme

1 teaspoon celery salt

1 tablespoon gluten-free Worcestershire sauce

3 cups gluten-free clam broth

1 (28-ounce) can chopped tomatoes with their juice

Freshly ground black pepper, to taste

Parsley, chopped, for garnish

1. Scrub the clams and place them in a large pot. Add 2 cups water, cover, and boil until the clams open. Remove them to a large bowl and let cool; reserve the juice. When cool, remove the clams, discard the shells, and chop the clams in a food processor.

2. In a soup pot, fry the salt pork until crisp. Drain on paper towels, while reserving 1 tablespoon salt pork grease to cook the vegetables.

3. Add the vegetables to the pot, and over medium heat, sauté them until soft, about 10 minutes. Blend in the cornstarch and cook for 2 more minutes, stirring continuously.

4. Add the reserved clam juice, bay leaves, dill weed, thyme, and celery salt to the pot.

5. Stir in the Worcestershire sauce, clam broth, the chopped clams, and the salt pork. Reduce the heat, cover and simmer for ½ hour. Add the tomatoes. Cover and simmer for another ½ hour.

6. Before serving, remove bay leaves. Add black pepper to taste, garnish with chopped fresh parsley, and serve hot.

Tomato or Cream in Your Clam Chowder?

Manhattan clam chowder, made with tomatoes, is a latecomer to the chowder arena. During the eighteenth and nineteenth centuries, tomato-based chowder was banned in New England. In fact, tomatoes were suspect for many years—it was the invention and distribution of ketchup in the early twentieth century that brought the tomato into its own in America.

SPAGHETTI SQUASH WITH CREAMY VODKA AND SHRIMP SAUCE

The squash can be prepared a day in advance. Spaghetti squash is extremely versatile and tastes wonderful in many sauces, from a tomato-filled marinara to a meaty Bolognese.

Serves 6

INGREDIENTS:

1 large (4–5 pound) spaghetti squash, cooked

2 minced shallots

1 clove garlic, minced

2 tablespoons extra-virgin olive oil

1 tablespoon butter

1 tablespoon cornstarch

½ cup vodka

1 (28-ounce) can crushed tomatoes

1 cup heavy cream

1½ pounds medium shrimp, peeled and deveined

Salt and plenty of freshly ground pepper, to taste

½ cup each, chopped fresh parsley and basil

¼ cup gluten-free prosciutto, minced, for garnish

1. Place the cooked squash in a large bowl and keep warm while you make the sauce.

2. In a large skillet, sauté the minced shallots and garlic in a mixture of oil and butter for 2–3 minutes. When soft, add the cornstarch. Cook and stir over low heat until well blended, for 3–4 minutes.

3. Add the vodka and tomatoes. Cover and simmer gently for 20 minutes.

4. Stir in the cream and heat slowly, then add the shrimp. *Do not boil* after the cream has been added. When the shrimp turns pink, after about 2–3 minutes, pour over the spaghetti squash, and add salt and pepper to taste. Garnish with parsley, basil, and prosciutto.

ZUCCHINI WITH SEAFOOD, TOMATO, AND BACON

*This recipe can use up to the baseball bat–sized zucchinis, but it's better with the medium ones, about 10–12"
each.*

Serves 6

INGREDIENTS:

6 medium zucchinis

1 small onion, peeled and minced

2 cloves garlic, peeled and minced

1 serrano pepper, cored, seeded, and
minced

2 tablespoons butter or olive oil

1 cup cooked rice

1 cup crushed tomatoes

1 pound crabmeat or imitation gluten-free
crabmeat

2 tablespoons freshly squeezed lemon
juice

2 large eggs

1 tablespoon dried oregano leaves or 2
tablespoons fresh oregano

Salt and pepper, to taste

6 strips of gluten-free bacon, for garnish

1. Cut the top quarter off of the zucchinis, lengthwise. Hollow
   out the zucchinis with the small side of a melon baller or
   with a half-teaspoon measuring spoon; reserve pulp.

2. In a large skillet, sauté the onion, garlic, pepper, and
   zucchini pulp in the butter until soft. Add all remaining
   ingredients but the bacon.

3. Preheat the oven to 350°F.

4. Divide the filling among the zucchini boats. Lay a bacon
   strip on top of each stuffed zucchini. Place in a baking dish
   that you have prepared with nonstick spray or oil. Bake until
   the "boats" are hot and the bacon is brown and crisp. Serve
   hot or at room temperature.

Stuffed Vegetables

There are many vegetables you can successfully stuff with lots of
different delicious ingredients. Chopped meat, shrimp, fish, and
crabmeat make wonderful stuffing. A baked clam-stuffed mushroom
is also a real treat. Ricotta cheese, used to stuff pastas such as ravioli
and lasagna, also makes an excellent stuffing.

CHAPTER 11

VEGETARIAN MAINS

VEGETABLE LASAGNA PRIMAVERA WITH PASTA SUBSTITUTE

This vegetarian dish takes very little time and is excellent for a big family dinner or a holiday.

Serves 6–8

INGREDIENTS:

4 large eggs

½ teaspoon table salt or sea salt, or to taste

¼ teaspoon pepper, or to taste

1½ cups fat-free milk or water

1 cup corn flour (masa harina)

Butter or oil for greasing the griddle

1 pound gluten-free ricotta cheese

2 cloves garlic, chopped

½ cup Parmesan cheese, freshly grated or gluten-free

2 cups chopped raw mixed fresh vegetables, such as scallions, zucchini, fresh spinach, and young peas

½ cup finely chopped fresh parsley

1½ cups Spicy Marinara Sauce (see recipe in Chapter 12)

1 cup shredded mozzarella cheese

1. Mix two eggs, salt, pepper, milk or water, and corn flour in the blender and process until smooth.

2. Using a well-greased griddle, pour the batter, fry until firm, and cut into 10" strips that are 2 inches wide. Turn using an extra-large, long spatula. As you finish, place the strips on a baking dish that has been prepared with nonstick spray. When the bottom of the baking dish is covered, fry the rest of the batter in the same way and save it for topping.

3. In a bowl, mix the ricotta, other two eggs, garlic, Parmesan, vegetables, and parsley. Spread in tablespoonfuls over the base in the pan. Cover with more of the pasta strips.

4. Add the marinara sauce to the pan and cover with shredded mozzarella. Bake for about 12 minutes. Serve hot.

STUFFED PORTOBELLO MUSHROOMS WITH ROASTED TOMATOES AND QUINOA

You can substitute rice for quinoa. However, you get a nice nutty flavor from the quinoa.

Serves 4

INGREDIENTS:

4 portobello mushrooms, about 4 to 5" in diameter, stemmed and brushed off

16 cherry tomatoes, cut in half

¼ cup olive oil

1 tablespoon minced garlic

2 cups cooked quinoa

¼ cup walnuts, finely chopped (almonds or pecans are fine)

4 tablespoons butter or margarine, melted

1 teaspoon turmeric

Salt and red pepper flakes, to taste

¼ cup capers (optional)

¼ cup golden raisins (optional), gluten-free

1 teaspoon lemon zest (optional)

1. Preheat the oven to 350°F. Place the mushrooms on a well-greased baking pan.

2. In shallow baking dish, sprinkle the tomatoes with oil and garlic. Roast them in oven for 20 minutes or until soft.

3. Mix the roasted tomatoes with the cooked quinoa, nuts, butter or margarine, and seasonings. Add optional ingredients if desired. Spoon into the mushrooms.

4. Bake the mushrooms for 30 minutes or until very hot and soft.

Do You Know Quinoa?

Rich, nutrient-filled quinoa is considered a "super grain," though it is not really a grain but the starchy seed of a plant related to spinach. The protein in quinoa is more complete than that of other grains, and contains the amino acid lysine, as does buckwheat and amaranth. The quality of quinoa's protein is equivalent to that of milk.

GRILLED PORTOBELLO MUSHROOMS

These big, meaty mushrooms are great sliced over salad, stuffed, or chopped into sauce.

Serves 4

INGREDIENTS:

4 large (4–5" in diameter) portobello mushrooms, stems removed, brushed off

1 cup balsamic vinaigrette

Salt and pepper, to taste

1. Marinate the mushrooms in the vinaigrette for 1–2 hours, covered, in the refrigerator.

2. Preheat your grill to glowing coals, or set your gas grill to low.

3. Grill mushrooms, then slice and serve. Use salt and pepper to taste.

Mushrooms and Protein

Mushrooms are not really high in protein, but they do have some and they are filling. The large portobello mushrooms are excellent for grilling or stuffing with all kinds of goodies. They make excellent bases for rice, quinoa, eggs, and vegetables.

STUFFED PORTOBELLO MUSHROOMS WITH ROQUEFORT AND SWEET RED PEPPERS

This is as good as it gets. Serve with salad or in an omelet.

Serves 4

INGREDIENTS:

4 large whole portobello mushrooms, marinated in balsamic vinaigrette

8 tablespoons crumbled Roquefort cheese

4 roasted red peppers, cut in strips (jarred is fine)

Salt and pepper, to taste

1. Preheat oven to 350°F. Place the marinated mushrooms on a baking sheet.

2. Place 2 tablespoons of cheese in each mushroom. Put the pepper strips on top. Sprinkle with salt and pepper. Bake for 20 minutes, until the cheese melts.

SWEET POTATO GRATIN WITH LEEKS AND ONIONS

The combination of sweet and savory makes this a fascinating, unique, and delicious dish.

Serves 6

INGREDIENTS:

2 leeks, white part only, rinsed and chopped

2 large sweet onions, such as Vidalia, peeled and finely chopped

2 stalks celery with tops, finely chopped

4 tablespoons olive oil

4 sweet potatoes, peeled and sliced thinly

1 teaspoon dried thyme

1 teaspoon salt

½ teaspoon ground black pepper

3 cups 1% milk

1½ cups gluten-free corn bread crumbs

2 tablespoons butter or margarine, cut in small pieces

1. In a skillet over medium heat, add the leeks, onions, celery, and olive oil and sauté for 3–5 minutes, until softened.

2. Grease a 4-quart slow cooker with nonstick cooking spray.

3. Layer the sweet potato slices in the slow cooker with the sautéed vegetables. Sprinkle thyme, salt, and pepper on each layer as you go along. Finish with a layer of potatoes.

4. Add the milk until it meets the top layer of potatoes. Then add the corn bread crumbs. Dot with butter or margarine.

5. Cover and cook on high for 4 hours or on low for 8 hours, until the potatoes are fork tender. In the last hour of cooking, vent the lid of the slow cooker with a chopstick or wooden spoon handle to allow excess condensation to escape.

Instead of . . .

Instead of gluten-free corn bread, you can also use crushed gluten-free corn tortillas as a topping. Several brands such as Utz and Food Should Taste Good actually have "This is a gluten-free food" listed on some of their products. If you have any questions about a product, make sure to call the company to ask about their gluten cross-contamination prevention policies.

CORN AND SPINACH POCKETS STUFFED WITH CHEESE AND ARTICHOKES

Simply because a dish is vegetarian does not mean it has to be tasteless. This recipe is a perfect example.

Serves 8

INGREDIENTS:

1 (10-ounce) box frozen artichoke hearts, thawed

1 (10-ounce) box frozen spinach, thawed, moisture squeezed out

1 cup gluten-free ricotta cheese

4 ounces cream cheese

¼ cup minced chives

1 clove garlic, chopped

¼ teaspoon freshly ground nutmeg

Salt and pepper, to taste

1 large egg

8 large (8–9" diameter) Corn Crepes (see recipe in Chapter 2)

Beaten egg for sealing pockets

1. Add the defrosted artichokes to a food processor with the spinach, process and slowly add the cheeses, chives, garlic, seasonings, and egg.

2. Preheat oven to 350°F. Lay out the crepes on a nonstick baking sheet or one covered with a sheet of aluminum foil.

3. Divide the filling among the crepes, spooning the mixture onto one half and leaving the other half plain.

4. Wet the rims of the crepes with beaten egg. Fold over and press lightly to seal, and then bake for 20 minutes or until well browned and filling is bubbling out.

Selecting and Preparing Artichokes

Look for artichokes that are tightly closed. Take a pair of kitchen scissors and clip off the sharp points. You can use a knife to cut off the tops. They are hearty when stuffed with many kinds of delicious foods. If you eat fish, salmon mixed with rice makes an excellent stuffing.

SPINACH WITH BAKED EGGS AND CHEESE

This is an excellent brunch, lunch, or supper. Everyone loves it, and even after a tough day, it's easy to put together.

Serves 4

INGREDIENTS:

1½ cups gluten-free corn bread crumbs

3 (10-ounce) packages frozen spinach, thawed, moisture squeezed out

2 tablespoons butter or margarine, melted

½ cup shredded Swiss cheese

½ teaspoon nutmeg

1 teaspoon salt

½ teaspoon ground black pepper

1 cup heavy cream

8 large eggs

1. Grease a 4-quart slow cooker with nonstick cooking spray. Sprinkle corn bread crumbs on the bottom of the slow cooker.

2. In a medium bowl, mix the spinach, butter, cheese, nutmeg, salt, and pepper together. Stir in the cream. Spread the spinach-cheese mixture on top of the corn bread crumbs.

3. Using the back of a tablespoon, make 8 depressions in the spinach mixture. Break open the eggs and place one egg in each hole.

4. Cover and cook on low for 3 hours or on high for 1½–2 hours, until the yolks are cooked through, but not hard. Serve with gluten-free toast and fresh fruit.

Herbs and Spices

People often confuse herbs with spices. Herbs are green and are the leaves of plants—the only herb (in Western cooking) that is a flower is lavender. Frequently used herbs include parsley, basil, oregano, thyme, rosemary, cilantro, and mint. Spices are roots, tubers, barks, or berries. These include pepper, cinnamon, nutmeg, allspice, cumin, turmeric, ginger, cardamom, and coriander.

CRISPY POTATO PANCAKES

This can be served traditionally with applesauce for an entrée, alongside of eggs for breakfast or brunch, or even as an appetizer with an aioli dipping sauce.

Makes about 10 pancakes

INGREDIENTS:

4 large Idaho potatoes, peeled and coarsely grated

2 medium mild onions, chopped fine

1 tablespoon parsley, finely chopped

½ cup scallions, chopped (including the green part)

2 large eggs, well beaten

½ cup potato flour

Salt and pepper, to taste

2 cups cooking oil (such as canola)

Gluten-free sour cream, applesauce, fruit preserves, gluten-free salsa, or chutney, for garnish

1. Mix the grated potatoes, onions, parsley, scallions, and eggs in a bowl. Sprinkle with potato flour, salt, and pepper. Form into cakes.

2. Heat the oil in a skillet to 350°F and spoon in the potato cakes, pressing down to make a patty.

3. Fry until golden, about 5 minutes per side. Drain on a paper towel, keep warm, and serve with gluten-free garnish of choice.

The Origins of Potato Pancakes

During the long winters in northern and eastern Europe, when fresh fruits and vegetables were not available, winter storage of carrots, potatoes, beets, Brussels sprouts, apples, and dried fruits was crucial to prevent scurvy, or ascorbic acid deficiency. As Mother Nature would have it, these vegetables are packed with vitamins and minerals. Potato pancakes with sour cream, applesauce, or fruit syrups became a staple in harsh climates.

POTATO FRITTATA WITH CHEESE AND HERBS

Use both nonstick spray and butter in this recipe, or the starch in the potatoes will stick. You can experiment with different herbs and cheeses.

Serves 4

INGREDIENTS:

1 large Yukon Gold potato, peeled

4 teaspoons butter, melted

6 large eggs

½ cup grated Parmesan cheese, fresh or gluten-free

6 sage leaves, minced

½ teaspoon salt

½ teaspoon pepper

Fresh herbs, extra cheese, gluten-free sour cream, for garnish

1. Using a mandoline, slice the potato as thinly as possible. Grease a 4-quart slow cooker with melted butter and with a spritz of nonstick cooking spray, and place the potatoes on the bottom in a thin layer.

2. In a medium bowl, beat the eggs well. Add the cheese, sage, salt, and pepper; stir to combine. Pour over the potatoes.

3. Cover and cook on high for 2 hours or on low for 4 hours.

4. Cut into squares and serve at once. Add chopped fresh herbs, additional shredded cheese, or gluten-free sour cream to garnish.

An Untraditional Frittata

Usually frittatas are open omelets that are started in a heavy skillet on the stove and then finished by broiling in the oven. Using this slow cooker method you can put together the frittata the night before, then get up early, place it in the slow cooker, and 2 hours later, breakfast is hot and ready!

TOFU AND VEGETABLES WITH MACADAMIA NUTS AND ASIAN CITRUS SAUCE

The tastes and textures come together beautifully in this Asian-inspired dish. Serve over rice.

Serves 4

INGREDIENTS:

1 tablespoon sesame seed oil

3 tablespoons peanut or other vegetable oil

1 bunch scallions, chopped

1 clove garlic, minced

1" piece gingerroot, peeled and minced

⅔ pound sugar snap peas, ends trimmed

2 cups mung bean sprouts

2 cups shredded Chinese cabbage

½ teaspoon brown sugar

½ orange, juice and rind, pulsed in the food processor

1 teaspoon gluten-free Asian five-spice powder

1 teaspoon gluten-free Chinese mustard or Japanese wasabi, or to taste

¼ cup sake or dry white wine

¼ cup light gluten-free soy sauce

1 pound satin tofu, cubed

1. Heat the oils in a wok. Add the scallions, garlic, and gingerroot. Lightly mix in the rest of the vegetables and toss in the oil for 3–4 minutes. Place the cooked vegetables in a large, warm serving bowl.

2. In a small bowl, mix together the brown sugar, orange juice and rind, five-spice powder, mustard or wasabi, sake or wine, and soy sauce.

3. Stir into the wok until blended. Add the tofu cubes and vegetables, and mix to coat. Serve hot.

A Source of Protein for Vegetarians

Tofu, long used in Asia because meat and milk were both scarce and expensive, has become an important part of the vegetarian diet. It can be flavored to taste like many kinds of meat. Or it can be sweetened and prepared with fruit for desserts. It's delicious in soups and with vegetables.

SPINACH-AND-CHEESE-STUFFED BAKED POTATOES

This is an American favorite, and if you enjoy anchovies, they make a delightful addition to this recipe.

Serves 4 as a meal, 8 as a snack

INGREDIENTS:

4 Idaho or Yukon Gold potatoes

1 (10-ounce) package frozen chopped spinach, thawed and moisture squeezed out

1 cup gluten-free sour cream

¼ teaspoon nutmeg

1 cup grated white American cheese

Salt and pepper, to taste

½ cup shredded sharp Cheddar cheese

1. Preheat the oven to 350°F.

2. Bake the potatoes for 40 minutes. Then cool the potatoes and split them in half lengthwise.

3. Spoon out the insides of the potatoes and place in a bowl; add the spinach. Stir in the sour cream and nutmeg. Add the American cheese. Season to taste with salt and pepper.

4. Restuff the potato skins. Arrange the Cheddar cheese on top. Bake for another 20 minutes and serve hot.

SWEET PEPPER AND GORGONZOLA OMELET

This omelet has a delightful flavor from the Gorgonzola cheese melting into the eggs. A nonstick pan takes all of the guesswork out of making omelets.

Serves 2

INGREDIENTS:

2 teaspoons unsalted butter

4 large eggs, well beaten

2 ounces crumbled Gorgonzola cheese

4 1" × 2" strips roasted red pepper

Salt and hot red pepper flakes, to taste

1. Heat a 10" nonstick pan over medium-high heat. Melt the butter and swirl to coat. Add the eggs and swirl to distribute evenly in pan.

2. Place the cheese and pepper strips on one side of the omelet. Season with salt and pepper flakes.

3. Cook until just set, when it has the consistency of custard (soft and creamy but not liquid or runny). Flip the plain side over the side with the cheese and peppers. Cut in half and serve on a warmed plate.

GREEK EGGPLANT AND OLIVE SAUCE

Here you have many of the flavors of Greece without the travel. Touches of garlic and mint do not overwhelm. Goes great over gluten-free pasta or rice.

Serves 4

INGREDIENTS:

2 tablespoons flax meal

½ cup rice flour mixed with 1 teaspoon salt

1 medium eggplant, peeled and cubed

⅓ cup extra-virgin olive oil

2 cloves garlic, minced

½ cup kalamata or other black, Greek olives, pitted and chopped

10 mint leaves, coarsely chopped

½ cup finely snipped chives

Juice of ½ lemon

Extra olive oil if sauce seems dry

1. Mix the ground flax with the flour and salt. Dredge the eggplant cubes in flour mixture.

2. In a saucepan, heat the olive oil over medium-high heat. Sauté the eggplant until brown.

3. When brown, lower heat and add the garlic; sauté for another 3 minutes.

4. Add the rest of the ingredients and serve.

GRILLED CHEESE ON TOASTED CORN BREAD SQUARES

This recipe is one of the hundreds of goodies you can make if you have Crunchy Corn Bread Squares in your fridge or freezer.

Makes 32 small squares

INGREDIENTS:

1 batch Crunchy Corn Bread Squares (see recipe in Chapter 3)

½ cup soft butter

1 cup cubed Monterey jack cheese

½ cup grated Parmesan cheese, fresh or gluten-free

½ cup red roasted peppers, jarred is fine

½ cup chopped sweet red onion

1. Arrange the corn bread squares on a baking sheet that you have prepared with nonstick spray. Preheat the oven to 350°F.

2. Whirl the rest of the ingredients in the food processor until mixed. Don't worry about making the cheese mixture smooth. Using a teaspoon, place a small mound of cheese/butter mixture on each corn bread square.

3. Bake until the cheese melts, about 10 minutes. You can vary this recipe by adding different herbs, chopped garlic, or any of your favorite flavors.

GRILLED EGGPLANT AND PEPPER SALAD

Grill the eggplant and peppers the day before the party, then, at the last minute, put the vegetables together, shave the provolone, and dress the salad.

Serves 12

INGREDIENTS:

⅓ cup balsamic or red wine vinegar

1 cup olive oil

1 teaspoon gluten-free Dijon-style mustard

Salt and pepper, to taste

1 medium eggplant

3 red bell peppers, cored and seeded, cut in half

1 bunch arugula or watercress, stems removed, washed

1 large head romaine lettuce, washed, dried, and chopped

4 ripe tomatoes, cored and chopped

2 ounces aged provolone cheese

1. To prepare the dressing, mix the first four ingredients together in a cruet. Shake well. Peel and slice the eggplant into ½" slices, brush with salad dressing, and grill for 3 minutes on each side. Cool and cut into cubes.

2. Grill the peppers on the skin side until charred. Place in a paper bag. Cool and pull the skin off. Cut into pieces.

3. Just before serving, toss the greens with the eggplant and peppers, add tomatoes, and shave the provolone over the top.

4. Whirl the prepared dressing in your blender. Pour over the salad.

LEEK, POTATO, AND CARROT POTAGE

Potage is a classic French home-style soup that is perfect for a blustery winter day.

Serves 6

INGREDIENTS:

4 cups sliced leeks

4 russet potatoes, peeled and cubed

2 carrots, diced

5 cups water

¼ teaspoon salt

½ teaspoon white pepper

1. Place all ingredients into a 4-quart slow cooker. Cook on low for 7 hours.

2. Purée using an immersion blender or purée in batches in a blender. Serve piping hot.

VEGETABLE STEW WITH CORNMEAL DUMPLINGS

The naturally gluten-free cornmeal dumplings perfectly complement the fall vegetables in this hearty stew, making it a complete meal in one pot.

Serves 6

INGREDIENTS:

1 teaspoon olive oil

3 russet potatoes, peeled and diced

3 carrots, cut into ½" chunks

2 stalks celery, diced

1 medium onion, diced

2 rutabagas or turnips, peeled and diced

1 cup cauliflower florets

2 quarts gluten-free vegetable broth

1 tablespoon fresh thyme

1 tablespoon fresh parsley

⅔ cup water

2 tablespoons canola oil

½ cup gluten-free cornmeal

2 teaspoons gluten-free baking powder

½ teaspoon salt

1. Heat the olive oil in a large nonstick skillet. Add all of the vegetables. Sauté until the onions are soft and translucent, about 3–5 minutes. Add to a 4-quart slow cooker.

2. Add the broth, thyme, and parsley. Stir. Cook for 4–6 hours on high or 8 hours on low, until the vegetables are fork tender. Stir.

3. In a medium bowl, stir the water, oil, cornmeal, baking powder, and salt. Drop in ¼-cup mounds in a single layer on top of the stew. Cover and cook on high for 20 minutes without lifting the lid. The dumplings will look fluffy and light when fully cooked.

Herbivore Versus Omnivore

To make this a non-vegetarian meal, use gluten-free beef broth instead of vegetable broth and add 1 pound diced, browned stew beef to the vegetables.

EGGPLANT PARMESAN

This popular Italian dish is transformed into an easy, healthy casserole.

Serves 10

INGREDIENTS:

2 medium eggplants, peeled and thinly sliced across the eggplant

1 teaspoon sea salt

3 large eggs, plus 2 egg whites, lightly beaten

2 cups gluten-free bread crumbs

¾ cup ground flaxseed

1 teaspoon oregano

4 cloves garlic, minced

½ cup Parmesan cheese, fresh or gluten-free, divided

6 cups Easy Pizza Sauce (see Chapter 4) or gluten-free spaghetti sauce

2 cups mozzarella cheese, shredded

1 tablespoon fresh basil

1. Preheat oven to 350°F.

2. Place eggplant slices in 9" × 13" casserole dish. Add salt to eggplant and let sit for 1 hour to let eggplant "sweat" out extra moisture. After the hour, put eggplant in colander and rinse off excess salt from eggplant slices and casserole. Pat dry with paper towels.

3. Place beaten eggs in shallow bowl.

4. In another shallow bowl, add the bread crumbs, flaxseed, oregano, garlic, and ¼ cup Parmesan cheese. Stir well to combine.

5. Spray a baking sheet with nonstick cooking spray. Dip eggplant in egg, then bread crumb mixture and place onto baking sheet. Bake for 10 minutes on each side.

6. Spread ½–¾ cup pizza sauce on the bottom of the casserole dish. Place a layer of eggplant on top of sauce layer. Sprinkle with Parmesan and ½ cup–¾ cup mozzarella cheeses. Repeat another layer of sauce, eggplant, and cheeses until ingredients run out.

7. Top with fresh basil. Bake for 20 minutes or until golden brown and cheese is melted.

Why Do You Need to "Sweat" Out Eggplant?

Eggplants are very bitter. Once you remove moisture from it, the eggplant will become less bitter. The salt helps remove the moisture from the eggplant. Just be sure to rinse it thoroughly so it isn't too salty.

ASPARAGUS, MUSHROOMS, EDAMAME, AND SUN-DRIED TOMATOES IN BALSAMIC GLAZE

This vegan entrée can be served either warm or cold. Fresh asparagus and mushrooms will work best in this recipe.

Serves 6

INGREDIENTS:

1 pound asparagus, ends trimmed and cut into 1" pieces

1 8-ounce package fresh sliced mushrooms, wiped clean and stems cut off

1 cup organic shelled and cooked edamame

½ cup sun-dried tomatoes (not in oil), sliced in halves

2 tablespoons extra-virgin olive oil

1 tablespoons balsamic vinegar

3 cloves garlic, crushed

½ teaspoon salt

⅛ teaspoon pepper

Fresh parsley, for garnish

1. Preheat the oven to 350°F.

2. Place the asparagus, mushrooms, edamame, and sun-dried tomatoes in a large zip-top bag.

3. In small bowl, mix the olive oil, vinegar, garlic, salt, and pepper together with wire whisk.

4. Pour marinade over vegetables in the bag. Close the bag and shake until evenly coated.

5. Place veggie mixture on baking sheet, top with chopped parsley. Roast for 45–60 minutes, checking periodically to turn veggies and to make sure they do not over brown.

What Are Edamame?

Edamame are actually immature, green soybeans. They are so versatile and super easy to add to all types of dishes. They are a favorite for vegans and vegetarians since they are a complete protein. Edamame are also packed with fiber, B vitamins, omega-3 fatty acids, iron, calcium, and zinc.

WARM CHICKPEA SALAD WITH SPINACH

Chickpeas (or garbanzo beans) are loaded with protein and fiber. If you use canned beans, make sure you rinse them thoroughly before using. Serve this with a green salad for a balanced meal.

Serves 4

INGREDIENTS:

1 tablespoon extra-virgin olive oil

4 cloves garlic, minced

½ medium onion, diced

2 cups fresh baby spinach

1 (12-ounce) can chickpeas, rinsed and drained thoroughly

½ teaspoon cumin

½ teaspoon salt

⅛ teaspoon gluten-free curry powder

Juice from ½ freshly squeezed lemon

¼ cup gluten-free vegetable broth

1. Heat the olive oil in a skillet over medium-low heat. Cook the garlic and onion in the oil until translucent, about 5 minutes.

2. Stir in the spinach, chickpeas, cumin, salt, and curry. Continue to stir for a few minutes. Add lemon juice and broth, and stir. Allow to cook until thoroughly heated.

The Benefits of Beans

Beans are low in fat and help regulate blood sugar levels. They are also high in dietary fiber, which studies have shown can help lower cholesterol, reduce blood pressure, and support proper digestive health.

INDIAN VEGETABLE CAKES

This is a great way to get kids to eat their veggies! A nonstick pan helps prevent sticking. Sour cream makes a very good garnish.

Serves 4–6

INGREDIENTS:

1 tablespoon extra-virgin olive oil

1 (10-ounce) package frozen chopped spinach, thawed and squeezed of excess moisture

5 ounces frozen baby peas, thawed

½ bunch scallions, chopped

1 teaspoon gluten-free curry powder

½ teaspoon turmeric

½ teaspoon ground black pepper

Salt and hot pepper sauce, to taste

¼ cup gluten-free cornmeal

5 extra-large eggs, well beaten

½ cup Parmesan cheese, fresh or gluten-free

1. Heat olive oil in a nonstick pan over medium heat.

2. In a large bowl, mix together all the ingredients except the Parmesan cheese. Form into patties.

3. Drop patties, 3 or 4 at a time, into the pan and fry until delicately browned, 3–4 minutes per side. Turn and sprinkle with cheese before serving.

Terrific Turmeric

Do you know about the health benefits of turmeric? Curcumin, a main ingredient in turmeric, has been shown to reduce inflammation. Some studies indicate that it may help ease the pain and symptoms of arthritis and rheumatoid arthritis. Other research shows that turmeric may protect against diseases, such as certain cancers, Alzheimer's disease, high cholesterol, and heart disease, to name a few. Try adding turmeric to your favorite dishes for some added health benefits.

SPINACH, TOMATOES, AND GNOCCHI IN CLASSIC PESTO SAUCE

This meal is so simple to prepare that you will be amazed how delicious it tastes. This would be wonderful with shrimp or sliced chicken as well for a non-vegetarian dish.

Serves 8

INGREDIENTS:

1 (12-ounce) package gluten-free gnocchi

1 (6-ounce) bag organic baby spinach

1 pint of organic grape tomatoes, halved

1 teaspoon extra-virgin olive oil

1 clove garlic, chopped

Classic Pesto Sauce (see recipe in this chapter)

Parmesan cheese, fresh or gluten-free, for garnish (optional)

1. Cook the gnocchi according to the package directions.

2. Place the spinach and grape tomatoes in a skillet with oil and garlic, and sauté until soft, about 2–3 minutes. Add in the gnocchi and stir until well blended.

3. Place everything in large bowl. Pour pesto on top. Stir to combine. Top with Parmesan if desired.

Gnocchi

Gnocchi is an Italian-style potato dumpling and can be substituted for pasta in many popular dishes. Be advised, just because you hear "potato" dumplings, don't assume they are gluten-free. Read your ingredient lists carefully because many of them are made with wheat flour. There are many brands of gluten-free gnocchi offered in specialty grocery stores and many local supermarkets.

CLASSIC PESTO SAUCE

This wonderful sauce takes only a few minutes to prepare. Feel free to double this recipe as it stores well in the freezer.

Serves 8

INGREDIENTS:

4 ounces extra-virgin olive oil

3 cloves garlic

1½ ounces pine nuts

2 ounces Parmesan cheese, fresh or gluten-free

2 ounces fresh basil leaves, torn

Salt and pepper, to taste (optional)

1. Add all the ingredients to a food processor or high-speed blender in the order listed.

2. Blend for 1 minute or until blended smooth. Depending on your blender or processor, you may need to also stir the pesto by hand to make sure all the ingredients are combined.

Pesto Possibilities

When it comes to pesto, try thinking outside of the box. You can substitute pine nuts with walnuts, cashews, pistachios, almonds, or even pumpkin seeds. To add different flavors and textures you can also add different vegetables and cheeses. The possibilities are endless!

PESTO, ARUGULA, AND YELLOW TOMATO PIZZA WITH CAULIFLOWER PIZZA CRUST

Pizza doesn't have to consist of just cheese and sauce. It's fun to be creative with different vegetables and sauces.

Serves 4

INGREDIENTS:

2 cups Easy Pizza Sauce (see recipe in Chapter 4)

1 Cauliflower Pizza Crust (see recipe in this chapter)

½ cup Classic Pesto Sauce (see recipe in this chapter)

3 cups fresh arugula

1 tablespoon extra-virgin olive oil

1 clove garlic, minced

1 cup part-skim mozzarella cheese, shredded or fresh

1 pint yellow cherry tomatoes, sliced in half

¼ cup freshly torn basil leaves

1. Preheat oven to 350°F.

2. Spread the pizza sauce evenly over the top of the cauliflower crust.

3. Spread the pesto evenly on top of the pizza sauce.

4. Sauté the arugula in a small pan with 1 tablespoon olive oil and garlic until wilted, about 1–2 minutes. Once done, pour evenly over pizza.

5. Sprinkle with the cheese, and add sliced tomatoes and fresh basil on top.

6. Bake for about 10–15 minutes, until the edges are browned.

7. Place under the broiler, on high heat, until cheese is melted, approximately 1–2 minutes.

CAULIFLOWER PIZZA CRUST

Being on a gluten-free diet doesn't mean you can't have pizza! This makes a 1"-thick crust but it can be doubled for a larger pizza.

Serves 4

INGREDIENTS:

1 cup raw cauliflower, grated (or chopped in food processor)

1 large egg

½ cup Parmesan cheese, fresh or gluten-free

1 teaspoon oregano

2 teaspoons parsley

Handful of fresh basil

1 clove garlic, finely diced

1. Preheat oven to 425°F. Spray a cookie sheet with nonstick spray or use parchment paper.

2. In a medium bowl, combine the cauliflower, egg, Parmesan cheese, and all the seasonings. Press evenly on baking pan or pizza stone. Bake for 15–20 minutes, until the edges start to brown. You may turn over once if desired.

3. Remove the pan from the oven. Add sauce and desired toppings.

4. Place under the broiler, on high heat, until cheese is melted.

Cauliflower Pizza Crust Tips

Approximately 2¼ cups of cauliflower, chopped into 1" pieces, would grate into 1 cup of grated cauliflower. Be careful not to spread the crust too thin, or it will fall apart and its edges will burn. Alternatively, spreading the crust too thick will leave the middle uncooked.

RAW BROCCOLI SLAW WITH FRUIT, VEGGIES, AND WALNUTS

Why not try a broccoli slaw without mayonnaise? This is perfect for outdoor picnics and cookouts.

Serves 6

INGREDIENTS:

1 (12-ounce) bag of broccoli slaw

1 cup diced organic Fuji apple, peeled

1 organic kiwi, peeled and sliced

1 organic red bell pepper, seeded and chopped

2 tablespoons gluten-free dried cranberries (unsweetened)

2 tablespoons sliced walnuts

Chia-Balsamic Vinaigrette (see recipe in this chapter)

1. Place broccoli slaw in large bowl. Add chopped apple, kiwi, and pepper. Mix it all together.

2. Top with cranberries and walnuts. Mix again. Add vinaigrette just before serving.

CHIA-BALSAMIC VINAIGRETTE

You can make more of this dressing and keep it in your refrigerator. It goes well with veggies, meats, and any kind of salad.

Serves 6–8

INGREDIENTS:

1 tablespoon gluten-free Dijon mustard

5 tablespoons balsamic vinegar

1 tablespoon extra-virgin olive oil, or oil of your choice

1 tablespoon chia seed, ground

Salt and freshly ground black pepper, to taste

1 large clove garlic, finely chopped

1–2 tablespoons fresh basil leaves

1. In a clean, empty jar or Tupperware container with a lid, add the mustard, balsamic vinegar, oil, chia seed, salt, and pepper.

2. Add the chopped garlic along with the fresh basil leaves.

3. Cover the jar and shake well to blend. Store up to 5 days in airtight container.

BROCCOLI-AND-CHEESE-STUFFED BAKED POTATOES

The whole family will love this recipe. You can experiment with a variety of vegetables and different cheeses too.

Serves 4 as a meal, or 8 as a snack

INGREDIENTS:

4 large Idaho or Yukon Gold potatoes

5 cups broccoli florets

1 cup gluten-free sour cream

¼ teaspoon nutmeg

1 cup grated white American cheese

3 cloves garlic, chopped

1 large onion, finely chopped

Salt and pepper, to taste

½ cup shredded sharp Cheddar cheese

1. Preheat the oven to 350°F.

2. Bake the potatoes in the oven for 40 minutes. Then cool the potatoes and split them in half lengthwise.

3. Steam broccoli until tender, about 5 minutes. Drain, rinse, and chop.

4. Spoon out the insides of the potatoes and place in a bowl; add the broccoli. Stir in the sour cream and nutmeg. Add the American cheese, garlic, and onion. Season to taste with salt and pepper.

5. Restuff the potato skins. Arrange the Cheddar cheese on top. Bake for another 20 minutes and serve hot.

STUFFED EGGPLANT WITH RICOTTA AND SPICES

This dish is also known as Eggplant Sicilian. It freezes beautifully and is very delicious.

Serves 4

INGREDIENTS:

2 medium eggplants, peeled, cut in 16 round slices (8 slices each, about ½" thick depending on size of eggplant) and salted

1 cup rice or corn flour

Freshly ground black pepper, to taste

¼ cup extra-virgin olive oil, or as needed

1 clove garlic, chopped

2 cups tomato sauce

1 pound gluten-free ricotta cheese

1 cup grated Parmesan cheese, fresh or gluten-free, divided

2 large eggs

1 teaspoon dried basil

1 tablespoon dried oregano

1 cup shredded mozzarella cheese

1. Stack the salted eggplant slices on a plate and put another plate with a weight on top to press the brown liquid out of them.

2. Mix the flour and pepper and use it for dredging the eggplant slices. Fry the slices in the olive oil and garlic, removing to paper towels as they are browned.

3. Preheat oven to 325°F. Prepare a 2-quart casserole dish or a 10" × 10" glass pan with nonstick spray and spread with a thin layer of tomato sauce.

4. In a large bowl, mix the ricotta cheese, ½ cup of the Parmesan, eggs, basil, and oregano. Place a tablespoon of the egg-cheese mixture on each slice of eggplant and roll, placing seam-side down in the baking dish.

5. Spread with remaining tomato sauce, sprinkle with the rest of the Parmesan cheese and the mozzarella cheese, and bake for 35 minutes.

Smaller Is Sweeter

The smaller eggplants now available are much sweeter and not old enough to have grown bitter. Also, many have few seeds. They come in pale cream, lavender, and purple, all the way from egg-sized to long and skinny. All are good!

SWEET PEPPER AND FETA OMELET

This omelet has a delightful flavor from the feta cheese melting into the eggs. A nonstick pan takes all of the guesswork out of making omelets.

Serves 2

INGREDIENTS:

2 teaspoons unsalted butter

4 large eggs, well beaten

2 ounces crumbled feta cheese

1 large red pepper, cut into thin strips, can use roasted or use raw

Salt and hot red pepper flakes, to taste

1. Heat a 10" nonstick pan over medium-high heat. Melt the butter and swirl to coat. Add the eggs and swirl to distribute evenly in pan.

2. Place the cheese and pepper strips on one side of the omelet. Season with salt and pepper flakes.

3. Cook until just set, when it has the consistency of custard (soft and creamy but not liquid or runny). Flip the plain side over the side with the cheese and peppers. Cut in half and serve on a warmed plate.

SPINACH, KALE, AND MUSHROOM PIZZA

This pizza goes beyond the typical red sauce and mozzarella cheese. Goat cheese makes a wonderful addition to this sauce-less pizza.

Serves 4

INGREDIENTS:

2 cups kale

2 cups spinach

1 cup sliced mushrooms

1 tablespoon grapeseed oil

2 cloves garlic, chopped

½ medium onion, chopped

Cauliflower Pizza Crust (see recipe in this chapter)

½ cup goat cheese, crumbled

Handful of fresh basil, torn

1. Place kale, spinach, and mushrooms in a skillet with grapeseed oil, garlic, and onion. Sauté for 3–4 minutes, until mushrooms soften and the greens wilt.

2. Place the vegetables on top of pizza crust. Next top with goat cheese and fresh basil.

3. Place in the broiler for 2 minutes until cheese is melted. Serve hot.

Pizza Is a Family Affair

Making pizzas can be a fun and easy family activity. Let the kids sprinkle the cheese, add the vegetables, or tear the basil. By doing simple prep work, it's an easy way to expose "future chefs" to the joy of cooking.

VEGAN QUINOA–BLACK BEAN CAKES

These are so light and tasty that they can be made with a green salad for an entrée or even served as an appetizer.

Makes 8 cakes

INGREDIENTS:

3 tablespoons grapeseed oil (or extra-virgin olive oil), divided

½ cup finely chopped green bell pepper

3 cloves garlic, chopped

1 medium onion, finely chopped

½ cup finely chopped plum (Roma) tomatoes

1 (15-ounce) can organic black beans, thoroughly rinsed and drained

2 cups quinoa, cooked in gluten-free vegetable broth

1 tablespoon fresh cilantro leaves

½ teaspoon cumin

½ teaspoon red pepper flakes

Salt and pepper, to taste

1 egg white, beaten

1 cup gluten-free bread crumbs

Fresh cilantro and diced tomatoes, for garnish (optional)

1. Heat 2 tablespoons of grapeseed oil in skillet; add the green pepper and sauté until soft, about 3 minutes.

2. Add the garlic, onion, and tomatoes, and continue to sauté until soft, about 3–4 minutes.

3. Remove from heat, combine with black beans, quinoa, cilantro, cumin, and red pepper flakes. Allow to cool for a few minutes. Add salt and pepper to taste. Place in food processor and pulse until chunky but not completely smooth.

4. Add the beaten egg white and mix well. Form into patties, dredge in bread crumbs, and place in heated skillet with 1 tablespoon grapeseed oil. Sauté at least 5 minutes on each side. Garnish with fresh cilantro and diced tomatoes.

ASIAGO QUINOA WITH PORTOBELLO MUSHROOMS

This dish can be kept vegetarian, or you can also include diced shrimp or chicken to add some protein. In addition, you can throw in whatever fresh vegetables you have on hand to add some color.

Serves 6

INGREDIENTS:

2 tablespoons extra-virgin olive oil, divided

1 shallot, chopped

2 cloves garlic, minced

1 cup portobello mushrooms, wiped clean, stems removed, and sliced

1 teaspoon thyme

1 teaspoon oregano

1½ cups uncooked quinoa, rinsed and drained

2½ cups gluten-free vegetable broth

2 tablespoons fresh basil, torn

⅓ cup Asiago cheese, grated

1. Heat 1 tablespoon of oil in a large skillet. Add the shallot, garlic, and mushrooms. Top with the thyme and oregano and cook until browned, about 5 minutes. Set aside.

2. Heat the other tablespoon of oil in a pot over medium-high heat. Add quinoa and let it brown, about 2–3 minutes. Pour in the vegetable broth and bring it to a boil. Cover and reduce heat to low. Simmer for 15–20 minutes, until all the liquid is absorbed.

3. Stir in mushroom mixture and top with basil and cheese.

Are Shallots the Same As Green Onions?

No, they are not. Shallots are often confused with green onions or scallions. They are, however, members of the onion family but have their own mild taste. Shallots look like small onions, which when peeled, have divided cloves like garlic. When a recipe calls for 1 shallot, they generally mean the entire shallot, not just one clove.

MUSHROOM AND SQUASH QUINOA RISOTTO

This dish has a unique twist on traditional risotto made with rice. This can be left vegetarian or would also taste wonderful with sliced sweet sausage added to it.

Serves 4–6

INGREDIENTS:

1 cup uncooked quinoa, rinsed

1½ cups gluten-free vegetable broth (can also use gluten-free chicken broth)

1 tablespoon butter

2 cloves garlic, minced

½ medium onion, minced

2 cups diced butternut squash

2 cups sliced mushrooms

1 tablespoon dried oregano

½ teaspoon dried marjoram

½ teaspoon dried sage

½ teaspoon cinnamon

½ cup dry white wine

¼ cup grated Parmesan cheese, fresh or gluten-free

1. Place quinoa and broth in a pot. Bring to a boil over medium heat. Cover and reduce heat to low. Simmer for 15–20 minutes until all liquid is absorbed.

2. While quinoa is cooking, place the butter, garlic, and onions in a large skillet. Cook over medium heat 3–4 minutes, until onions are translucent.

3. Add squash and let cook for 10 minutes or until squash softens.

4. Add mushrooms and seasonings; stir to combine.

5. Pour in the white wine and mix. Let cook for a few minutes until all the wine is absorbed. Add cooked quinoa to skillet and thoroughly combine.

6. Top with grated cheese and serve immediately.

STUFFED PEPPERS WITH VEGGIE-BURGER FILLING AND SPICES

Veggie burgers can be a great alternative to regular meats, although this recipe can also be prepared using ground beef, chicken, or turkey if eating non-vegetarian.

Serves 4

INGREDIENTS:

4 large cloves garlic, minced

1 large onion, minced

¼ cup extra-virgin olive oil

1 tablespoon Asian sesame oil

1 pound gluten-free veggie burgers

Salt and pepper, to taste

4 large green or red bell peppers

1. In a skillet over medium heat, sauté the garlic and onion in the olive and sesame oils until soft, about 3–4 minutes.

2. Add the veggie burgers, break them up into pieces with a wooden spoon, and stir. Add salt and pepper.

3. Preheat oven to 350°F. Prepare a baking sheet with nonstick spray.

4. Cut the peppers in half lengthwise and scoop out seeds and cores. Fill with the burger mixture. Place on the baking sheet.

5. Bake for 25 minutes. Serve hot.

Dry Veggie Burgers?

You can do several things to keep veggie burgers moist. Mixing a bit of chopped fresh tomato into the mix is one option. Another is to add olive oil, milk, or cream before grilling. A bit of cooked, mashed potatoes also adds bulk and moisture. Add about a tablespoon of tomato, oil, milk, or mashed potato per burger.

QUINOA "MAC AND CHEESE" IN TOMATO BOWLS

These yummy broiled tomatoes make delicious little bowls for this tasty quinoa dish.

Serves 4

INGREDIENTS:

¼ cup uncooked quinoa, rinsed and drained

1 tablespoon grapeseed oil

2 tablespoons pine nuts

2 cloves garlic, minced

1 cup fresh spinach leaves

Juice of ½ fresh lemon

¼ cup freshly grated cheese of your choice

4 organic beefsteak tomatoes, top 1" sliced off, pulp and seeds scooped out (retain tomato tops)

1. Bring a pot of lightly salted water to a boil over high heat. Add the quinoa, and cook until the quinoa is tender, 15–20 minutes. Drain in a mesh strainer, and rinse until cold; set aside.

2. Heat the grapeseed oil in a skillet over medium heat, stir in pine nuts, and cook until lightly toasted, about 2 minutes.

3. Stir in the garlic, and cook until the garlic softens, about 2 minutes. Stir in the quinoa and spinach; cook and stir until the quinoa is hot, and the spinach has wilted, about 3–4 minutes. Stir in the lemon juice, and the cheese.

4. Meanwhile place tomatoes in a baking dish and place sliced top back on top of the tomato. Place in broiler for 5 minutes until they soften slightly but still remain intact.

5. Take tomatoes out and place the quinoa mixture inside the tomato, using them like bowls. The juices of the tomato will combine with the quinoa mixture and taste delicious.

Quinoa's Superpowers

Quinoa has been popular lately because it is so versatile and can be used in so many different ways. Quinoa is actually a seed that is loaded with magnesium, iron, and calcium. Quinoa is just like a grain, but it is the only one to have all nine essential amino acids, which also makes it the only one to be a complete protein. It is low calorie, has a lot of fiber, and is also wheat and gluten-free.

TRICOLOR QUINOA SALAD WITH VEGETABLES, CRANBERRIES, AND ALMONDS

This salad is perfect for cookouts or potlucks when you want to have something a little different.

Serves 4

INGREDIENTS:

1 cup uncooked tricolor quinoa, rinsed well and drained

¾ teaspoon kosher salt, divided, plus more for seasoning

2 tablespoons extra-virgin olive oil, divided

½ cup shredded carrots

1 (8½-ounce) can artichokes, rinsed, drained well, and sliced

½ cup cherry tomatoes, sliced

1 cup baby spinach

2 tablespoons coarsely chopped toasted almonds

½ lemon

¼ teaspoon basil

¼ teaspoon ground cumin

¼ teaspoon sweet paprika

1 medium firm-ripe avocado, pitted, peeled, and cut into ½" chunks

1 medium scallion, white and light green parts only, thinly sliced

2 tablespoons fresh cranberries

Freshly ground black pepper, to taste

1. In a 2-quart saucepan, bring 2 cups water, the quinoa, and ½ teaspoon salt to a boil over high heat. Cover, reduce the heat to medium low, and simmer until the water is absorbed and the quinoa is translucent and tender, about 10–15 minutes. Immediately fluff the quinoa with a fork, and allow it to cool to room temperature.

2. In a sauté pan, place 1 tablespoon oil with the carrots, artichokes, tomatoes, and spinach. Sauté until the vegetables soften, about 3–4 minutes. Add chopped almonds, and stir for 1 minute, until well mixed. Remove from heat.

3. Finely grate the zest from the lemon and then squeeze 1 tablespoon juice. In a small bowl, whisk the lemon zest and juice with the remaining tablespoon of olive oil, basil, cumin, paprika, and ¼ teaspoon salt.

4. In a large bowl, toss the lemon juice mixture with the quinoa, avocado, scallions, and cranberries.

5. Add the vegetable mixture, season to taste with salt and pepper, and serve.

CHAPTER 12

PASTA AND RICE

CHESTNUT CANNELLONI WITH SAGE, MUSHROOMS, AND WINE SAUCE

The number of cannelloni you make depends not on the recipe but how large and thick you make them. Plan on two stuffed tubes per person.

Serves 6

INGREDIENTS:

4 large eggs

1 teaspoon salt

Freshly ground white pepper, to taste

1 cup fat-free milk

1 cup Italian chestnut flour

Vegetable oil or unsalted butter for cooking

1 cup gluten-free ricotta cheese

¼ teaspoon nutmeg

½ cup gluten-free smoked ham, thinly sliced and shredded

½ cup chopped fresh Italian flat-leaf parsley

½ cup freshly grated Parmesan cheese

2 shallots, minced

2 cups mushrooms, sliced

½ cup olive oil

1 tablespoon cornstarch

1 cup dry white wine

½ cup gluten-free chicken broth

10 fresh sage leaves, chopped

Salt and pepper, to taste

Grated Parmesan, fresh or gluten-free, for the topping

1. Put 2 of the eggs, salt, pepper, milk, and flour into the blender or food processor and whirl until smooth.

2. Heat plenty of oil or butter in a nonstick pan over medium heat. Pour the batter into the hot pan, moving the pan around in circles to evenly spread the batter.

3. Fry for a few minutes per side; don't over- or undercook or the pasta will tear. Stack on sheets of wax paper and store in a plastic bag in the refrigerator until ready to use (if making it in advance).

4. Preheat oven to 350°F.

5. Mix the ricotta, the remaining 2 eggs, nutmeg, ham, parsley, and Parmesan in a bowl and, laying out the cannelloni, spread a tablespoon of the mixture across one edge. Carefully roll the pasta into a tube and place in a buttered baking dish. Repeat until filling is gone.

6. Sauté the shallots and mushrooms in the olive oil. Add the starch and stir until thickened. Blend in the wine and broth, the sage, and salt and pepper. Pour over the cannelloni and sprinkle with cheese. Bake for 30 minutes.

Variation on a Theme

This is wonderfully delicious and easy to make in advance, storing the pasta for future use. A fine variation is to add some spinach to the ricotta stuffing. You can also substitute prosciutto for regular ham.

SAVORY RICE AND SAUSAGE

This is so easy and really great for any time when you are really busy. Kids love it and grownups do too.

Serves 4–6

INGREDIENTS:

1 pound gluten-free Italian sausage, sweet or hot, cut into 1" pieces

1 medium onion, chopped fine

2 cloves garlic, chopped

1 cup uncooked rice

2¾ cups gluten-free chicken broth

1 teaspoon dried rosemary, or 1 tablespoon fresh rosemary

Parmesan cheese, fresh or gluten-free and chopped fresh parsley, for garnish

1. Brown the sausage pieces, onion, and garlic. If the sausage is very lean, add a bit of olive oil to prevent the food from sticking.

2. Stir in the rice and toss with the sausage and vegetables. Add the broth and rosemary and cover. In a broiler-safe skillet or casserole dish, cook on very low heat or place in a 325°F oven for 45–60 minutes, depending on the type of rice you are using. (Do not use Minute Rice.)

3. Just before serving, sprinkle the top with Parmesan cheese and brown under the broiler. Add the chopped parsley and serve.

MEXICAN CHICKEN AND RICE

This dish is not too spicy, but it is well seasoned. To save time, cook the rice while the chicken is simmering.

Serves 4–6

INGREDIENTS:

½ cup corn flour

¼ teaspoon salt

½ teaspoon pepper

1 (3½-pound) chicken, cut in serving-sized pieces, rinsed and dried on paper towels

½ cup corn oil

4 cloves garlic, peeled and cut into thick slices

1 large red onion, chopped coarsely

4 tomatillos, peeled and chopped

1 hot pepper, such as serrano or poblano, cored, seeded, and chopped

1 sweet red pepper, cored, seeded, and chopped

½ cup frozen corn

10 mushrooms, chopped

1½ cups chopped fresh or canned tomatoes

1 cup dry red wine

1 lemon, thinly sliced, seeded

½ teaspoon cinnamon

1 cup short-grained rice, uncooked

2 cups gluten-free chicken broth

½ cup chopped flat-leaf parsley or cilantro

1. Mix the corn flour, salt, and pepper on a sheet of wax paper. Dredge the chicken in it.

2. Heat the oil in a large frying pan or Dutch oven over medium-high heat. Brown the chicken, for 5–7 minutes. Remove the chicken from the pan and drain on paper towels.

3. Add the garlic, onion, tomatillos, hot pepper, sweet pepper, corn, and mushrooms. Sauté until soft, about 10 minutes.

4. Add the tomatoes, wine, lemon, and cinnamon. Mix well.

5. Return the chicken to the pan and add uncooked rice and broth. Bring to a boil. Then reduce heat to low, cover, and simmer for 45 minutes.

6. Just before serving, add the parsley or cilantro. Serve immediately.

Texas Influence

Mexican cooking is well seasoned, with layers of flavors coming from herbs, aromatic vegetables, and, yes, some spices. It's the Texas influence and the American passion for burning up the taste buds that has given Mexican cooking a reputation for being overly spiced.

HAWAIIAN-STYLE RICE WITH PINEAPPLE, MANGO, AND MACADAMIA NUTS

This is perfect with grilled or roasted ham, pork chops, or pork tenderloin. You can also add crumbled crisp bacon as an interesting garnish.

Serves 6

INGREDIENTS:

1 cup water

1½ cups orange juice

1½ cups uncooked short-grained rice

Minced zest of 1 orange

1 teaspoon salt

⅛ teaspoon Tabasco sauce

½ cup chopped pineapple

1 ripe mango, peeled and diced

2 tablespoons butter

½ cup toasted macadamia nuts

1. Bring the water and juice to a boil in a saucepan. Stir in the rice and then add mixture to a greased 2½-quart slow cooker. Cook on high for 2 hours or on low for 4 hours.

2. Add the rest of the ingredients on top of the rice and cook an additional 30 minutes until warmed through.

WILD RICE SALAD WITH RASPBERRY VINAIGRETTE

This is just as good on a summer picnic as it is a wintry side dish. It's filling and delightful.

Serves 6

INGREDIENTS:

4 cups water

¾ cup uncooked wild rice

1 teaspoon salt and black pepper, to taste

1 small red onion, chopped

3 stalks celery, rinsed and chopped finely

1 cup water chestnuts, drained and chopped

1 cup jicama, peeled and chopped

1 small apple, cored and chopped

⅔ cup olive oil

⅓ cup raspberry vinegar

½ cup fresh Italian flat-leaf parsley, rinsed, dried, and chopped

6 ounces fresh raspberries, rinsed and set on paper towels to dry

1. Bring water to a boil and add the rice; return to a rolling boil and then reduce heat to simmer and cover tightly. After 30 minutes, add salt and pepper.

2. When the rice has bloomed but is still hot, add the vegetables and apple. Taste and add additional salt and pepper if needed.

3. Mix the olive oil and vinegar together with the parsley and combine with the rice and vegetables. Place in a large serving dish and serve warm or chilled. Sprinkle with berries at the last minute.

Cooking Wild Rice

Disregard the directions on the package of wild rice. They tell you to cook for 30–40 minutes, when it takes closer to 90 minutes for it to bloom and soften. When cooking, just keep adding liquid if the rice dries out, and keep simmering until it "blooms" or the grains open up.

RISOTTO WITH RADICCHIO AND GORGONZOLA CHEESE

This is very nicely pungent and good as a side with game or seafood.

Serves 4

INGREDIENTS:

5 cups gluten-free canned or homemade chicken, fish, or vegetable broth

2 tablespoons butter

2 tablespoons olive oil

½ cup finely chopped sweet onion

1 head radicchio, rinsed and chopped finely

1½ cups uncooked arborio rice

Salt and freshly ground black pepper

¼ cup crumbled Gorgonzola cheese

Roasted red pepper strips and chopped parsley, for garnish

1. Bring the broth to a slow simmer in a saucepan and keep hot.

2. Heat the butter and oil in a large, heavy pan; add the onion and radicchio and sauté until softened, about 8 minutes. Add the rice and stir. Add salt and pepper.

3. Add the broth, ¼ cup at a time, until it is all gone, stirring constantly. This will take about 35 minutes. If the risotto is still not done, add water, ¼ cup at a time.

4. When the rice is done, stir in the Gorgonzola cheese and garnish with strips of roasted red pepper and parsley. Serve hot.

Flavoring with Bacon

Bacon is an excellent garnish. It also can add flavor to soups and stews, and fat for sautéing vegetables, mushrooms, etc. A little goes a long way. If you are watching your diet, just drain the bacon well on paper towels and crumble it. Then, sprinkle it on soups, salads, vegetables, pasta, and rice. Be sure the package states "gluten-free."

PUMPKIN AND BACON RISOTTO

A boon to the cook is fresh pumpkin, peeled, seeded, and cut up, in supermarkets. This saves endless time and energy. This is a fine fall/winter side and great with turkey.

Serves 4

INGREDIENTS:

2 cups fresh pumpkin, peeled, seeded, and diced

Water to cover the pumpkin

1 tablespoon salt

4 strips gluten-free bacon

5 cups gluten-free canned or homemade chicken broth

4 tablespoons butter

½ cup finely chopped sweet onion

2 teaspoons dried sage or 1 tablespoon chopped fresh

½ teaspoon dried oregano or 2 teaspoons chopped fresh

1½ cups uncooked arborio rice

Salt and freshly ground black pepper

½ cup Parmesan cheese, fresh or gluten-free

¼ cup pepitas, for garnish

1. Put the diced pumpkin in a saucepan with water to cover and some salt. Simmer until the pumpkin is just tender, drain, and set aside, reserving the pumpkin liquid.

2. While the pumpkin is cooking, fry the bacon and drain it on paper towels. Crumble when cool. Heat the chicken broth in a large saucepan and keep at a low simmer.

3. Melt the butter in a big, heavy pot and add onion; sauté until soft. Add the sage, oregano, rice, salt, and pepper.

4. Slowly add the broth, ¼ cup at a time. When the pot hisses, add more broth, ¼ cup at a time. Repeat until broth is gone and then, if still dry, add some of the pumpkin liquid.

5. Stir in the pumpkin, Parmesan cheese, and bacon. Add extra pepper or butter if desired. Garnish with a sprinkle of pepitas and serve immediately.

Pumpkins

When you can get fresh pumpkin, peeled, seeded, and chopped, at the grocery store, go for it! Otherwise, it's easy to cut a pumpkin in half, remove the seeds, and place it cut-side down in a baking dish. Add ½ inch water, cover with foil, and roast it for an hour or more in a 250°F oven. Then it's easy to purée. That is an excellent way to prepare pumpkin for pies and soups.

BAKED MUSHROOM AND FONTINA RISOTTO

You can add so many other ingredients—cubes of cooked chicken or turkey, chopped pears or apples, and your favorite herbs.

Serves 6–8

INGREDIENTS:

3 tablespoons butter, divided

3 tablespoons extra-virgin olive oil

1 small onion, minced

2 cloves garlic, minced

½ teaspoon salt

½ teaspoon pepper

½ teaspoon ground oregano

6 large leaves fresh sage, ripped or cut up, or 2 teaspoons dried sage, crumbled

1 cup uncooked long grain rice

2½ cups gluten-free chicken broth

½ cup white vermouth

8 ounces mixed mushrooms (shiitake, porcini, morels, chanterelles), sliced

⅓ cup grated fontina cheese

1. Preheat the oven to 350°F.

2. Heat 1 tablespoon butter and the olive oil in an ovenproof casserole. Sauté the onion and garlic over a low flame until softened, about 2–3 minutes.

3. Add the salt, pepper, oregano, sage, and rice. Stir to coat the rice. Add the broth and vermouth. Cover the dish and place in the oven.

4. After the rice has cooked for 20 minutes, heat the remaining butter in a skillet and sauté the mushrooms for 3–4 minutes.

5. Stir the mushroom/butter mixture into the rice. Re-cover the casserole and continue to cook for 15 minutes.

6. Just before serving, stir in the fontina cheese.

A Misunderstood Italian Staple

Most cooks think that risotto is simply rice that has been boiled with broth and herbs. But it's so much more—the technique for making risotto is simple but demanding. The secret is the rice and how it's slow cooked, using a bit of liquid until it's absorbed and then a bit more. It's been said that the rice will tell you when to add liquid—it hisses and sizzles, asking for the broth!

MOROCCAN HOT AND TASTY WHITE RICE

Harissa is a classic Moroccan chili paste that comes in tubes. You can substitute quinoa, an ancient Aztec grain that is also gluten-free, for rice.

Serves 4

INGREDIENTS:

3 cups water

2 teaspoons salt

1 cup uncooked white rice

2 cloves garlic, finely minced

1 medium onion, finely minced

½ cup olive oil

6 gluten-free dried apricots, quartered and soaked in ⅔ cup warm water

1" harissa (squeezed from tube)—more if you like it really hot. Make sure it's gluten-free.

1 teaspoon dried thyme

Salt, to taste

½ cup parsley or cilantro, rinsed and chopped

1. Bring water to a boil and add salt and rice. Reduce heat, cover, and cook until tender, about 25 minutes.

2. In a skillet, sauté the garlic and onion in the olive oil over low heat.

3. Add the remaining ingredients (including the parsley), and simmer, stirring occasionally, for 10 minutes.

4. When the rice is done, mix with the sauce and serve.

CONFETTI AND RICE PASTA WITH CHICKEN

This is fun to eat and pretty to look at. The "confetti" is minced vegetables. Lots of Parmesan cheese completes the dish.

Serves 4

INGREDIENTS:

½ cup extra-virgin olive oil

½ cup finely chopped sweet red pepper

½ cup finely chopped yellow summer squash

½ cup zucchini squash, finely chopped

1 bunch scallions, chopped fine

2 cloves garlic, chopped fine

½ cup rice or corn flour

1 teaspoon salt

½ teaspoon pepper, or to taste

½ teaspoon dried thyme

¾ pound boneless, skinless chicken breast, cut into bite-sized pieces

½ cup gluten-free chicken broth

8 ripe plum (Roma) tomatoes, chopped, or 1½ cups canned

1 teaspoon dried oregano

1 teaspoon dried basil

1 tablespoon red pepper flakes, or to taste

1 pound rice pasta, cooked

1 cup freshly grated Parmesan cheese

1. In a large skillet over medium heat, heat the olive oil and add the pepper, squash, scallions, and garlic. Sauté, stirring frequently, for 3–4 minutes.

2. While the vegetables are sautéing, mix the flour, salt, pepper, and thyme on a piece of wax paper.

3. Dredge the chicken in the flour mixture and add to the pan along with the vegetables.

4. Add the broth, tomatoes, oregano, basil, and plenty of red pepper flakes. Cook, uncovered, for 10 minutes to make sure the chicken is done.

5. Add the rice pasta to the pan of sauce and mix. Sprinkle with plenty of Parmesan cheese and serve.

Rice Pasta

Rice pasta is available online and at Asian markets. Many supermarkets also carry it. Soba—Japanese noodles—have both buckwheat flour and wheat flour in them and sometimes the contents are listed in Japanese characters.

PAELLA

You need a really big pan for this—you can get paella pans made of heavy metal that have been coated with enamel.

Serves 10–16

INGREDIENTS:

2 medium-sized chickens cut into 10 pieces

1 pound chorizo (Spanish sausage) or sweet Italian sausage, cut into bite-sized pieces, gluten-free

½ cup olive oil

1 large onion, diced

2 cloves garlic, minced

3 cups uncooked rice

5½ cups gluten-free chicken broth

Pinch saffron

2 tomatoes, cored and chopped

1 (10-ounce) box tiny frozen peas (petit pois)

18 littleneck clams, scrubbed

18 mussels, scrubbed and debearded

1½ pounds jumbo shrimp, peeled and deveined

½ cup chopped fresh parsley

1. Preheat the oven to 350°F.

2. In paella pan or very large skillet, brown the chicken and chorizo in the olive oil and push them to the side of the pan. Add the onion, garlic, and rice, stirring to soften the onion and garlic and to coat the rice.

3. Add the broth, saffron, and tomatoes. Mix well, including the chicken and chorizo.

4. Bake in a preheated oven at 350°F for 20 minutes or until the rice begins to take up the broth. Add the peas.

5. The order in which you add the seafood is crucial. Always add the ones that take the longest to cook first, adding the more tender pieces at the end. Start by arranging the clams on top. When they start to open, add the mussels. When both are open, add the shrimp and simply mix them into the rice—shrimp take only 2–3 minutes to cook. Sprinkle with parsley and serve in the cooking pan.

Check Your Mussels

You must be sure that your mussels are alive. This means they are shut tightly and when you tap two together, you get a sharp click, not a hollow thump. Often, they will be slightly open but close when tapped—that's fine. Just don't use any that are cracked, open, or hollow-sounding. The same is true for clams. Always scrub clams and mussels with a stiff brush under cold running water.

LASAGNA WITH SPINACH

There is no need to precook the gluten-free noodles in this recipe.

Serves 10

INGREDIENTS:

28 ounces low-fat gluten-free ricotta cheese

1 cup defrosted and drained frozen cut spinach

1 large egg

½ cup part-skim shredded mozzarella cheese

8 cups (about 2 jars) gluten-free marinara sauce

½ pound uncooked gluten-free lasagna noodles

1. In a medium bowl, stir the ricotta, spinach, egg, and mozzarella.

2. Ladle a quarter of the marinara sauce along the bottom of a greased 6-quart slow cooker. The bottom should be thoroughly covered in sauce. Add a single layer of lasagna noodles on top of the sauce, breaking noodles if needed to fit in the sides.

3. Ladle an additional quarter of sauce over the noodles, covering all of the noodles. Top with half of the cheese mixture, pressing firmly with the back of a spoon to smooth. Add a single layer of lasagna noodles on top of the cheese, breaking noodles if needed to fit in the sides.

4. Ladle another quarter of the sauce on top of the noodles, and top with the remaining cheese. Press another layer of noodles onto the cheese and top with the remaining sauce. Take care that the noodles are entirely covered in sauce.

5. Cover and cook for 4–6 hours, until cooked through.

EASY ITALIAN SPAGHETTI

It doesn't get any easier than this. Because this meal cooks so quickly, you can put it together as soon as you get home from work.

Serves 4

INGREDIENTS:

1 pound lean ground beef, browned

1 (16-ounce) jar gluten-free marinara sauce

1 cup water

8 ounces gluten-free pasta, uncooked

½ cup grated Parmesan cheese, fresh or gluten-free

Add browned ground beef, marinara sauce, and water to a greased 4-quart slow cooker. Cook on high for 2 hours or on low for 4 hours. About 45 minutes prior to serving, stir dry gluten-free pasta into meat sauce. The pasta will cook in the sauce. Serve with Parmesan cheese sprinkled on top of each serving.

CLASSIC ITALIAN RISOTTO

Risotto should be very creamy on the outside, yet firm on the inside of each grain of rice.

Serves 4

INGREDIENTS:

5 cups gluten-free canned or homemade chicken or vegetable broth

2 tablespoons butter

2 tablespoons extra-virgin olive oil

½ cup finely chopped sweet onion

2 stalks celery, finely chopped

¼ cup celery leaves, chopped

2 cloves garlic, minced

1½ cups uncooked arborio rice

⅓ cup dry white wine

1 teaspoon salt, or to taste

⅔ cup freshly grated Parmesan cheese

¼ cup chopped parsley

Freshly ground black pepper, to taste

1. In a medium saucepan, bring the broth to a slow simmer over low heat and keep it hot.

2. Place the butter and oil in a heavy-bottomed pot, melt butter, and add the onion, celery, celery leaves, and garlic. Cook for 8–10 minutes.

3. Add the rice and stir to coat with butter and oil. Add white wine and salt.

4. In ¼-cup increments, start adding hot broth. Stir until the broth has been absorbed into the rice. Add another ¼ cup, stirring until all of the broth is absorbed. Repeat this process until all of the hot broth is gone. It must be stirred constantly and takes about 35 minutes.

5. When all of the broth is gone, taste the rice for desired consistency. If it needs more broth or water, add it and keep stirring. Add the cheese, parsley, and pepper. Serve immediately.

Parmesan Cheese

Always grate Parmesan cheese yourself as you need it. Buy it in 1-pound blocks and keep well sealed with plastic wrap in the refrigerator. Try using a box grater for a coarse cheese with lots of body.

ONE-POT SPAGHETTI AND MEATBALLS

Here's a classic comfort food the whole family will enjoy. It takes a little extra work to make the homemade gluten-free meatballs, but your family will agree it's well worth the effort when they taste this fabulous one-pot meal.

Serves 4

INGREDIENTS:

1 slice gluten-free bread, torn in very small pieces

¼ cup 2% milk

1 pound lean ground beef

½ teaspoon salt

½ teaspoon pepper

1½ teaspoons dried onion

1 large egg

1 tablespoon olive oil

1½ cups gluten-free prepared spaghetti sauce

⅓ cup water

4 ounces gluten-free spaghetti, uncooked and broken into small pieces

1. In a large bowl, mix together bread and milk. Set aside for 5 minutes. Add ground beef, salt, pepper, dried onion, and egg. Mix well and roll into small meatballs.

2. In a skillet over medium heat, cook the meatballs in small batches in the olive oil until they are browned, approximately 5–6 minutes. Add meatballs to a greased 2½-quart slow cooker.

3. Add spaghetti sauce and water to the slow cooker. Cook on high for 4 hours or on low for 8 hours.

4. An hour before serving, add the spaghetti pieces and stir into the sauce. Cook spaghetti for an hour. Try not to overcook the pasta, as it will become mushy.

GARLIC AND ARTICHOKE PASTA

Artichoke hearts give this sauce a unique and savory flavor perfect for gluten-free pasta or rice.

Serves 6

INGREDIENTS:

2 (14½-ounce) cans diced tomatoes with basil, oregano, and garlic

2 (14-ounce) cans artichoke hearts, drained and quartered

6 cloves garlic, minced

½ cup heavy cream

3 cups cooked gluten-free pasta

1. Pour tomatoes, artichokes, and garlic into a 4-quart slow cooker. Cook on high for 3–4 hours or on low for 6–8 hours.

2. Twenty minutes prior to serving, stir in cream.

3. Serve over hot gluten-free pasta.

Can't Find Seasoned Canned Tomatoes?

If you can't find diced tomatoes with herbs and spices in your grocery store, use regular diced tomatoes and add 2 teaspoons of Italian seasoning to your sauce.

QUINOA WITH CHORIZO

Try this quinoa side dish as an alternative to rice. Chorizo has a savory, smoky, and garlicky flavor, which adds zest to the mildness of quinoa. The sausage also adds a nice red color to this dish due to the paprika (also known as "pimenton") used to season it.

Serves 4

INGREDIENTS:

½ cup (or 1 link) Spanish-style chorizo, gluten-free

½ cup onions, diced

1 cup uncooked quinoa, rinsed

2 cups water or gluten-free chicken broth

1. Sauté the chorizo and onions in a small, nonstick skillet over medium heat until the onions are soft. Drain off any excess fat.

2. Add to a greased 2½-quart or smaller slow cooker, along with quinoa and water or chicken broth.

3. Cover and cook on low for 2 hours or on high for 1 hour, until quinoa is soft and fluffy.

RED RICE AND SAUSAGE

This is so easy—and perfect for when you are low on time. Kids love it and grownups do too.

Serves 4–6

INGREDIENTS:

1 pound gluten-free sweet or hot Italian sausage, cut into 1" pieces

1 medium onion, chopped fine

2 cloves garlic, chopped

1 cup red rice, uncooked

2¾ cups gluten-free chicken broth

1 teaspoon dried rosemary or 1 tablespoon fresh rosemary

½ cup grated Parmesan cheese, fresh or gluten-free

¼ cup chopped fresh parsley

1. Brown the sausage pieces, onion, and garlic in oven-safe skillet over medium-high heat for 5–8 minutes. If the sausage is very lean, add a bit of olive oil to prevent sticking.

2. Stir in the rice and toss with the sausage and vegetables. Add the broth and rosemary and cover. Cook on very low heat or place in a 325°F oven for 45–60 minutes.

3. Just before serving, sprinkle the top with Parmesan cheese and brown under the broiler. Add the chopped parsley and serve.

What Is Red Rice?

Yes there is more out there than white or brown rice! Red rice is often found in Europe, Southeast Asia, and India. Red rice has similar nutritional information as brown rice, as they are both high in fiber.

BROWN RICE PILAF WITH TOASTED ALMONDS

For best results, soak the brown rice overnight to help make it softer and lighter. This can be served as a side dish or paired with beans to create a perfect main dish.

Serves 6

INGREDIENTS:

⅓ cup almonds, slivered

1 tablespoon extra-virgin olive oil

1 large onion, finely chopped

3 cloves garlic, minced

1½ cups uncooked long grain brown rice

1 teaspoon dried parsley

3½ cups gluten-free vegetable broth or low-sodium chicken broth

2 teaspoons dried marjoram, minced

Salt and pepper, to taste

1. Place the almonds in medium-sized dry skillet over medium heat, stirring constantly for 3–4 minutes, until lightly browned. Place almonds in a small bowl.

2. In the same skillet, sauté the onion and garlic in oil. Cook until onion is translucent, about 5 minutes.

3. Add the rice and stir until thoroughly mixed, about 1 minute.

4. Add parsley, broth, and marjoram; cover and reduce heat to low.

5. Simmer until all the water is absorbed and the rice is fully cooked, about 45–50 minutes.

6. Uncover, fluff with fork and let stand for a few minutes. Stir in toasted almonds. Add salt and pepper to taste.

ASPARAGUS, MUSHROOMS, AND YELLOW TOMATOES WITH BROWN RICE PASTA

Fresh vegetables work best in this dish. This dish is packed with flavor and full of color.

Serves 6

INGREDIENTS:

1 (16-ounce) package of brown rice pasta

1 tablespoon extra-virgin olive oil

2 cloves garlic, chopped

1 pound fresh asparagus, cut in half

1 pint yellow tomatoes, sliced in half

1 organic yellow pepper, sliced in strips

1 organic orange pepper, sliced in strips

1 cup mushrooms, sliced

½ cup gluten-free vegetable broth (or broth of your choice)

1 tablespoon Parmesan cheese, grated, fresh or gluten-free

Salt and pepper, to taste

1. Prepare the brown rice pasta according to the instructions on the package. This pasta should be prepared al dente. Rinse thoroughly with cool water to stop the cooking process and drain.

2. Place the oil, garlic, and vegetables in a large skillet and sauté for 3–4 minutes, until they soften. Add vegetable broth and stir until well blended. Let cook for another 2–3 minutes, until the vegetables are tender.

3. Place the vegetables on top of the brown rice pasta and top with freshly shaved Parmesan cheese. Season with salt and pepper to taste if desired.

Brown Rice Pasta

Make sure you cook your brown rice pasta according to the instructions. If it is overcooked, it becomes mushy and hardly palatable. If it is undercooked, it becomes chewy. It may take a few times to get the perfect, al dente, brown rice pasta.

CORN PASTA IN RICH CREAM SAUCE WITH PROSCIUTTO, GORGONZOLA, AND WALNUTS

This is a delicious variation on the basic cream sauce. Feel free to lighten this up using half-and-half.

Makes 2½ cups

INGREDIENTS:

1 (10-ounce) package corn pasta

3 tablespoons unsalted butter

3 tablespoons corn flour

2 cups medium cream, warmed

2 tablespoons gluten-free minced prosciutto

½ cup crumbled Gorgonzola or blue cheese

¼ teaspoon ground nutmeg

½ cup walnut pieces, toasted

Salt and pepper, to taste

1. Cook corn pasta according to instructions on the package.

2. Melt the butter in a large skillet and stir in the flour. Sauté, stirring for 4–5 minutes over medium-low heat. Add the warm cream, whisking constantly until thickened to desired consistency.

3. Remove from the heat and stir in the prosciutto, cheese, nutmeg, walnuts, salt, and pepper. Serve immediately.

Rich Cream Sauces Are Versatile

You can add herbs, broth, or even bacon to a rich cream sauce. You can add cheese such as mascarpone or some prosciutto. The addition of mushrooms adds body and flavor too! You can adapt a cream sauce to loads of fish, meat, and vegetable dishes and benefit from the lush flavors.

RICE PASTA IN SPICY SPINACH AND LOBSTER SAUCE

Rice pasta is found in Asian markets and some specialty supermarkets.

Serves 4

INGREDIENTS:

1 (16-ounce) package rice pasta

1 (1½-pound) lobster; if imitation, make sure it is gluten-free

2 tablespoons butter

2 tablespoons cornstarch

1 cup gluten-free hot chicken or clam broth

1 cup heavy cream

3 cups fresh baby spinach, rinsed and stems trimmed

1 tablespoon dry sherry

Pinch ground nutmeg

1 teaspoon hot red pepper flakes or gluten-free cayenne pepper

Salt and pepper, to taste

1. Cook rice pasta according to instructions.

2. Plunge the lobster into plenty of boiling salted water. Cook for 15 minutes. Cool; crack the shell and remove the meat. Set the meat aside.

3. In a large saucepan, melt the butter and add the cornstarch, stirring until smooth. Whisk in the broth. Add the cream and heat.

4. Stir in the spinach and cook until wilted. Add the sherry, nutmeg, red pepper flakes, and reserved lobster. Sprinkle with salt and pepper. Serve over the rice pasta.

ZUCCHINI PASTA WITH PARMESAN AND SPICY MARINARA SAUCE

This is such a fun substitution for regular noodles or pasta. This dish is also a perfect way to eat more vegetables.

Serves 4

INGREDIENTS:

4 large zucchini

1 tablespoon grapeseed oil

2–3 cloves garlic, minced

Salt and black pepper, to taste

3 tablespoons Parmesan cheese, grated, fresh or gluten-free

Spicy Marinara Sauce (see recipe in this chapter)

1. Cut the zucchini into thin, noodle-like strips using a peeler or mandoline.

2. Heat the oil in a large skillet over medium-high heat. Add zucchini and garlic; cook and stir until just tender, about 5 minutes. Season to taste with salt and pepper.

3. Sprinkle with Parmesan cheese. Top with Spicy Marinara Sauce.

SPICY MARINARA SAUCE

This sauce is perfect for many various dishes. You can adjust the spiciness by increasing or decreasing the red pepper flakes.

Serves 10

INGREDIENTS:

3 tablespoons extra-virgin olive oil

1 medium onion, finely chopped

6 cloves garlic, minced

1 teaspoon oregano, dried

1 teaspoon parsley, dried

¾ teaspoon rosemary, dried

1 cup fresh basil leaves, torn

¾ teaspoon marjoram

½ teaspoon crushed red pepper flakes

2 (28-ounce) cans crushed tomatoes

1 red bell pepper, seeded and finely chopped

½ cup dry white wine

Salt and pepper, to taste

1. Heat the olive oil in a large pan. Add onion, garlic, and seasonings. Cover and cook for 10 minutes.

2. Add all other ingredients and simmer gently for 75 minutes.

SPRING VEGETABLES WITH PESTO AND PASTA

This dish is so easy to prepare and tastes wonderful with grilled chicken, shrimp, or steak.

Serves 4

INGREDIENTS:

½ medium onion, sliced

1 tablespoon extra-virgin olive oil

1 bunch asparagus, trimmed and cut into 1" pieces

3 large carrots, peeled and sliced

1 cup arugula

½ cup shelled English peas

Gluten-free pasta of your choice

Classic Pesto Sauce (see Chapter 11)

1. Place the onion in a large skillet with oil. Sauté for 3–4 minutes, until translucent.

2. Add asparagus and carrots. Cook for 5 minutes, until their colors brighten and they become tender.

3. Add arugula and peas, and stir to combine for 1 minute until arugula wilts. Remove from heat and place in a large bowl.

4. Cook pasta according to instructions. When finished cooking, toss vegetables and pasta together. Add the amount of pesto to your liking.

QUINOA ANGEL HAIR WITH BOLOGNESE SAUCE

Quinoa pasta has become more popular for its added protein and wonderful texture. Most grocery stores and specialty markets carry quinoa pasta. If you can't find it, feel free to substitute with another gluten-free pasta or rice.

Serves 4–6

INGREDIENTS:

1 tablespoon extra-virgin olive oil

2 cloves garlic, chopped

½ medium onion, chopped

1 pound lean ground beef, turkey, or chicken

2 ounces gluten-free diced pancetta

½ cup lean ground pork

½ cup chopped mushrooms

½ cup chopped carrots

Spicy Marinara Sauce (see recipe in this chapter)

1 (8-ounce) package quinoa angel hair pasta

Parmesan cheese, for topping (optional), fresh or gluten-free

1. In a large skillet over medium heat, place the oil, garlic, and onion. Sauté for 3–4 minutes, until onions are translucent and tender.

2. Add the ground beef, pancetta, and ground pork and brown over medium heat until no longer pink, about 5–8 minutes.

3. Once the meat is cooked, add mushrooms and carrots and cook for 3–4 minutes, until they soften.

4. Add Spicy Marinara Sauce (you can adjust the spices, when preparing the Spicy Marinara Sauce, according to your tastes) and let simmer over low heat for 20–25 minutes, stirring occasionally.

5. Cook quinoa angel hair according to instructions. Place Bolognese sauce on top. Add grated Parmesan cheese if desired.

PASTA PRIMAVERA WITH SUMMER VEGETABLES

This dish can be served over brown rice pasta, quinoa pasta, rice, or even quinoa. Feel free to add some shrimp or chicken to it if you'd like.

Serves 6

INGREDIENTS:

16 ounces gluten-free pasta of your choice

3 tablespoons extra-virgin olive oil

½ green onion, chopped

2 cloves garlic, minced

1 large carrot, peeled and diced

1 large zucchini, peeled and diced

1 summer squash, peeled and diced

½ medium green bell pepper, seeded and diced

½ medium red bell pepper, seeded and diced

½ cup chopped green beans

½ small eggplant, peeled and cut crosswise into ¼" slices

½ cup sliced plum (Roma) tomatoes

½ cup Spicy Marinara Sauce (see recipe in this chapter)

Grated Parmesan cheese, fresh or gluten-free, for topping (optional)

Salt and pepper, to taste

1. Cook pasta according to package instructions. Rinse with cool water and set aside.

2. In a large skillet over medium heat, add the oil, onion, and garlic. Cook for 2–3 minutes, until onions and garlic become tender.

3. Add the vegetables and stir to combine. Cook vegetables about 10 minutes, until they soften. Remove from heat.

4. Add the marinara sauce to the vegetables and stir to combine. Add pasta and stir once again. Top with grated Parmesan cheese and salt and pepper to taste.

BROWN RICE WITH BABY SPINACH, TOMATOES, AND GRILLED TURKEY SAUSAGE

This dish will be a family favorite. It's so simple to make and can be made ahead of time.

Serves 6

INGREDIENTS:

1½ cups brown rice, uncooked

1 (16-ounce) package turkey sausage, gluten-free

¼ teaspoon grapeseed oil

2 cloves garlic, chopped

2 cups organic baby spinach

½ pint grape or cherry tomatoes, sliced in half

1 yellow pepper, cut in 1" slices

¼ cup gluten-free chicken broth

½ teaspoon sea salt

Pepper, to taste

½ teaspoon oregano

1 tablespoon fresh basil, torn

1. Cook rice according to instructions.

2. Grill sausage in a grill pan or on the grill for 5–8 minutes, until browned and no longer pink. Set aside.

3. In a saucepan over medium heat, place oil and garlic, and sauté for 1–2 minutes, until garlic softens.

4. Add the spinach, tomatoes, and pepper and cook for 3–4 minutes, until vegetables are tender.

5. Add the chicken broth, salt, pepper, and oregano, turn heat to low, and let simmer for 3–4 more minutes.

6. Add cooked sausage and stir to combine. Pour sausage/vegetable mixture over rice and serve immediately. Top with fresh basil.

PERSIAN RICE WITH SAFFRON AND SOUR CHERRIES

This is excellent with duckling, turkey, or chicken. It has a slight bite to it and a nice tang. It's a simple recipe, but most delicious, and quite different from other side dishes.

Serves 6–8

INGREDIENTS:

1 tablespoon extra-virgin olive oil

1½ cups uncooked basmati or other long-grain rice

2½ cups gluten-free chicken broth

1 teaspoon saffron threads

1 (8-ounce) jar imported Iranian sour cherries, blanched, with juice

1 tablespoon butter

1 teaspoon salt

Freshly ground pepper, to taste

½ cup slivered almonds, toasted, for garnish

1. Heat the oil in a large skillet and add the rice; cook, stirring, for 6 minutes.

2. Add the chicken broth and bring to a boil. Reduce heat to low and add all remaining ingredients, except the almonds.

3. Cover and simmer for 25 minutes, or until the rice is tender. Check the rice every 10 minutes to make sure it does not dry out. If the rice is stubbornly tough, add more broth, or water.

4. Place in a warm serving bowl and sprinkle with almonds.

Rice and Fruit

You can also use a 15-ounce can unsweetened sour cherries or 1 pound sour red pie cherries, but do not use sweetened pie cherries in this recipe. Interestingly, you can use summer fruit, tropical fruit, dried fruit, and just about any kind of nut with white rice or wild rice.

BEEF-FLAVORED WHITE RICE WITH ASIAN SPICES

This is the perfect side dish to complement any Asian-style stir-fry or grilled meat or fish. Five-spice powder is available at some supermarkets and at most Asian markets.

Serves 4

INGREDIENTS:

½ cup gluten-free soy sauce

¼ cup dry white wine or sake

1 tablespoon freshly grated gingerroot

1 tablespoon Asian sesame seed oil

1 teaspoon gluten-free Asian five-spice powder

2 cloves garlic, minced

4 scallions, minced

⅔ cup gluten-free beef broth

3 cups hot, cooked white rice

Mix together all ingredients, except the rice, to make a sauce. Boil for 3 minutes to reduce. Then mix in the rice, and serve hot.

A Grass, Not a Rice

Many people may be surprised to know that wild rice is not rice at all but a grass. Wild rice (*Zizania aquatica*) is really an annual aquatic seed found mostly in the upper freshwater lakes of North America. It was used by tribes such as the Algonquin and Ojibwa as an important food source, and it was a staple in their ritual harvest feasts. Stores of wild rice nourished them during the long winters.

SPANISH-STYLE RICE

This is an excellent side to pair with a steak. Perfect for entertaining, it can be made in advance and then reheated just before serving time.

Serves 4

INGREDIENTS:

3 cups water

2 teaspoons salt

1 cup white rice, uncooked

½ cup extra-virgin olive oil

1 large onion, chopped

1 clove garlic

½ teaspoon oregano, dried

2 jalapeño or poblano peppers, cored, seeded, and chopped

1 roasted red pepper, from a jar or your own, chopped

4 ripe plum (Roma) tomatoes, cored and chopped

1 teaspoon lemon zest

10 black olives, sliced

Freshly ground black pepper, to taste

1. In a large saucepan, bring the water to a boil, and add the salt and the rice. Reduce the heat to low, cover, and simmer until tender, about 25 minutes.

2. While the rice is cooking, heat the oil in a large frying pan.

3. Add the onion, garlic, oregano, and hot peppers. Sauté over low flame for 8–10 minutes.

4. Mix in the rest of the ingredients and simmer for 10 minutes.

5. Add to the hot rice and serve.

Ground Pepper

You can get pink, white, and black peppercorns. Some cooks like to mix them. Some say there is a taste difference among the three. Other cooks use white pepper in white food so you won't see the black specks. Try a coarsely ground pepper in recipes like the one above. To coarsely grind, place 6–8 peppercorns between two pieces of wax paper. Use a heavy frying pan to press down on the corns until they are cracked and in coarse pieces. Don't just lay them on a board and hit them with the pan or they will fly all over the kitchen.

RANGOON RICE CAKES

These are spicy and need a nice cold cucumber salad or some chutney on the side. Serve with chicken, shrimp, or fish.

Serves 6

INGREDIENTS:

6 cups cooked rice

½ cup minced red onion

1 clove garlic, chopped

1" fresh gingerroot, peeled and minced

1 tablespoon gluten-free madras curry powder

½ teaspoon cinnamon

2 large eggs

½ cup heavy cream

1 teaspoon salt and black pepper, to taste

¼–½ cup cooking oil, as needed

2 cups gluten-free bread crumbs

½ cucumber, chopped

½ cup plain gluten-free yogurt

Juice of ½ lemon

12 mint leaves, for garnish

1. In a large bowl, mix the rice, onion, garlic, gingerroot, and spices together.

2. Add the eggs and cream and keep mixing. Sprinkle with salt and pepper to taste and combine well.

3. Form into 12 small cakes. (The recipe can be made up to this point in advance and refrigerated for up to a day.)

4. Heat oil in a frying pan over high heat. Cover the cakes with crumbs and fry until golden. Place on paper towels to drain, and then on a warm platter.

5. Mix chopped cucumber, yogurt, and lemon. Place in a bowl on the side of the dish of rice balls. Serve rice balls with a mint leaf on top of each cake.

Rice and Wild Rice

Native Americans in the Northwest gathered wild rice in lakes. These days most basmati rice is grown in Texas. Always give wild rice extra time—it needs to be fully cooked and to grow in size to about six times what you started with.

WILD RICE STUFFING FOR POULTRY

This can be baked inside the bird or in a separate casserole dish. Allow about ¾ cup stuffing per pound of bird.

Makes enough stuffing for a 12-pound turkey

INGREDIENTS:

¼ pound butter

1 large onion, chopped

3 stalks celery with their tops, rinsed and chopped

1 teaspoon each: dried thyme, dried rosemary, dried sage, salt, and pepper

1 cup walnut halves, toasted and chopped

3 tart apples, peeled, cored, and chopped

½ cup dry white wine

½ cup fresh parsley, rinsed and chopped

6 cups cooked wild rice

1. In a large skillet, melt the butter and add onion, celery, herbs, salt, and pepper. Sauté until vegetables are softened, about 5 minutes. Add the walnuts and apples as well as wine and parsley.

2. Mix all of the ingredients in a large bowl, tossing with the wild rice until well combined.

3. Either stuff it into the turkey or spoon it into a casserole dish and bake at 350°F for 30 minutes, covered with aluminum foil.

LEMON RICE WITH TOASTED PINE NUTS

This dish can easily be made into a meal by simply adding chicken or sausage. The lemon flavor is so light and can easily go alongside most entrées.

Serves 4

INGREDIENTS:

1 cup uncooked arborio rice

1½ cups water

1 tablespoon grapeseed oil

Juice from ½ lemon

1 clove garlic, finely chopped

Salt and pepper, to taste

Zest from 1 lemon

¼ cup fresh parsley

1 tablespoon pine nuts, toasted

1 tablespoon Parmesan cheese, fresh or gluten-free (optional)

1. In a large saucepan, combine the rice with water over high heat and bring to a boil. Reduce heat to medium, stirring continuously until the water is absorbed.

2. In ¼ cup increments, add an additional 3 cups of water to the saucepan. Continue to stir constantly while adding the water and until all 3 cups of water have been absorbed. Drain well in case any liquid is left, but do not rinse.

3. In a small bowl, mix the oil and lemon juice.

4. Transfer the rice to a medium-sized serving bowl. Add garlic, lemon juice mixture, and season with salt and pepper.

5. Add the lemon zest, parsley, and pine nuts, and toss. Top with Parmesan cheese if desired.

Arborio Rice

Arborio rice cooks much differently than other varieties of rice. Arborio rice is typically used in risotto dishes, which require a creamier texture. By slowly adding the water and continuously stirring, the rice releases starches, which make the texture much more creamy.

CHEESY BROCCOLI RICE

You will find that many other broccoli rice casseroles use canned creamed soups. Be careful cooking with those as they contain a lot of sodium and fat and can contain gluten.

Serves 10

INGREDIENTS:

2 cups water

1 cup uncooked jasmine rice, rinsed

1 teaspoon, plus 2 tablespoons, butter

4 slices gluten-free bacon

4 cups broccoli florets and stems, cleaned and trimmed, finely chopped

1 medium onion, chopped

2 cloves garlic, minced

½ cup mushrooms, diced

1 tablespoon gluten-free cornmeal

1½ cups fat-free milk

2 cups shredded Gouda cheese (you can also use Cheddar, Swiss, or provolone), divided

1. Preheat oven to 350°F.

2. In a large saucepan, place 2 cups of water and rice over high heat and bring to a boil. Cover, reduce heat to low and simmer about 10 minutes, until all the liquid has been absorbed and rice is tender. Remove from heat and fluff with fork. Cover again and let sit 5 minutes.

3. In a large skillet, melt 1 teaspoon butter over medium-high heat. Add bacon and cook until crisp while turning over several times. Remove bacon from skillet and place on paper towels to drain.

4. Place broccoli in large saucepan, and add water to cover broccoli. Bring to boil over high heat and reduce heat to medium. Cook for 3–4 minutes, until broccoli is bright green and tender. Remove from heat, drain, and place broccoli in a 1½-quart casserole dish. Crumble bacon into small pieces.

5. In same skillet that you cooked bacon, add 2 tablespoons butter, onion, garlic, and mushrooms. Cook for 2–3 minutes, until mushrooms are softened.

6. Add cornmeal and mix to combine. Slowly add milk, and continue stirring until sauce thickens, about 4 minutes.

7. Add 1½ cups cheese and crumbled bacon. Stir.

8. Combine rice and cheese sauce with broccoli in casserole dish. Top with remaining ½ cup cheese. Bake for 20 minutes, or until cheese is completely melted and golden brown.

WILD RICE PILAF

Wild rice is a perfect side dish for the gluten-free diet. It's naturally gluten-free and is actually in the grass family. Wild rice has a rustic, earthy flavor that's a nice alternative to plain white rice.

Serves 6

INGREDIENTS:

2 tablespoons butter

½ cup finely chopped onion

2 cups wild rice, uncooked

½ teaspoon salt

½ teaspoon pepper

2 (14-ounce) cans gluten-free chicken broth

½ cup water

1 (4-ounce) can sliced mushrooms, undrained

1 teaspoon dried thyme

1 teaspoon dried oregano

1. Pour rice into a mesh colander and rinse.

2. Add butter to a frying pan and heat until sizzling. Add chopped onion and wild rice. Cook over medium-high heat for 3–4 minutes, until rice has a slightly nutty, toasty aroma, and onions are translucent.

3. Grease a 4-quart slow cooker with nonstick cooking spray. Add toasted rice and onions to slow cooker. Add remaining ingredients and mix well.

4. Cover and cook on high for 3 hours or on low for 6 hours until rice has absorbed most of the liquid. If rice is not absorbing the liquids fast enough, vent the lid of the slow cooker with a chopstick or wooden spoon handle.

CHAPTER 13

BEANS AND LENTILS

BISTRO LENTIL SALAD

This is a favorite in French bistros and Greek tavernas. In either case, the seasonings are only slightly different, in all cases delicious.

Serves 6

INGREDIENTS:

1 (16-ounce) package red lentils or small French ones

2 cups gluten-free chicken broth

Water, as needed

2 cloves garlic, smashed and peeled

2 whole cloves

4 slices gluten-free smoked bacon

½ cup finely chopped sweet red onion

1 sweet red bell pepper, roasted, peeled, and chopped

2 stalks celery, washed and finely chopped

½ cup chopped fresh parsley

2 teaspoons dried oregano

1 teaspoon prepared gluten-free Dijon mustard

2 tablespoons lemon juice

2 tablespoons red wine vinegar

⅔ cup extra-virgin olive oil

Salt and freshly ground pepper, to taste

1. In a large saucepan, combine the lentils and broth, and add water to cover. Add the garlic and cloves. Bring the lentils to a boil and reduce heat to simmer. Cook until tender, about 20 minutes. Drain and place in a large serving bowl. Remove garlic and cloves.

2. Cook bacon, and drain on paper towels.

3. Mix the rest of the ingredients with the lentils and chill for 2–3 hours. Just before serving, heat for a few seconds in the microwave. Or serve well chilled with shredded lettuce. Garnish with crisp chopped bacon.

The Lovely Lentil

Lentils are a staple in India, where many people need to be fed on little money. You can become a gourmet on a budget, experimenting with many varieties of lentils. Substitute them for pasta and use them in soups, stews, and salads.

TUSCAN BEAN, TOMATO, AND PARMESAN CASSEROLE

This is fantastic comfort food. If you are looking for a satisfying, warming, and delicious meal, this is it!

Serves 4–6

INGREDIENTS:

4 slices gluten-free bacon

¼ cup extra-virgin olive oil

4 cloves garlic, chopped coarsely

1 medium onion, peeled and chopped coarsely

½ fresh fennel bulb, coarsely chopped

1 tablespoon rice flour

2 (15-ounce) cans white beans, drained and rinsed

16 ounces tomatoes, chopped (canned is fine)

1 medium zucchini, chopped

1 tablespoon chopped fresh basil

1 teaspoon dried oregano

1 teaspoon dried rosemary

½ cup fresh Italian parsley, rinsed and chopped

1 teaspoon dried red pepper flakes, or to taste

1 teaspoon salt, or to taste

½ cup freshly grated Parmesan cheese, fresh or gluten-free

2 tablespoons unsalted butter, cut into small pieces

1. Preheat oven to 350°F.

2. Fry the bacon in a skillet until almost crisp. Place on paper towels to drain. Remove all but 1 teaspoon of bacon fat from pan. Chop bacon and set aside.

3. Add the oil, garlic, onion, and fennel to the skillet. Sauté over low heat for 10 minutes, or until softened but not browned.

4. Blend the flour into the mixture and cook for 3 minutes, mixing well.

5. Add the beans, tomatoes, and zucchini. Mix well and pour into a casserole dish.

6. Add the herbs, red pepper flakes, and salt, and stir. Mix in the reserved chopped bacon.

7. Sprinkle Parmesan cheese and butter over the top and bake for 25 minutes, or until the cheese is lightly browned.

Eat More Beans

There are more varieties of legumes than it's possible to list here. They are delicious and loaded with protein, vitamins, minerals, and fiber. If a culture, or a household, needs to stretch its food supply, beans are the answer. They come in red and pink, green and orange, black and white, speckled or solid. Some have black eyes and others look like cranberries. Beans—legumes—are available in many sizes and shapes, from tiny peas to big kidneys.

INDIAN-STYLE CHICKEN WITH LENTILS

In countries with huge populations, it's both wise and popular to stretch meat, fish, and seafood with all kinds of legumes.

Serves 4–6

INGREDIENTS:

1 cup uncooked lentils

3 cups water

Salt and red pepper flakes, to taste

2 cloves garlic, peeled and minced

1 medium onion, peeled and finely minced

2 tablespoons lemon juice

1 teaspoon cumin

½ cup chopped fresh parsley

1 pound boneless, skinless chicken breasts, cut into bite-sized pieces

1 cup plain gluten-free yogurt

1 tablespoon gluten-free curry powder

Salt and Tabasco sauce, to taste

1. Place the lentils and water in a saucepan. Bring to a boil, reduce heat, and simmer.

2. Just before the lentils are cooked (when barely tender, after about 25 minutes), add the salt and pepper flakes, garlic, onion, lemon juice, cumin, and parsley until the onion is soft and lentils are finished cooking.

3. Toss the chicken with the yogurt, curry powder, salt, and Tabasco. Place on aluminum foil and broil for 5 minutes per side.

4. Mix the chicken into the lentils and serve with rice.

Lentils Are Versatile!

Lentils are a form of bean, and they come in many colors—the red ones are particularly pretty in any dish. The yellow, green, and gray varieties are also just as delicious.

THICK AND CREAMY CORN AND LIMA BEAN CASSEROLE

This makes a satisfying meal and can be made with chopped ham, for added flavor and a serving of protein. Simply add 1–2 cups of chopped gluten-free ham into the slow cooker with the ingredients in Step 2 and cook as directed.

Serves 4

INGREDIENTS:

2 tablespoons butter

½ sweet onion, finely chopped

½ cup minced celery

¼ cup minced roasted red pepper

½ cup gluten-free chicken broth

1 (10-ounce) package frozen lima beans

1 (10-ounce) package frozen corn kernels

2 large eggs, well beaten

1½ cups heavy cream or evaporated milk

1 teaspoon salt

1 teaspoon paprika

1 teaspoon ground black pepper

1 teaspoon ground coriander

½ teaspoon ground allspice

1 cup gluten-free bread crumbs

1. Melt butter in a large skillet. Sauté onion and celery until softened, about 3–5 minutes.

2. Grease a 4-quart slow cooker. Add sautéed onions and celery. Add remaining ingredients to slow cooker, except for bread crumbs. Stir together and sprinkle bread crumbs on top.

3. Cover and vent the lid with a chopstick. Cook on low for 6 hours or on high for 3 hours.

Better Than Canned

Stay away from canned creamed corn (as it contains wheat flour) and stick with fresh or frozen, and make your own cream sauce. It's easy and gluten-free, and tastes so much better than the ones made with soups or mixes.

RED BEANS AND RICE

You can add an additional boost to the flavor of this dish by substituting spicy tomato-vegetable juice for the broth or water.

Serves 6

INGREDIENTS:

1 tablespoon olive oil

1 cup converted long-grain rice, uncooked

1 (15-ounce) can red beans, rinsed and drained

1 (15-ounce) can pinto beans, rinsed and drained

½ teaspoon salt

1 teaspoon gluten-free Italian seasoning

½ tablespoon dried onion flakes

1 (15-ounce) can diced tomatoes

1¼ cups gluten-free vegetable broth or water

1. Grease a 4-quart slow cooker with nonstick spray. Add the oil and rice; stir to coat the rice in the oil.

2. Add the red beans, pinto beans, salt, Italian seasoning, onion flakes, tomatoes, and vegetable broth or water to the slow cooker. Stir to combine. Cover and cook on low for 6 hours or until the rice is tender.

WHITE BEAN CASSOULET

The longer you cook this cassoulet, the creamier the beans become. Try serving this meal with toasted gluten-free croutons on top.

Serves 8

INGREDIENTS:

1 pound dried cannellini beans

2 leeks, sliced

1 teaspoon canola oil

2 parsnips, diced

2 carrots, diced

2 stalks celery, diced

1 cup sliced baby bella mushrooms

½ teaspoon ground fennel

1 teaspoon crushed rosemary

1 teaspoon dried parsley

⅛ teaspoon ground cloves

¼ teaspoon salt

¼ teaspoon freshly ground black pepper

2 cups gluten-free vegetable broth

1. The night before making the soup, place the beans in a 4-quart slow cooker. Fill with water to 1" below the top of the insert. Soak overnight.

2. Drain and rinse the beans and return them to the slow cooker.

3. Slice only the white and light-green parts of the leeks into ¼" rounds. Cut the rounds in half.

4. Heat the oil in a nonstick skillet. Add the parsnips, carrots, celery, mushrooms, and sliced leeks. Sauté for 1 minute, just until the color of the vegetables brightens. Add vegetables to the slow cooker along with the broth, herbs, and spices.

5. Cook on low for 8–10 hours.

SLOW-COOKED SOUTHERN LIMA BEANS WITH HAM

Lima beans are a Southern favorite and can withstand extremely long cooking periods without being mushy. In this traditional recipe, lima beans are flavored with bite-sized pieces of ham and simmered in savory tomato-based sauce.

Serves 8

INGREDIENTS:

1 pound dry lima beans, soaked for 6–8 hours and rinsed with cold water

2 cups gluten-free cooked ham, diced

1 sweet onion, chopped

1 teaspoon dry mustard

1 teaspoon salt

½ teaspoon freshly ground pepper

2 cups water

1 (15½-ounce) can tomato sauce

1. Drain and rinse soaked lima beans. Add beans to a greased 4–6-quart slow cooker. Add all remaining ingredients. If needed add additional water to cover the beans by 1".

2. Cook on high for 4 hours or on low for 8 hours. Serve over cooked rice or gluten-free pasta.

CURRIED LENTILS

Serve this Indian-style dish with freshly cooked rice. Aromatic varieties such as jasmine or basmati pair well with curry dishes.

Serves 6

INGREDIENTS:

2 teaspoons canola oil

1 large onion, thinly sliced

2 cloves garlic, minced

2 jalapeños, seeded and diced

½ teaspoon red pepper flakes

½ teaspoon ground cumin

1 pound uncooked yellow lentils

6 cups water

½ teaspoon salt

½ teaspoon ground turmeric

4 cups chopped fresh spinach

1. Heat the oil in a nonstick pan. Sauté the onion slices until they start to brown, about 8–10 minutes.

2. Add the garlic, jalapeños, red pepper flakes, and cumin. Sauté for 2–3 minutes. Add the onion mixture to a 4-quart slow cooker.

3. Sort through the lentils and discard any rocks or foreign matter. Add the lentils to the slow cooker.

4. Add the water, salt, and turmeric to the slow cooker and stir to combine. Cook on high for 2½ hours.

5. Add the spinach. Stir and cook on high for an additional 15 minutes.

EASY "REFRIED" BEANS

Some cooks like to mash the onion, jalapeño pepper, and garlic into the cooked beans; others prefer to discard them once the beans are cooked. (They've pretty much given up their flavors to the beans at this point anyhow.)

Serves 8

INGREDIENTS:

3 cups dried pinto beans

1 large onion, peeled and halved

½ fresh jalapeño pepper, seeded and chopped

6 cloves garlic, peeled and minced

⅛ teaspoon ground cumin

9 cups water

1 teaspoon salt

½ teaspoon freshly ground black pepper

1. Rinse and drain beans and place them in a bowl or saucepan. Add enough water to cover the beans by 2 inches. Cover and let soak overnight or for 8 hours. Drain the beans, then rinse and drain again.

2. Add the soaked beans, onion, jalapeño, garlic, and cumin to a 6-quart slow cooker. Pour in the water and stir to combine. Cover and, stirring occasionally, and adding more water as needed, cook on high for 8 hours or until the beans are cooked through and tender. (If you have to add more than 1 cup of water during cooking, lower the temperature to low or simmer.)

3. Once the beans are cooked, strain them, reserving the liquid. Mash the beans with a potato masher, adding some of the reserved water as needed to attain desired consistency. Add salt and pepper.

Reheating Refried Beans

Refried beans can be reheated in the microwave or by using any other traditional method that you use to warm up leftovers. However, if you want to add a touch of authentic flavor (and fat) to them, melt some lard in a nonstick skillet over medium heat, stir in the beans, and sauté until heated through.

BETTY'S BEANS GALORE

You may know this dish as cowboy beans, ranch beans, or glorified baked beans—but I call them Betty's Beans for my dear friend who shared this recipe with me. The wonderful combination of spices, brown sugar, molasses, beans, and ground beef make for a filling and delicious one-pot meal.

Serves 8

INGREDIENTS:

½ pound gluten-free bacon

1 pound lean ground beef

1 medium onion, chopped

¼ cup brown sugar

¼ cup white sugar

¼ cup gluten-free ketchup

¼ cup gluten-free barbecue sauce

1 teaspoon dry mustard

2 tablespoons molasses

½ teaspoon gluten-free chili powder

½ teaspoon ground pepper

1 teaspoon salt

2 (15-ounce) cans gluten-free pork and beans (do not drain)

1 (15-ounce) can red kidney beans (do not drain)

1 (15-ounce) can lima beans (do not drain)

1. Fry bacon in a skillet until crisp. Drain on paper towels. Crumble bacon and add to a greased 4–6-quart slow cooker. Brown ground beef in skillet, drain of grease, and add to slow cooker.

2. Add remaining ingredients to slow cooker. Cook on high for 4–6 hours or on low for 8–10 hours. Serve with Gluten-Free Corn Bread (see recipe in Chapter 3).

Make It Healthier

Feel free to use half the sugar called for in this recipe. It's quite sweet as is, and the tangy flavor will not be compromised if you decrease the amount of sugar. Also, feel free to use turkey bacon and extra-lean ground beef for an even healthier meal.

SPICY BEANS AND RICE CASSEROLE

Using salsa, instead of tomatoes and added spices, makes this casserole super easy to put together. It's delicious topped with a dollop of sour cream.

Serves 8

INGREDIENTS:

1 (15-ounce) can whole kernel corn, drained

1 (15-ounce) can black beans, rinsed and drained

1 (10-ounce) can diced tomatoes with green chilies

1 cup brown rice, uncooked

2¼ cups gluten-free chicken broth or water

1 cup gluten-free salsa

1 cup Cheddar cheese, shredded

¼ cup chopped fresh cilantro, for garnish

1. Grease a 4-quart slow cooker. Add corn, beans, tomatoes, rice, chicken broth or water, and salsa. Cover and cook on high for 3 hours or on low for 6 hours.

2. Once rice has absorbed water and is fully cooked, stir in Cheddar cheese. Cook an additional 20 minutes on high to melt cheese, and serve. Garnish with cilantro.

Instead of Salsa . . .

For an Italian/Tuscan flavor variation, use cannellini beans instead of black beans, use your favorite gluten-free marinara sauce or gluten-free spaghetti sauce in place of the salsa, and garnish with freshly chopped parsley instead of cilantro.

TUSCAN CHICKEN AND WHITE BEANS

Hearty white beans with warm Tuscan spices and tomatoes make this super-easy slow-cooked chicken special enough for company!

Serves 4

INGREDIENTS:

3 large boneless, skinless chicken breasts

1 (15½-ounce) can white beans, drained and rinsed

1 (14½-ounce) can diced tomatoes

1 (4-ounce) can mushrooms, drained

¼ cup Spanish olives stuffed with pimientos, sliced in half

2 teaspoons onion powder

1 teaspoon garlic powder

1 teaspoon basil

1 teaspoon oregano

1 teaspoon ground pepper

½ teaspoon salt

2 teaspoons olive oil

1. Cut chicken breasts into large chunks and place in a greased 4-quart slow cooker.

2. Add beans, tomatoes (including the juice), mushrooms, and olives. Add onion powder, garlic powder, basil, oregano, ground pepper, and salt.

3. Mix all ingredients together in the slow cooker. Drizzle olive oil over the top of the chicken and vegetables.

4. Cook on high for 3½–4 hours or on low for 6 hours. Serve over cooked rice or gluten-free pasta, if desired.

White Beans

White beans, which are also called navy beans, Boston beans, or Yankee beans, are small, lightly colored beans that are very mild in taste and work well in a variety of recipes. If you don't have white beans available, cannellini beans or northern beans, which are slightly larger, are excellent substitutes.

LEMON-GARLIC GREEN BEANS

Lemon zest and sliced garlic add a fresh and bright flavor to these slow-cooked green beans.

Serves 4

INGREDIENTS:

1½ pounds fresh green beans, trimmed

3 tablespoons olive oil

3 large shallots, cut into thin wedges

6 cloves garlic, sliced

1 tablespoon grated lemon zest

½ teaspoon salt

½ teaspoon pepper

½ cup water

1. Place green beans in a greased 4-quart slow cooker. Add remaining ingredients over the top of the beans.

2. Cook on high for 4–6 hours, or on low for 8–10 hours. If you like your beans crisper, check them on high after about 3½ hours or on low after about 6 hours. Fresh green beans are sturdy enough to withstand very long cooking temperatures without getting mushy.

CLASSIC BEANS AND FRANKS

Use your favorite gluten-free hot dogs in this recipe. All-beef hot dogs in particular have a wonderfully rich taste that pairs well with the salty sweet baked beans!

Serves 6

INGREDIENTS:

¼ cup onion, finely diced

2 teaspoons butter

1 (16-ounce) can gluten-free baked beans

1 (16-ounce) package gluten-free hot dogs, cut into ½" slices

⅓ cup brown sugar

1 teaspoon ground mustard

1 teaspoon celery salt

1. In a small glass or microwave-safe bowl, cook onion and butter on high for about 1 minute until onion is soft. Pour into a greased 2½-quart slow cooker.

2. Add baked beans, hot dogs, brown sugar, mustard, and celery salt to the onions and mix well.

3. Bake for 4 hours on high or for 8 hours on low.

Coleslaw in a Jiffy

In a large bowl mix together ½ cup gluten-free mayonnaise, 2 tablespoons sugar, 1 tablespoon apple cider vinegar, 1 teaspoon salt, 1 teaspoon pepper, and 1 tablespoon gluten-free creamy horseradish. Stir in 4½ cups shredded cabbage and ½ cup shredded carrots. Chill for 3–4 hours before serving.

PINTO BEAN–STUFFED PEPPERS

Stuffed peppers are most often filled with a ground meat mixture, but this recipe is an easy vegetarian option that will please the pickiest of diners.

Serves 4

INGREDIENTS:

1 cup cooked rice

1 (15-ounce) can pinto beans, drained and rinsed

1 (15-ounce) can tomato sauce

1 packet gluten-free taco seasoning

4 medium red, yellow, or green peppers

1. In a large bowl mix together the rice, pinto beans, tomato sauce, and taco seasoning.

2. Carefully remove the tops, seeds, and membranes of the peppers. Fill each pepper with ¼ of the pinto bean mixture.

3. Place the stuffed peppers in a greased 4-quart slow cooker. Add ⅓ cup of water around the bottom of the stuffed peppers.

4. Cook on high for 3–4 hours or on low for 6–8 hours until peppers are softened.

BARBECUE CHICKEN AND BEANS

Barbecue sauce can make any meal taste like a cookout! Homemade gluten-free barbecue sauce can be used with any of your favorite barbecue recipes. It's cheaper than store-bought sauce, and you can feel safe knowing it's gluten-free.

Serves 4

INGREDIENTS:

3–4 chicken breasts, cut into 1" pieces

1 (14½-ounce) can red kidney beans, drained and rinsed

2 teaspoons gluten-free Worcestershire sauce

1 cup gluten-free homemade or store-bought barbecue sauce

2 cups cooked white rice

1. Add all ingredients, except rice, to a greased 2½-quart or larger slow cooker.

2. Cook on high for 4 hours or on low for 8 hours. Serve over rice.

Quick Homemade Barbecue Sauce

Mix together 1 cup gluten-free ketchup, ¼ cup apple cider vinegar, 2 tablespoons brown sugar or molasses, 1 tablespoon gluten-free Dijon mustard, 1 tablespoon water, ½ teaspoon salt, and ½ teaspoon black pepper. Cook over medium heat for 3–5 minutes and let cool. Use as you would any barbecue sauce. Store in an airtight container or in a washed, recycled plastic bottle in the refrigerator for up to 1 month.

BLACK BEAN AND CHEESE TACOS

No one will guess how fast and easy this vegetarian taco filling is to make. Serve with guacamole and gluten-free sour cream.

Serves 4

INGREDIENTS:

1 (15-ounce) can black beans, drained and rinsed

¾ cup mild gluten-free salsa

8 gluten-free corn taco shells

1 cup shredded Cheddar cheese

1 heart of romaine lettuce, shredded

1. Add black beans and salsa to a greased 2½-quart slow cooker. Cook on high for 3–4 hours or on low for 6–8 hours.

2. Fill each taco shell with several tablespoons black bean filling, several tablespoons of shredded cheese, and a handful of shredded lettuce.

Guacamole in a Minute

Halve and seed 2 large avocados. Scoop the avocado pulp into a bowl. Add 2–3 tablespoons lime juice, a few halved grape tomatoes, 1 clove garlic (minced), ½ teaspoon salt, and ¼ teaspoon Goya Adobo sin Pimiento (all-purpose Hispanic seasoning—check label to ensure it is gluten-free). Mash together and serve with gluten-free chips or tacos.

THREE BEAN SALAD

This vegan salad is not too sweet and not too tangy, like other bean salads. It tastes even better when marinated overnight.

Serves 8

INGREDIENTS:

1 (15-ounce) can black beans, thoroughly rinsed and drained

1 (15-ounce) can red kidney beans, thoroughly rinsed and drained

1 (15-ounce) can chickpeas (garbanzo beans), thoroughly rinsed and drained

1 green pepper, finely diced

2 medium red onions, finely diced

⅓ cup cider vinegar

¼ cup extra-virgin olive oil

1 clove garlic, finely diced

1 tablespoon honey

½ teaspoon ground mustard

½ teaspoon salt

½ teaspoon black pepper

Handful of fresh cilantro, chopped

1. In a large bowl, mix the black beans, red kidney beans, and chickpeas. Add the diced pepper and onions and mix well.

2. In a small bowl, combine the vinegar, oil, garlic, honey, mustard, salt, and black pepper. Once thoroughly mixed, pour over bean mixture.

3. Add cilantro and refrigerate for 3–4 hours before serving.

TRICOLOR TOMATO-BEAN SALAD

Take advantage of local summer produce to create this perfect, light salad.

Serves 6

INGREDIENTS:

3 plum (Roma) tomatoes, seeded and chopped

1 green tomato, seeded and chopped

1 yellow tomato, seeded and chopped

1 small cucumber, peeled and chopped into 1" wedges

1 (15-ounce) can small white beans, thoroughly rinsed and drained

½ red onion, finely chopped

3 tablespoons extra-virgin olive oil

2 tablespoons balsamic vinegar

2 cloves garlic, crushed

1 teaspoon gluten-free Dijon mustard

1. Place the tomatoes, cucumber, beans, and onion in medium-sized bowl.

2. In a small bowl, whisk together the oil, vinegar, garlic, and mustard until completely blended.

3. Pour oil and vinegar mixture over chopped vegetables. Stir to thoroughly combine. Refrigerate for at least 1 hour or overnight.

Visit Your Local Farmers' Market

If available, your local farmers' market is the best place to buy the freshest fruit and veggies. Shopping at your local farmers' market will not only support local farmers, but it will also stimulate your town's economy.

HEALTHY MEXICAN CASSEROLE

This one-dish meal is so easy and delicious your family will ask you to make it again and again. Serve the casserole with Baked Corn Tortilla Chips (see recipe in Chapter 4).

Serves 8

INGREDIENTS:

1 tablespoon extra-virgin olive oil

1 pound lean ground turkey

½ teaspoon cumin

¼ teaspoon gluten-free chili powder

¼ teaspoon red pepper flakes

⅛ teaspoon coriander

2 tablespoons water

1 (15-ounce) can black beans, rinsed thoroughly and drained

1 (15-ounce) can pinto beans, rinsed thoroughly and drained

4–5 plum (Roma) tomatoes, chopped and seeds removed

1 teaspoon chopped chili peppers

½ cup frozen corn

¼ cup Mexican blend shredded cheese

1. Preheat the oven to 350°F.

2. Heat the oil in a large skillet over medium-high heat. Cook turkey in hot oil for 5–8 minutes, until the meat is browned.

3. Stir in cumin, chili powder, red pepper flakes, coriander, and water.

4. Add black and pinto beans, tomatoes, chili peppers, and corn. Stir well.

5. Place the meat mixture in a 9" × 13" casserole dish and add cheese on top.

6. Bake for 20 minutes until cheese is melted.

THICK AND CREAMY CORN AND BLACK BEAN CASSEROLE

This makes a satisfying meal and can be kept vegetarian, or add some gluten-free ham for extra flavor. Feel free to substitute half-and-half for the whipping cream to lighten it up.

Serves 4–5

INGREDIENTS:

2 tablespoons unsalted butter

½ sweet onion, chopped fine

½ cup minced celery

½ cup minced celeriac (celery root)

¼ cup sweet red pepper, roasted and chopped

2 tablespoons corn flour, potato flour, or cornstarch

½ cup rich gluten-free chicken broth

1 (15-ounce) can black beans, thoroughly rinsed and drained

1 (10-ounce) package frozen corn kernels

2 large eggs, well beaten

1½ cups whipping cream

1 teaspoon salt

1 teaspoon sweet paprika

1 teaspoon ground black pepper

1 teaspoon ground coriander

½ teaspoon ground allspice

1 cup gluten-free bread crumbs

1 cup grated Cheddar cheese

1. Preheat the oven to 350°F.

2. Melt the butter in a large ovenproof casserole. Add the onion, celery, celeriac, and red pepper and sauté over low heat until vegetables are soft, about 10 minutes.

3. Mix in the corn flour or starch and stir, cooking gently for 3 minutes.

4. Add the chicken broth, black beans, and corn. Bring to a boil, and then lower the heat to a simmer and cook until the black beans are slightly softened, about 20 minutes. Take off the heat.

5. In a small bowl, mix together the eggs and cream. Blend the mixture quickly into the vegetables. Mix in the salt and spices.

6. Place in a well-buttered casserole or keep in the same ovenproof pan that you've been using for cooking. Sprinkle the top with bread crumbs and cheese.

7. Bake until golden brown and bubbling, about 15 minutes. Serve hot.

Better Than Canned

Stay away from canned creamed corn and stick with fresh or frozen, making your own cream sauce. It's easy and gluten-free, and tastes so much better than the ones made with soups or mixes.

WARM TOMATO BEAN SALAD

This salad can be served as a light side dish or as a delightful first course.

Serves 4

INGREDIENTS:

1 tablespoon grapeseed oil

3 cloves garlic, chopped

1 (15-ounce) can white cannellini beans, rinsed and drained

5 plum (Roma) tomatoes, chopped

1 cup baby spinach

1. Heat the grapeseed oil in a skillet over medium-high heat, and sauté the garlic for 1–2 minutes, until soft.

2. Pour the beans and chopped tomatoes into the skillet. Reduce heat to medium-low and simmer for 5–10 minutes, until the tomatoes are soft.

3. Remove from heat and stir in spinach until wilted.

4. Serve over chicken or as a side dish.

What Is Grapeseed Oil?

Grapeseed oil is extracted from the seeds of grapes. It has a very high smoke point, which makes it optimal for sautéing and frying foods. It has a clean, light taste that blends nicely with foods. Grapeseed oil also works well in baked goods. It is packed with vitamins and healthy omega fatty acids.

FIESTA LIME-LENTIL SALAD

This is the perfect meatless dish that even carnivores will love.

Serves 8

INGREDIENTS:

1 (16-ounce) bag dried lentils

4 cups water

½ teaspoon sea salt

2 tablespoons freshly chopped cilantro

1 tablespoon grapeseed oil

½ cup broccoli, chopped

¼ cup carrots, sliced

½ cup green cabbage, chopped

¼ cup radish, chopped

½ green pepper, chopped

1 celery stalk, chopped

2 cloves garlic, minced

¼ teaspoon ground chili pepper

½ teaspoon dried oregano

1 teaspoon dried basil

1 teaspoon dried cumin

½ teaspoon dried paprika

½ teaspoon ground gluten-free cayenne pepper

Juice of 1 lime

1. Rinse the lentils under running water and pick through them to remove any bits of soil or rocks.

2. Add the lentils and water to a saucepan (with a lid) and bring to a boil. Turn heat down to low and cover to let the lentils simmer, but leave the lid ajar a bit so that they don't boil over. Check on them occasionally to make sure the water has not boiled down below the level of the lentils; add more water as needed. When the lentils are tender and can easily be mashed with a fork, they are done. It usually takes about 30–45 minutes for them to cook.

3. Add salt and cilantro in about the last 15 minutes of cooking time—when the lentils are starting to get soft. (Cooking often neutralizes the taste of the salt, so if you add it at the start, you end up having to add more salt to get the same flavor.)

4. When they are finished cooking, take the saucepan off the heat and cover tightly with the lid. Let sit for 5–10 minutes. The lentils will absorb more of the water, making them juicier and more tender.

5. In a large skillet over medium heat, add the oil and chopped veggies and sauté for 5 minutes.

6. Add lentils and seasonings and stir. Let sit on medium-low heat for 5–8 minutes until the veggies soften.

7. Remove from heat, add fresh lime juice, and stir until well blended.

Steamed Lentils Save Time

Do you want to save time and preparation? Purchase steamed lentils, which are available in the refrigerated section of most grocery stores. Simply take the steamed lentils out of their container and add to sautéed vegetables (Step 5) and follow the rest of the instructions.

QUINOA PILAF WITH LENTILS AND SPINACH

This dish is loaded with protein; it makes the perfect vegetarian dish.

Serves 4

INGREDIENTS:

1 tablespoon butter

½ medium onion, finely chopped

1 clove garlic, minced

½ cup uncooked quinoa, rinsed and drained

1½ cups gluten-free vegetable broth

½ cup uncooked lentils, rinsed and dried

1 tablespoon extra-virgin olive oil

1 cup water

2 carrots, finely chopped

1 teaspoon oregano, dried

1 teaspoon basil, dried

4 cups baby spinach

Salt and pepper, to taste

¼ cup toasted almonds, for garnish (optional)

1. Place butter in large skillet over medium heat. Add onion and garlic and cook 3–4 minutes, until onion is translucent.

2. Add rinsed quinoa and let sit for 1 minute until brown. Add broth and bring to a boil. Reduce heat, cover, and let simmer on low heat until all broth is absorbed, about 15–20 minutes.

3. While quinoa is cooking, place dried lentils and olive oil in a small skillet. Add water, carrots, oregano, and basil. Bring water to slight boil over medium-high heat, then reduce heat to low. Cook lentils for 20–30 minutes, until tender.

4. When quinoa is finished cooking, stir in baby spinach. Add salt and pepper.

5. Combine lentil mixture and quinoa together. Garnish with toasted almonds if desired.

Watch the Dates on Your Lentils

Try not to mix older lentils with fresh ones. Older lentils may take longer to cook than the newer ones because they have lost moisture. This will leave the fresh lentils overcooked and mushy.

BLACK BEAN–QUINOA CHILI

This comforting dish can be made in a slow cooker or on the stove in a Dutch oven. This also freezes well.

Serves 10

INGREDIENTS:

1 cup uncooked red quinoa, rinsed and drained

2 cups gluten-free vegetable broth

1 tablespoon canola oil

1 green onion, chopped

5 cloves garlic, chopped

1 tablespoon gluten-free chili powder

1 tablespoon cumin, ground

1 teaspoon coriander, ground

2 cups plum (Roma) tomatoes, diced

2 cans black beans, rinsed and drained

1 green bell pepper, chopped

1 jalapeño pepper, seeded and chopped (optional)

1 tablespoon dried chipotle pepper

1 zucchini, chopped

1 teaspoon dried oregano

½ teaspoon dried cinnamon

Salt and ground black pepper, to taste

1 cup frozen corn

1 cup portobello mushrooms, chopped

¼ cup fresh cilantro, chopped

Sliced avocado, plain gluten-free Greek yogurt, and shredded Cheddar cheese for topping

1. Place quinoa and broth in a medium saucepan over high heat and bring to a boil. Cover, reduce heat to medium-low, and let simmer for 15–20 minutes, until all the broth is absorbed. Set aside.

2. Heat oil in a large skillet. Add the onion and garlic, and sauté for 3–4 minutes, until soft. Add the chili powder, cumin, and coriander. Stir to combine.

3. Add the tomatoes, beans, peppers, zucchini, oregano, and cinnamon. Mix well and season with salt and pepper. Bring to a boil over high heat, reduce to low heat, cover, and let simmer for 20 minutes.

4. After 20 minutes, add the quinoa, corn, and mushrooms, and cook for an additional 5 minutes to soften corn and mushrooms. Remove from heat.

5. Top with sliced avocado, a dollop of plain Greek yogurt, cilantro, and shredded cheese.

Slow Cook It!

This dish can be made easily in a 4-quart slow cooker. Sauté onion and garlic in a skillet for 3–4 minutes, until soft. Add chili powder, cumin, and coriander and mix thoroughly. Add all the other ingredients except the corn and mushrooms. Cook on low for 5–6 hours. Add corn and mushrooms in the last hour and garnish with toppings.

SPICY QUINOA BEAN BURGERS

Even meat lovers will love these burgers! The patties can be made ahead of time and then refrigerated until ready to cook.

Makes 6 burgers

INGREDIENTS:

½ cup uncooked quinoa, rinsed and drained

1 cup gluten-free vegetable broth

1 (15-ounce) can black beans, rinsed and drained

1 (15-ounce) can red kidney beans, rinsed and drained

1 cup baby spinach

¾ cup cornmeal or gluten-free bread crumbs

¼ cup red bell pepper, chopped

¼ cup frozen corn, defrosted

¼ cup mushrooms, finely diced

1 shallot, minced

1 clove garlic, minced

1 teaspoon gluten-free chili powder

½ teaspoon red pepper flakes

1 teaspoon cumin

1 teaspoon paprika

1 teaspoon fresh cilantro, chopped

1 teaspoon gluten-free hot sauce

1 large egg

Juice of ½ fresh lime

Fresh avocado slices and tomato slices for topping

1. Preheat the oven to 375°F.

2. Place the quinoa and broth in a small saucepan and bring to a boil. Cover, reduce heat to low, and simmer for 15–20 minutes, until all the broth is absorbed.

3. Place the beans and spinach in blender or food processor and process for 1 minute allowing for some pieces of whole beans to remain.

4. Place the quinoa in a medium-sized bowl. Add the beans/spinach mixture, cornmeal, bell pepper, corn, mushrooms, shallot, garlic, seasonings, cilantro, hot sauce, egg, and fresh lime juice. Thoroughly mix with your hands to combine. If you have time, sit bowl in the refrigerator for a few minutes. This allows for easier forming of the patties.

5. Form the quinoa/bean mixture into 6 patties. Line baking sheet with aluminum foil and place patties on top. Bake for 30 minutes, making sure to turn them over after first 15 minutes.

6. Serve on top of rice or sautéed spinach and top with avocado and tomato slices. You can also eat these burgers with a gluten-free bun or in a gluten-free wrap or wrap each one in a giant lettuce leaf.

No Wheat-Free Bread Crumbs in the House?

Ground rolled oats are a wonderful substitution for gluten-free bread crumbs. Just make sure you read your labels to guarantee your rolled oats are pure and gluten-free!

SUN-DRIED TOMATO–ARTICHOKE PASTA WITH WHITE BEANS

Although this dish is vegetarian, cooked chicken or gluten-free sausage would be a nice addition.

Serves 6

INGREDIENTS:

1 tablespoon grapeseed oil

3 cloves garlic, finely chopped

1 cup sun-dried tomatoes, sliced

2 cups chopped mushrooms

1 (9-ounce) box frozen artichoke hearts, rinsed and drained

1 (15-ounce) can small white beans, rinsed thoroughly and drained

2 cups gluten-free vegetable broth

3 cups arugula

1 (16-ounce) package brown rice pasta

2 tablespoons freshly shaved Parmesan cheese (optional)

1. Place the oil and garlic in large skillet and let simmer for 1–2 minutes, until the garlic softens.

2. Add the sun-dried tomatoes, mushrooms, artichoke hearts, and beans, and let simmer for 3–4 minutes, until they soften.

3. Add broth and let simmer for 3–4 minutes. Add arugula, mix well, and remove from heat. You do not want the arugula to get too soft.

4. Cook the brown rice pasta according to instructions. Rinse pasta with cool water and drain.

5. Mix pasta with broth and veggie mixture. Top with shaved Parmesan if desired.

SWEET POTATO AND BLACK BEAN HASH

This is a wonderful side dish and leftovers can easily be wrapped up in gluten-free tortillas. Feel free to add chorizo or any kind of gluten-free sausage to make a complete meal.

Serves 4

INGREDIENTS:

2 tablespoons extra-virgin olive oil

1 medium onion, thinly sliced

2 cloves garlic, minced

1 small yellow pepper, chopped

2 medium sweet potatoes, peeled and diced into ½" cubes

1 jalapeño pepper, seeded and minced (optional)

1½ teaspoons cumin

1 teaspoon coriander

⅛ teaspoon gluten-free cayenne pepper

½ teaspoon gluten-free chili powder

¾ cup gluten-free vegetable broth

1 (15-ounce) can black beans, rinsed thoroughly and drained

2 tablespoons fresh cilantro, diced

Salt and pepper, to taste

Sliced avocado, lime wedges, diced scallions, and gluten-free sour cream, for garnish (optional)

1. Heat the olive oil over medium heat in a large skillet. Add onions and garlic and cook for 3–4 minutes.

2. Add the yellow pepper and cook another 2 minutes until they all start to brown.

3. Add the sweet potatoes and continue to stir while they brown. Cook for another 5 minutes. Add jalapeño pepper (if using), cumin, coriander, cayenne pepper, and chili powder. Stir to combine.

4. Add broth and continue to stir for 3–4 minutes, until liquid is absorbed.

5. Add beans and continue to stir, making sure everything is completely mixed. Add cilantro, and season with salt and pepper.

6. Can be served warm or cold. Garnish with sliced avocado, lime wedges, diced scallions, or sour cream, if desired.

SPICY MEXICAN BLACK BEAN SOUP

This traditional soup is easy but takes quite a while to make. It freezes beautifully, so make a lot. If ham hocks are hard to find, or you would like a vegetarian option, use vegetable broth in place of the beef broth, and add 1 teaspoon liquid smoke or smoked paprika at the end, in place of the ham hocks.

Makes about 3 quarts

INGREDIENTS:

1 pound ham hocks, split

1 pound dried black beans, soaked in fresh water overnight

2 medium onions, chopped

4 cloves garlic, minced

2 cups gluten-free beef broth

Juice of 1 fresh lime

1 large (½ pound) Idaho or Yukon Gold potato, peeled and chopped

2 medium carrots, peeled and cut up

2 jalapeño peppers, cored, seeded, and chopped

1 tablespoon ground cumin

½ teaspoon gluten-free cayenne pepper, ground

1 tablespoon ground coriander

Salt and freshly ground black pepper, to taste

½ cup chopped fresh Italian flat-leaf parsley or cilantro

1 cup golden rum

Gluten-free sour cream and thinly sliced lemon or lime, for garnish

1. In a large stockpot or Dutch oven, cover the ham hocks with cold water, bring to a boil, cover, and lower heat to simmer. Simmer for 4 hours. Remove the ham hocks from the pot and reserve the cooking liquid. Remove the meat from the bones, discard the skin and bones, chop the meat, and set aside. Drain the beans. Add the beans to the reserved cooking liquid from the ham.

2. Stir the onion, garlic, beef broth, lime juice, vegetables, spices, salt, and pepper into the pot with the beans and cooking liquid. Add enough water to make 3½ quarts. Cover and simmer for 5 hours.

3. Stir in parsley or cilantro, taste for seasonings, and add additional salt and pepper if necessary.

4. Place mixture in the blender and purée the soup in batches, or use an immersion blender directly in soup pot. Return to the pot to heat. Return the meat to the pot.

5. Either add all of the rum at once and serve, or you can add it to individual bowls of soup. Top each bowl of soup with gluten-free sour cream and a slice of lemon or lime.

Soaking Beans: The Long and Short of It

Our fast-food culture has moved the packagers of many varieties of dried beans to tell the consumer to boil, then soak for a short period of time. Sounds like a good idea; however, this method soon separates the bean from its skin and it just does not make for a good texture, whether you are leaving the beans whole or puréeing them. If you are short on time, use canned beans.

LENTIL-SPINACH SOUP

Nothing warms you up like a warm bowl of comforting soup loaded with healthy vegetables and beans. This freezes wonderfully so go ahead and double the recipe.

Serves 6

INGREDIENTS:

1 tablespoon extra-virgin olive oil

2 medium onions, finely chopped

4 cloves garlic, minced

3 large carrots, chopped

3 stalks celery, diced

1 medium zucchini, diced

2 teaspoons oregano, dried

2 teaspoons basil, dried

1 teaspoon cumin

1 cup grape or cherry tomatoes, halved

1½ cups brown lentils, dried

4 cups gluten-free vegetable broth (you can also use gluten-free chicken broth)

4 cups water

1 bay leaf

Rind of Parmesan cheese (optional)

3 cups fresh spinach

1 tablespoon lemon juice

Salt and pepper, to taste (optional)

1. Heat the oil in a large pot over medium heat. Add the onions, garlic, carrots, celery, and zucchini. Cook for 3–4 minutes, until vegetables soften.

2. Add oregano, basil, and cumin. Stir to combine and cook for 3–4 minutes.

3. Add tomatoes, lentils, broth, water, bay leaf, and Parmesan cheese rind, if using. Bring to a boil.

4. Reduce heat and let simmer 50–60 minutes, or until lentils are soft.

5. Right before ready to serve, add spinach and lemon juice. Stir well until spinach wilts.

6. Season with salt and pepper, if desired. Remove Parmesan cheese rind and bay leaf before serving.

For the Carnivores . . .

This is a delightful vegetarian soup. If you are a meat eater and are looking for a heartier soup, add some cooked gluten-free bacon, ham, sausage, chicken, or turkey at the end. You can add some small gluten-free noodles, potatoes, or corn as well for a more substantial meal.

KALE, SQUASH, AND BEAN MEDLEY

This makes a wonderfully well-balanced vegetarian meal. This can also be a lovely addition to a hearty steak or poultry dish.

Serves 6–8

INGREDIENTS:

1 cup butternut squash, peeled and cut into 1" cubes (about ¾ pound)

¼ cup gluten-free vegetable broth

1 teaspoon fresh gingerroot

1 teaspoon rosemary, dried

2 tablespoons butter

3 cups kale, trimmed and washed

¼ cup gluten-free dried cranberries

¼ cup chopped pecans, toasted

½ cup white beans, rinsed and drained

1 teaspoon salt

1. In a large skillet, cook squash with vegetable broth, gingerroot, and rosemary over medium-low heat for about 8–10 minutes, until squash becomes tender.

2. Stir in butter, kale, cranberries, pecans, beans, and salt. Toss to coat. Serve immediately.

CHAPTER 14

SIDE DISHES

SNOW PEAS WITH WATER CHESTNUTS AND GINGER

This tasty side dish is very fast and good. It's a boon to the busy working person who wants fresh but has little time.

Serves 4

INGREDIENTS:

1 pound snow pea pods, ends trimmed

½ cup peanut oil

1 (8-ounce) can water chestnuts, drained, rinsed, and sliced

½ cup unsalted peanuts

2 tablespoons gluten-free soy sauce

1 teaspoon lemon juice

1 tablespoon minced fresh gingerroot

Tabasco or other red pepper sauce, gluten-free

1. Place the snow pea pods in a hot wok or frying pan with the oil. Stir to coat, then add the water chestnuts and peanuts, stirring again.

2. Continue cooking, and after 5 minutes, add the rest of the ingredients. Mix well and serve hot or at room temperature.

Cheese and Milk in Asian Cooking

The reason that cheese and milk are practically nonexistent in Asian cooking is that Asian countries do not have many dairy cows. In some areas, water buffalo work hard and produce milk too. Water buffalo in Italy provide the milk for a wonderful mozzarella cheese. Asians substitute tofu for meat, and what meat they do eat is stretched with vegetables and rice. Fish is popular in lake and seaside communities. Americans have adapted Asian flavors in a popular fusion food.

CHINESE CABBAGE WITH SESAME

Chinese cabbage, also called Napa cabbage, is wonderful cooked, or served raw in salads. It's pale green, mild, leafy, and very good for you!

Serves 4

INGREDIENTS:

2 tablespoons sesame seed oil

2 tablespoons canola or other light oil

1 tablespoon sesame seeds

1 (1½-pound) head Chinese (Napa) cabbage, washed and thinly sliced

Juice of ½ lemon

2 cloves garlic, minced

Salt, pepper, and gluten-free soy sauce, to taste

1. Place the oils in a hot wok or frying pan. Add the sesame seeds and toast for 2 minutes.

2. Stir in the cabbage, lemon juice, and garlic. Toss until just wilted, about 4 minutes. Add the seasonings and serve.

GOLDEN CORN FRITTERS

Fritters are really fun to make and to eat. They can be as plain or as interesting as you want. The idea is to make them really creamy on the inside and golden on the outside.

Makes 12–14 fritters

INGREDIENTS:

1 large egg

⅓ cup milk or gluten-free beer

⅔ cup cornstarch or corn flour

1½ teaspoons gluten-free baking powder

½ teaspoon salt

Red pepper flakes and/or ground black pepper, to taste

⅛ teaspoon freshly grated nutmeg

1 cup fresh corn, cut off the cob, or frozen

Peanut, canola, or other cooking oil (not olive oil)

1. Starting with the egg and milk, place everything but the corn and oil in a food processor and blend until smooth. Scrape into a bowl; fold in the corn.

2. Heat about 1 inch of oil to 350°F.

3. Drop the fritters by the tablespoonful into the hot oil. Drain on paper towels and serve hot.

Frittering Away

You can vary your fritters by using chopped clams instead of corn. They are fine with eggs for breakfast or as a side dish with chicken or steak. They are good with syrup or herb-savory with gluten-free gravy. You can also use them as hors d'oeuvres to dip in gluten-free salsa.

CLASSIC POLENTA WITH HERBS AND PARMESAN

By using the slow cooker to make this creamy homemade polenta, you don't have to stand over the stove for nearly 2 hours stirring the pot.

Serves 6

INGREDIENTS:

7 cups water

2 tablespoons salt

2 cups yellow gluten-free cornmeal

2–4 ounces unsalted butter

1 teaspoon dried basil

1 teaspoon dried parsley

1 teaspoon crushed rosemary

½ teaspoon freshly ground black pepper

½ cup freshly grated Parmesan cheese

1. Add all ingredients except cheese to a greased 4-quart slow cooker.

2. Whisk together thoroughly. Cover and cook on low for 6–7 hours or on high for 3–4 hours.

3. Thirty minutes prior to serving, stir in Parmesan cheese.

ROASTED WINTER VEGETABLES

This is a perfect side dish to roast chicken or roast beef. To make sure all the vegetables cook evenly, cut into small cubes that are similar in size. If you find the vegetables are becoming too dry, add in about ½ cup gluten-free vegetable broth, a little at a time, until they are as moist as you would like them to be.

Serves 4

INGREDIENTS:

5–6 cups cubed root vegetables

2 tablespoons olive oil

½ teaspoon salt

1 teaspoon freshly ground pepper

1. Place cubed vegetables in a greased 4-quart slow cooker.

2. Drizzle with olive oil and sprinkle with salt and pepper.

3. Cover and cook on high for 3½–4 hours or on low for 7–8 hours until vegetables are fork tender. Stir vegetables every hour or so to prevent them from over browning on the bottom.

Winter Root Vegetables

Use a variety of your favorite root vegetables such as carrots, turnips, sweet potatoes, white potatoes, parsnips, or onions. If using turnips, rutabagas, or sweet potatoes, make sure to peel the tough skin off before adding to the other vegetables.

BOSTON BAKED BEANS

This comfort food is made with nutritious northern beans and smoked bacon and simmered in a tangy homemade barbecue sauce. If you don't have time to precook the northern beans simply use 3 (15-ounce) cans of northern beans that have been drained and well rinsed.

Serves 8

INGREDIENTS:

6 cups precooked northern beans (see sidebar)

½ pound raw gluten-free bacon, diced

1 medium onion, finely diced

3 tablespoons molasses

1½ teaspoons ground pepper

½ teaspoon dry mustard

½ cup gluten-free ketchup

1 tablespoon gluten-free Worcestershire sauce

¼ cup brown sugar

1. Layer cooked northern beans, bacon, and onions in a greased 4-quart slow cooker.

2. In a bowl or glass measuring cup, whisk together the molasses, ground pepper, dry mustard, ketchup, Worcestershire sauce, and brown sugar.

3. Pour sauce over the layered beans. Cover and cook on high for 4–5 hours or on low for 8–10 hours.

Preparing Great Northern Beans

Presoaking beans removes the enzymes that make them difficult for some people to digest. Rinse and drain the amount of beans called for in the recipe and then add them to a bowl or saucepan. Add enough water to cover the beans by 2 inches. Cover and let soak overnight or for 8 hours. Drain the beans, then rinse and drain again. Add the beans to a saucepan with enough water to cover the beans by 2 inches. Bring to a boil over high heat, and then reduce the heat and simmer the beans for 40–60 minutes, or until they just begin to become tender. Drain, and add to the slow cooker according to the recipe instructions.

STEAMED SPAGHETTI SQUASH

People are often intimidated by cooking spaghetti squash, but by using your slow cooker it's an incredibly easy process. Serve this freshly cooked squash instead of pasta for a healthy gluten-free main dish.

Serves 4

INGREDIENTS:

1 large spaghetti squash

¾ cup water

1. Place whole spaghetti squash and water in a 4-quart or larger greased slow cooker.

2. Cook on high for 4 hours or on low for 8 hours until squash is fork tender or a knife can be inserted in the center easily.

3. Remove the squash carefully from the slow cooker. Allow to cool for several minutes. With a sharp knife cut top and bottom off of squash, then cut in half lengthwise. Scoop seeds out of the center of the squash, and use a fork to remove the noodle-like threads of the spaghetti squash.

4. Serve as a side dish topped with butter, salt, and pepper or as the base of a gluten-free meal in place of pasta.

Safely Cutting Winter Squashes

You can cook any type of winter squash (such as acorn squash, butternut squash, or pumpkins) using this method with the slow cooker. Because these squashes are rock hard when fresh, they can be extremely hard to cut, even with a very sharp knife. The possibility of cutting yourself once they are soft after being cooked is much less likely.

SLOW COOKER BAKED POTATOES

Here's a great way to keep your kitchen cool on a warm summer day. Serve these baked potatoes with grilled steaks or salmon.

Serves 4–6

INGREDIENTS:

4–6 medium-sized baking potatoes

1 tablespoon butter, per potato

¼ teaspoon salt, per potato

¼ teaspoon ground pepper, per potato

1. Wrap potatoes in aluminum foil and place in a 4-quart or larger slow cooker.

2. Cover and cook on high for 4 hours or on low for 8 hours until potatoes are fork tender.

3. When ready to serve, remove potatoes from cooker; remove foil, and cut potatoes in half. Add butter, salt, and pepper for each serving.

APPLE AND SWEET POTATO CASSEROLE

This sweet side dish would be perfect for Thanksgiving or even as a dessert with a scoop of gluten-free ice cream.

Serves 6

INGREDIENTS:

4 large sweet potatoes, peeled and sliced

1 (15-ounce) can gluten-free apple pie filling

2 tablespoons butter, melted

¼ teaspoon salt

1. Grease a 4-quart slow cooker with nonstick cooking spray. Place sweet potatoes in the bottom of the slow cooker.

2. Add apple pie filling, butter, and salt. Cover and cook on high for 3–4 hours until sweet potatoes are fork tender.

Canned Shortcuts

Using apple pie filling in this recipe is an easy way to add apples, spices, and sugar without a lot of hassle. Most canned, prepared apple pie fillings are made with cornstarch instead of wheat, but always read the nutrition label to make sure. Apple pie filling is good not only with sweet potatoes, but also in oatmeal, in a cake, or as a topping for a cheesecake.

GRANDMA'S GREEN BEANS

This recipe is easy to double if you need extra servings for a church social or buffet. Serve these green beans with meat loaf or any grilled meat.

Serves 6

INGREDIENTS:

1 (1-pound) bag frozen green beans, thawed

1 medium sweet onion, peeled and diced

6 medium red potatoes

1 teaspoon sugar

½ teaspoon salt

½ teaspoon freshly ground black pepper

6 strips of gluten-free bacon

1. Add the green beans and onion to a 4-quart or larger slow cooker.

2. Depending on your preference, you can either scrub and dice the potatoes or peel and dice them. Add the potatoes to the slow cooker along with the sugar, salt, and pepper.

3. Dice the bacon and add ⅔ of it to the slow cooker. Stir to mix well.

4. Sprinkle the remaining bacon pieces over the top of the bean mixture. Cover and cook on low for 4 hours or until the potatoes are cooked through. Taste for seasoning and add additional salt and pepper if needed.

Fresh Green Beans

You can substitute 1–1½ pounds of freshly washed, trimmed, and cut green beans for the frozen green beans. Increase the cooking time to 6 hours if you do.

SCALLOPED POTATOES WITH BACON

Scalloped potatoes is an ideal dish for the slow cooker. Potatoes cooked slowly over low heat are extremely tender and delicious.

Serves 8

INGREDIENTS:

2 tablespoons cornstarch

1 teaspoon salt

½ teaspoon pepper

2 cups fat-free milk

4 cups potatoes, thinly sliced (about 6–8 medium potatoes)

½ pound gluten-free bacon, cooked and crumbled

3 tablespoons butter, cut in small pieces

½ cup Cheddar cheese, shredded

½ cup scallions, sliced

1. Grease a 4-quart slow cooker with nonstick cooking spray.

2. In a small bowl, mix together the cornstarch, salt, pepper, and milk.

3. Place ⅓ of the potatoes in the bottom of the slow cooker. Pour ⅓ of the milk mixture over the potatoes. Sprinkle ⅓ of the bacon over the milk. Continue to layer ingredients, finishing with potato slices.

4. Dot butter over potatoes. Cover slow cooker and cook on low for 6–8 hours, until potatoes are tender.

5. Thirty minutes prior to serving, sprinkle cheese and green onions on top of potatoes. Allow cheese to melt and then serve.

Make It Dairy-Free

A recipe like this you can easily make dairy-free by using coconut oil or olive oil in place of the butter, coconut milk or almond milk in place of the dairy milk, and Daiya (soy-free, gluten-free, and dairy-free cheese product) in place of the dairy cheese.

FINGERLING POTATOES WITH HERB VINAIGRETTE

Fingerling potatoes are small new potatoes. It's fun to use fingerling potatoes, because often they are small enough that they do not have to be chopped or diced. This dish is also delicious served cold as a potato salad.

Serves 4

INGREDIENTS:

2 pounds red or yellow fingerling potatoes, scrubbed

1 teaspoon salt

¼ cup lemon juice

⅓ cup extra-virgin olive oil

1 small shallot, minced (about 2 tablespoons)

1½ teaspoons minced fresh thyme leaves

1 tablespoon minced fresh basil leaves

1 tablespoon minced fresh oregano leaves

½ teaspoon gluten-free Dijon mustard

1 teaspoon sugar

1. Place potatoes in a medium pot and cover with cold water. Bring to a boil and add salt to the water. Cook potatoes for 6–8 minutes, until fork tender.

2. Drain potatoes and place in a greased 4-quart slow cooker.

3. In a small bowl whisk together lemon juice, olive oil, shallot, thyme, basil, oregano, mustard, and sugar. Drizzle vinaigrette over potatoes.

4. Cook on low for 4 hours or on high for 2 hours.

RATATOUILLE

Ratatouille, a rich and savory vegetable casserole, comes out surprisingly crisp-tender when made in the slow cooker.

Serves 6

INGREDIENTS:

1 medium onion, roughly chopped

1 unpeeled eggplant, sliced horizontally into ½" slices

2 zucchini, sliced into ½" rounds

1 green, red, or yellow pepper, seeded and sliced into thin strips

3 tomatoes, cut into wedges

2 tablespoons minced fresh basil

2 tablespoons minced fresh Italian parsley

¼ teaspoon salt

½ teaspoon freshly ground black pepper

3 ounces tomato paste

¼ cup water

1. Grease a 4-quart slow cooker with nonstick cooking spray. Place the onion, eggplant, zucchini, pepper, and tomatoes into the slow cooker. Sprinkle with basil, parsley, salt, and black pepper.

2. Whisk the tomato paste and water in a small bowl. Pour the mixture over the vegetables. Stir to combine.

3. Cook on low for 4 hours or until the eggplant and zucchini are fork tender.

What Is Ratatouille?

Ratatouille is a traditional vegetable stew that originated in France in the city of Nice. The full name of the dish is *ratatouille niçoise*. The recipe has experienced a revival in the past few years after the success of a popular Disney movie of the same name. In the movie, a rat named Remy makes the dish for a particularly picky French restaurant critic.

SWEET AND SOUR RED CABBAGE

Cabbage is often overlooked when it comes to weekly meals, which is unfortunate considering how nutritious it is. The tart apples, sugar, and apple cider vinegar give the cabbage a tangy pickled flavor. Try this recipe as a side to roast pork.

Serves 6

INGREDIENTS:

1 large head red cabbage, sliced

2 medium onions, chopped

6 small tart apples, cored and quartered, and peeled (if preferred)

2 teaspoons salt

1 cup hot water

1 cup apple juice

⅓ cup sugar

⅔ cup apple cider vinegar

½ teaspoon caraway seeds

6 tablespoons butter, melted

1. Place cabbage, onions, apples, and salt into a greased 4-quart slow cooker.

2. In a bowl, whisk together water, apple juice, sugar, vinegar, and caraway seeds. Pour over the cabbage.

3. Drizzle butter over everything and cover slow cooker. Cook on high for 3–4 hours or on low for 6–8 hours. Stir well before serving.

A Little about Red Cabbage

Red cabbage gets its unique color from a pigment in the plant leaves. The color will vary depending on the pH values of the soil it's grown in. Red cabbage juice can actually be used as a homemade pH indicator, turning red in acidic solutions and blue in basic solutions. Red cabbage usually turns blue when cooked. This recipe, however, uses apple cider vinegar not only to give the dish a tangy flavor, but to retain the reddish/purple color of the vegetable.

SIMPLE GARLIC MASHED POTATOES

Everybody loves mashed potatoes! The only problem is you generally have to plan to make them right before dinner or they will get cold. Instead, put mashed potatoes in the slow cooker, and you'll have them hot and ready whenever it's time for dinner!

Serves 8

INGREDIENTS:

5 pounds red potatoes, peeled and cut into cubes

½ cup butter, melted

3 tablespoons gluten-free mayonnaise

2 teaspoons garlic powder

1½ teaspoons salt

1 teaspoon pepper

½ cup 2% milk

⅓ cup green onions, sliced

1. Cook potatoes in a large pot in salted water until very tender, about 15–20 minutes.

2. Drain potatoes. Place in a clean bowl or add back to the cooking pot. Mash potatoes with a potato masher. Stir in butter, mayonnaise, garlic powder, salt, pepper, and milk.

3. Spoon mashed potatoes into a greased 2½- or 4-quart slow cooker. Cover and either keep on warm setting for up to 2 hours or on low for 2–4 hours. Before serving, sprinkle on green onions. If potatoes seem dry, stir in more milk before serving.

SWEET POTATO CASSEROLE

This is a welcome side dish at almost any holiday buffet.

Serves 8

INGREDIENTS:

2 (29-ounce) cans sweet potatoes

⅓ cup plus 2 tablespoons butter, melted

2 tablespoons white sugar

2 tablespoons plus ⅓ cup brown sugar

1 tablespoon orange juice

2 large eggs, beaten

½ cup whole milk

⅓ cup chopped pecans

2 tablespoons brown rice flour

1. Drain the sweet potatoes, add to a bowl, and mash them together with ⅓ cup butter, white sugar, and 2 tablespoons brown sugar.

2. Stir in orange juice, eggs, and milk. Transfer the sweet potato mixture into a greased 4-quart slow cooker.

3. In a small bowl, mix together 2 tablespoons butter, ⅓ cup brown sugar, pecans, and flour. Use a fork to thoroughly blend. Sprinkle over the sweet potatoes. Cover and cook on low for 6 hours.

HOT GERMAN POTATO SALAD

Serve this with grilled brats and chilled mugs of ice cold gluten-free beer, such as Red Bridge, Bard's Tale, or New Grist.

Serves 6

INGREDIENTS:

6 baking potatoes

1 small red onion, peeled and diced

3 stalks celery, diced

1 small green bell pepper, seeded and diced

¼ cup apple cider vinegar

½ cup water

¼ cup light olive or vegetable oil

2 tablespoons sugar

½ teaspoon celery seeds

¼ cup fresh flat-leaf parsley, minced

6 strips gluten-free bacon, cooked until crisp, drained, and crumbled

1 teaspoon salt

½ teaspoon freshly ground black pepper

1. Scrub the potatoes; slice them into ¼" slices and add to a greased 6-quart slow cooker. Add the onion, celery, and bell pepper; stir to mix.

2. In a small bowl combine the vinegar, water, oil, sugar, and celery seeds. Whisk to mix and then pour into the slow cooker.

3. Cover and cook on low for 4 hours or until the potatoes are cooked through.

4. Stir in the parsley and crumbled bacon. Season with salt and pepper. Serve hot.

Swap Bacon for Sausage

You can omit the oil and bacon and instead add 8 ounces of diced gluten-free smoked sausage in Step 1. The fat that renders from the sausage should be sufficient to offset the vinegar; however, if you think it's too tart when you taste the dish for seasoning, you can stir in a little vegetable oil when you add the salt and pepper.

SLOW COOKER STUFFING

Thanksgiving simply wouldn't be complete without stuffing on the table. The key to a really good gluten-free stuffing is to find or make a gluten-free bread that is very dry and somewhat dense.

Serves 6

INGREDIENTS:

6 cups toasted, cubed, and very dry gluten-free bread

½ cup butter

1 cup diced onion

1 cup diced celery

1½ teaspoons salt

1 teaspoon pepper

2 tablespoons gluten-free poultry seasoning

1 pound gluten-free mild pork sausage

2½ cups gluten-free chicken broth

1. Place bread cubes in a very large bowl and set aside. Melt butter in a large sauté pan over medium-high heat. When warm and sizzling, add onion and celery. Sauté until onion is translucent, about 3–5 minutes. Add salt, pepper, and poultry seasoning. Pour onion and butter mixture over bread cubes in bowl.

2. Add sausage to the sauté pan, breaking it up into small pieces. Brown sausage until completely cooked through. Pour sausage into stuffing mixture in bowl. Stir together thoroughly.

3. Pour stuffing into a greased 4-quart slow cooker. Slowly add chicken broth. If you prefer a moister dressing, add additional chicken broth, until desired consistency is reached.

4. Cook stuffing on high for 3–4 hours or on low for 6–8 hours. During the last 90 minutes of cooking, vent the lid of the slow cooker with a chopstick to let excess moisture escape.

Gluten-Free Bread—Worth the Expense?

Store-bought gluten-free bread is expensive. It's less expensive to buy gluten-free baking ingredients, but either way, you're spending more money than you would have for wheat bread. If you plan on keeping gluten-free bread in your diet (and sometimes that sandwich is just worth it!), make sure to save leftovers in a zip-top bag in your freezer for recipes like this.

SCALLOPED POTATOES WITH LEEKS AND PROSCIUTTO

This is the ideal comfort food. It's filling and tasty and is an excellent brunch or supper dish.

Serves 6

INGREDIENTS:

1½ cups grated Parmesan cheese, fresh or gluten-free

1 cup coarsely grated fontina cheese

½ cup corn flour

½ teaspoon salt

½ teaspoon freshly ground pepper

6 large Idaho or Yukon Gold potatoes, peeled and sliced thinly

4 leeks, thinly sliced crosswise, white parts only

1 pound prosciutto, diced, gluten-free

3 cups fat-free milk

4 tablespoons butter (for greasing baking dish and dotting on potatoes)

1. Grease a 9" × 13" baking dish or prepare it with nonstick spray. Preheat oven to 350°F.

2. Mix together the cheeses, corn flour, salt, and pepper.

3. Place a layer of potatoes in the baking dish, then one of leeks, and dab with bits of prosciutto. Sprinkle with the mixture of cheeses, corn flour, and seasonings. Repeat until you get to the top of the baking dish. Add the milk, sprinkle with cheese mixture, and dot with butter.

4. Bake for about 90 minutes. The top should be brown and crispy, the inside soft and creamy.

ZUCCHINI WITH TOMATO AND BACON

This recipe is best when made with medium-sized zucchini, about 10–12" each and can also easily be made vegetarian by omitting the bacon.

Serves 6

INGREDIENTS:

6 medium zucchini

1 small onion, peeled and minced

2 cloves garlic, peeled and minced

1 serrano pepper, cored, seeded, and minced

2 tablespoons butter or extra-virgin olive oil

1 cup cooked rice

1 cup crushed tomatoes

2 tablespoons freshly squeezed lemon juice

2 large eggs, slightly beaten

1 tablespoon dried oregano leaves or 2 tablespoons fresh oregano

½ teaspoon salt

½ teaspoon pepper

6 strips gluten-free bacon

1. Preheat the oven to 350°F. Spray a 9" × 13" baking dish with nonstick spray or oil.

2. Cut the top quarter off the zucchini, lengthwise. Hollow out the zucchini with the small side of a melon baller or with a half-teaspoon measuring spoon; reserve the pulp.

3. In a skillet over medium heat, sauté the onion, garlic, pepper, and zucchini pulp in the oil until soft, about 3–4 minutes. Add all the remaining ingredients except the bacon.

4. Divide the filling among the zucchini boats. Lay a bacon strip on top of each stuffed zucchini. Place in the prepared baking dish. Bake until the "boats" are hot and the bacon is brown and crisp, about 10–12 minutes. Serve hot or at room temperature.

Stuffed Vegetables

There are many vegetables you can successfully stuff with lots of different, delicious ingredients. Chopped meat, shrimp, fish, and crabmeat all make wonderful stuffing. A baked clam–stuffed mushroom is also a real treat. Ricotta cheese, used to stuff pastas such as ravioli and lasagna, also makes an excellent stuffing.

SPAGHETTI SQUASH WITH MARINARA SAUCE

Spaghetti squash holds endless possibilities for a nutritious, gluten-free diet. It's delicious and so easy to prepare.

Serves 6–8

INGREDIENTS:

1 (4-pound) spaghetti squash, rinsed

1 cup freshly grated Parmesan cheese, fresh or gluten-free

1 clove garlic, minced

Garnish of fresh herbs such as parsley, basil, and oregano

2 cups of your favorite jarred, gluten-free marinara sauce

1. Preheat oven to 275°F.

2. Make a boat of aluminum foil and place the squash in the center and place on a baking sheet. Pierce the squash in several places with a knife to let the steam escape. Sprinkle with water. Tent with more foil and roast for 2 hours. The squash is done when you can insert a fork easily.

3. Cool the squash so you can handle it. Cut it in half and scoop out the seeds. Using a fork, run it through the flesh and it will turn into "spaghetti."

4. Mix the squash and most of the cheese together in a medium bowl and reheat. Sprinkle with the remaining cheese, garlic, and herbs, toss with marinara, and serve.

Freshly Grated Cheese

Blocks of Parmesan cheese will keep for a week, tightly wrapped, in the refrigerator. It is so easy to grate exactly the amount you need, when you need it, and it tastes 100 percent better than the grated cheese you get in a box or jar. Use a box grater and place a piece of wax paper on a cutting board. Grate away, then remove the grater, make a funnel of the paper, and slide the cheese into a bowl or add it to what you are preparing. You can also use Romano, fontina, or Cheddar cheese in this way and enjoy them so much more.

AUTUMN ROOT VEGETABLES AND QUINOA

This really does taste better the next day. Don't be alarmed if your quinoa turns pink because of the beets!

Serves 4–6

INGREDIENTS:

2 medium sweet potatoes, peeled and diced

2 medium red potatoes, peeled and diced

3 small beets, peeled and chopped

3 large carrots, peeled and chopped

½ medium red onion, chopped

4 cloves garlic, chopped

Juice of ½ lemon

1 teaspoon basil, dried

1 teaspoon parsley, dried

½ teaspoon thyme, dried

2 tablespoons extra-virgin olive oil

2 cups gluten-free chicken broth

1 cup uncooked quinoa, rinsed and drained

1 cup chickpeas, rinsed and drained (optional)

Salt and pepper, to taste

1. Preheat the oven to 375°F.

2. Place chopped vegetables, lemon juice, seasonings, and olive oil in sealable plastic bag. Close the bag and shake vigorously to make sure the vegetables are evenly coated.

3. Spread the vegetables on a baking sheet evenly, making sure they are in one layer. Roast in the oven for 40 minutes, stirring occasionally.

4. Place broth in a small saucepan and bring to a boil. Add quinoa, cover, and reduce heat to low. Cook for 15–20 minutes until all broth is absorbed. Fluff with a fork when done.

5. In large serving bowl, mix roasted vegetables with quinoa mixture. Add chickpeas (if using). Season with salt and pepper if desired. Serve warm or cold.

QUINOA, KALE, AND ROASTED TOMATO SALAD WITH FETA CHEESE

The roasted tomatoes bring out a magnificent flavor in this salad. The feta melts wonderfully!

Serves 4

INGREDIENTS:

1 pint grape or cherry tomatoes, halved

1 tablespoon honey

4 sprigs of fresh thyme, chopped and stems removed

1 tablespoon extra-virgin olive oil

Salt and pepper, to taste

2 cups gluten-free vegetable broth

1 cup uncooked quinoa, rinsed and drained

4 cups kale, stems removed and chopped

½ cup feta cheese, crumbled

2 tablespoons fresh parsley, chopped, for garnish (optional)

1. Preheat the oven to 350°F.

2. In a large resealable bag, place the tomatoes, honey, thyme, olive oil, salt, and pepper. Seal the bag and shake to combine.

3. Place tomato mixture on a baking sheet lined with parchment paper and roast for 1 hour, until the tomatoes become wrinkled and shriveled.

4. While the tomatoes are roasting, place vegetable broth and quinoa in a saucepan and bring to a boil. Cover, reduce heat to low, and continue to cook 15–20 minutes, until all the broth is absorbed. Fluff with a fork.

5. Immediately add the roasted tomatoes, kale, and feta cheese to the hot quinoa. The kale will soften and the feta will melt. Garnish with fresh parsley.

SOUTHERN FRIED GREEN TOMATOES

Use tomatoes that are very firm. They usually aren't very large, so count on two per person. Serve with thick slices of country ham or Irish bacon.

Serves 4

INGREDIENTS:

1 cup corn flour

Salt and coarse, freshly ground black pepper, to taste

1 cup gluten-free cornmeal

2 large whole eggs whisked in a large flat soup bowl

8 green tomatoes, cores trimmed, cut in ⅓" slices

Oil for frying

1. Spread the flour, mixed with salt and pepper, on one sheet of wax paper and the cornmeal on another. Place the whisked eggs in a bowl between the two.

2. Dip the tomato slices first in the flour, then in the egg, and coat them with cornmeal.

3. Heat ½" of oil in a frying pan and heat to 350°F. Slide the tomato slices in and fry for 4 minutes or until well browned. Turn and finish frying, about 3–4 minutes.

4. Drain on paper towels. Serve as a side dish with eggs and gluten-free bacon. This dish is perfect for brunch.

BALSAMIC ROASTED VEGETABLES

This is the perfect side dish that can be made with any vegetable you have on hand. You can make double the amount and add roasted vegetables to omelets or pizza—or even on top of sandwiches.

Serves 12

INGREDIENTS:

1 head of broccoli crowns, chopped

2 red bell peppers, seeded and diced

1 large sweet potato, peeled and cubed

4 large carrots, peeled and chopped

1 bunch asparagus, ends trimmed and chopped

1 medium red onion, quartered

1 tablespoon chopped fresh thyme

2 tablespoons chopped fresh rosemary

3 tablespoons olive or grapeseed oil

2 tablespoons balsamic vinegar

Salt and freshly ground black pepper, to taste

1 tablespoon fresh lemon juice (juice of 1 lemon)

1 tablespoon balsamic vinegar

1. Preheat oven to 475°F.

2. In a large bowl, combine the broccoli, red bell peppers, sweet potatoes, carrots, and asparagus.

3. Separate the red onion quarters into pieces, and add them to the mixture.

4. In a small bowl, stir together the thyme, rosemary, oil, 2 tablespoons balsamic vinegar, salt, and pepper. Toss with vegetables until they are coated.

5. Spread vegetables evenly on a large roasting pan. Roast for 25–30 minutes, stirring every 10 minutes, or until vegetables are cooked through and browned.

6. Top with fresh lemon juice and 1 tablespoon balsamic vinegar.

SIMPLE ZUCCHINI-PARMESAN STICKS

This is an easy, delicious side dish that complements any entrée. These are also perfect for a light, healthy snack.

Serves 4

INGREDIENTS:

1 cup zucchini, sliced into 2–3" sticks

Nonstick cooking spray

Misto sprayer filled with extra-virgin olive oil

1 tablespoon shaved Parmesan cheese, fresh

Salt and pepper, to taste

1. Preheat oven to broil. Line baking sheet with aluminum foil. Spray nonstick cooking spray on aluminum foil to prevent sticking.

2. Place sliced zucchini sticks on aluminum foil and spray lightly with olive oil sprayer.

3. Sprinkle Parmesan cheese on top. Season with salt and pepper.

4. Broil for a few minutes until cheese melts and turns light brown, about 2 minutes.

DELICIOUS GARLIC BUTTERNUT SQUASH

The name says it all! This is perfect, simple, and delicious. Butternut squash is low in calories and rich in vitamins and minerals. It's a wonderful alternative to potatoes.

Serves 6

INGREDIENTS:

2 tablespoons minced fresh parsley

1 tablespoon grapeseed oil

2 cloves garlic, minced

¼ cup grated Parmesan cheese, fresh

½ teaspoon rosemary, dried

½ teaspoon kosher salt

½ teaspoon pepper

3½ pounds butternut squash, peeled and cut into 1" cubes

1. Preheat oven to 400°F.

2. In a large bowl, combine the parsley, oil, garlic, cheese, rosemary, salt, and pepper. Add the squash and toss to coat.

3. Transfer to an ungreased shallow 2-quart baking dish. Bake, uncovered, for 50–55 minutes or until squash is just tender.

Butternut Squash

Butternut squash is a type of winter squash that is similar to pumpkin. Cutting up butternut squash can be a little intimidating. First, cut off ¼" from both ends. Use a sharp vegetable peeler and peel the outer layer of squash. Once completely peeled, slice squash in half from top to bottom. Next, scoop out the seeds and gummy pulp inside the squash. Cut each half in half again, making quarters. Then chop each quarter into strips. Finally, slice each strip into cubes.

RISOTTO WITH SPINACH AND GORGONZOLA CHEESE

This is a wonderful complement to any poultry or seafood dish.

Serves 4

INGREDIENTS:

5 cups gluten-free canned or homemade chicken, fish, or vegetable broth

2 tablespoons butter

2 tablespoons extra-virgin olive oil

½ cup finely chopped sweet onion

1½ cups arborio rice, uncooked

Salt and freshly ground black pepper, to taste

10 ounces fresh spinach, rinsed and chopped finely

¼ cup crumbled Gorgonzola cheese

Roasted red pepper strips and chopped parsley, for garnish

1. Bring the broth to a slow simmer in a saucepan and keep hot.

2. Heat the butter and oil in a large, heavy pan; add the onion and sauté until softened, about 8 minutes. Add the rice and stir. Add salt and pepper.

3. Add the broth, ¼ cup at a time, until it is all gone, stirring constantly. This will take about 35 minutes. If the rice is still not done, add water, ¼ cup at a time. When rice is cooked, add spinach, one handful at a time. Stir to combine.

4. Stir in the Gorgonzola cheese and garnish with strips of roasted red pepper and parsley. Serve hot.

CORN SOUFFLÉ

This is a tasty side dish with roast turkey or pork. Just make sure the oven is very hot. The herbs and seasonings can be adjusted to suit your tastes.

Serves 4–6

INGREDIENTS:

½ cup corn or rice flour

¼ cup 2% milk or light cream

3 large eggs, separated

3 teaspoons gluten-free baking powder

2 tablespoons finely grated fresh Parmesan cheese

1 clove garlic, minced

Salt, pepper, and 1 teaspoon of your favorite herbs, to taste

1 cup fresh corn, cut off the cob, or frozen

1. Preheat the oven to 375°F.

2. Place the flour, milk, egg yolks, baking powder, cheese, garlic, salt, pepper, and herbs in a food processor and blend together. Place in a bowl and add the corn.

3. In a separate bowl, beat the egg whites until stiff and fold them into the corn mixture.

4. Grease or use nonstick spray on a 2-quart soufflé mold. Pour the mixture into the mold, and place in the middle of the oven for 25–30 minutes, until brown and puffed. Serve hot.

GARLICKY PARMESAN ROASTED POTATOES

This side dish is a perfect companion to any meat or poultry dish. These potatoes also make a wonderful accompaniment to eggs for breakfast or brunch. Using fresh herbs and Parmesan cheese is definitely better when roasting.

Serves 4

INGREDIENTS:

2 tablespoons extra-virgin olive oil

2 cloves garlic, minced

1 medium onion, finely chopped

1 teaspoon fresh basil, diced

1 teaspoon fresh rosemary, chopped

1 teaspoon fresh parsley, chopped

2 tablespoons fresh Parmesan cheese, grated

⅛ teaspoon crushed red pepper flakes

½ teaspoon salt

4 large red potatoes, scrubbed clean and sliced into cubes

1. Preheat oven to 450°F.

2. Place all the ingredients in a large resealable plastic bag. Close the bag and shake to evenly coat potatoes.

3. Spray a baking sheet with nonstick cooking spray. Spread potato mixture in an even layer on baking sheet. Place in oven for 40 minutes, making sure to stir potatoes occasionally.

4. Place oven on broil and cook potatoes 1–2 minutes, until they become browned and crispy. Remove from oven. Serve immediately.

Dried Herbs

If you would like to use dried herbs or don't have fresh herbs on hand, remember less is more. Dried herbs are usually stronger than fresh ones. Typically, you can cut the amount in half when using dried herbs.

GARLIC AND PARMESAN MASHED POTATOES

These mashed potatoes are so flavorful you don't need any gravy. This dish goes wonderfully with fish, steak, meat loaf, chicken, or turkey. The possibilities are endless.

Serves 6

INGREDIENTS:

4 cloves garlic, minced and divided

2½ pounds Yukon Gold potatoes, scrubbed clean, unpeeled and quartered

2 tablespoons butter, softened

½ cup buttermilk

2 tablespoons gluten-free sour cream

1 teaspoon salt

½ teaspoon sage

¼ cup Parmesan cheese, freshly grated

Chopped green onion, for garnish

1. Place 2 cloves of garlic and the potatoes in a large saucepan. Cover with water and bring to a boil over high heat. Once boiling, cover and reduce heat to low and simmer 20–25 minutes, until the potatoes are fork tender.

2. Drain the potatoes thoroughly and place back into saucepan.

3. In a small bowl, add 2 remaining cloves minced garlic, butter, buttermilk, sour cream, salt, and sage. Stir to combine.

4. Add cheese and stir well. Place garlic sauce over potatoes and mix well. Mash with potato masher or hand mixer on medium-high speed until desired consistency. Top with chopped green onions. Serve immediately.

Be Creative with Potatoes

Let your imagination go wild with potatoes! Gone are the days when you think of boring, lumpy, instant potatoes. Making your own mashed potatoes is easy. You can add whatever seasonings and additions you'd like.

CHEDDAR AND BACON MASHED POTATOES

Another lovely variation of typical mashed potatoes, this side dish will surely impress your guests.

Serves 6

INGREDIENTS:

1 tablespoon butter

4 slices applewood smoked gluten-free bacon

2½ pounds russet potatoes, unpeeled, scrubbed clean and cut into quarters

1 clove garlic, minced

1 cup sharp Cheddar cheese, shredded

¾ cup fat-free milk

1 medium onion, chopped finely

2 tablespoons gluten-free sour cream

Salt and pepper, to taste

1 teaspoon chives, minced

1. Melt butter in large skillet over medium-high heat. Add bacon and cook, turning over several times, until crisp. Drain bacon on paper towels.

2. Place potatoes and garlic in a large saucepan. Cover with water and bring to a boil over high heat. Once boiling, cover and reduce heat to low, and simmer for 20–25 minutes, until potatoes are fork tender.

3. Drain potatoes thoroughly and place back into saucepan.

4. Crumble bacon into small pieces.

5. In a medium bowl, mix cheese, milk, onion, crumbled bacon, and sour cream. Stir well and pour mixture on top of potatoes. Mix thoroughly and mash with potato masher or hand mixer on medium-high speed until desired consistency is reached.

6. Add salt and pepper to taste and serve with chives on top. Serve immediately.

BALSAMIC ROASTED BRUSSELS SPROUTS

Even those who do not typically like Brussels sprouts will love these! This is a simple and tasty dish, delicious enough for a holiday dinner.

Serves 6

INGREDIENTS:

3 tablespoons extra-virgin olive oil

2 tablespoons balsamic vinegar

1 clove garlic, minced

1 teaspoon sweet paprika

1½ pounds Brussels sprouts, bottoms trimmed, outer leaves removed, and halved

4 shallots, thinly sliced

Salt and pepper, to taste

1. Preheat the oven to 400°F.

2. In a small bowl, mix together the oil, balsamic vinegar, garlic, and paprika.

3. Place Brussels sprouts, shallots, and oil/vinegar mixture in a large resealable plastic bag. Make sure the bag is closed and shake to coat sprouts evenly. Season with salt and pepper.

4. Place sprouts and shallots on a baking sheet that is coated with nonstick cooking spray. Roast sprouts for 35 minutes, shaking pan every 5–8 minutes to make sure they are evenly browning.

5. Remove from oven when finished; season with some more salt. Serve immediately.

The Many Benefits of Brussels Sprouts

Brussels sprouts are part of the cabbage family and actually look like little cabbages. Brussels sprouts were first grown in Brussels, Belgium, hence the name. These sprouts are packed with vitamins C, A, and B.

CREAMED SPINACH

This recipe is wonderful and can easily be doubled to feed a larger group. You can substitute half-and-half for the heavy cream to lighten this up.

Serves 10

INGREDIENTS:

3 (10-ounce) bags fresh spinach, chopped

¼ cup butter

3 cloves garlic, minced

½ teaspoon nutmeg

1 medium-sized shallot, minced

½ cup heavy cream

4 ounces Asiago cheese

½ cup Parmesan cheese, freshly grated

Salt and pepper, to taste

1. Place spinach in a large stockpot, cover with water, and cook over medium-high heat until wilted, about 2–3 minutes. Remove from heat and drain in colander until most of the liquid is gone.

2. Place butter in large skillet and melt over medium heat. Add garlic, nutmeg, and shallot, and cook 3–4 minutes, until shallot is translucent.

3. Add spinach and slowly pour in heavy cream. Sprinkle in Asiago and Parmesan cheeses. Continue to stir until sauce thickens, about 4–5 minutes. Season with salt and pepper. Serve warm or hot.

TROPICAL FRUIT SALSA

The sweet blend of fruits and vegetables makes a wonderful and unique salsa. Try it with pork, lamb, or any kind of fish. It is also great eaten with Brown Rice Chips (see recipe in this chapter).

Makes about 1½ cups

INGREDIENTS:

1 large mango, peeled, seeded, and diced

1 cup fresh pineapple, diced

½ red bell pepper, seeded and diced

¼ cup minced red onion

½ teaspoon freshly grated lime zest

Juice of ½ lime

Salt, to taste

Mix all ingredients in a bowl and cover. Refrigerate for 2 hours. Serve at room temperature.

Does slicing onions make you cry?

Place peeled and unsliced onions in a bowl of water for a few minutes before slicing. This little soaking helps reduce some of the onion's harsh acids, which can cause tearing.

BROWN RICE CHIPS

These chips will be a favorite in your house. They will stay fresh in an airtight container for up to a week.

Serves 8

INGREDIENTS:

1 package brown rice tortillas

1 tablespoon cinnamon

1 tablespoon turbinado sugar

½ teaspoon cloves

½ teaspoon all spice

1. Preheat oven to 350°F. Cut the tortillas into slices.

2. In a small bowl combine the cinnamon, sugar, and spices together.

3. Lay tortilla slices out in a single layer on a baking sheet and sprinkle with cinnamon spice/sugar mixture.

4. Bake 8–12 minutes, until chips start to lightly brown. Repeat with remaining tortilla slices. Let cool 10 minutes and serve with chilled Tropical Fruit Salsa (see recipe in this chapter).

CHAPTER 15

DESSERTS

CHOCOLATE MINT SWIRL CHEESECAKE WITH CHOCOLATE NUT CRUST

This is incredibly rich and delicious. It is definitely a special-occasion cake with layers of deep flavor.

Serves 10–12

INGREDIENTS:

1½ cups ground walnuts (the food processor works well)

½ cup sugar

⅓ cup unsalted butter, melted

4 ounces semisweet chocolate, melted

4 large eggs, separated

3 (8-ounce) packages cream cheese (not low- or nonfat)

1 cup gluten-free sour cream

¾ cup sugar

1½ teaspoons pure vanilla extract

1 teaspoon salt

2 tablespoons chestnut flour

4 ounces semisweet chocolate

2 tablespoons peppermint schnapps

Whipped cream for topping (optional)

1. In medium bowl, mix the first four ingredients together. Spray a 9" springform pan with nonstick spray and press the walnut mixture into the bottom to make a crust. Chill for at least 1 hour.

2. Preheat the oven to 350°F. In a clean bowl, beat the egg whites until stiff. In a separate large bowl, using an electric mixer, beat the cream cheese, sour cream, sugar, vanilla, salt, and chestnut flour. Melt 4 ounces semisweet chocolate with the schnapps.

3. With the motor running, add the egg yolks, one at a time, beating vigorously. Fold in the stiff egg whites. Using a knife, swirl the chocolate and schnapps into the bowl.

4. Pour into the springform pan and bake for 1 hour. Turn off the oven, and with the door cracked, let the cake cool for another hour. Chill before serving. You can add whipped cream to the top before serving.

Baking with Cream Cheese

It's best to use cream cheese that is not low- or nonfat. The lower the fat content, the more chemicals are in the cheese to make it work for spreading. When baking, use the purest ingredients, as heat will change the consistency of anything artificial.

CHERRY VANILLA CHEESECAKE WITH WALNUT CRUST

This is a fine combination with a delightful flavor and smooth consistency.

Serves 10–12

INGREDIENTS:

1½ cups ground walnuts

½ cup sugar

½ cup unsalted butter, melted

4 large eggs, separated

3 (8-ounce) packages cream cheese

1 cup gluten-free sour cream

2 teaspoons pure vanilla extract

1 teaspoon salt

2 tablespoons rice flour

⅔ cup cherry preserves, melted

1. Mix together the walnuts, sugar, and melted butter. Prepare a springform pan with nonstick spray and press the nut mixture into the bottom to form a crust. Chill for at least 1 hour.

2. Preheat oven to 350°F. Beat the egg whites until they form peaks and set aside. In a large bowl, using an electric mixer, beat the cream cheese, sour cream, vanilla, salt, and rice flour together.

3. Add the egg yolks, one at a time, while beating. When smooth, fold in the egg whites and mix in the cherry preserves.

4. Pour into springform pan and bake for 1 hour. Turn off oven and crack the door. Let cake cool for another hour. Chill before serving.

Nut Crusts for Cheesecake

We specify walnuts because they are probably the least expensive shelled nut and work well in these recipes. However, you can substitute hazelnuts, almonds, or pecans. Pecans add a Southern touch and are really good—and expensive. Grinding nuts is simple—just use your food processor.

LEMON CHEESECAKE WITH NUT CRUST

This cheesecake is light, with an intense lemon flavor. It's a good summer cheesecake that will make your guests ask for more.

Serves 10–12

INGREDIENTS:

1¼ cups ground walnuts (or whatever nuts you like)

½ cup sugar

½ cup unsalted butter, melted

5 egg whites

3 (8-ounce) packages cream cheese

1 cup gluten-free sour cream

⅔ cup sugar

2 tablespoons rice flour

1 teaspoon salt

3 egg yolks

Juice of one lemon

Minced rind of 1 lemon

Extra nuts to sprinkle on top of cake, paper-thin lemon slices

1. Mix together the ground nuts, sugar, and melted butter. Use nonstick spray on a springform pan. Press the nut mixture into the bottom to form a crust, and chill.

2. Preheat oven to 350°F. Beat the egg whites until stiff and set aside. Using an electric mixer, beat the cheese, sour cream, sugar, flour, salt, and egg yolks, adding the yolks one at a time. Beat in the lemon juice and lemon rind.

3. Gently fold in the egg whites. Pour the cheese/lemon mixture into the springform. Bake for 1 hour. Turn off oven and crack the door, letting cool for another hour. Chill before serving. The chopped nuts and thinly sliced lemon add a nice touch.

Stiffly Beaten Egg Whites

Be very careful not to get even a speck of egg yolk in the whites to be beaten stiff. Even a drop of egg yolk will prevent the whites from stiffening. And always use clean beaters. Any fat or oil will prevent the whites from fluffing up. You can use a drop of vinegar or lemon juice to help them stiffen up.

MOLTEN LAVA DARK CHOCOLATE CAKE

For such an easy recipe, it comes off as elegant. It just tastes more complex than it is to make. The nice thing is that chestnut flour gives a wonderful underlying flavor.

Serves 8

INGREDIENTS:

8 teaspoons butter to grease custard cups

8 tablespoons sugar to coat buttered custard cups

8 ounces semisweet baking chocolate

6 ounces unsalted butter

3 large eggs

3 egg yolks

⅓ cup sugar

1 tablespoon chestnut flour

1 teaspoon vanilla

1 quart raspberry sorbet

1. Prepare the insides of 8 (6-ounce) custard cups with butter and sugar. Preheat oven to 425°F. Over very low heat, melt the chocolate and butter in a heavy saucepan.

2. In a large bowl, using an electric mixer, beat the eggs, egg yolks, sugar, flour, and vanilla for about 10 minutes. Add the chocolate mixture by the tablespoonful until the eggs have absorbed some of the chocolate. Fold in the rest of the chocolate/butter mixture.

3. Divide the mixture between the custard cups. Place the cups on a cookie sheet and bake for 12–13 minutes. The sides should be puffed and the center very soft. Serve hot with raspberry sorbet spooned into the "craters."

Chocolate Sauce

When you make a thick chocolate sauce, you need to remember that it is best made with real chocolate blocks, not with cocoa. When you melt the chocolate, use a heavy pan or the top of a double boiler. If necessary, you can add a teaspoon of butter or water to the chocolate.

MOLTEN SWEET WHITE CHOCOLATE CAKE

This is delicious with fresh berries and whipped cream spooned into the "craters."

Serves 8

INGREDIENTS:

8 teaspoons butter to grease custard cups

8 tablespoons sugar to coat buttered custard cups

8 ounces unsweetened white baking chocolate

6 ounces unsalted butter

3 large eggs

3 egg yolks

⅓ cup sugar

1 tablespoon chestnut flour

1 teaspoon vanilla

½ teaspoon salt

2 cups mixed berries, such as strawberries, raspberries, and blueberries

1. Prepare the insides of 8 (6-ounce) custard cups with butter and sugar. Preheat oven to 425°F. Melt the chocolate and butter over low heat in a heavy saucepan. In a large bowl, using an electric mixer, beat together the eggs, egg yolks, sugar, and flour. Add vanilla and salt.

2. Keep beating and slowly add, by the tablespoonful, ¼ of the white chocolate mixture. When well blended, add the rest of the chocolate mixture, very slowly.

3. Divide between the custard cups, place on a cookie sheet, and bake for about 12 minutes. Serve with mixed berries in the "craters." You can also vary this by using shaved bittersweet chocolate in the craters, or you can spoon in gluten-free ice cream or sorbet.

ORANGE CARROT CAKE

This delicious cake has a nice zing with the addition of a little lemon juice and the grated orange rind. The gingerroot adds an appealing sophistication.

Serves 8–10

INGREDIENTS:

4 large eggs, separated

½ cup brown sugar

1½ cups grated carrots

1 tablespoon lemon juice

Grated rind of ½ fresh orange

½ cup corn flour

1" fresh gingerroot, peeled and minced

1½ teaspoons baking soda

½ teaspoon salt

1. Liberally butter a springform pan and preheat oven to 325°F. Beat the egg whites until stiff and set aside.

2. Beat the egg yolks, sugar, and carrots together. Add lemon juice, orange rind, and corn flour. When smooth, add the gingerroot, baking soda, and salt. Gently fold in the egg whites.

3. Pour the cake batter into the springform pan and bake for 1 hour. Test by plunging a toothpick into the center of the cake—if the pick comes out clean, the cake is done.

What's Up, Doc?

Carrot cake was devised during World War II when flour and sugar were rationed. The sweetness of carrots contributed to this cake, and when oranges were available, it became a feast. Cooks used their fuel carefully too, baking and making stews and soups in the oven all at the same time. Sometimes, hard times make for sweet endings.

CLASSIC PAVLOVA CAKE

This light, beautiful, delicate, and delicious cake is enhanced by sweet bananas and strawberries.

Serves 6

INGREDIENTS:

4 egg whites

1 teaspoon vinegar

4 ounces sugar

1 cup heavy cream

3 tablespoons confectioners' sugar

½ teaspoon vanilla

1 banana, sliced

1 quart strawberries, washed, hulled, and halved, 8 left whole for decoration

1. Preheat oven to 200°F.

2. Whip the egg whites, and as they stiffen, add the vinegar and slowly add the sugar. Pour into a 9" glass pie pan that you've treated with nonstick spray.

3. Bake the meringue for 2 hours. Then, turn off the oven and crack the door. Let the meringue rest for another hour. It should become very crisp and lightly browned. Do not store it if the weather is humid.

4. Whip the cream and mix in the confectioners' sugar and vanilla. Slice a layer of bananas onto the bottom of the cooled meringue crust. Add a layer of whipped cream. Sprinkle with halved strawberries.

5. Add another layer of whipped cream and decorate with the whole strawberries. Serve immediately or it will get soggy.

Origins of the Pavlova

There is some discussion as to who invented this cake. It was designed to honor the famed ballerina Anna Pavlova, whose admirers came from around the world. Some say it was devised in Australia; others say the cake was born in the United States.

CHESTNUT COOKIES

These cookies are delicious around the holidays. They are so unique and delightful the whole family will love them.

Make about 48 cookies

INGREDIENTS:

1 (2-ounce) can chestnuts, roasted, peeled, and packed in water

1½ cups chestnut flour

½ cup fat-free milk

2 egg yolks

1 teaspoon vanilla

½ teaspoon nutmeg

1 teaspoon salt

2 teaspoons gluten-free baking powder

½ cup granulated sugar

½ cup unsalted butter, melted

3 egg whites, beaten stiff

1. Preheat the oven to 350°F.

2. Drain the chestnuts and chop in the food processor. Place in the bowl of an electric mixer. With the motor on low, add the chestnut flour, milk, egg yolks, vanilla, nutmeg, salt, baking powder, sugar, and melted butter.

3. Fold the egg whites into the chestnut mixture. Drop by the teaspoonful on cookie sheets lined with parchment paper.

4. Bake for 12–15 minutes. Cool and place on platters for immediate use, or store in tins for later use.

Chestnuts—Raw, Jarred, or Canned?

Preparing chestnuts can be a real pain! You have to make cross slits in each, then either boil or roast them, and get the shells off. Then, you have to peel off the skins. This process is time consuming. However, you can buy prepared chestnuts in jars and cans and avoid all that work. Of course, your house won't smell like roasted chestnuts, but you'll have more time to enjoy them.

CHOCOLATE MERINGUE AND NUT COOKIES

These are crisp and delicious. The nuts add a wonderful crunch. Use either blanched almonds or hazelnuts.

Makes about 40 cookies

INGREDIENTS:

½ cup sugar, divided

¼ cup unsweetened cocoa powder

⅛ teaspoon salt

3 egg whites (from extra-large eggs)

⅛ teaspoon cream of tartar

½ cup hazelnuts, lightly toasted, skinned, and coarsely chopped

1. Preheat oven to 275°F. Line two cookie sheets with parchment paper. Sift ¼ cup of sugar and ¼ cup of cocoa together in a bowl. Add salt.

2. Beat egg whites with cream of tartar. When peaks begin to form, add the remaining ¼ cup sugar, a teaspoon at a time. Slowly beat in the cocoa mixture. The meringue should be stiff and shiny.

3. Add chopped nuts. Drop by teaspoonfuls on the parchment paper. Bake for 45–50 minutes. Cool on baking sheets. You can place these in an airtight cookie tin or serve them the same day.

Ugly, but Good!

These cookies are known in Italy as "ugly but good"! Other, kinder descriptions include "kisses" and "crisps." They are a bit dumpy looking, but just try one. This recipe is a simplification of the original, far more time-consuming, one.

APPLE COBBLER WITH CHEDDAR BISCUIT CRUST

This cobbler is very easy to make in advance—just bake it the last hour before serving.

Serves 8–10

INGREDIENTS:

2 cups corn flour

½ teaspoon salt

4 teaspoons gluten-free baking powder

½ teaspoon gluten-free cayenne pepper

¼ cup margarine, softened

¾ cup buttermilk

¾ cup grated sharp Cheddar cheese

8 large tart apples such as Granny Smiths, peeled, cored, and sliced

⅓ cup lemon juice

2 teaspoons cinnamon

¼ teaspoon nutmeg

1½ tablespoons cornstarch

¼ cup dark brown sugar

¼ cup white sugar

Pinch salt

4 tablespoons butter

1. Preheat the oven to 325°F. In a large bowl, mix the flour, salt, baking powder, and pepper. Cut in the margarine with a large fork until it looks like oatmeal. Add the buttermilk and stir. Add the cheese and set aside.

2. Place the apples in a large baking dish, about 9" × 13", or a 2-quart casserole. Sprinkle them with lemon juice.

3. Mix together the spices, cornstarch, sugars, and salt. Toss the apples with this mixture. Dot with butter. Drop the cheese mixture by the tablespoonful over the top.

4. Bake for 50 minutes, or until crust is browned and the apples are bubbling. Serve with extra slices of cheese or with vanilla ice cream.

BLUEBERRY-PEACH COBBLER

This smells and tastes like August; however, if you blanch and freeze your peaches and buy frozen blueberries, you can reminisce over a past August in January.

Serves 10

INGREDIENTS:

6 ripe peaches, blanched in boiling water, skinned, pitted, and sliced

½ cup fresh lemon juice

1 cup sugar, divided

1 pint blueberries, rinsed and picked over, stems removed

1 stick (½ cup) unsalted butter, melted

½ teaspoon salt

1½ cups rice flour or quinoa flour

1 tablespoon gluten-free baking powder

1 cup buttermilk

1. Preheat the oven to 375°F. Place sliced peaches into a bowl and sprinkle with lemon juice and ½ cup sugar. Add the blueberries and mix well.

2. Prepare a 9" × 13" baking dish with nonstick spray. Spread the peaches and blueberries on the bottom. Pour the melted butter into a large bowl. Add the remaining ½ cup sugar and salt and whisk in the flour and baking powder. Add the buttermilk and stir; don't worry about lumps.

3. Drop the batter by tablespoonfuls over the fruit. Bake for 35–40 minutes. Cool for 25 minutes. Serve with gluten-free vanilla ice cream or whipped cream.

Freezing Fruit in Its Prime

There's nothing like blueberry pie in January, and I'm not talking about the fruit that comes all ready and loaded with sugar syrup in a can. When fresh blueberries are available, just rinse a quart and dry on paper towels. Place the berries on a cookie sheet in the freezer for a ½ hour and then put them in a plastic bag for future use.

ORANGE CORNMEAL COOKIES

This is an adaptation of a classic Italian cookie. You will love them for the kids and can add currants, raisins, or dried apple chips. Make sure your dried fruits are labeled gluten-free.

Makes 30 cookies

INGREDIENTS:

3 large eggs

1 cup sugar

1½ cups gluten-free cornmeal (yellow)

1¼ cups corn flour

½ teaspoon salt

¾ teaspoon xanthan gum

1½ sticks (¾ cup) unsalted butter, melted

1 tablespoon concentrated orange juice

Zest of ½ orange, minced very finely

1. Whirl the eggs and sugar in the bowl of your food processor. Slowly add the rest of the ingredients, stopping occasionally to scrape the bowl.

2. Don't over process. When the dough comes together, remove from the food processor and place in plastic wrap. Refrigerate for 1–2 hours.

3. Preheat oven to 350°F. Prepare a cookie sheet with nonstick spray or parchment paper.

4. Shape the dough into a flat oval. Break off a small piece and roll into a ball. Flatten to about ¼" to ½" and place on cookie sheet. Repeat until all of the dough is used. Bake for 10 minutes, or until golden.

INDIAN PUDDING WITH WHIPPED CREAM

If you make too much, let it firm up and fry in butter, making sweet griddle cakes for breakfast the next day.

Serves 8

INGREDIENTS:

4 cups fat-free milk, divided

¼ cup white or yellow gluten-free cornmeal

⅓ cup dark brown sugar

¼ cup white sugar

1 teaspoon salt

1 teaspoon cinnamon

¼ teaspoon ground nutmeg

1 teaspoon minced fresh gingerroot

¼ cup molasses

1. Preheat the oven to 250°F. Heat 2 cups milk. Place the cornmeal and the rest of the dry ingredients, the gingerroot, and molasses in the top of a double boiler.

2. Whisk the hot milk into the mixture, cooking and stirring over simmering water for 10 minutes or until smooth. Prepare a 2-quart casserole dish with butter or nonstick spray.

3. Whisk the cold milk into the hot mixture and pour into the baking dish. Bake for 3 hours. Serve hot or at room temperature with whipped cream.

SWEDISH FRUIT PUDDING (KRAM)

Children and adults like this equally well. It's tangy and very bright red. Serve it in wine glasses with a spoonful of whipped cream on top.

Serves 4

INGREDIENTS:

1 (10-ounce) box frozen strawberries

1 (10-ounce) box frozen raspberries

¼ cup lemon juice

1½ tablespoons arrowroot flour or cornstarch

Pinch salt

¼ cup sugar, or to taste

2 tablespoons orange liqueur (optional)

Whipped cream or gluten-free ice cream

1. Place the thawed berries in a saucepan. Drain off the juice that is produced from thawing into a bowl. Mix in the lemon juice. Add the arrowroot or cornstarch to the mixture.

2. Stir the mixture and a pinch of salt and sugar to taste into the berries. Cook over low heat until the mixture starts to thicken. Add the liqueur. Cool and serve in wineglasses with whipped cream

STRAWBERRY CLOUDS

These fluffy delights are cool and refreshing. Garnish with sprigs of mint. The recipe is a cross between a Bavarian cream and a mousse.

Serves 4

INGREDIENTS:

1 (¼-ounce) package unflavored gelatin

¼ cup cold water

1 cup boiling water

1 pint strawberries, rinsed and hulled

Sugar, to taste

2 egg whites, beaten stiff

½ cup heavy cream, beaten stiff with 1 tablespoon sugar

1. Place the gelatin and cold water in the bowl of your blender. Let stand for 5 minutes so the gelatin can "bloom." With the motor running, slowly pour in the boiling water.

2. Add strawberries and sugar, and whirl until smooth, stopping to scrape down the sides of the jar.

3. When the berries have cooled, fold in the egg whites and whipped cream. Refrigerate until chilled, mixing occasionally.

Clouds

You can use berries as a flavoring for clouds, but peaches, blanched and mashed, are also very good, as are pears. Try making a cloud with fresh, spicy applesauce for fall. The basic principle works with all fruits. Just vary the amount of sugar to suit the type of fruit; that is, if the fruit is very sweet, use less sugar.

CHOCOLATE MOUSSE

The classic darling of the French bistro, this is a fresh take on an old favorite.

Serves 6–8

INGREDIENTS:

4 squares semisweet chocolate

¼ cup rum or cognac

½ cup sugar, or to taste

1 teaspoon instant coffee powder

¼ cup boiling water

5 large eggs, separated

1 cup heavy cream, whipped stiff with 1 tablespoon sugar

1. Combine the chocolate, rum or cognac, and sugar in a heavy saucepan or the top of a double boiler. Mix the coffee powder with boiling water and add to the chocolate mixture.

2. Cook over very low heat, stirring from time to time, until the chocolate melts. Remove from the heat and cool for 3 minutes. Slowly, beat in the egg yolks, one at a time.

3. Let cool and fold in the egg whites that are beaten until stiff. Spoon into a serving bowl or dessert glasses. Chill for 4–6 hours. Serve with whipped cream.

Garnishes for Chocolate Mousse

Fresh raspberries are a perfect garnish for chocolate mousse, as is a sprig of mint. You can also pour a bit of peppermint schnapps over each serving for an added kick. Chambord (raspberry liqueur) is also good added to the mousse when you are making it.

CHOCOLATE-RASPBERRY SOUFFLÉ

Chocolate and raspberries are a heavenly combination. Serving a soufflé is grand enough, but adding fresh raspberries to the mix is very special.

Serves 4

INGREDIENTS:

2 squares bittersweet chocolate

½ cup sugar

1 tablespoon butter plus 1 tablespoon for soufflé dish

2 tablespoons Chambord (raspberry liqueur)

3 tablespoons rice flour or cornstarch

3 tablespoons cold fat-free milk

4 egg yolks

5 egg whites

Pinch cream of tartar

½ pint fresh raspberries, rinsed and allowed to dry on paper towels

1. Preheat the oven to 375°F.

2. In a medium-sized, heavy saucepan, melt the chocolate with the sugar, butter, and Chambord. Remove from heat. In small bowl, whisk the flour and milk together and add to the chocolate mixture.

3. Beat the egg yolks, one at a time, into the chocolate mixture. In separate bowl, whip the egg whites and cream of tartar together until stiff. Fold the egg whites into the chocolate mixture and pour into a buttered 1½-quart soufflé dish.

4. Bake for 35–40 minutes, or until puffed and brown. Pour fresh raspberries over each portion and garnish with whipped cream if desired.

The Creative Soufflé

The variety of soufflés you can make is limited only by the availability of ingredients and your imagination. You can substitute mashed bananas for the chocolate, or mangoes, for that matter. The soufflé makes a marvelous presentation, but it must be served immediately or it will sou-flop.

HALF-FROZEN MOCHA MOUSSE

Mocha, the combination of coffee and chocolate, is said to be an aphrodisiac. And when it's frozen enough to be icy cold and very dark, it could evoke Eros.

Serves 4

INGREDIENTS:

2 tablespoons espresso powder

4 tablespoons pure Dutch cocoa powder

⅓ cup ice water

⅔ cup sugar

1 teaspoon vanilla

½ teaspoon salt

1 cup heavy cream

1. Blend the espresso powder, cocoa powder, and water together until smooth. Add sugar, vanilla, and salt.

2. Whip the cream and fold the cocoa mixture into it, mixing gently but thoroughly.

3. Place in a bowl in the freezer for 1 hour, stirring occasionally; do not freeze hard. Serve in balloon wine glasses with shaved chocolate sprinkled over the top.

PUMPKIN CUSTARD

You can substitute frozen winter (butternut) squash for the pumpkin with good results. Canned pumpkin is very heavy and strong, so try to avoid it.

Serves 6–8

INGREDIENTS:

2 cups cubed fresh pumpkin, steamed in 1 cup water, or 2 (12–13-ounce) packages frozen winter squash, thawed

½ cup brown sugar

¼ cup white sugar

½ teaspoon each: ground ginger, ground cloves, ground nutmeg

1 teaspoon ground cinnamon

3 large eggs, beaten

1 cup heavy cream

1. Preheat oven to 325°F. Purée the pumpkin in your blender or food processor. Slowly add the rest of the ingredients.

2. Pour into a buttered casserole dish. Place a roasting pan of hot water in the middle of the oven. Put the bowl of pumpkin custard in the roasting pan and bake for 50–60 minutes. A nice variation is to add a cup of pecan pieces and let them bake right in the custard.

RICE PUDDING WITH APRICOTS

The classic dish is to mix canned cherries in heavy syrup with the rice pudding. This is a bit different and, we think, better.

Serves 6–8

INGREDIENTS:

1 cup gluten-free dried apricots, cut into quarters

1 cup water

½ cup sugar

1 cup uncooked rice (basmati is preferable)

2½ cups fat-free milk

1 teaspoon vanilla

⅛ teaspoon nutmeg

½ cup sugar, more to taste

1 cup heavy cream, whipped stiff

8 ounces blanched almonds, toasted, for garnish

1. In a small saucepan, bring the apricots, water, and ½ cup sugar to a boil. Turn down heat and simmer until the apricots are plump and the sauce syrupy.

2. In a large, heavy pot, mix the rice and milk. Bring to a boil, then turn down heat to simmer, and cook for about 60 minutes, stirring occasionally.

3. Add the vanilla, nutmeg, and ½ cup sugar, stirring. Cool slightly. Fold the whipped cream into the pudding. Fold the apricots into the pudding. Top with toasted almonds.

Long Grain Versus Short-Grain

"Long grain" is simply a classification for milled rice that is 3 times long as it is wide. Common varieties are basmati, jasmine, or Texmati. Short grain and medium grain rice are *less* than 3 times long as they are wide. Short grains are often more starchy and can be considered "sticky" rice. A common medium grain rice is arborio, while a common short grain rice is sushi rice.

CRUSTLESS APPLE PIE

You may need to adjust the cooking time depending on the type of apples you use. A softer Golden Delicious should be cooked through and soft in the recommended cooking times, but a crisper Granny Smith, Roma, or Gala apple may take longer.

Serves 8

INGREDIENTS:

8 medium apples, cored, peeled, and sliced

3 tablespoons orange juice

3 tablespoons water

½ cup pecans, chopped

⅓ cup brown sugar

¼ cup butter, melted

½ teaspoon cinnamon

2 cups whipped heavy cream

1. Treat a 4-quart slow cooker with nonstick spray. Arrange apple slices on the bottom of the slow cooker.

2. In a small bowl combine the orange juice and water; stir to mix. Evenly drizzle over the apples.

3. In a separate bowl combine the pecans, brown sugar, butter, and cinnamon. Mix well. Evenly crumble the pecan mixture over the apples. Cover and cook on high for 2 hours or on low for 4 hours.

4. Serve warm or chilled, topped with whipped cream.

BAKED STUFFED APPLES

You can serve these baked apples as a warm dessert with some gluten-free vanilla ice cream or along with some gluten-free coffee cake for breakfast.

Serves 4

INGREDIENTS:

4 large tart baking apples

½ cup light brown sugar

4 teaspoons grated orange zest

1 teaspoon cinnamon

¼ cup golden seedless raisins, gluten-free

4 teaspoons frozen orange juice concentrate

4 teaspoons butter

½ cup apple cider or juice

1. Wash the apples and remove the core and the stem, but don't peel them.

2. Add the brown sugar, orange zest, and cinnamon to a small bowl; stir to mix.

3. Fill each apple with a tablespoon of raisins, a teaspoon of orange juice concentrate, and a generous tablespoon of the brown sugar mixture. Top the filling in each apple with a teaspoon of butter.

4. Pour the cider or juice into the slow cooker. Carefully place the apples upright in the slow cooker. Cover and cook on low for 5 hours or until the apples are cooked through and tender.

5. Use tongs and a spatula to remove the apples to dessert plates. Serve warm.

SPICED WINTER FRUIT COMPOTE

Warm fruit that's spiced with ginger, cardamom, and nutmeg: This would be perfect spooned over toasted gluten-free pound cake or even gluten-free ice cream.

Serves 8

INGREDIENTS:

3 medium pears, peeled if desired, cored, and cubed

1 (15½-ounce) can pineapple chunks, undrained

1 cup gluten-free dried apricots, quartered

½ cup gluten-free dried cranberries

3 tablespoons frozen orange juice concentrate

2 tablespoons packed brown sugar

3 tablespoons tapioca starch

½ teaspoon ground ginger

¼ teaspoon cardamom

½ teaspoon freshly grated nutmeg

2 cups frozen unsweetened pitted dark sweet cherries

½ cup toasted flaked coconut

½ cup toasted pecans

1. In a greased 4-quart slow cooker combine pears, pineapple, apricots, and cranberries.

2. In a small bowl, whisk together orange juice concentrate, brown sugar, tapioca starch, ginger, cardamom, and nutmeg. Pour orange juice mixture over fruit.

3. Cover and cook on low for 6–8 hours or on high for 3–4 hours. Stir in cherries 1 hour prior to serving.

4. To serve, spoon warm compote into dessert dishes. Top with coconut and nuts.

Make It Even Easier

Don't want to go to the trouble of preparing all the fruit called for in this recipe? Use 2–3 cans of drained mixed fruit (packed in its own juice), or 2 bags of mixed frozen fruit.

OLD-FASHIONED RICE PUDDING

This creamy delicious rice pudding can be served hot or cold. Top it with sweetened whipped cream for a special treat.

Serves 6

INGREDIENTS:

¾ cup uncooked long grain rice

3 cups whole milk

¾ cup granulated sugar

¾ teaspoon ground cinnamon

1 pinch salt

⅛ cup butter, melted

1. In a colander, rinse rice with cold water, until water runs clear.

2. Pour rice into a greased 4-quart slow cooker. Add remaining ingredients and stir to combine.

3. Cover and cook on high for 2½–3 hours, until rice has absorbed the liquid.

4. Serve warm or refrigerate until cold.

CINNAMON-VANILLA TAPIOCA PUDDING

Tapioca pudding is a favorite among children. This dessert can be made overnight and placed in the refrigerator to serve as a cold afternoon snack.

Serves 4

INGREDIENTS:

4 cups whole milk

⅔ cup white sugar

2 large eggs, lightly beaten

½ cup small pearl tapioca

½ teaspoon cinnamon

1 tablespoon vanilla

1. In a greased 2½-quart or 4-quart slow cooker, whisk together all ingredients.

2. Cover and cook on high for 2½–3 hours or on low for 6 hours, stirring occasionally.

3. Serve warm or cold.

GINGERBREAD PUDDING CAKE

This cake may not be the prettiest cake you'll ever make, but the warm spices, paired with gluten-free vanilla bean ice cream, is an excellent combination.

Serves 6

INGREDIENTS:

½ cup brown rice flour

½ cup arrowroot starch

½ cup sugar

1 teaspoon gluten-free baking powder

¼ teaspoon baking soda

1¼ teaspoons ground ginger

½ teaspoon ground cinnamon

¾ cup 2% milk

1 large egg

½ cup raisins, gluten-free

2¼ cups water

¾ cup packed brown sugar

½ cup butter

1. Grease a 4-quart slow cooker with nonstick cooking spray. In a medium bowl, whisk together flour, arrowroot starch, sugar, baking powder, baking soda, ginger, and cinnamon.

2. Stir milk and egg into dry ingredients. Stir in raisins (batter will be thick). Spread gingerbread batter evenly in the bottom of the prepared cooker.

3. In a medium saucepan, combine the water, brown sugar, and butter. Bring to a boil; reduce heat. Boil gently, uncovered, for 2 minutes. Carefully pour water/brown sugar mixture over the gingerbread batter.

4. Cover and vent lid with chopstick or the end of a wooden spoon. Cook on high for 2–2½ hours until cake is cooked through and a toothpick inserted about ½" into the cake comes out clean. (The cake may not look like it's cooked all the way through.)

5. Remove slow cooker insert from the metal cooker. Allow to cool for 45–60 minutes to allow "pudding" to set beneath the cake.

6. To serve, spoon warm cake into dessert dishes and spoon "pudding sauce" over the warm cake.

APPLESAUCE CAKE

A lightly spiced cake that can be frosted with whipped vanilla icing or eaten plain, this cake would also be delicious with Spiced Winter Fruit Compote (see recipe in this chapter) spooned over each serving.

Serves 9

INGREDIENTS:

½ cup brown rice flour

½ cup plus 2 tablespoons arrowroot starch

½ cup sugar

1 teaspoon gluten-free baking powder

½ teaspoon baking soda

½ teaspoon xanthan gum

¼ teaspoon salt

1 teaspoon cinnamon

½ teaspoon ground nutmeg

¼ teaspoon ground cloves

2 tablespoons canola oil

1 cup applesauce, no sugar added

2 large eggs

1. In a large bowl, whisk together flour, arrowroot starch, sugar, baking powder, baking soda, xanthan gum, salt, cinnamon, nutmeg, and cloves. Mix together thoroughly.

2. In a smaller bowl, mix together the oil, applesauce, and eggs.

3. Mix wet ingredients into dry ingredients with a fork, until you have a thick batter.

4. Grease 3 emptied and cleaned (15-ounce) aluminum cans and place ⅓ of the cake batter into each can. Place the cans into a 4-quart slow cooker.

5. Cover the slow cooker and vent the lid with a chopstick. Cook on high for 3–3½ hours or on low for 6–7 hours. Cakes should rise and become golden brown on top when done.

6. Remove cans of cake carefully from slow cooker and allow to cool before removing from cans. Slice each canned cake into 3 round pieces of cake. These pieces can be placed in cupcake liners and served as cupcakes.

Make a Round or Oval Cake

If you can't find any aluminum cans to use for this recipe, you can pour the batter into the bottom of a 4-quart slow cooker that's been lined with parchment paper. Cover, vent the lid, and cook on high for 2–2½ hours or until cake is cooked through in the middle. You'll have to watch the cake carefully as it could burn at the edges and on the bottom.

CHOCOLATE BREAD PUDDING

Fat-free evaporated milk gives this bread pudding a creamy texture, but it has several dozen fewer calories than heavy cream.

Serves 10

INGREDIENTS:

4 cups cubed gluten-free bread, day-old and toasted

2⅓ cups fat-free evaporated milk

2 large eggs

⅓ cup light brown sugar

¼ cup unsweetened cocoa powder

1 teaspoon vanilla extract

1. Grease a 4-quart slow cooker with nonstick cooking spray. Add the bread cubes.

2. In a medium bowl, whisk the evaporated milk, eggs, brown sugar, cocoa, and vanilla extract until the sugar and cocoa are dissolved. Pour over the bread cubes.

3. Cover and cook on low for 5 hours or until the pudding no longer looks wet.

EASY CHOCOLATE CAKE

This chocolate cake is easy to mix together to make a batch of cupcakes. To make your own chocolate cake mix, simply whisk together all dry ingredients and place in a sanitized glass jar with a tight-fitting lid. Little jars of gluten-free cake mix make a nice homemade gift.

Serves 9

INGREDIENTS:

⅓ cup brown rice flour

⅓ cup arrowroot starch

⅓ cup sorghum flour

½ teaspoon xanthan gum

¾ cup sugar

¼ cup unsweetened baking cocoa

1 teaspoon gluten-free baking powder

¼ teaspoon baking soda

¼ cup oil

¾ cup almond milk

½ teaspoon vanilla extract

2 large eggs, slightly beaten

1. In a large bowl whisk together brown rice flour, arrowroot starch, sorghum flour, xanthan gum, sugar, cocoa, baking powder, and baking soda. Mix together thoroughly.

2. In a smaller bowl whisk together the oil, almond milk, vanilla extract, and eggs.

3. Mix wet ingredients into dry ingredients with a fork until you have a thick cake batter.

4. Grease 3 emptied and cleaned (15-ounce) aluminum cans and place ⅓ of the cake batter into each can. Place the cans in a 4-quart slow cooker.

5. Cover the slow cooker and vent the lid with a chopstick. Cook on high for 3–3½ hours or on low for 6–7 hours. Cakes should rise and about double in size and become a dark brown on top when done.

6. Remove cans of cake carefully from slow cooker and allow to cool before removing from cans. Slice each canned cake into 3 round pieces of cake. These pieces can be placed in cupcake liners and served as cupcakes. Eat plain or frost with your favorite icing.

Everybody Loves Chocolate Chips

Mini chocolate chips make a nice addition to this cake. The Enjoy Life Company makes gluten-free and dairy-free mini chocolate chips.

CRUSTLESS LEMON CHEESECAKE

Cheesecake bakes perfectly in the slow cooker. In this recipe, the slow cooker is lined with parchment paper, which makes for a very easy cleanup!

Serves 8

INGREDIENTS:

16 ounces cream cheese, softened

⅔ cup sugar

2 large eggs

1 tablespoon cornstarch

1 teaspoon fresh lemon zest

2 tablespoons fresh lemon juice

1. In a large bowl beat cream cheese and sugar together until smooth.

2. Beat in eggs and continue beating on medium speed of a handheld electric mixer for about 3 minutes.

3. Beat in remaining ingredients and continue beating for about 1 minute.

4. Line a 4-quart slow cooker with parchment paper. Pour batter onto the parchment paper.

5. Cover and cook on high for 2½–3 hours or until cheesecake is set. Remove slow cooker insert and place in fridge to chill for 2–6 hours. Slice to serve.

RIGHT-SIDE-UP PINEAPPLE CAKE

This is a fun and pretty cake to make, and it turns out beautifully in the slow cooker!

Serves 9

INGREDIENTS:

½ cup plus 1 tablespoon fine brown rice flour

½ cup arrowroot starch

½ cup sugar

1 teaspoon gluten-free baking powder

½ teaspoon baking soda

½ teaspoon xanthan gum

¼ teaspoon salt

¼ cup oil

¾ cup 2% milk

2 large eggs

1 teaspoon vanilla extract

6 pineapple rings

6 maraschino cherries

¼ cup pecans, chopped

¼ cup brown sugar, lightly packed

2 tablespoons butter, melted

1. In a large bowl whisk together flour, arrowroot starch, sugar, baking powder, baking soda, xanthan gum, and salt. Mix together thoroughly.

2. In a smaller bowl whisk together the oil, milk, eggs, and vanilla extract.

3. Mix wet ingredients into dry ingredients with a fork until you have a thick cake batter.

4. Line a 4-quart slow cooker with parchment paper. Spray with nonstick cooking spray. Pour cake batter onto the parchment paper and spread evenly.

5. Gently place the pineapple rings on top of cake. Add a cherry to the middle of each slice. Sprinkle pecans and brown sugar over cake. Drizzle melted butter over cake.

6. Cover the slow cooker and vent the lid with a chopstick. Cook on high for 2½–3 hours. Cake should rise and become golden brown when done.

CRANBERRY-APPLE GRANOLA COOKIE BARS

These bars are like a cookie and a granola bar in one. There is no need to buy the store-bought granola bars anymore. These are healthy and delicious.

Makes 25 bars

INGREDIENTS:

3 cups gluten-free pure rolled oats

¾ cup walnuts, finely chopped

¾ cup ground flaxseed

⅓ cup almond meal

½ cup shredded coconut

⅛ teaspoon kosher salt

1¼ cups honey

1 teaspoon vanilla extract

2 ounces gluten-free dried cranberries, unsweetened

2 ounces gluten-free dried apple slices, unsweetened

1. Preheat the oven to 350°F.

2. In a large bowl, mix the oats, walnuts, flax, almond meal, coconut, and salt. Place on baking sheet and roast in the oven for 15 minutes, stirring occasionally.

3. Dissolve honey and vanilla extract in saucepan over low heat.

4. Remove dry ingredients from the oven and pour into a bowl. Lower oven to 300°F. Grease a 9" × 13" glass dish with cooking spray.

5. Mix honey mixture into bowl with dry ingredients; add the cranberries and apples.

6. Pour into greased dish and, using rubber spatula, spread out and press down evenly. Bake for 30–40 minutes, until golden brown.

7. Let cool for at least 1½–2 hours to harden. Cut into about 25 bars.

STRAWBERRY-VANILLA CHEESECAKE WITH WALNUT CRUST

This is a fine combination with a delightful flavor and smooth consistency.

Serves 10–12

INGREDIENTS:

1½ cups ground walnuts

½ cup sugar

½ teaspoon cinnamon, ground

½ cup unsalted butter, melted

4 large eggs, separated

3 (8-ounce) packages cream cheese

1 cup gluten-free sour cream

2 teaspoons vanilla extract

1 teaspoon salt

2 tablespoons rice flour

⅔ cup strawberry preserves, melted

1. Mix together the walnuts, sugar, cinnamon, and melted butter. Prepare a springform pan with nonstick spray and press the nut mixture into the bottom to form a crust. Chill for at least 1 hour.

2. Preheat oven to 350°F.

3. Beat the egg whites until stiff and set aside.

4. In a large bowl, using an electric mixer, beat the cream cheese, sour cream, vanilla, salt, and rice flour together.

5. Add the egg yolks, one at a time, while beating. When smooth, fold in the egg whites and mix in the strawberry preserves.

6. Pour into the springform pan and bake for 1 hour. Turn off oven and crack the door. Let cake cool for another hour. Chill before serving.

Nut Crusts for Cheesecake

This recipe specifies walnuts because they are probably the least expensive shelled nut and work well in these recipes. However, you can substitute hazelnuts, almonds, or pecans. Pecans add a Southern touch and are really good (see the Pumpkin Pie with Pecan Crust recipe in this chapter). Grinding nuts is simple—just use your food processor.

CRISPY CHOCOLATE-MINT MERINGUE COOKIES

These are crisp and delicious. The nuts add a wonderful crunch. Use either blanched almonds or hazelnuts.

Makes about 40 cookies

INGREDIENTS:

½ cup sugar, divided

¼ cup unsweetened cocoa powder

⅛ teaspoon salt

3 egg whites (from extra-large eggs)

⅛ teaspoon peppermint extract

⅛ teaspoon cream of tartar

½ cup hazelnuts, lightly toasted, skinned, and coarsely chopped

1. Preheat the oven to 275°F. Line two cookie sheets with parchment paper.

2. Sift ¼ cup of sugar and ¼ cup of cocoa together in a bowl. Add salt.

3. In a separate bowl, beat egg whites, mint extract, and cream of tartar. When peaks begin to form, add the remaining ¼ cup sugar, a teaspoon at a time. Slowly beat in the cocoa mixture. The meringue should be stiff and shiny.

4. Add chopped nuts. Drop by teaspoonfuls on the parchment paper. Bake for 45–50 minutes. Cool on baking sheets. You can place these in an airtight cookie tin or serve them the same day.

FROZEN CHOCOLATE-COVERED BANANA BITES

These are the perfectly portioned snack or dessert. Children and adults alike love these little treats.

Makes 30 bites

INGREDIENTS:

2 ripe bananas (not too ripe or they won't work)

1 cup gluten-free baking chocolate

1 tablespoon milk

Shredded coconut, slivered almonds, or toffee bits for toppings (optional)

1. Line a baking sheet with wax or parchment paper.

2. Cut bananas into ½" thick slices and place them on the lined baking sheet. Place them in the freezer on the tray while you melt the chocolate.

3. Place the chocolate in a small saucepan and melt over low heat while stirring continuously. Add milk and continue to stir until completely melted. Remove from heat.

4. Place a toothpick (or you can use a fork) in each banana slice and dip into melted chocolate. Place on lined baking sheet.

5. You can pour some extra melted chocolate on top of banana slices. Sprinkle with shredded coconut, slivered almonds, or whatever topping you like.

6. Transfer tray to freezer for a minimum of 1 hour or until completely frozen. Store in an airtight container in the freezer.

RASPBERRY-BLUEBERRY COULIS

This is wonderful not only on gluten-free crepes but on gluten-free ice cream and gluten-free pancakes as well. You can also mix it into Rice Pudding (see recipe in this chapter) for a different take on an old-fashioned dessert.

Makes 1½ cups

INGREDIENTS:

½ pint fresh blueberries, rinsed

½ pint fresh raspberries, rinsed

¼ cup water

¼ cup sugar

1" × ½" strip orange rind

Place all of the ingredients in a medium-sized saucepan and bring to a boil. Remove from heat and cool. Whisk until smooth. Serve warm or cool.

APPLE COBBLER

This smells like autumn but tastes wonderful any time of the year.

Serves 10

INGREDIENTS:

8 large tart apples such as Granny Smiths, peeled, cored, and sliced

½ cup fresh lemon juice

1 teaspoon cinnamon, ground

1 cup sugar, divided

1 stick (½ cup) unsalted butter, melted

½ teaspoon salt

1½ cups rice flour or quinoa flour

1 tablespoon gluten-free baking powder

1 cup buttermilk

1. Preheat the oven to 375°F.

2. Place apples in a bowl and sprinkle with lemon juice, cinnamon, and ½ cup sugar. Mix well.

3. Prepare a 9" × 13" baking dish with nonstick spray. Spread the apples on the bottom.

4. Pour the melted butter into a large bowl. Add the remaining ½ cup sugar and salt, and whisk in the flour and baking powder. Add the buttermilk and stir; don't worry about lumps.

5. Drop the batter by tablespoonfuls over the fruit. Bake for 35–40 minutes. Cool for 25 minutes. Serve with gluten-free vanilla ice cream or whipped cream.

RICE PUDDING

This classic dessert is an extremely popular dessert in many restaurants. You can save some calories and fat by using reduced-fat milk and cut back on the sugar to ¼ cup.

Serves 6

INGREDIENTS:

1 tablespoon butter

1½ cups water

¾ cup arborio rice, uncooked

1 large egg

2 cups whole milk, divided

⅓ cup turbinado sugar

¼ teaspoon salt

½ cup golden raisins, gluten-free

1 teaspoon cinnamon

½ teaspoon nutmeg

½ teaspoon vanilla extract

1. Melt the butter in a medium saucepan. Add 1½ cups water and bring to boil. Stir rice into boiling water. Reduce heat to low, cover, and simmer about 20 minutes, until all water has been absorbed.

2. Place the egg in a small bowl and beat. Slowly add ½ cup of milk to the egg. Set aside.

3. Add 1½ cups milk, sugar, and salt to the cooked rice. Cook over medium heat about 30 minutes, until it begins to get thicker and creamier.

4. Slowly add in egg/milk mixture making sure to stir constantly.

5. Add raisins, cinnamon, nutmeg, and vanilla. Continue to cook another 2 minutes, while stirring constantly. Serve warm or cold.

Temper, Temper

What does it mean to "temper an egg"? It simply means to slowly add the beaten egg to the hot milk while stirring. If you just dump the egg mixture in, you could end up with scrambled eggs in the mixture, which wouldn't be tasty in a rice pudding.

PEANUT BUTTER COOKIES

These are quite addictive. You might find it difficult to eat just one! These are equally as delicious with or without chocolate chips.

Makes 2–3 dozen cookies, depending on size

INGREDIENTS:

1 cup gluten-free natural peanut butter, well stirred

½ cup turbinado sugar

⅓ cup brown sugar

1 large egg, beaten

½ teaspoon vanilla extract

½ teaspoon baking soda

1 cup gluten-free chocolate chips (optional)

½ cup almonds or nut of your choice, finely diced

1. Preheat oven to 350°F.

2. In a medium-sized mixing bowl, combine the peanut butter, sugars, egg, vanilla extract, and baking soda. Mix thoroughly. Add chocolate chips and diced nuts if desired.

3. Line a baking sheet with parchment paper. Spoon cookie dough by tablespoonfuls onto baking sheet. Bake for 12–15 minutes, until centers are cooked and edges are lightly browned. Let them cool on the sheet for 5–10 minutes before transferring to a wire rack to cool completely.

PAVLOVA WITH CHOCOLATE AND BANANAS

Pavlova is a meringue dessert cake with a whipped cream topping. Place the whipped cream on the pavlova right before serving, as it will become soft and doesn't usually hold for more than a few hours.

Serves 6

INGREDIENTS:

4 egg whites

1 teaspoon vinegar

½ teaspoon vanilla extract

½ cup sugar

3 squares semisweet chocolate

½ cup unsalted butter

⅓ cup sugar

2 bananas, kept in the freezer for 20 minutes to firm

1 cup heavy cream, whipped with 2 teaspoons confectioners' sugar

1. Preheat the oven to 200°F.

2. Whip the egg whites, and as they stiffen, add the vinegar and vanilla extract, and slowly add the ½ cup sugar. Pour into a 9" glass pie pan that you've treated with nonstick spray.

3. Bake the meringue for 2 hours. Then, turn off the oven and crack the door. Let the meringue rest for another hour. It should become very crisp and lightly browned. Do not prepare ahead of time if the weather is humid.

4. Melt the chocolate, butter, and ⅓ cup sugar. Cool until it's still liquid but room temperature.

5. Peel and slice 1 banana in single layer into the meringue crust. Spoon half of the chocolate sauce over banana slices. Slice the other banana into another layer over chocolate sauce, then spoon the remaining sauce on top of bananas, and top with whipped cream.

NATURALLY RED VELVET CUPCAKES WITH CREAM CHEESE FROSTING

There is no need for artificial colors in these cupcakes. Beets make these cupcakes a wonderful red color.

Makes 12 cupcakes

INGREDIENTS:

1¼ cups gluten-free, all-purpose flour

½ teaspoon, plus ⅛ teaspoon, xanthan gum

¾ cup turbinado sugar

2 tablespoons cocoa powder, unsweetened

1 teaspoon gluten-free baking powder

¼ teaspoon salt

6 beets, steamed

¼ cup 100% pure maple syrup

⅓ cup unsweetened applesauce

2 tablespoons lemon juice (juice from about 1 large lemon)

1½ teaspoons vanilla extract

Cream Cheese Frosting (see recipe in this chapter)

1. Preheat the oven to 350°F. Line 12 cupcake tins with liners.

2. In a large bowl, whisk together the flour, xanthan gum, sugar, cocoa, baking powder, and salt so that all of the ingredients are evenly dispersed throughout the mixture. Set aside.

3. Place the beets into your food processor or blender, slowly adding small amounts of water if it becomes too thick. Process the beets for a solid 2–4 minutes, depending on how powerful your machine is, until completely smooth.

4. Add the maple syrup, applesauce, lemon juice, and vanilla extract, and pulse briefly to incorporate. If you are not using a high-efficiency blender, add 1 tablespoon of water at a time if mixture is too thick.

5. Pour the beet mixture into the bowl of dry ingredients, and mix just enough to combine.

6. Equally distribute the batter between your prepared tins, and bake for 18–22 minutes, until a toothpick inserted into the center comes out clean. Let cool completely before frosting.

CREAM CHEESE FROSTING

This frosting can be a wonderful topping for any cake or cookie. Unlike the store-bought varieties, this simple frosting only has 4 ingredients.

Makes frosting for 15–18 cupcakes

INGREDIENTS:

2 tablespoons unsalted butter, softened

3 ounces cream cheese, softened

½ teaspoon vanilla extract

1 cup powdered sugar

1. In a large mixing bowl, mix the butter, cream cheese, and vanilla extract until smooth with a handheld blender.

2. Add the powdered sugar and beat until smooth.

3. Store any frosting in airtight container in the refrigerator for 3–5 days.

PUMPKIN PIE WITH PECAN CRUST

This pie is a perfect dessert any time of year, not just during the holidays. You can use nonfat milk in this recipe to lighten it up, and it will still taste delicious.

Serves 8

INGREDIENTS:

15 ounces pumpkin

¾ cup fat-free milk

¾ cup 100% pure maple syrup

3 large egg, whites

2 teaspoons cinnamon

1 teaspoon pumpkin pie spice

1 Pecan Crust (see recipe in this chapter)

1. Preheat the oven to 350°F.

2. Mix all the ingredients together in a medium-sized mixing bowl until well combined.

3. Pour batter into prepared pecan crust. Bake about 55–60 minutes, or until a toothpick inserted into the center comes out clean.

PECAN CRUST

Anyone eating this pie crust will not believe this is made with pecans. So simple and tasty, and gluten-free.

Serves 8

INGREDIENTS:

¾ cup pecans

1 cup blanched almond flour

⅛ teaspoon salt

¼ teaspoon baking soda

½ teaspoon cinnamon

½ teaspoon pumpkin pie spice (cinnamon, ginger, allspice, and nutmeg)

1 teaspoon vanilla extract

4 tablespoons coconut oil (or cold butter)

3 tablespoons 100% pure maple syrup

1 large egg

1. Preheat oven to 350°F.

2. Place the pecans in a food processor and process until you have a coarse flour.

3. Add the almond flour, salt, baking soda, cinnamon, pumpkin pie spice, vanilla extract, coconut oil, maple syrup, and egg, and pulse until a ball of dough forms.

4. Using the palms of your hands, press the dough into the bottom and up the sides of a pie pan. Spread into a thin layer throughout the sides and bottom. Bake for 10 minutes.

MINI APPLE-CRANBERRY CRISPS WITH QUINOA CRUMBLE TOPPING

Your house will smell heavenly while this is cooking! You can substitute or add different fruits if you'd like as well.

Makes 4 Mini Apple-Cranberry Crisps

INGREDIENTS:

For the crisp:

3 tart apples, cored and chopped into 1" pieces

2 tablespoons unsweetened gluten-free dried cranberries

1 tablespoon 100% pure maple syrup

1 tablespoon lemon juice or juice of ½ fresh lemon

1 tablespoon cinnamon

1 tablespoon almond flour

1 tablespoon unsalted butter, melted

For the topping:

½ cup quinoa, rinsed and uncooked

½ cup gluten-free pure rolled oats

1 tablespoon chia seeds

1 teaspoon cinnamon

1 tablespoon 100% pure maple syrup

1 tablespoon unsalted butter, melted

1. Preheat oven to 350°F.

2. Place chopped apples, cranberries, maple syrup, lemon juice, cinnamon, almond flour, and butter in a medium bowl. Mix thoroughly until well combined. Pour the apple mixture evenly into 4 mini greased ramekins.

3. In a medium-sized bowl, place quinoa, oats, chia seed, cinnamon, maple syrup, and butter. Stir until completely mixed. Sprinkle on top of the apple mixture in each ramekin.

4. Bake for 35 minutes or until topping is golden brown. Serve immediately with gluten-free vanilla ice cream or whipped topping if desired.

QUINOA PUMPKIN CHOCOLATE CHIP SQUARES

Quinoa adds a wonderful texture, protein, antioxidants, and fiber to these squares. You won't feel guilty having your second!

Makes 20 squares

INGREDIENTS:

2 cups gluten-free all-purpose flour

½ cup ground flaxseed

1 teaspoon pumpkin pie spice

1½ teaspoons cinnamon

1 teaspoon baking soda

½ teaspoon salt

2 tablespoons turbinado sugar

3 tablespoons 100% pure maple syrup

½ cup butter, room temperature

1 large egg

1 cup cooked quinoa, cooled

1½ teaspoons vanilla extract

1½ cups pumpkin purée

¾ cup dark chocolate chips

1. Preheat oven to 350°F. Spray a 9" × 9" or 9" × 13" baking dish with nonstick cooking spray.

2. Mix flour, flax, pumpkin pie spice, cinnamon, baking soda, and salt in a medium-sized bowl. Set the bowl aside.

3. In a large bowl, mix the sugar, syrup, and butter until thoroughly combined. Add egg, quinoa, and vanilla extract, and mix again.

4. Slowly add in pumpkin and continue to mix well. Once completely mixed, slowly add flour mixture. Add small amounts of water in increments of 1 teaspoon if batter seems too thick.

5. Once the flour mixture is thoroughly mixed, add chocolate chips and mix well.

6. Pour into baking dish, and bake for 40 minutes or until you place a toothpick in the center and it comes out clean. Allow to cool for 15 minutes before cutting into squares.

BAKED RICOTTA TORTE WITH CANDIED ORANGE PEEL AND CHOCOLATE CHIPS

This is an adaptation of an Italian Christmas torte; it's rich and an easy-to-make finale for a big family dinner.

Serves 6–8

INGREDIENTS:

5 large eggs

1 pound whole-milk gluten-free ricotta cheese

4 ounces cream cheese (not low- or nonfat)

1 teaspoon vanilla extract

1 teaspoon salt

¾ cup candied orange peel, chopped

1 cup chocolate bits

1. Preheat oven to 350°F. Separate the eggs and beat the whites until stiff. Set aside. Put the yolks, cheeses, vanilla extract, and salt in the food processor and whirl until smooth.

2. Place in a bowl and fold in the egg whites, the orange peel, and the chocolate bits. Prepare a pie plate (preferably glass) with nonstick spray. Pour in the egg mixture and bake for 45 minutes or until set and golden on top.

Ricotta Cheese and Cottage Cheese

You can substitute cottage cheese for ricotta in any recipe. Just be sure to use the small-curd, low-salt variety. Cottage cheese may be a bit moister than ricotta—you can drain it by using a sieve and letting the fluid run out, or you can wring it out in cheesecloth.

VANILLA POACHED PEARS

Slow poaching makes these pears meltingly tender and infuses them with a rich vanilla flavor.

Serves 4

INGREDIENTS:

4 Bosc pears, peeled

1 vanilla bean, split

2 tablespoons vanilla extract

2 cups water or apple juice

1. Stand the pears up in a 4-quart slow cooker. Add the remaining ingredients.

2. Cook on low for 2 hours or until the pears are tender. Discard all cooking liquid prior to serving.

In a Pinch . . .

If you need an easy dessert, but don't have fresh fruit, use a large can of sliced or halved pears. Drain and rinse them thoroughly. Make the recipe as written, except use only ½ cup of water or apple juice.

METRIC CONVERSION CHART

VOLUME CONVERSIONS

U.S. Volume Measure	Metric Equivalent
⅛ teaspoon	0.5 milliliter
¼ teaspoon	1 milliliter
½ teaspoon	2 milliliters
1 teaspoon	5 milliliters
½ tablespoon	7 milliliters
1 tablespoon (3 teaspoons)	15 milliliters
2 tablespoons (1 fluid ounce)	30 milliliters
¼ cup (4 tablespoons)	60 milliliters
⅓ cup	90 milliliters
½ cup (4 fluid ounces)	125 milliliters
⅔ cup	160 milliliters
¾ cup (6 fluid ounces)	180 milliliters
1 cup (16 tablespoons)	250 milliliters
1 pint (2 cups)	500 milliliters
1 quart (4 cups)	1 liter (about)

WEIGHT CONVERSIONS

U.S. Weight Measure	Metric Equivalent
½ ounce	15 grams
1 ounce	30 grams
2 ounces	60 grams
3 ounces	85 grams
¼ pound (4 ounces)	115 grams
½ pound (8 ounces)	225 grams
¾ pound (12 ounces)	340 grams
1 pound (16 ounces)	454 grams

OVEN TEMPERATURE CONVERSIONS

Degrees Fahrenheit	Degrees Celsius
200 degrees F	95 degrees C
250 degrees F	120 degrees C
275 degrees F	135 degrees C
300 degrees F	150 degrees C
325 degrees F	160 degrees C
350 degrees F	180 degrees C
375 degrees F	190 degrees C
400 degrees F	205 degrees C
425 degrees F	220 degrees C
450 degrees F	230 degrees C

BAKING PAN SIZES

U.S.	Metric
8 x 1½ inch round baking pan	20 x 4 cm cake tin
9 x 1½ inch round baking pan	23 x 3.5 cm cake tin
11 x 7 x 1½ inch baking pan	28 x 18 x 4 cm baking tin
13 x 9 x 2 inch baking pan	30 x 20 x 5 cm baking tin
2 quart rectangular baking dish	30 x 20 x 3 cm baking tin
15 x 10 x 2 inch baking pan	30 x 25 x 2 cm baking tin (Swiss roll tin)
9 inch pie plate	22 x 4 or 23 x 4 cm pie plate
7 or 8 inch springform pan	18 or 20 cm springform or loose bottom cake tin
9 x 5 x 3 inch loaf pan	23 x 13 x 7 cm or 2 lb narrow loaf or pate tin
1½ quart casserole	1.5 liter casserole
2 quart casserole	2 liter casserole

INDEX